AF768050

Ius Gentium: Comparative Perspectives on Law and Justice

Volume 67

Series editors

Mortimer Sellers, University of Baltimore
James Maxeiner, University of Baltimore

Board of Editors

Myroslava Antonovych, Kyiv-Mohyla Academy
Nadia de Araújo, Pontifical Catholic University of Rio de Janeiro
Jasna Bakšic-Muftic, University of Sarajevo
David L. Carey Miller, University of Aberdeen
Loussia P. Musse Félix, University of Brasilia
Emanuel Gross, University of Haifa
James E. Hickey Jr., Hofstra University
Jan Klabbers, University of Helsinki
Cláudia Lima Marques, Federal University of Rio Grande do Sul
Aniceto Masferrer, University of Valencia
Eric Millard, West Paris University
Gabriël A. Moens, Curtin University
Raul C. Pangalangan, University of the Philippines
Ricardo Leite Pinto, Lusíada University of Lisbon
Mizanur Rahman, University of Dhaka
Keita Sato, Chuo University
Poonam Saxena, University of Delhi
Gerry Simpson, London School of Economics
Eduard Somers, University of Ghent
Xinqiang Sun, Shandong University
Tadeusz Tomaszewski, Warsaw University
Jaap de Zwaan, Erasmus University Rotterdam

More information about this series at http://www.springer.com/series/7888

Tania Sourdin · Archie Zariski
Editors

The Responsive Judge

International Perspectives

Springer

Editors
Tania Sourdin
Newcastle Law School
University of Newcastle Australia
Newcastle, NSW
Australia

Archie Zariski
Athabasca University
Edmonton, AB
Canada

ISSN 1534-6781 ISSN 2214-9902 (electronic)
Ius Gentium: Comparative Perspectives on Law and Justice
ISBN 978-981-13-1022-5 ISBN 978-981-13-1023-2 (eBook)
https://doi.org/10.1007/978-981-13-1023-2

Library of Congress Control Number: 2018944352

© Springer Nature Singapore Pte Ltd. 2018
This work is subject to copyright. All rights are reserved by the Publisher, whether the whole or part of the material is concerned, specifically the rights of translation, reprinting, reuse of illustrations, recitation, broadcasting, reproduction on microfilms or in any other physical way, and transmission or information storage and retrieval, electronic adaptation, computer software, or by similar or dissimilar methodology now known or hereafter developed.
The use of general descriptive names, registered names, trademarks, service marks, etc. in this publication does not imply, even in the absence of a specific statement, that such names are exempt from the relevant protective laws and regulations and therefore free for general use.
The publisher, the authors and the editors are safe to assume that the advice and information in this book are believed to be true and accurate at the date of publication. Neither the publisher nor the authors or the editors give a warranty, express or implied, with respect to the material contained herein or for any errors or omissions that may have been made. The publisher remains neutral with regard to jurisdictional claims in published maps and institutional affiliations.

Printed on acid-free paper

This Springer imprint is published by the registered company Springer Nature Singapore Pte Ltd.
The registered company address is: 152 Beach Road, #21-01/04 Gateway East, Singapore 189721, Singapore

To all judges who aspire to respond to the hope and trust placed in them by the people they serve.

Foreword

How one becomes a judge differs among countries. In some countries, becoming a judge is a career path. In others, becoming a judge is a mid-career or even end-of-career job change. Some places have a vigorous vetting process and some places elect judges. So what binds this disparate group into becoming effective judges? There are some countries which have quite similar rules of procedure albeit the nomenclature is different. And there are places which have radically different rules of procedure. Are there values or approaches to being a judge that transcend these differences that define how to be a very good judge?

Former US Congresswoman Barbara Jordan once said, "What the people want is simple. They want an America as good as its promise." The same can be said of what the people want of their courts and judges. They want a judiciary as good as its promise. A judiciary that is as good as its promise is known not just for speed and efficiency (heaven knows many judges are good at that) but also for other less quantifiable aspects of justice—things like fairness and respect, attention to human equality, a focus on careful listening, and a demand that people leave our courts understanding our orders. Judges cannot be satisfied with being quick nor complacent about being slow. Nor can we be satisfied with being clever. We must strive to be fully just towards every person who enters the courthouse. The volume of work makes undivided attention to justice seem at times to be an unattractive goal, and so too often we rest on measuring our speed or casting blame on others for the faults of our justice system.

With the mantle of leadership that is given to those who get to become a judge comes the responsibility to deliver—or in the words of this book, to be responsive. Throughout the world there are challenges to judges. Some of these challenges are threats to judicial independence. Some are threats driven by the public's misunderstanding or lack of understanding about what it is to be a judge. Enhancing the public's understanding of what judges do and why begins with attention to the details of doing well with those that appear before us. The high volume of cases can be seen as a strength, not a weakness, of the judiciary. We need to confront the notion that although judges at every level must be neutral, neutrality does not mean that we mask that we care. The people who come into our courthouses and the community that we serve must know that judges care about them as individuals. And to achieve that, insight into what it means to be a responsive judge is the perfect starting point.

Judges go through stages of development. A new judge may have doubts and uncertainties. As time goes by, judges begin to experience their own limitations as well as a sense of the professional self. How they handle both the limits and strengths of their own abilities defines a professional "judicial self." Judges learn in this stage of their career how they are like and different from other judges. The job of being a judge feels less and less as though it is "coming at" him or her. For most judges at this stage of their careers, judicial job stress feels under control or at least bearable. However, failure at this stage of judicial development leads to chronic feelings of inferiority, vulnerability, and defensiveness.

There is a point in most judges' careers where they settle in terms of who they are, who they know, what they are known for, and what they enjoy about the job. As judges begin for the first time to view retirement on the horizon, they see their career as finite and many begin to reflect on it anew. Hopefully, they view their career as gratifying and experience satisfaction, fulfillment, and a sense of ownership of their identity. Some, though, may see their ambitions not fulfilled and the opportunities not taken, and will become disheartened as they experience regret and possibly despair.

Why do some judges discover new vitality and creativity towards the end of their days, while others go to seed long before? We have all known judges who run out of steam before they reach their career's halfway mark. There are judges who stop learning or growing because they have adopted the fixed attitudes and opinions that all too often come with the passing of years. Stages of development are not limited to judges. All of us have the capacity to run out of steam at the halfway mark. To avoid that you should read this book. Understanding systems different than ours not only enriches us but it gives us an opportunity to think about how to make the system we work in better.

It is not trite to say that judges play an indispensable role in preserving freedom. We most definitely do. Although you can go through an entire career and not decide any case of historical significance, each case a judge decides is a critical human event. Taken together, the decisions judges make day in and day out have the potential to affirm the public's faith in the strength and decency of our courts—or to shake that faith. What the people want is simple. They want a court system—they want its judges—as good as its promise.

Minneapolis, USA

Judge Kevin S. Burke
Hennepin County District Court

Preface

In the second decade of the twenty-first-century judges, courts, and legal systems face a new existential challenge—that of remaining relevant to the public they are entrusted to serve. The crisis of access to justice has become so endemic and permanent in many countries that, with few exceptions, today only large corporations can make effective and full use of traditional civil legal systems and a civil trial. Individuals and smaller corporate entities seeking justice are instead participating in alternative dispute resolution ("ADR") processes, private dispute resolution systems which have attained the force of law, utilizing complaint and Ombuds procedures, and undertaking social media action. Increasingly, justice is being "crowdsourced" through viral social media appeals which enlist public opinion and consumer action to achieve redress. Some such campaigns descend into dangerous vigilantism, but new "social law" based upon mores and norms shared online together with online processes that can span borders may soon overshadow both established domestic common and civil law trial processes.

This latest crisis to impact legal systems is largely unrelated to historic concerns about maintaining the legitimacy of judges and courts. Judges in most countries continue to be treated with respect and trusted for their honesty and impartiality. But the public never see them at work because the courts can be perceived to be inaccessible, and thus their perceived connection with justice in practical terms can also be perceived to be weak. Judges, of course, have been concerned with the resistant problem of access to justice from the beginning. However, the initiatives they and others have taken to provide initially, access to lawyers, and next, access to courts, have not had a significant impact. Some jurisdictions have started to report declines in the number of civil cases being filed, signaling a shift in public perception away from viewing courts as being the principal sources of justice. In this environment, many judges are beginning to recognize that the only remaining tool left to them with which to reclaim for the courts their historic role of providers of justice is themselves. Access to justice today must therefore include an important focus on "access to judges".

Traditionally, judges have tended to distance themselves from the public they serve to preserve both the substance and appearance of their independence and impartiality. Many modern civil litigation systems were similarly designed with lawyers in mind as expert intermediaries between disputants and judges. Today, however, the cost of legal representation has, at times, removed this mediating element, leaving litigants (when they manage to appear) and judges face to face. Further, judges must convince those who are skeptical of the value of the courts that judges are accessible and amenable to closer contact and interaction in the joint pursuit of justice. In such situations, judges have been searching for a new understanding of their role in achieving justice and the skills and techniques to implement it. This new role calls for a "responsive judge".

We are once again writing a Preface to a book that considers judicial innovation and the role of judges as we travel across different countries to engage with and learn more about how judges work and respond to people across the globe. This is a privilege and we thank all those who have engaged with us, in this work and in our other practice areas that have caused us to reflect and consider how disputes can be effectively resolved by judges in a responsive manner. Our respective work in this field has led us to deeply appreciate the different approaches and perspectives that judges bring to their work, the extent that it is shaped by social and political domestic cultures and we hope that this book will enable some challenging, important and at times innovative judicial approaches to be considered by a wider audience.

Systems of justice vary from place to place, and in this work, how judges work in a responsive way is explored from the perspective of judges, scholars, and thinkers. This approach has led to the book presenting a smorgasbord of comparative and diverse processes related to the theme of responsiveness. We have been conscious to ensure that our view of these developments is not constrained by an Anglo-American focus and we hope that this will provide the reader with a different view about how judicial responsiveness can reflect the cultural nuances of different societies.

In considering innovations in judging and particularly judicial responsiveness, it is both challenging and fruitful to gather together expert commentators to discuss such developments because so often there are somewhat idiosyncratic approaches in different cultures. For that reason, we are particularly grateful to the Law and Society Association who sponsored our International Research Collaborative (IRC) in relation to judicial responsiveness. Through a grant program, the Law and Society Association and the United States National Science Foundation provided some financial support for the conference attendance of several authors to enable them to meet and confer with our collaborative research network (CRN) at a Conference held in Mexico City in June 2017.

This work is a collaborative effort, and we have greatly relied on the expertise of others to bring these writings together and to support the development of the book. This was achieved largely through our contributing authors who enthusiastically engaged with the theme, discussed, developed, and created this joint work. The book would also not have been possible without the wise guidance, magnificent editing, and tireless work of Jacqueline Meredith, a Senior Researcher at the University of Newcastle, Australia. We also appreciate the initial hard work done by Stanley Mak, another wonderful researcher from the University of Newcastle, Australia, who helped to bring the beginnings of the book together.

We now understand far more about judicial responsiveness and are indebted to those who have contributed to this book. We are hopeful that these perspectives will enable readers to think about and consider these trends and the issues presented in differing jurisdictions. In this regard, we are particularly grateful for the perceptive and thoughtful Foreword written by Judge Kevin Burke who is a leader in judicial education which provides an insightful perspective of the range of views that exist about judicial responsiveness.

As with any new work we also wish to thank the pioneers in this field, judges, scholars, and legal practitioners, many of whom are referred to throughout this book. Their groundwork in identifying theoretical constructs, practical measures, questions, issues, and processes is invaluable in the context of future developments in this field.

Our families and friends have also aided us, and we thank them for unfailingly supporting our efforts particularly as we may have been less than responsive while working on this book!

Lastly, we wish to thank our universities for their support and encouragement—Tania, the University of Newcastle, Australia and Archie, Athabasca University, Canada particularly for providing research and study leave.

Kuala Lumpur, Malaysia
March 2018

Tania Sourdin
Archie Zariski

Contents

What Is Responsive Judging? 1
Tania Sourdin and Archie Zariski

Part I Theoretical and Conceptual Contributions to Responsive Judging

The Responsive Tribunal: Robust Processes; Fair and Timely Outcomes 41
Helen Shurven and Clair Berman-Robinson

Settlement Adjudication and Judicial Responsiveness: The Choice Between a Wide and a Narrow Model 61
Karni Perlman

Do Judges Need to Be Human? The Implications of Technology for Responsive Judging 87
Tania Sourdin and Richard Cornes

The High Court and the Cocktail Party from Hell: Can Social Media Improve Community Engagement with the Courts? 121
Andrew Henderson

Sustainable Justice, A Social Responsible Focus on Innovation in Justice 143
Alexander F. de Savornin Lohman and Jaap van Straalen

Part II Comparative Approaches to Responsive Judging

Inside Out or Outside In?: Looking at Judges' Relations with the Public in Canada and China 175
Archie Zariski and Changqing Shi

Judicial Practice in Action: Court Reform and Responsive Judges in Canada 217
Toby S. Goldbach

Judging in a Therapeutic Way: TJ Audit of Juvenile, Probation and Criminal Procedure Law in Pakistan with Reference to Therapeutic Design and Therapeutic Application of Law 241
Muhammad Amir Munir

The #BlueWhale Challenge to the Indian Judiciary: A Critical Analysis of the Response of the Indian Higher Judiciary to Risky Online Contents with Special Reference to the BlueWhale Suicide Game 259
Debarati Halder

The Responsive Judge: Comparative Perspectives of Korea and Japan 277
Young Hoa Jung

Mansfield, Atkin, Weinstein: Three Responsive Judges at the Nexus of Law, Politics, and Economy 311
Archie Zariski

Index 335

Editors and Contributors

About the Editors

Tania Sourdin is the Dean of the University of Newcastle Law School and was previously the Foundation Chair and Director of the Australian Centre for Justice Innovation (ACJI) at Monash University in Australia. Professor Sourdin has led national research projects and produced important recommendations for ADR and justice reform. In the past two decades, she has conducted qualitative and quantitative research projects into aspects of the dispute resolution and justice system systems in 12 Courts and Tribunals and six external dispute resolution schemes. Other research has focussed on justice innovation, technology, delay and systemic reforms. Professor Sourdin is the author of a number of books (the 5th Edition of her book "Alternative Dispute Resolution" was released in February 2016), articles and papers, and has published and presented widely on a range of topics including ADR, justice innovation, justice issues, mediation, conflict resolution, collaborative law, artificial intelligence, technology and organizational change.

Archie Zariski is Professor of Legal Studies at Athabasca University, Canada, a lawyer and an experienced mediator. He has created and taught courses in ADR, negotiation and mediation at Athabasca and at Murdoch Law School, Australia. His research includes exploring the roles of lawyers and judges in dispute resolution processes. Archie is co-editor of the book *The Multi-Tasking Judge: Judicial Dispute Resolution in Comparative Perspective* and the author of *Legal Literacy: An Introduction to Legal Studies*. He is a member of the ADR Institute of Canada, and the Resolution Institute (Australia).

Contributors

Clair Berman-Robinson National Native Title Tribunal, Brisbane, Australia

Richard Cornes University of Essex, Colchester, UK

Toby S. Goldbach University of British Columbia Allard School of Law, Vancouver, Canada

Debarati Halder Unitedworld School of Law, Gandhinagar, India

Andrew Henderson Australian National University, Canberra, Australia; University of Canberra, Canberra, Australia

Young Hoa Jung Chonbuk National University, Jeonju, South Korea

Muhammad Amir Munir Punjab Judicial Academy, Lahore, Pakistan

Karni Perlman College of Management Academic Studies, Rishon Lezion, Israel

Alexander F. de Savornin Lohman Center for Sustainable Justice, Utrecht, The Netherlands

Changqing Shi Shanghai University, Shanghai, People's Republic of China

Helen Shurven National Native Title Tribunal, Brisbane, Australia

Tania Sourdin University of Newcastle, Newcastle, Australia

Jaap van Straalen Center for Sustainable Justice, Utrecht, The Netherlands

Archie Zariski Athabasca University, Athabasca, Canada

What Is Responsive Judging?

Tania Sourdin and Archie Zariski

Abstract In this chapter the Editors introduce the concept of responsive judging, examine its historical roots, and explore some of its manifestations in courts and judiciaries today. In general terms, judicial responsiveness is an acknowledgement by judges that the law is not an autonomous field of activity answerable only to its own norms, but is rather a semi-autonomous practice embedded in society which answers to the desire for justice of members of that society. Such a conception of responsiveness is compared to more traditional jurisprudential analyses of law and a view of law as intersecting and interacting with society is preferred. Some elements of responsiveness are explored including accountability, concern for consequences of decisions and the experiences of litigants, as well as the need for open communication with the public. Critiques of responsive judging are examined and answered. The chapter concludes with an overview of the aspirations and examples of responsive judging which appear in the following chapters.

1 Introduction

Judges in both Western judicial traditions, the civil and the common law, have always been responsive in several crucial respects.[1] They: (1) finalise all disputes brought before them; (2) consider the submissions of litigants concerning a dispute or case; (3) use those submissions in making decisions; and (4) explain and justify their decisions in relation to the submissions. This may be called the "classic" or "passive" model of responsive judging which has historically predominated in Western legal systems.

[1] The following description of "classic" responsive judging is largely based on Fuller (1978) and Eisenberg (1978).

T. Sourdin
University of Newcastle, Newcastle, Australia
e-mail: tania.sourdin@newcastle.edu.au

A. Zariski (✉)
Athabasca University, Edmonton, Canada
e-mail: archiez@athabascau.ca

© Springer Nature Singapore Pte Ltd. 2018

T. Sourdin and A. Zariski (eds.), *The Responsive Judge*, Ius Gentium: Comparative Perspectives on Law and Justice 67, https://doi.org/10.1007/978-981-13-1023-2_1

This book is concerned with an expanded or enhanced mode of responsive judging, observed in the work of exemplary judges of the past and present. We consider such an approach to be a "progressive" or "active" form of judicial responsiveness which incorporates the classic elements described above plus one or more of the following: (1) responsiveness to accountability for public investment in the legal system and the demand for justice; (2) responsiveness to the problems of interdependent, network society; (3) responsiveness to litigants' experiences of the legal system and courts; and (4) active responsiveness in the context of public attention. In the words of one contemporary responsive judge, these features present a contrast between "the passive and the passionate models of adjudication" (Weinstein 1995, 102). Some of these practices of responsive judging are associated more with courts than individual judges, but we point to the intimate interrelation between the two: responsive judges support responsive courts, and responsive courts encourage responsive judging.

Thus, today's fully responsive judge, in addition to adhering to the essential principles of fidelity to law, impartiality, and integrity, is also:

- a cost-conscious manager of litigation with a concern for ensuring access to justice
- a quick learner with the curiosity and patience to inquire into the foreseeable consequences of her decisions
- a student of human nature who values and works at establishing respectful relations with litigants and colleagues
- a public figure comfortable in the roles of ambassador for justice and public legal educator.

These key elements of progressive, active responsive judging will be examined in more detail below. From here on we will simply use the term *responsive judging* as meaning this expanded or enhanced mode of judging.

Responsive judging as a description of, and normative model for, the work of judges, has a history going back to the late nineteenth century. We would describe the distinguished American jurist Oliver Wendell Holmes Jr. as the "grandfather" of the modern era of responsive judging (Goldberg 2015). Holmes observed that the core activity of legal systems is judicial decision making and admonished judges doing that work to be concerned about, and take into consideration, the foreseeable effects on society of their decisions. As he put it, "… judges themselves have failed adequately to recognize their duty of weighing considerations of social advantage. The duty is inevitable, and the result of the often proclaimed judicial aversion to deal with such considerations is simply to leave the very ground and foundation of judgments inarticulate, and often unconscious …" (Holmes 1897, 467). Following in his footsteps the American Realist scholars and jurists promoted a pragmatic, results-oriented view of legal decision making. Felix Cohen described this as the functional approach and admonished judges to deal frankly with "the social forces which mold the law and the social ideals by which the law is to be judged" (Cohen 1935, 812). Llewellyn (1930) highlighted judges' freedom of action in applying law to achieve social goals, describing what we consider to be a responsive judge as one "… who loves creativeness, who can without loss of sleep combine risk-taking with responsibility, who sees and feels institutions as things built and to be built to serve functions, and who sees the functions as vital and law as a tool to be eternally reoriented to justice and to general welfare." (Llewellyn 1950, 397). Jerome Frank brought to public awareness the common humanity of judges (Frank 1930) and opened the way to a more realistic view of the judiciary than that reflected in traditional judicial roles.

Responsive judging became more common in America later in the twentieth century during the era of the civil rights movement, and the deep involvement of the judiciary in helping to desegregate schools and reform other institutions. Chayes described a new role for judges as "the dominant figure in organizing and guiding the case" and as "the creator and manager of complex forms of ongoing relief" (Chayes 1976, 1284). During the 1970s the so-called "litigation explosion" triggered public concern for the viability of legal systems and the need to manage courts more efficiently (Burger 1976). The ADR movement contemporaneously promised both to help lift the case load burden on judges by diverting parties to alternative processes, and at the same time to provide litigants with better solutions to their problems (Sander 1976). "Access to justice" became a global concern as the cost of hiring lawyers rose and triggered new approaches to the design of justice systems and court processes. Later, the research and scholarship of "procedural justice" (Thibaut and Walker 1975) led to re-envisioning the relations between litigants, courts and judges. In all of these developments judges have been both champions and skeptics, although the prevailing trend has been change in judicial roles and practices. Together, these changes have resulted in modern responsive judging.

In diverse ways many judges today are actively responsive to the parties before them, to wider communities of interest, and to societies which require much of their judges in a complex interconnected world. We examine each of these developments in the practices of judging in more detail below.

2 Responsiveness and the Jurisprudence of Judging

Clearly the concept of responsive judging is multi-faceted and includes the notion that Judges may consider matters beyond a strict or existing legal rationale in order to determine or resolve a dispute (de Hoon and Verberk 2013). It requires that, as part of this work, a judge may attend to and explore human relationships between individual disputants and organizations and within society more generally, and consider the impact of a decision in the context of the development of the whole legal system (see Zariski later in this work). A responsive judge, therefore may, from time to time, be appropriately engaged in issues that relate to public policy. As Stępień has noted:

> More precisely, the responsive ruling may result from an analysis of the future situation of the parties involved in the particular case (individual responsiveness), take into account the anticipated impact of the decision on the whole legal system (intrinsic legal responsiveness) or even involve the consideration of the macro-economic and macro-societal consequences of arriving at the particular decision (social responsiveness). (Stępień 2013, 140–1)

At this same time, judicial responsiveness is not only concerned with a judicial ruling and adjudicated outcome. It requires that a judge consider the perspective of participants in a legal dispute as well as others when dealing with a dispute, and incorporates the notion that a responsive Judge reshape the processes used within a court by recognising that the dignity, participation and voice of a participant in a legal dispute and that such factors relevant in determining and resolving disputes. Judicial responsiveness can also be linked to how a Judge supports those who are in dispute. It may require an understanding of support structures and referral opportunities, collaboration with those who may not necessarily be involved in a dispute (such as drug and alcohol counsellors in a criminal matter) as well as a developed understanding about referral to alternative dispute resolution processes or other processes that may enable disputants to achieve better or lasting outcomes.

The concept of a responsive judge does not necessarily challenge important notions relating to jurisprudence of judging if jurisprudence is explored in the context of its most narrow and literal definition. This is partly because the essence of jurisprudence is the study, knowledge and science of the law and responsive judges are arguably engaged in this unrelenting quest and consider that social and other sciences can inform them in this task and in the judicial processes that they adopt. However, there exists some significant jurisprudential debate about responsiveness in general and the extent to which judges should be socially or legally responsive. Whilst, in the past formalists (such as Dworkin) would suggest that judges should treat law as a logical discipline or science, realists (such as Roscoe Pound) suggest that judges use a process of inductive reasoning which may permit either creativity or a consideration of broader societal well-being (Posner 1990, 73).

Naturally, jurisprudential debate involves an additional range of varying schools of theory including the naturalists (who might assume that objective morality can exist and that law should be just) and positivists who have continued to challenge formalist perspectives. In recent years, however, it appears to have been accepted that the dominant jurisprudential approaches can be framed within realist or positivist theoretical schools of thought (Tamanaha 2015) (see further discussion below). To some, both realist and positivist jurisprudential approaches support responsive judging:

> 'Over the past century, the Legal Process school of law, as well as many realists and pragmatists, promoted a notion of decision-making in law based on purposive interpretation… Judges under this perception mediate social goals when they apply rules'. (Sinai and Alberstein 2016, 237–8)

However, regardless of the jurisprudential theory adopted or developed, responsive judging has the capacity to reignite debates in jurisprudence between realists and positivists in part because the role of the judge must necessarily extend beyond determination or adjudication. Although, as discussed further below, a third and arguably compelling theory—the social jurisprudential theory—arguably tethers both realist and positivist theoretical elements (Tamanaha 2015) and is supportive of responsive judging (see below). From a pragmatic perspective, as Sourdin and Cornes note in their Chapter later in this work, there are good reasons to reject previously ascendant theoretical approaches as more formalist and even realist and positivist approaches may ignore the broader work undertaken by judges (which includes managing cases, contributing to education and debate and facilitating settlements). In respect of adjudication, an acceptance of, for example, more formalist jurisprudential approaches, arguably raises the prospect of potential judicial redundancy as Judge Artificial Intelligence (AI) becomes more feasible.

As some commentators have noted, the responsive judge concept may signal the continuing ascendancy of the realist jurisprudential approaches or may, as Tamanaha has suggested, support a third theoretical approach (Tamanaha 2015) (see below). At its simplest, however, responsive judging could be regarded as an essentially pragmatic approach to judging, that requires judicial consideration of matters beyond those who are in dispute and requires consideration of a broader societal impact. As noted by Aldisert:

> I believe that judges today do consider the pragmatic effects of alternative courses of decision. In their declarations of public policy, they attempt to accommodate the social needs of all who would be affected **by** their decisions, irrespective of whether those affected were the litigants before them…They consider economic forces, scientific developments, and identifiable expressions of public opinion. To be sure, this decisional process has deontological as well as axiological overtones. It bears a remarkable resemblance to classic natural law. (Aldisert 2009, 245)

A responsive judge must reject, rather than adhere to the Latin phrase: *Fiat justicia pereat mundus* (let there be justice, though the world may perish) as the responsive judge must accept that there is a judicial responsibility "to society and its values" (The Art of Justice 2012, 13). Whilst judges remain conscious of and bound by the law, responsive judges may go further and consider how the law is applied, developed (with a conscious consideration of societal wellbeing and operation) and how engagement with litigants and others takes place (see Kouroutakis 2014).

The potential difficulties that can surface in respect of responsive judging are mainly related to a separation of powers concern regarding political structures: essentially that judges should not interfere with the making of law which is intended to remain in most societies within the executive arm of government (often an assembly of some description). Coupled with this is a fear concerning "judge made law" which underpins much jurisprudential squabbling. In this regard, it is clear that judges within a court structure play an integral role in the government of democratic societies. Judges and courts are intended to provide an open forum to which citizens may come to assert or establish legal rights and to receive an enforceable determination of these rights. The process is subject to review through public scrutiny and a hierarchy of appellate courts. Judges therefore provide a medium through which law is created, explained and applied. From this perspective, responsive judging processes and proceedings could be seen as "threatening the essential role of judges which is 'not to maximise the ends of private parties, nor simply to secure the peace, but to explicate and give force to values embodied in authoritative texts such as the Constitution and statutes'" (Australian Law Reform Commission 1997, referring to Fiss 1984) partly because there might be a suggestion that responsive judges might depart from previously authoritative approaches.

However, it must be noted that responsive judging need not involve any rejection of these values or indeed a focus on private interests at the cost of important public interests. Rather, responsive judging invites a consideration of the judicial function and role in the context of societal values and assumes that judges, and those they deal with, are human beings who vary, and have "messy" problems where simple solutions may be unattainable. As responsive judging processes may be diverse and include facilitative and other components, there is, however, a risk that a focus on the needs of an individual may obscure a focus on broader societal values (discussed further below). However, responsive judging may incorporate the need for broader enquiry about the impact of decisions and actions. In addition, judicial activity, in terms of engagement and empathy, rather than passivity, does not equate to a shift to a primary focus on individual needs. For example, responsive judges may use facilitative processes when encouraging settlement in civil disputes—these may vary from a discussion of the "issues" and a suggestion that settlement be attempted to judges providing a preliminary view (an evaluation) on issues that have been raised and the evidence that may be required. Other responsive judges may use facilitative processes and techniques of summary and reframing when conducting concurrent evidence ("hot tub") processes or when involved in specialist "problem solving" courts. Others may use therapeutic jurisprudence techniques to support offenders in a more collaborative court environment. Whilst the dominant characteristic or feature of these responsive judging interactions involves judicial activity rather than passivity, the responsive Judge retains an overarching focus on the application of the written law together with an appreciation of societal impact.

A fear relating to "judge made law" may drive some confusion and concern about the nature and approach of a responsive judge. It must be made clear, however, that a responsive judge, remains quite properly constrained by law. As Colby has noted, a responsive judge is appropriately and properly supportive of legal doctrine as:

> In brief, legal doctrine, at both the constitutional and subconstitutional level, is permeated with reasonableness and balancing tests and other doctrinal mechanisms that can- not possibly be employed effectively unless judges are able to gain an empathic appreciation of the case from the perspective of all of the litigants. A judge can neither craft nor employ legal doctrine competently if she is not willing and able to understand the perspectives of, and the burdens upon, all of the parties. (Colby 2012, 1946)

This perception, or view of responsive judging resonates with what has been described as the third branch of jurisprudential theory. Tamanaha has suggested that the conventional jurisprudential narrative has been described (roughly speaking) as the debate between natural lawyers and legal positivists (Tamanaha 2015). In proposing a social legal approach to jurisprudence, a wide and diverse range of social theories can be used to support jurisprudential approaches and two propositions are critical: That "…law is social in nature and is best understood through an empirically-focused lens" (Tamanaha 2015, 32). It is this acknowledgment of the social interaction and social aspect of judging that is central to an exploration of responsive judging. In addition, a social legal jurisprudential approach can accommodate both positivist and natural law approaches, whilst providing more insights into how and why responsive judging can work.

Exploring key aspects of responsive judging with a social theory jurisprudential lens enables a consideration of how interactions take place and provides support for the development of empirical approaches to examine those interactions. As authors in later Chapters in this book have noted, there can be key areas of difference in terms of responsive judging in the context of impartiality, transparency and overarching objectives that have so far received little empirical attention. Given the diversity of approaches adopted by judges, some relevant issue areas have been summarized below.

2.1 Norms of Judging: Impartiality

In most jurisdictions, it is expected that a judge will be impartial. There are, however, fundamental differences within and between jurisdictions about what this may mean. In some jurisdictions, for example, impartiality may be linked to bias whilst in others it may be equated to indifference in the context of an outcome. In some jurisdictions it may be accepted that a judge will act "without fear of favour", whilst in others, it is expected that a judge may uphold the political belief system that may or may not be clearly articulated. There are also significant differences in the context of what a responsive judge may do.

During a hearing the processes used by a responsive judge can vary according to the circumstances and could involve a decision-maker adopting a facilitative stance and using many of the techniques of introduction, understanding and questioning more commonly regarded as therapeutic or ADR techniques. The timing of questions can be an important issue in determinative processes. Such an approach must also be balanced with natural justice requirements.[2] The rules in relation to natural justice impact upon the way in which material can be presented to a decision-maker, and also impact upon the nature and communication of decisions. Recently, natural justice and bias concerns have been re-examined as judges and others have become increasingly involved in case management processes and intervention at trial (Moore 2003).

---

[2]For judicial pronouncements on the rule against bias, see R v Watson (1976), Livesey v New South Wales Bar Association (1983), Vakauta v Kelly (1989).

In addition, at hearing, the identification of issues can also be crafted by a responsive judge in a neutral way, as would be the case in a facilitative process, however, the issues will often also be determined by some external criteria such as legislation (that defines the legal rights). For example, issues that relate to future relationships or communication may not be dealt with in the substance of the decision (clearly such matters will be of central importance in relation to some decisions). Such an approach may not raise issues about bias, however, it could be suggested that in some jurisdictions this somewhat managerial approach is contrary to adversarialism (see Thornburg 2010; Hughes and Bryden 2017).

At the end stages of hearing a dispute, responsive process approaches may also be useful in assisting to identify and express issues. For example, the analytical stage in adjudication will clearly involve a weighing up of relevant material. Unlike facilitative processes, this focus will usually be upon materials that are relevant to the determination of legal rights rather than needs or interests. However, the broader needs and interests can be considered to ensure that the decision that is made is crafted to ensure that the parties understand and appreciate that they have been heard.

In terms of the delivery and composition of a decision, responsive techniques can be useful in ensuring that the decision is conveyed in a sensitive, serious and appropriate manner. The extent to which the decision refers to evidence or material put by various parties can also assist to determine the extent to which the parties accept the decision. These issues have been largely unexplored in any research about judicial decision-making. Perceptions of litigants, for example, as well as their future actions, may in part be formed by the quality of the decision and the manner in which it is rendered. Other factors may relate to the personal attributes of the decision-maker or adviser and the way in which the decision is rendered. The degree of eye contact, the pitch and tone of the voice, and whether the decision is rendered in person or 'on paper' may all be relevant factors in determining whether or not the decision will be accepted or complied with.

Essentially, the responsive judge, insofar as an individual dispute is concerned, may use a blend of skills to communicate, manage and determine a dispute. One area where blending the functions has been more actively developed is within the context of "problem solving courts" (Phelan 2004). In this context, it is expected that a judge will adopt responsive skills in order to "hear" a dispute and explore options and community concerns. Problem solving courts have been defined in policy framework as "specialist tribunals established to deal with specific problems, often involving individuals who need social, mental health, and/or substance abuse treatment services" (Courts and Programs Development Unit 2006). In recent years, problem solving courts have emerged in a number of jurisdictions. Seventeen countries now have a problem solving court of some description and in the United States (where problem solving courts were created) there are over seven hundred problem solving courts in operation.[update] Australia has also piloted and implemented a number of specialist courts for disadvantaged or specified members of the community. In the last two decades, Indigenous courts, domestic (or family) violence courts and sexual offences courts have been introduced and operate around Australia.

Problem solving courts have been defined as courts that:

> … use their authority to forge new responses to chronic social, human and legal problems. They seek to broaden the focus of legal proceedings from adjudicating past facts and legal issues to changing the future behavior of litigants and ensuring the future of well-being of communities. (Berman and Feinblatt 2004, 126)

Problem solving courts aim to use the legal process to create and advance the opportunities for treatment and rehabilitation of offenders (Indermaur and Roberts 2003; Wexler 1995). The key element of a problem solving court, as opposed to specialist courts which employ therapeutic jurisprudence practices, is that problem solving court judges are responsible for post-adjudication services, including the creation, development and monitoring of treatment for participants (Belenko 1998).

As with all applications of therapeutic jurisprudence, the criticisms of problem solving courts center around breaches of constitutional barriers relating to the separation of powers and judicial independence, ex parte communications with defendants, impartiality and natural justice (Hoffman 2000; Freiberg 2001). As Richard Cappalli notes, relevant to problem solving courts is the question of whether offenders are coerced into participation and thus, whether they are truly consenting to their involvement (Berman 2000). This is of particular concern as the length of the program an offender enters into is often undefined at the outset and participants may be asked to sign a waiver, which requires their involvement in the program for an indeterminate period (Nolan 2003). Moreover, the presiding judge is responsible for setting treatment goals and boundaries for program participants. This requires an awareness of cultural and other background influences which may affect the person's participation in the program, and although this is done in consultation with a court team,[3] ultimately it is the judge's decision as to what limitations and expectations are set (King and Wager 2005). The broader social responsiveness that is required is a hallmark of judicial responsiveness practice in that it applies beyond the individuals involved in a dispute.

2.2 *Norms of Judging: Independence and Transparency*

Whilst some responsive judging approaches will raise issues about impartiality, others may raise issues about independence and transparency. As noted above, such issues may be more pronounced where some responsive functions are concerned. Judicial mediation, for example, that does not take place within an open court may legitimately raise both issues (Sourdin 2014). Where a judge is collaborating with others, for example in a problem solving or therapeutic court context, to ensure that services are aligned, available and supportive, questions might also be raised about judicial independence if a responsive judge fails to separate and focus on general process rather than individual matters which can be dealt with in open court.

---

[3] A court team usually consists of a variety of professionals from different backgrounds including defense lawyers, community support agents and treatment providers such as psychologists, social workers etc.

In terms of communication skills that take place within an open court, one question is whether open communication or the use of empathy might suggest that a judge is no longer independent. As Colby has noted:

> the argument here is neither grounded in extralegal, touchy-feely notions of humanity and compassion nor based on some sort of radical vision of wealth redistribution through activist courts. Nor, for that matter, does it spring from a post-Realist rejection of "law" as a legitimate constraining force on judges. Quite to the contrary, the argument is grounded in a firm commitment to the rule of law and a deep-seated appreciation of—rather than rejection of—legal doctrine. In brief, legal doctrine, at both the constitutional and subconstitutional level, is permeated with reasonableness and balancing tests and other doctrinal mechanisms that can- not possibly be employed effectively unless judges are able to gain an empathic appreciation of the case from the perspective of all of the litigants. A judge can neither craft nor employ legal doctrine competently if she is not willing and able to understand the perspectives of, and the burdens upon, all of the parties. (Colby 2012, 1946)

The central task of the responsive judge and the requirement of independence are not necessarily at odds. As Colby has also noted:

> But the law is not mechanical; judging requires judgment. And judgment requires empathy. To understand why, we must explore the nature of the legal doctrine that judges are called upon to apply. (Colby 2012, 1965)
>
> A judge who believes in the popular portrait of judges as umpires, and who rejects as illegitimate calls for judicial empathy, will "call 'em like he sees'em"—applying the law as he understands it to the facts as he perceives them. What he will fail to realize is that he is seeing the case from a particular perspective—his own—and is mistaking that perspective for an unbiased, neutral one. What he views as the disinterested, "correct" answer will in fact in many close cases just be the contingent answer that he arrives at after unintentionally privileging his own perspective—subconsciously empathizing with those whose experiences he shares, whose perspective comes naturally to him, and whose plight strikes a chord with him. (Colby 2012, 1992)

Some writers draw a distinction in terms of empathy and independence between determining what the law is and the application of law within the courtroom. As Chin (2012) has noted:

> "Empathy, of course, should play no role in a judge's determination of *what* the law is…Nonetheless, there is a place within the law for empathy and emotion. In my view, empathy is an essential characteristic for a judge" (1563–4) and "emotion—some emotion, emotion both ways, emotion not alone but in combination with the law, logic, and reason—helps judges get it right". (1580–81)

The consideration of the distinction between process, substantive law and outcome highlights the more humane approach taken by responsive judges. It involves considering and applying the law:

> Judges are not totally free, nor are they totally bound. They are trained in law and legal argument, they influence and are influenced by legal materials and legal culture. Judges would not be judges, and lawyers would not be lawyers, if they did not acknowledge or consider the laws, doctrines, and principles that are the very nature of their enterprise. But perhaps they can listen to and use the materials more effectively and more humanely, if they do not try to take refuge in the pretension of "pure reason" alone. (Henderson 1988, 147–8)

Again, some theorists note that this approach is central to a consideration of the jurisprudence of judging and critical in terms of a consideration of responsive judging. Brennan has noted that this may involve a judicial internal dialogue of "reason and passion" that may not necessarily be translated into courtroom interventions or approaches but which may result in a responsive decision:

> By "passion" I mean the range of emotional and intuitive responses to a given set of facts or arguments, responses which often speed into our consciousness far ahead of the lumbering syllogisms of reason. Two hundred years ago, these responses would have been called the responses of the heart rather than the head...An appreciation for the dialogue between head and heart is precisely what was missing from the formalist conception of judging. (Brennan 1988, 9)

2.3 *Civil and Common Law Traditions and Objectives*

The development of responsive judging can also be viewed from the perspective of the development of justice objectives. The evolution of justice objectives has according to many commentators undergone a rapid development over the past two decades (Sourdin 2016a) so that justice objectives are no longer perceived to only apply to courts and judicial processes. These shifts have enabled in part the development of more socially responsive justice objectives. There is also often a distinction made between civil and criminal justice objectives. In the criminal sphere, past justice objectives might be both utilitarian, and focused on reducing and preventing crime, and non-utilitarian, where justice serves to articulate and enunciate what is right or wrong behavior. In contrast, in the civil sphere, justice objectives have included resolving or limiting disputes, rule-making and providing outcomes that are consistent with law and social policy, articulating and enouncing the law and, in recent years, a greater focus on doing so efficiently and fairly (Sourdin 2016b).

In the context of responsive judging, a greater consideration of "wellness" as well as social impact has emerged that supports a broader range of processes and outcomes. There are a number of examples of this changing focus. From Australia, Draft Civil Justice Objectives (2012) state:

> Draft Objectives for the Australian Civil Justice System
>
> The Australian civil justice system contributes to the well-being of the Australian community and fosters social stability and economic growth.
>
> 1. People[4] are empowered and have the capacity to solve their problems before they become disputes
> 2. People can expediently resolve disputes at the earliest opportunity
> 3. People are treated fairly and have access to legal processes that are just
> 4. People can resolve their disputes at a reasonable cost

---

[4]The term 'People' in this context is understood as including any legal entity which may use services provided by the civil justice system including corporations, incorporated associations etc.

5. People have equitable access to the civil justice system irrespective of their personal, social or economic characteristics or background
6. People benefit from a civil justice system that contributes to the well-being of those who use it
7. People can be confident that the civil justice system is built on and continuously informed by a solid evidence base.

Such objectives with a focus on well-being at both an individual and societal level may support responsive judging practices. As Stępień has noted:

> According to the responsive model one could weigh and anticipate the consequences of a certain choice by considering the level of legitimisation, public trust in the court system, or a specific measure of social prosperity such as increase in satisfaction, social utility, welfare or Gross Domestic Index…Responsive adjudication guarantees a larger extent of flexibility and a better adjustment of the decision to the specific circumstances and context. (Stępień 2013, 140–1)

In addition, a focus on "access" over the past three decades imports a broader discussion as access might not only involve the removal of barriers and consideration of the cost of justice, but may also include considering whether people understand justice processes and outcomes, thus supporting more responsive judicial practices that incorporate social understanding, communication skills and knowledge beyond the law.

Similarly, efficiency may require a broader societal perspective. The Australian Law Reform Commission (ALRC) (1997, [3.14]) has noted:

> Efficiency can be viewed from a number of perspectives including
>
> - the need to ensure appropriate public funding of courts and dispute resolution processes that avoid waste
> - the need to reduce litigation costs and avoid repetitive or unnecessary activities in case preparation and presentation
> - the need to consider the interests of other parties waiting to make use of the court or other dispute resolution process.

Efficiency can also refer to long-term gains, rates of compliance, and the broader costs of unresolved conflict. Using these broader notions of efficiency, responsive processes might arguably meet efficiency objectives more readily than conventional litigation or non-integrative processes. In addition, some of the possible benefits of responsive judging are difficult to measure. For example, the increased use of responsive judging may lead to a decrease in litigious or adversarial behaviour,[5] foster better relationships between parties to disputes, or result in higher levels of compliance with outcomes.

---

[5]It has been suggested that those exposed to cooperative dispute resolution processes develop more constructive communication patterns and less obstructive behaviour: Wanger (1994).

The ALRC (1998, 27) has also noted that:

> Effectiveness implies that
>
> - the process should ensure, or at least, encourage a high degree of compliance with the outcome
> - at the conclusion of the process, there should be no need to resort to another forum or process in order to finalise the dispute
> - the process should promote certainty in the law.

In terms of responsive judging and effectiveness, the extent to which the process can or should promote satisfaction is relevant. Satisfaction could be a criterion to be considered when determining whether or not a process is effective. For example, can a process be regarded as effective if all concerned with the process are unsatisfied?

Effectiveness as an objective can also be considered in the context of the debate about the role of courts and their objectives has also occurred in the context of problem solving courts and notions of integrated therapeutic justice. As Phelan has noted, the emergence of problem solving courts has:

> ... challeng[ed] the nature of courts and represent[ed] something of a revolution in the way that courts might operate in modern, democratic societies. Problem solving courts are examples of courts working in partnership with other agencies, both inside and out of conventional justice fields and with "the community" to produce better social outcomes. (Phelan 2004, 137)

Arguably responsive judges are already grappling with an expanded perspective of the objectives of the litigation system designed to promote more satisfying, party and future focussed outcomes which may challenge more traditional perspectives of judicial and court functions.

3 Elements of Responsiveness

The rationale for an increasing judicial focus on responsiveness can partly be explained by societal, court, justice sector and other factors that are responsible for re-interpreting the judicial role. A modern society increasingly requires that judges respond to factors that were previously less relevant to the judicial role. Core elements of such responsiveness are set out in Table 1 and are discussed in detail in the following section.

3.1 Responding to Accountability

In the 1970s, particularly in America, the public perception arose that an overly litigious society was filling the courts with a volume of civil claims which could not be expeditiously resolved (Church 1982). At the same time, the rights of a criminal

Table 1 Potential responsive judging elements

In court engagement—individual and social responsiveness	Decision making—individual, social and legal system responsiveness	External court engagement—social and legal system responsiveness
Use of empathy and therapeutic jurisprudential approaches	Articulation of decision considering the needs of participants	Engaged in public policy debates and legislative reform
Refined and supportive communication skills	Checking understanding and framing decisions appropriately	Involved in public education
Referral of participants to support services	Considering broader social and legal system impacts including the cost of, and access to justice	Use of social and other media
Settlement functions that could extend to judicial mediation	Drawing attention to shortfalls in policy or legislation	Collaboration in problem solving court environments
Robust engagement with the social factors that led to offending or the dispute	Developing and articulating legal theory	Awareness and collaboration with drug, alcohol and mental health services
Consideration of those not present in court	Analysis and reasoning that incorporates a wider social view	Articulating an agenda for reform

accused to stand trial within a reasonable time had to be given preference. Consequently, the courts were seen to be overburdened and the legal system to be in need of reforming which was the preferred response to simply appointing more judges (Burger 1976). Courts were challenged to become more efficient and effective in resolving cases with a view to maintaining “proportionality” between the costs and benefits of litigation (Uzelac 2014).

One of the court reforms pursued as a result of these critiques was to empower judges to take a more active role in managing the pretrial phase of civil litigation (Baicker-McKee 2015; Federal Rules 2017). Through amendments to court rules judges were given the authority to control processes such as disclosure and exchange of documents and information (“discovery” in the common law tradition), and to initiate and promote settlement activity (Brazil 1985; Elliott 1986; Rabinovich-Einy and Sagy 2016; Zimmerman 2017). Some commentators have noted that the development in common law courts of judicial management of litigation can be described as actual or potential convergence of expectations of the judicial role in common law and civil law systems (Hazard and Dondi 2006; Rowe 2007; Dodson and Klebba 2011; Emerson 2015). Particularly when judges were assigned a case from start to finish (“individual calendaring”) this resulted in judges becoming intimately acquainted with the litigation before them at an early point, and to a depth that was unprecedented, at least in the common law world.

Also as part of the drive for efficiency in court operations judicial performance indicators and evaluation systems were also introduced together with new technologies that enabled continuous scrutiny (Fix-Fierro 2003). Judges could manage more easily the pace of litigation on their calendars, and Chief Judges could monitor the resolution rate of claims maintained by individual judges in their courts (Kourlis and Singer 2007, 2010). Consequently, rather than waiting for parties to be ready for trial, judges became proactive in moving matters along, and assisting in various ways to enhance the prospects for settlement (Langbein 2012). Judges began to actively shape cases with the likelihood of settlement in mind (Infante 1997). Reforms and changes in judicial practice similar to these in the United States subsequently occurred in most other common law jurisdictions. In civil law systems judges have always been expected to take early control of the trial process, particularly in relation to evidence gathering (Langbein 1985), so such changes were not very pertinent in those jurisdictions, although similar judicial performance evaluation systems were in place there.

Frank Sander's seminal call for a "multi-door courthouse" (Sander 1976) foresaw a place for courts as screening points in the growing movement for alternative dispute resolution (ADR), but it did not envision a new role for judges. As ADR proliferated in the business world and local communities, however, calls to institutionalize alternative processes in courts were heard and answered. Court-connected mediation and arbitration programs were introduced, usually under the supervision and direction of judges (Kessler and Finkelstein 1988; Kaufman 1990; Stempel 1996; Brazil 1999; French 2009). Eventually, some judges began to offer their services to litigants as mediators or conciliators over and above their role as mere proponents of settlement (Galanter 1986; Colatrella 2000; Alexander 2009). Judges with extensive knowledge of the litigation on their calendars became even more privy to the merits of the cases through acting as mediator or dispute resolver. Such active involvement of judges prior to trial raises ethical questions of impartiality and confidentiality which remain contentious today. However, in many jurisdictions such as Canada and Singapore, the role of judicial mediator is now well established. Judges who embrace this function see it as another way of meeting litigants' needs for resolution through processes that are not win or lose as trial inevitably is. In some civil law jurisdictions, a similar active role in facilitating settlement is expected of judges (Haavisto 2002). Judges providing ADR is another example of responding accountably to the public for the expeditious resolution of disputes with the possible additional benefit of more tailored, flexible solutions to underlying problems, thus combining efficiency with effectiveness.

Accountability of judges may also be seen in some jurisdictions which have vested more management authority over the courts in judicial officers (Forde 2001). In many cases as well, courts and judges have embraced advanced technologies such as online filing of documents, videoconferencing of hearings, and digitally enhanced trials as responses to the demand for cost-effective proceedings.

Judicial responses to the call for access to justice have become even more urgent in recent times as large numbers of litigants enter courts without lawyers. Access to justice originally meant access to legal representation, but has grown to include many barriers to effective participation in litigation, some related to the absence of legal advice and assistance. Judges in many jurisdictions have taken the lead in sponsoring programs and services that assist litigants in navigating the legal system which can take the form, for instance, of public legal education, court helpdesks, and improved court design and signage (Lippman 2014; Rogers 2015). Once in the courtroom, however, it is judges themselves who must respond directly to those seeking justice. The traditional role of a common law judge as a passive "umpire" between the parties is not a viable one when one, or both, of the parties are self-represented.[6] Newer concepts of judging such as "active adjudication" have been formulated to describe the function of a judge in assisting parties without becoming their advocate and losing the appearance of impartiality in doing so (Flaherty 2015; Cook 2017; Hughes and Bryden 2017). Responsive judging in this mode is fraught with ethical difficulties that are still being debated, but it is an attempt to ensure that everyone has effective access to the courts. Civil law judges can rely on a tradition of being more active in the presentation of cases, but may still encounter complaints of bias if they appear to unduly assist an unrepresented party.

In all these ways many judges today are responding accountably to society for the efficient and effective administration of justice for all.

3.2 *Responding to a Networked Society*

Taking their cue from Oliver Wendell Holmes Jr. and the American Realist scholars and jurists, responsive judges today are attentive to the foreseeable effects of their decisions not only on the litigants before them, but also on wider communities of interest and, indeed, society as a whole. This is an approach to judicial decision making which has been variously described as "pragmatic", "functional", or "contextual". As applied to the task of interpretation of law, it is also known as a "purposive" approach which tries to take into account the purpose of the law and the intent of lawmakers in dealing with distinct social problems. The more traditional approach to judging is often described as "formalist" and is primarily concerned with justifying decisions as being consistent with established rules and principles without much regard for the actual impact of the judgments handed down (Arvind 2012). By contrast, a responsive legal system and its judges try to balance the requirement of fidelity to law with the need to be open to social pressures and needs (Hutchinson 1979; Selznick 1980, 2003). Gélinas et al. (2015) describe the challenge of judging as an ongoing tension between satisfying the parties and preserving the integrity of the judicial system. One exemplary responsive judge, Jack Weinstein, pointed to the dilemma of maintaining equality before the law with concern for the unique individuality of people facing the court (Weinstein 2015). Sometimes, a notably responsive

[6]However, as noted by McGuire and Macdonald (1996) even judges who are given an explicit mandate to assist self-represented parties still find it difficult to abandon the role of passive "umpire". See also Steinberg (2016).

judge may acquire a reputation for being "crusading" (Galanter et al. 1979; Galanter 2014), "entrepreneurial" (Cates and McIntosh 1995), "strategic" (Morris 2015) or "activist" (Shetreet 1980) as a result of their non-traditional approach.

Responsive judicial decision making today is a direct challenge to Lon Fuller's theory of what he called "polycentric" problems (Fuller 1978). According to Fuller, social problems which involved many interconnected actors, interests, and policy considerations were best dealt with by administrative agencies rather than the judicial branch. However, even before Fuller's theory was published posthumously, United States courts had started to deal with just such problems in the school desegregation cases and other litigation which required massive judicially mandated structural changes to institutions and organizations. Later, the mass tort cases such as *Agent Orange* continued the trend for American courts to become involved in disputes which could clearly be described as polycentric. Thus, many courts today have become more used to adjudicating disputes which are recognized to have many wider ramifications beyond the outcome for the immediate parties before the court (Allison 1994). This is recognized in such practices as judges appointing court experts, and allowing intervenors and *amicus curiae* to assist the judge through representing interests and perspectives beyond those of the immediate parties to the litigation (Weinstein 1995).

Judges today cannot help but recognize that they live in network societies with multifold intensive intimate connections and extensive global interdependencies. This has fostered the willingness of judges to look beyond the immediate disputes before the courts and consider them in wider contexts of interpersonal conflict and social disruption (Sinai and Alberstein 2016; Alberstein and Zimerman 2017). The conceptual framework of dispute resolution advanced as part of the ADR movement has also helped to broaden the judicial perspective beyond narrow legal issues of law and fact. This contextual approach to framing disputes and their potential resolution can operate within a wide range of scope, from families to communities, cultural and religious affiliations, and national organizations, up to the widest and most inclusive international obligations and aspirations. Responsive judges try to determine the most appropriate context within which to frame disputes and provide decisions which meet the needs of those identified as necessarily and properly concerned. To do this properly, judges need to be learners and students of society as well as of law (Weinstein 1994a, b). In Judge Weinstein's words, "Judges must be free to inform—and to be informed by—the society around them" (Weinstein 1994b, 41).

Responsive contextual judging takes many forms. As mentioned above, it can include complex multi-party litigation, and broad constitutional issues affecting many people in diverse situations. Racial and gender discrimination are examples of endemic problems which judges are sometimes called upon to respond to with knowledge of their embeddedness in society (Greenberg 2017). Feminist judging is one response to the need to bring a new perspective to how mostly male judges have typically framed many problems faced by women with a view to providing more informed, engaged and effective legal redress (Hunter et al. 2016; Feminist Judgments 2017; McLoughlin 2017). As Judith Resnik puts it, "Judgment is an expression of connection of self to others. Thus I suggest that the aspirations for judges be altered, that we talk about judicial independence and dependence, disengagement and connection, compassion and dispassion, and celebrate the dailiness of these activities" (Resnik 1990, 37–38).

But contextual judging can also be very intimately focussed as in the practices of family court judges who work with other professionals to prevent children's lives being destroyed in the crossfire of warring parents. At the local community level, judges with a restorative justice orientation and problem solving courts try to assist victims, offenders, and their communities gain healing and peace. Indigenous justice practices such as sentencing circles incorporate responsive judges within traditional native approaches to restoring harmony in communities. In all these ways responsive judges are embracing the challenge to look beyond the courtroom and the immediate dispute before them with knowledge that unrepresented others, sometimes many of them, will be affected by their decision making.

3.3 Responding to Litigants

"Objectivity" is a cardinal virtue in the traditional approach to judging, signifying the absence of sympathy, empathy or enmity in a judge who employs a strictly rational mode of thinking with an emphasis on the use of logic and deductive reasoning (Fish 2009). Today, such a judge would be more likely to be criticized as being aloof, apathetic, and unengaged in the hard work, both mental and emotional, of judging (Roach Anleu et al. 2016). Such a critique largely stems from newer insights into the subjective states of both judges and litigants which place both in an interpersonal framework that is not adequately described by reference to formal procedures alone. Responsive judges today embody a growing appreciation of the need to move beyond traditional procedural formalism towards greater acknowledgement of the subjective perceptions and preferences of all involved in litigation (Mack and Roach Anleu 2011). This development can be described as an evolution in adjudication from reliance on routine "due process" to an aspiration to provide more individualized "fair process" for litigants.

The evolution of a more subjectively oriented understanding of legal processes can be traced back to the scholarship of the American realists, in particular Jerome Frank, who brought Freudian psychoanalysis to the study of the legal system (Frank 1930). He famously asked the question "Are judges human?" (Frank 1931a, b) and gave the inevitable answer "yes", urging that we should study them as such rather than as superhuman oracles of the law. Frank pursued his own study of the human failings and mistakes which were endemic to legal fact finding through the presentation of evidence in an adversary system (Frank 1949), but few followed in his scholarly footsteps. In the United States, investigations of the judicial mind were largely preoccupied for many decades with attempting to trace the influence of judges' political background and leanings on their decision making.

In 1965, however, in a prescient article, Ehrenzweig (1965) advocated thorough psychological research into peoples' perceptions and preferences regarding justice.

He believed such investigations might help to clear away some of the conceptual confusion and obfuscation that plagued debates amongst schools of jurisprudence. Within a decade, the research Ehrenzweig envisioned had commenced and bore fruit in the findings of Thibaut and Walker (1975). They found that subjective perceptions of the way legal processes were conducted affected peoples' evaluations of the justice of the result. When procedures were considered "fair" outcomes were more likely to be considered "just". Thibaut and Walker's work helped to create a distinct field of research based on the concept of "procedural justice", a term used to describe and evaluate adjudication and other legal processes from the standpoint of the perceptions of litigants. This was a move beyond proceduralism founded on following objectively prescribed steps in litigation and trial to consideration of the subjective impact of legal processes on those involved in them. A key insight of procedural justice research thus has been that fairness lies in the eye of the beholder. Lind and Tyler (1988) have also contributed much to our understanding of the interaction between subjective human factors and objective outcomes in peoples' interaction with legal systems.

Some other important findings in procedural justice research highlight the interpersonal relationship between litigants and decision makers. Being listened to, and heard by, a judge who treats you with respect is apparently the essence of having one's "day in court" for many people. Whether that encounter occurs in a courtroom in the context of a trial, in a conference session in the judge's office, or elsewhere, seems to be relatively inconsequential in relation to people's perception of being treated justly and fairly. The results of procedural justice research therefore argue for responsive judges who can demonstrate strong interpersonal and communication skills such as empathy and active listening (Greenberg 2017). This is a vision of judging far removed from the austere, unapproachable authority figure of the traditional judge on a high bench. Judges are now encouraged to take steps to foster positive interactions with litigants based on the findings of procedural justice research (Burke and Leben 2007; Tyler 2007; Rottman 2007; Sivasubramaniam and Heuer 2007; Tyler and Sevier 2013; LaGratta 2017; Procedural Fairness 2017).

The unremarkable finding that "judges are human" has now been extended to the observation that "litigants are human too". One of the earlier applications of this insight is the law and economics approach which has analyzed the behavior of disputing parties through the lens of their subjective preferences for risk, loss, cost and benefit. Many judges in turn have embraced such analysis in their settlement practices, encouraging parties to weigh the risks and rewards of proceeding to trial. This is an example of responsive judging in the light of extra-legal economic incentives and disincentives.

Another example of the incorporation of subjective perspectives in adjudication is the therapeutic jurisprudence movement. Starting with an acknowledgement that traditional legal processes may have an adverse impact on the mental health and wellbeing of those who come to court, therapeutic jurisprudence advocates changes that are informed by psychology and other health disciplines. Wexler (2007) and others (Stobbs 2017) perceive a complementary relationship between concerns for procedural justice and therapeutic jurisprudence initiatives. The respect and attention of judges contribute both to perceptions of fairness and positive self-regard among litigants. Drug treatment and other specialized courts employ the principles of therapeutic jurisprudence and require responsive judges who are knowledgeable and supportive in the area of mental health. Responsive judges in such courts go well beyond traditional interactions with the people who come before them, often developing long term relationships involving supervision and encouragement with those they are called on to judge (Goldberg 2011; Wexler 2016; Kaiser and Holtfreter 2016).

Researchers have helped to put a human face on the judiciary (Guthrie et al. 2001; Darbyshire 2011; Fielding 2011) and there is renewed attention today to the role of emotion in judging (Wistrich et al. 2015) and of the value of empathy for understanding the diverse parties who appear before the court. Judicious empathy and the ability to convey appropriate emotions in the course of judging are now more readily accepted attributes of a wise responsive judge (Bandes 2015; Roach Anleu et al. 2016).

Responsive judges today accept and welcome the challenge of a judicial role which is both more expansive and more modest than in the past. Judges are now called on to respond to expectations of the parties before them that go beyond following strict procedure and require more flexible human interaction such as privately interviewing children in family law cases (Caldwell 2011). This is particularly the case with litigants who do not have lawyers. At the same time, judges are expected to be more willing to admit their own humanity and reveal it appropriately in court. In all such ways responsive judging can be described as more humane judging (Weinstein 2000). A leading judicial educator describes the qualities and attributes required of judges today in these words: "Our view is that a judge is not just a person who is learned in the law and who is really good at writing. We assume that's all in there. What you really want are people who are wise, who can balance justice and compassion. We want people who listen well, who have patience, who are respectful—this whole list of qualities" (Fogel and Strong 2016, 278).

Courts have also responded to the challenge of understanding and responding to litigants' experiences. This new perspective has been described as necessary to make courts more "agile" through "reimagining the court system as one that views its role from the outside in, from the perspective of court users, and revises or radically changes its system and business processes accordingly" (Rickard 2017, 236). Extensive research has been conducted into the legal needs of the public and how those with disputes interact with the legal system (American Bar Association 1994; Parker 1998; Genn 1999; Genn and Paterson 1999; van Velthoven and ter Voert 2004; Galligan 2005; Legal Services 2006; Billingsley et al. 2006; Coumarelos et al. 2006; Sossin 2010; Pleasence et al. 2013). Many courts have recognized the need for continuing input from the public and have integrated feedback into court operations through such mechanisms as court user advisory groups and surveys of court attendees (Nejelski 1977). Courthouse design and operating procedures have been influenced by the information and perspectives thus obtained. Courts are trying to demonstrate responsiveness to users' needs (Quintanilla 2017; Rickard 2017) in many ways including holding hearings out of normal office hours (Bernal 2017) and creating "pop-up" courts (Bowen 2017).

3.4 *Responding to Public Attention*

Public scrutiny of politicians, professionals, and indeed everyone in positions of power, authority or prestige in society is more intense and omnipresent today than ever before. Social media have activated the public gaze as the leader of attention in contrast to more traditional media which determined what was newsworthy for a more passive public. Those caught in this new wave of public attention have responded in kind, entering the sphere of social debate and discussion with initiatives of their own. The "Twitter presidency" of Donald Trump is just a rather extreme example of public figures becoming involved in the contemporary "global village" formed by blogs, twitter feeds, and chat and sharing services of all kinds. Courts and judges are not immune to this trend to more active participation in public forums (Weinstein 2011; Browning 2016) and research has identified the various "audiences" to whom judges might appeal and respond (Baum 2006; Garoupa and Ginsburg 2009).

Traditionally, most judges have shunned public attention, preferring to be seen and heard only in court, letting their judgments speak for themselves. This behavior was thought to preserve the dignity and decorum of the judiciary and protect judges from hazarding their reputation for impartiality in the cut and thrust of public debate. Thus, the image of the judge as a cloistered monk was maintained with the hope that it would preserve public trust and confidence in a judiciary that was above involvement in the everyday affairs of society. In a consumer oriented world, however, such obscurity and opaqueness is more apt to lead to suspicion than confidence on the part of the public. Courts, and many judges, have therefore emerged from this self-imposed exile from public life with a view to demonstrating the transparency of the judiciary and fostering better understanding of the judicial role.

Leading judges have often taken the lead in speaking more directly to the public. Lord Denning of England, an outspoken jurist and author of several books, gave innumerable public speeches and media interviews. His opinions were not always in accord with prevailing public opinion, but he nevertheless gained a reputation as "the people's judge". Judge Albie Sachs of South Africa was a leading opponent of apartheid and became recognized worldwide for this support of human rights. Michael Kirby of Australia, former judge of its High Court, is also an internationally acclaimed human rights advocate, particularly in support of gay rights. He currently maintains a personal website (Kirby 2017). Recently retired United States Judge Richard Posner authored more than thirty books (including *How Judges Think*—Posner 2008), was a leading exponent of economic analysis of law, and one of America's best known judges (Domnarski 2016). Former Justice of the Supreme Court of Canada, Louise Arbour, has played a leading role on the international stage including as special prosecutor for international war crimes and as United Nations

High Commissioner for Human Rights. She maintains an active Twitter account (Arbour 2017). In addition to these individual examples of responsive judges in the public eye, associations formed by judges and lawyers have become public spokespersons for justice. The International Commission of Jurists (2017) is just one example.

Courts have also embraced the challenge of constant communication with the public in order to demonstrate transparency and to educate citizens about the operation of the legal system. Graff (2012), for instance, describes courts as "conversations" and advocates their use of social media. Today many courts have employed dedicated information officers to act as public spokespersons and as an interface between judges and the media, both traditional and social. Some courts have adopted explicit communication plans and that of the Florida State Courts is a good example. It includes the following strategies:

- building relationships with key audiences (the public, court users, the media, state lawmakers, justice system partners, teachers, civic organizations, and the business community);
- increasing public awareness about court services and performance;
- providing information to court users to ensure understanding of court processes and services;
- involving the public to improve court processes;
- educating the public about the judicial branch by improving outreach efforts; and
- training judges and court staff in media relations (Labarga et al. 2016, 69).

The mission and vision statement of this court is also an exemplar of what is expected from responsive courts and judges today. It reads: "Mission—To protect rights and liberties, uphold and interpret the law, and provide for the peaceful resolution of disputes. Vision—Justice in Florida will be accessible, fair, effective, responsive and accountable" (Labarga et al. 2016, 68).

Responsive judging in the cyberworld of today necessarily involves courts and judges in more, and more direct communication with the public. To the extent that this enhanced engagement in the public sphere demonstrates transparency and a willingness to respond to the needs of society it will bolster the reputations and credibility of judges and courts, thereby enhancing the perceived legitimacy of the legal systems they represent.

4 Critiques of Responsiveness

There are four prominent critiques of the practice of responsive judging. In the following section we explore and answer them.

4.1 The Exceptionalism/Personalism Critique

Some critics of responsive judging admit that some good results may be obtained by exceptional responsive judges (for example Judge Weinstein as described in Zariski's chapter) but the necessary personal and professional abilities and qualities they possess are not shared by all judges. The argument goes that in less capable hands, bad results my often flow from responsive judging practices.

Richard Marcus, discussing the actions of Judge Jack Weinstein in settling the "Agent Orange" litigation levels such a criticism: "If there is an apocalyptic vision to be drawn from the Agent Orange litigation, it is that less talented judges may regularly use such prods to coerce acceptance of the results they conclude are more just than formal adjudication would probably yield." (Marcus 1987, 1270). He goes on:

> But is this judging? What standards did Judge Weinstein use in fashioning the critical allocation formula? Were they "legal"? In a sense, these episodes suggest a model of judging that depends more on the personality of the judge than on his position in the institutional hierarchy. Judge Weinstein could do it but Judge Pratt, perhaps, could not. It is nice to have charismatic judges, but this is hardly a trend to be embraced; as Max Weber observed long ago, in a complex society it is necessary to shift authority from a charismatic to an institutionalized leadership. [footnotes omitted] (Marcus 1987, 1293)

Stephen Burbank offers a similar view:

> I recognize how difficult it is to be a judge today, particularly a federal judge with Jack Weinstein's personality, life experiences, and belief structure. If I pause over certain aspects of his judicial behavior that I find problematic, it is to honor our shared commitment to the pursuit of knowledge. None of us would want to be emulated in every facet of our professional lives. (Burbank 1997, 1974)

This argument amounts essentially to a negative assessment of the "scalability" of a responsive judging approach: the achievements of an exceptional responsive judge cannot be reliably replicated by the majority of judges. One answer to this critique is that the foundations of responsive judging may be taught and are not just personal qualities possessed by extraordinary individuals. Education and training in increasingly being offered to judges including the following:

- "social context" education to provide judges with information and insight into sectors of society or social situations of which they have no personal exposure or knowledge
- training in mediation techniques and other settlement practices which expand judges' repertoire beyond decision-making
- education in the psychology of procedural justice and training in interpersonal and courtroom management skills in order to satisfy litigants' need for respect and recognition in their interactions with the court
- education and training in developing and expressing empathy towards litigants and other courtroom participants, especially when judges confront minorities or victims of discrimination with whom they have previously had little or no contact

- education in the psychology and behaviour associated with domestic violence and sexual crimes which require insight and understanding in order to be justly dealt with by the court
- training in the techniques of monitoring and support associated with problem solving and therapeutic jurisprudence oriented courts.

Although not all judges may be capable of exemplary responsive judging it seems nevertheless appropriate to offer these types of support, education, and training to all judges in the expectation that the majority are capable of putting at least some of these practices and principles to use in their courts.

4.2 The Judicial Function Critique

Another critique of responsive judging is that it diverts and distracts judges from their core judicial function of adjudication. Associated with this argument is the adverse consequence of depriving the public and the legal system of precedents and authoritative statements of public values (Fiss 1979, 1984; Farrow 2014). Such criticisms are also connected to the critique of a settlement orientation on the part of the judiciary and the participation of judges in ADR activities such as judicial mediation and other settlement efforts (see Senft and Savage 2003).

One answer to such criticisms is that judges have always been engaged in ancillary activities beyond merely sitting in court presiding over trials and other proceedings and issuing judgments and orders accordingly. From the time of King Solomon judges have been "nudging" disputants towards a just result (recall the "tentative judgment" to split the baby) and otherwise overseeing the progress of litigation. Although it is only relatively recently that formal case management and settlement procedures have been adopted by many courts it is not revolutionary to involve judges in such processes.

Furthermore, given the burgeoning digital legal environment we now live in it is arguable whether we now have more or less precedents to deal with. Surely, cases which present intractable and significant legal problems will continue to proceed to judgment, and appeal if necessary. By the same token, parties who discover mutually acceptable solutions to their conflicts should not be hindered in doing so by judges who are intent on adjudication.

Although fewer judges and prospective judicial appointees may now have significant trial experience it has been demonstrated that this is not a serious shortcoming through the appointment of legal academics to the judiciary and their subsequent success in the new role.

We recognize that some jurisdictions may face constitutional and other legislative restrictions on the functions which judges may perform, and that this may place limits on some activities associated with responsive judging (see for instance Luban 1997). However, we also believe that many ostensible restrictions on the role of judges and the functions they may perform stem largely from tradition and force of habit, rather than real legal impediments. Judges everywhere who value responsiveness will continue to find ways to combine their fidelity to law and judicial ethics with a desire to serve society more responsively.

4.3 *The Judicial Activism Critique*

The term 'judicial activism' has been poorly defined in the literature relating to judging (see Kmiec 2004; Fisher 2014; Mate 2014; Hansford 2014; Tahiri 2016; Cheema 2016). Those that criticize judicial activism overwhelmingly consider that judges act 'beyond the law'. These concerns are discussed to some extent above however specific concerns often revert to a formalist/realist jurisprudential debate. One noted critic of judicial activism has defined it as follows:

> The expression "judicial activism" is here used to mean using judicial power for a purpose other than that for which it was granted, namely doing justice according to law in the particular case. It means serving some function other than what is necessary for the decision of the particular dispute between the parties. Often the illegitimate function is the furthering of some political, moral or social program: the law is seen not as the touchstone by which the case in hand is to be decided, but as a possible starting point or catalyst for developing a new system to solve a range of other cases. (Heydon 2003)

One observer has proposed a more discerning analysis of judicial behaviour than merely "passive" or "active". Yung (2013) has studied judicial decision making in the appellate courts of the United States and classified nine judging styles: "trail-blazing, consensus building, stalwart, regulating, steadfast, collegial, incrementalist, minimalist, and error correcting" (Yung 2013, 1781). He found that activism as traditionally defined was a key characteristic of several of these judicial "types". This research underlines our belief that responsiveness in judging may be manifested by judges in different ways which reflect their personal and institutional differences.

At the same time, criticisms of those who consider that judicial activism is in appropriate point to the difficulties that judges have in not engaging more broadly with a range of issues. Hutchinson notes that "Even in a perfectly functioning constitutional democracy in which the legislature truly represented the genuine public interest, it is far from obvious why citizens would want courts to apply the rules of yesteryear to the problems of today…Moreover, it seems a flat rejection of political reality to maintain, as Heydon does, that all common law rules that are not directly overruled by a hobbled and over-stretched legislature are thereby approved" (Hutchinson 2003). In short, many commentators consider that it is not appropriate for a judge to not be active. For example in quoting Justice McHugh, Barker notes that 'While stare decisis is a sound policy because it promotes predictability of judicial decision and facilitates the giving of advice, it should not always trump the need for desirable change in the law. In developing the common law, judges must necessarily look to the present and to the future as well as to the past' (Barker 2005).

Whilst discussion about judicial activism is at times framed as a concern about 'judge made law' (see previous discussion) and maintaining the separation of powers, it has also at times become synonymous with a more liberal and value focused approach where the core values and overarching principles enable judges to consider disputes in a responsive manner (Kirby 1997). Importantly, as Kirby points out, proponents of judicial restraint might appropriately consider appropriate limitations in relation to judicial activism that can be grouped into four key areas relating to opportunity, need, inclination and methodology. It is suggested here that these four elements also guide the responsive judge who must have an appropriate dispute, a need for judicial innovation, individual judicial inclination whilst maintaining an appropriate judicial methodology. One observer has described such a responsive approach as "principled judicial activism" (Barnett 1987).

4.4 The Impartiality Critique

Responsive judging does not necessarily invoke a concern that a judge has ceased to be impartial. However, the spectre of impartiality may arise where there is a perception that a judge has "gone too far". For example, where judges act as mediators, in many jurisdictions they are unlikely to proceed to "hear" the case or a related dispute (see Deason 2017 and below). However, even with this limitation, concerns about the judicial role and whether it can include mediation are often expressed and often these concerns can be linked to a concern that objectivity has been lost and a judge may no longer be impartial. For a mediator judge, the concern can be linked to whether a judge has heard something in the absence of another party, where a relationship develops that is not the result of an open court process, potentially leading to allegations of impartiality or bias.

What constitutes bias? The situation appears clearer where adjudication has taken place although even in such a circumstance there may be questions about impartiality. In court proceedings in Australia, judicial comments before or during the trial about the credit of witnesses will often raise an inference of bias (R v Watson 1976), as will excessive intervention in the parties' conduct of the litigation (Jones v National Coal Board 1957; Tousek v Bernat 1959; Rogers 1993).

These determinations may have meant that judges in the past have been reluctant to "enter into the fray" and intervene to prevent proceedings from continuing for too long or to prevent a party pursuing a topic that is clearly irrelevant. However, the Australian High Court has made it clear that the bias rule should not prevent appropriate levels of intervention from occurring:

> It seems to us that a trial judge who made necessary rulings but otherwise sat completely silent throughout a non-jury trial with the result that his or her views about the issues, problems and technical difficulties involved in the case remained unknown until they emerged as final conclusions in his or her judgment would not represent a model to be emulated. (Vakauta v Kelly 1989, [3])

Similarly, Kirby P, then President of the New South Wales Court of Appeal, in Australia indicated that contemporary civil litigation requires greater judicial intervention and this should not be seen as opening judges to accusations of bias:

> It has become more common for judges to take an active part in the conduct of cases than was hitherto conventional. In part, this change is a response to the growth of litigation and the greater pressure of court lists….In part, it arises from a growing appreciation that a silent judge may sometimes occasion an injustice by failing to reveal opinions which the party then affected has no opportunity to correct or modify. In part, it is simply a reflection of the heightened willingness of judges to take greater control of proceedings for the avoidance of injustices that can sometimes occur from undue delay or unnecessary prolongation of trials… The conduct of criminal trials, particularly with a jury, remains subject to different and more stringent requirements. (Galea v Galea 1990, 281–282)

This relaxation in the bias rule has occurred as judges have increased their levels of participation in civil trials. Other forms of intervention, such as calling or questioning witnesses by the judge, are also recognized in some jurisdictions as acceptable practices to ensure just outcomes and to expedite trials (Ipp 1995; Davies and Sheldon 1993).

Issues associated with a judge mediating a matter and then proceeding to hear that matter or a related dispute have been specifically considered in some jurisdictions. In Australia, in the Duke Group (in Liq) v Alamein Investments Ltd. and ors (2003), this issue was considered by Justice Debelle, in relation to a successful application to disqualify himself from hearing a matter. The application related to a mediation conducted nine years prior to the court hearing that involved the same plaintiff and might involve similar issues in relation to fiduciary duties. His Honour had, "…no memory of the details." However, His Honour disqualified himself on the basis that, "A reasonable bystander might apprehend that, in the course of meeting the directors separately, I might have received information which would cause me to have a view about the merits of the claim against the directors which might affect the exercise of my discretion…"

In considering issues relating to bias Justice Debelle noted that,

> …When a judge acts as a mediator, the judge sheds, as it were, the judicial mantle for the duration of the mediation and acts in a manner inconsistent with the role of a judge by seeing the parties in private. In doing so, the judge acts in a manner contrary to the fundamental principle of natural justice that a judge must not hear representations from one party in the absence of the other. It is for that reason that the judge will not in any respect adjudicate in that action except with the consent of the parties. It is for that reason that Rule 56A.05 of the Supreme Court Rules provided:
>
>> '56A.05 A judicial officer who has presided over a mediation in an action shall, ipso facto, be disqualified from thereafter hearing or determining the action or any issue arising in the course thereof which is directed to be tried separately.'
>
> The principle is based upon the need for public confidence in the administration of justice. The judge is disqualified because a fair-minded lay observer might reasonably apprehend that the judge might not bring an impartial and unprejudiced mind to the resolution of the question the judge is required to decide: Johnson v Johnson (2000) 201 CLR 488 at [12]; Ebner v Official Trustee in Bankruptcy (2000) 205 CLR 337 at [33]. The fair-minded observer might apprehend that the judge has been told something by one party in the absence of the other and that information may affect his reasoning. [pinpoint]

Justice Debelle also made some instructive comments about his perception of the role and integrity of the Court:

> In the result, I believe that what is at stake is the integrity of the Court engaging in two forms of dispute resolution and the public interest in upholding the integrity of the Court and public confidence in the Court. It is necessary to uphold public confidence in the integrity of the mediation process. It is equally important to uphold the public confidence in the integrity of the process of adjudication by the Court. It is important that nothing should occur which would suggest any breach of the obligation of confidence attaching to a mediation. Those who engage in mediation should be entirely confident that in no respect will anything said in confidence be revealed. Secondly, the public should have confidence in its judges knowing that, when they adjudicate issues, they are not influenced by anything which might have occurred in a mediation. [pinpoint]

It has been argued that responsive judging (in its aspect of managing litigation) corrupts the qualities we traditionally expect of judges, most importantly impartiality, when they become overly engaged in the cases they hear (Resnik 1982); this can be linked as well to critiques of "active adjudication" in cases of self-represented litigants (see above). One response to such a criticism is advocacy of the concept of "substantive impartiality" within the practice of active adjudication in place of traditional "formal impartiality" (Flaherty 2015).

5 Studies of Responsiveness—Overview of the Chapters

This book is divided into two parts. Part I presents a variety of theoretical and conceptual contributions to the notion of responsive judging. In the Chapter "The Responsive Tribunal: Robust Processes; Fair and Timely Outcomes", Helen Shurven and Clair Berman-Robinson explore the practical ways in which tribunals can be responsive to participants. Using case studies to illustrate real world examples, the authors canvass various strategies to increase tribunal responsiveness, from the appropriate use of discretion, to designing the decision-making process to fit the particular dispute and disputants. In the second part of their chapter, Shurven and Berman-Robinson outline the importance of providing participants with the opportunity to resolve their dispute by agreement. By paying attention to these aspects of responsive practice, it is argued that decisions reached in a tribunal context will be fairer and more effective. Whilst this chapter draws on its authors' knowledge of the decision-making processes in Australia's Commonwealth National Native Title Tribunal, the chapter proffers comments and analysis that can be usefully applied to a much broader range of tribunals.

In the Chapter "Settlement Adjudication and Judicial Responsiveness: The Choice Between a Wide and a Narrow Model", Karni Perlman also discusses responsiveness in the context of litigants' experiences of the legal system and courts. Focusing on judges in Israel and Anglo-American law countries, Perlman compares and contrasts two models of settlement judging, each of which presents a different measure of judicial responsiveness: a 'narrow model' which is primarily concerned with considerations of efficiency, and a 'wide model' which takes into account additional needs and interests, from the psychological well-being of litigants, to the welfare of the wider community. After outlining the advantages and disadvantages of each model, Perlman argues for the application of the latter, asserting this model of judging can alleviate many of the concerns raised about the expansive use of settlement adjudication. The chapter concludes by offering a number of useful suggestions for increasing the use of the 'wide model' in dispute settlement.

In the Chapter "Do Judges Need to Be Human? The Implications of Technology for Responsive Judging", one of the Editors, Tania Sourdin, teams with Richard Cornes to present a thought-provoking discussion on the topic of whether or not judges need to be human. The authors encourage us to ponder the extent to which the judicial role will change as many aspects of human activity, including the work of judges, are taken over by replacement technologies. Whilst the chapter outlines the many ways in which artificial intelligence can beneficially contribute to the work of courts and judges, the authors apply insights from psychoanalytical thought to caution us against conceptualising the judicial role as akin to "a single data processing unit to be adequately represented in code". Rather, the chapter urges us to develop a more holistic appreciation of the judicial role which "requires at its heart the organic home of a *human* mind".

In the Chapter "The High Court and the Cocktail Party from Hell: Can Social Media Improve Community Engagement with the Courts?", Andrew Henderson examines the potential for social media to be utilised by the courts as a means of becoming more responsive to the views of the wider community. This chapter complements the previous Chapter "Do Judges Need to Be Human? The Implications of Technology for Responsive Judging" in its analysis of judicial responsiveness in the context of an interdependent, network society. In order to test the potential for Twitter to serve as a platform for community engagement, Henderson examines the volume and content of Twitter commentary about a recent decision of the High Court of Australia. With billions of items of information exchanged every day on social media, Henderson's chapter invites us to consider both the advantages and challenges which arise when courts become actively involved in this "cocktail party from hell".

In the Chapter "Sustainable Justice, a Social Responsible Focus on Innovation in Justice", the final chapter of this part, Alexander F. de Savornin Lohman and Jaap van Strallen discuss the substantive and organisational aspects of an internationally coordinated and planned approach to sustainable development. The authors outline the benefits that can stem from both the top-down and bottom-up organisation of the legal system, in which judges contribute to better solutions. After providing an overview of some examples of socially sustainable justice system projects that have already been realised, the authors offer a number of suggestions for the successful mainstreaming of these, and similar, practical initiatives. Overall, the chapter reminds us that a justice system which prioritises principles of social sustainability will have a positive impact both inside and outside the legal system.

In Part II of this book, comparative approaches to responsive judging are presented. In the Chapter "Inside Out or Outside In?: Looking at Judges' Relations with the Public in Canada and China", the other Editor, Archie Zariski, teams with Shi Changqing to present a comparative case study of relations between members of the judiciary and the wider public in Canada and China. This Chapter employs a theoretical and conceptual perspective to compare participant and observer perceptions of the social legitimacy of courts and their judges. By examining the careers of several prominent judges and their responses to high profile cases, the authors explore the conditions necessary for society to "believe in the wisdom and justness of its judges". In applying their analytical lens to the Canadian and Chinese judiciaries, Zariski and Changqing highlight the importance of striking an appropriate balance between judicial independence and impartiality on the one hand, and judicial engagement with public needs and concerns on the other.

In the Chapter "Judicial Practice in Action: Court Reform and Responsive Judges in Canada", Toby Goldbach adopts a socio-legal empirical approach to the study of responsive judging, examining the everyday activities and practices of Canadian judges outside of the courtroom. Goldbach's aim is to highlight the ways in which Canada's judges have responded to various challenges "behind the scenes" by "innovating, adapting, and reforming the practices and operation of activities at court". Two key examples of judicial responsiveness in this jurisdiction are explored—first, the incorporation of alternative dispute resolution mechanisms into conventional court procedures; and second, the implementation of culturally appropriate architectural design and procedures for delivering Aboriginal justice within the courthouse. In presenting these examples of judicial responsiveness, Goldbach's chapter provokes legal scholars to reflect on the various sites of judicial law-making, as well as the intermingling of law and politics.

In the Chapter "Judging in a Therapeutic Way: TJ Audit of Juvenile, Probation and Criminal Procedure Law in Pakistan with Reference to Therapeutic Design and Therapeutic Application of Law", Muhammad Amir Munir examines the therapeutic jurisprudence practices of judges in Pakistan. Looking at three specific Pakistani laws, Munir highlights the discrepancy which arises when laws which have been designed therapeutically are not applied in a therapeutic manner. The reason for this, Munir explains, is a lack of training and orientation of judges and prosecutors in Pakistan. Drawing on his own experience as a therapeutic jurisprudence practitioner, Munir provides some useful suggestions for mainstreaming therapeutic jurisprudence practice and increasing legal and judicial education so that "welfare and well-being and rehabilitation in society are the prime objectives for administering the law."

In the Chapter "The #BlueWhale Challenge to the Indian judiciary: A Critical Analysis of the Response of the Indian Higher Judiciary to Risky Online Contents with Special Reference to the BlueWhale Suicide Game", Debarati Halder shifts our focus to India's judiciary and its response to a notorious online suicide game. Halder praises the Indian judiciary for its thoughtful and therapeutic response to this issue, and willingness to engage with both public and private stakeholders to spread awareness about the perils of the dangerous online game. At the same time, however, Halder outlines the need for stricter judicial decision-making attitudes towards the liability of foreign hosted Internet service providers, and explains how India's judges can do more to take advantage of developing judicial mechanisms. As with the previous chapter, the importance of further judicial training and education is once again highlighted.

In the Chapter "The Responsive Judge: Comparative Perspectives of Korea and Japan", Young Hoa Jung compares and contrasts the practices of Korea's Constitutional Court with Japan's Supreme Court, examining the judicial responsiveness of each through judicial review of legislation. This chapter highlights the activism and autonomy of Korea's judiciary in constitutional matters, as well as the more responsive approach to alternative dispute resolution which has been taken by Japan's judiciary in civil litigation. In comparing the approaches taken to the adjudication of litigants' rights in these two jurisdictions, Jung reminds us of the wide-range of factors and considerations at play, from the democratic history of each country, to socio-economic factors, and each country's commitment to guaranteeing fundamental human rights.

In the Chapter "Mansfield, Atkin, Weinstein: Three Responsive Judges at the Nexus of Law, Politics, and Economy", the final chapter of this book, Archie Zariski surveys three leading cases of responsive judging to draw out commonalities and lessons for the future. The chosen case studies are tied together by their demonstration of active responsiveness in the context of public attention to civil litigation normally considered to be of a "private" nature. In such cases, Zariski contends that judges have an additional responsibility and opportunity to be responsive. After outlining the background to each of the three cases, Zariski highlights the ways in which each judge was able to successfully balance their legal skills, social knowledge, and human responsiveness to ultimately "navigate the nexus between law and justice". In an era of pervasive social media and the increasing openness of courts, Zariski posits that these cases may provide valuable guidance for judges seeking to secure a substantively just result within the limits of the law.

References

Alberstein M, Zimerman N (2017) Constructive plea bargaining: towards judicial conflict resolution. Ohio State J Dispute Resolut 32:279–294

Aldisert RJ (2009) Judicial declaration of public policy. J Appellate Pract Process 10(2):229–245

Alexander N (2009) International and comparative mediation: legal perspectives. Kluwer, Alphen ann den Rijn

Allison JWF (1994) Fuller's analysis of polycentric disputes and the limits of adjudication. Camb Law J 53(2):367–383

American Bar Association Consortium on Legal Services and the Public (1994) Legal needs and civil justice. American Bar Association, Chicago. http://www.americanbar.org/content/dam/aba/migrated/legalservices/downloads/sclaid/legalneedstudy.authcheckdam.pdf. Accessed 11 Feb 2018

Arbour L (2017) @louise_arbour. https://twitter.com/louise_arbour?lang=en. Accessed 5 Oct 2017

Arvind TT (2012) 'Though it shocks one very much': formalism and pragmatism in the *Zong* and *Bancoult*. Oxf J Legal Stud 32(1):113–151

Attorney General's Department, Australia (2012) Draft objectives for the civil justice system. https://www.ag.gov.au/LegalSystem/Documents/Draft%20objectives%20for%20the%20civil%20justice%20system.pdf. Accessed 21 Feb 2018

Australian Law Reform Commission (1997) Review of the adversarial system of litigation: rethinking the federal civil litigation system (Issues Paper No. 20). Australian Law Reform Commission, Sydney

Australian Law Reform Commission (1998) Review of the adversarial system of litigation: ADR—its role in federal dispute resolution (Issues Paper No 25). Australian Law Reform Commission, Canberra
Baicker-McKee S (2015) Reconceptualizing managerial judges. Am Univ Law Rev 65:353–398
Bandes SA (2015) Empathy and Article III: Judge Weinstein, cases and controversies. DePaul Law Rev 64:317–339
Barnett RE (1987) Foreword: judicial conservatism v. a principled judicial activism. Harvard J Law Public Policy 10:273–294
Barker L (2005) Judicial activism in Australia: a perspective, 79 Aust Law J, 783
Baum L (2006) Judges and their audiences: a perspective on judicial behavior. Princeton University Press, Princeton
Belenko S (1998) Research on drug courts: a critical review. Natl Drug Court Inst Rev 1(1):1–27
Berman G (2000) What is traditional justice anyway? Problem solving in the state courts. Judicature 8:78–85
Berman G, Feinblatt J (2004) Therapeutic Jurisprudence: the role of forensic psychology. In: Sarre R, Tamaino J (eds) Key issues in criminal justice. Australian Humanities Press, Unley, pp 166–191
Bernal D (2017) Taking the court to the people: real-world solutions for nonappearance. Ariz Law Rev 59:547–571
Billingsley B, Lowe D, Stratton M (2006) Civil justice system and the public: learning from experiences to find practices that work. Canadian Forum on Civil Justice. http://www.cfcj-fcjc.org/sites/default/files/docs/2006/cjsp-learning-en.pdf. Accessed 4 Oct 2017
Bowen P (2017) Building trust: how our courts can improve the criminal court experience for Black, Asian and Minority Ethnic defendants. Centre for Justice Innovation. http://justiceinnovation.org/portfolio/building-trust/. Accessed 4 Oct 2017
Brazil WD (1985) Settling civil suits: litigators' views about appropriate roles and effective techniques for federal judges. American Bar Association, Chicago
Brazil WD (1999) Comparing structures for the delivery of ADR services by courts: critical values and concerns. Ohio State J Dispute Resolut 14:715–811
Brennan WJ Jr (1988) Reason, passion, and the progress of the law. Cardozo Law Rev 10:3–23
Browning JG (2016) The judge as digital citizen: pros, cons, and ethical limitations on judicial use of new media. Faulkner Law Rev 8:131–156
Burbank S (1997) The courtroom as classroom: independence, imagination and ideology in the work of Jack Weinstein. Columbia Law Rev 97:1971–2009
Burger WE (1976) 70 F.R.D. 83. Agenda for 2000 A.D.-a need for systematic anticipation. Global Pound Conference. http://baltimore2017.globalpoundconference.org/Documents/1976%20Addresses%20Delivered%20at%201976%20Pound%20Conference.pdf. Accessed 15 Sept 2017
Burke K, Leben S (2007) Procedural fairness: a key ingredient in public satisfaction. Court Rev 44:4–25. University of Nebraska. http://digitalcommons.unl.edu/ajacourtreview/226/. Accessed 4 Oct 2017
Caldwell J (2011) Common law judges and judicial interviewing. Child Fam Law Q 23:41–62
Cates CL, McIntosh WV (1995) Retail jurisprudence: the judge as entrepreneur in the marketplace of ideas. J Law Polit 11:709–750
Chayes A (1976) The role of the judge in public law litigation. Harvard Law Rev 89(7):1281–1316
Cheema MH (2016) The 'Chaudhry court': deconstructing the 'judicialization of politics' in Pakistan. Pac Rim Law Policy J 25:447–488
Chin D (2012) Sentencing: a role for empathy. Univ Penn Law Rev 160(6):1561–1584
Church TW Jr (1982) The 'old and the new' conventional wisdom of court delay. Justice Syst J 7:395–412
Cohen FS (1935) Transcendental nonsense and the functional approach. Columbia Law Rev 35(6):809–849
Colatrella MT Jr (2000) 'Court-performed' mediation in the People's Republic of China: a proposed model to improve the United States federal district courts' mediation programs. Ohio State J Dispute Resolut 15:391–423

Colby TB (2012) In defense of judicial empathy. Minn Law Rev 96:1944–2015
Cook B (2017) Active adjudication: improving access to justice. Society of Ontario Adjudicators and Regulators. https://soar.on.ca/system/files/documents/cook-presentation-session2-ontario.pdf. Accessed 4 Oct 2017
Coumarelos C, Wei Z, Zhou AZ (2006) Justice made to measure: NSW legal needs survey in disadvantaged areas. Law and Justice Foundation of New South Wales, Sydney. http://www.lawfoundation.net.au/report/survey2006. Accessed 11 Feb 2018
Courts and Programs Development Unit (2006) Policy framework to consolidate and extend problem-solving courts and approaches. Department of Justice, Melbourne
Darbyshire P (2011) Sitting in judgment. Hart Publishing, Portland
Davies G, Sheldon S (1993) Some proposed changes in civil procedure: their practical benefits and ethical rationale. J Judicial Adm 3:111–127
de Hoon M, Verberk S (2013) Judicial conflict management: what brings litigants to court? In: Sourdin T, Zariski A (eds) The multi-tasking judge: comparative judicial dispute resolution. Thomson Reuters, Sydney, pp 87–102
Deason EE (2017) Beyond 'managerial judges': appropriate roles in settlement. Ohio State Law J 78:73–144
Dodson S, Klebba JM (2011) Global civil procedure trends in the twenty-first century. Boston Coll Int Comp Law Rev 34:1–26
Domnarski W (2016) Richard Posner. Oxford University Press, New York
Duke Group (in Liq) v Alamein Investments Ltd. and ors (2003) SASC 272
Ehrenzweig AA (1965) Psychoanalytic jurisprudence: a common language for Babylon. Columbia Law Rev 65:1331–1360
Eisenberg MA (1978) Participation, responsiveness, and the consultative process: an essay for Lon Fuller. Harvard Law Rev 92:410–432
Elliott ED (1986) Managerial judging and the evolution of procedure. Univ Chicago Law Rev 53:306–336
Emerson RW (2015) Judges as guardian angels: the German practice of hints and feedback. Vanderbilt J Transnational Law 48:707–752
Farrow TCW (2014) Civil justice, privatization, and democracy. University of Toronto Press, Toronto
Federal Rules of Civil Procedure (2017) Cornell Law School Legal Information Institute. https://www.law.cornell.edu/rules/frcp. Accessed 4 Oct 2017
Feminist Judgments Project (2017) https://www.kent.ac.uk/law/fjp/. Accessed 4 Oct 2017
Fielding NG (2011) Judges and their work. Soc Legal Stud 20:97–115
Fish S (2009) Empathy and the law. New York Times. https://opinionator.blogs.nytimes.com/2009/05/24/empathy-and-the-law/. Accessed 4 Oct 2017
Fisher F (2014) Moving toward a more perfect world: achieving equal access to justice through a new definition of judicial activism. City Univ N Y Law Rev 17:285–308
Fiss OM (1979) Foreword: the forms of justice. Harvard Law Rev 93(1):1–58
Fiss OM (1984) Against settlement. Yale Law J 93:1073–1090
Fix-Fierro H (2003) Courts, justice and efficiency. Hart, Oxford
Flaherty M (2015) Self-represented litigants, active adjudication and the perception of bias: issues in administrative law. Dalhousie Law J 38:119–146
Fogel J, Strong SI (2016) Judicial education, dispute resolution and the life of a judge: a conversation with Judge Jeremy Fogel, director of the Federal Judicial Center. J Dispute Resolut 2016:259–280
Forde HMW (2001) What model of court governance would optimize the expeditious delivery of justice, judicial independence and the accountability of Queensland's court system? Presented at Conference on Governance and Justice, Griffith University, Brisbane, 9 July. http://archive.sclqld.org.au/judgepub/forde090701.pdf. Accessed 5 May 2012
Frank J (1930) Law and the modern mind. Brentano's, New York
Frank J (1931a) Are judges human? Part one: the effect on legal thinking of the assumption that judges behave like human beings. Univ Penn Law Rev 80:17–53

Frank J (1931b) Are judges human? Part two: as through a glass darkly. Univ Penn Law Rev 80:233–267
Frank J (1949) Courts on trial: myth and reality in American justice. Princeton University Press, Princeton
Freiberg A (2001) Problem-oriented courts: innovative solutions to intractable problems? J Judicial Adm 11:8–27
French HR (2009) Perspectives on court annexed alternative dispute resolution. High Court of Australia.http://www.hcourt.gov.au/assets/publications/speeches/current-justices/frenchcj/frenchcj27july09.pdf. Accessed 5 May 2012
Fuller LL (1978) The forms and limits of adjudication. Harvard Law Rev 92:353–409
Galanter M (1986) The emergence of the judge as a mediator in civil cases. Judicature 69:257–262
Galanter M (2014) Snakes and ladders: *suo moto* intervention and the Indian judiciary. Florida Int Univ Law Rev 10:69–84
Galanter M, Palen FS, Thomas JM (1979) The crusading judge: judicial activism in trial courts. South Calif Law Rev 52:699–742
Galea v Galea (1990) 19 NSWLR 263
Galligan TC Jr (2005) Understanding the unrepresented. Tenn Bar J 41:14–29
Garoupa N, Ginsburg T (2009) Judicial audiences and reputation: perspectives from comparative law. Columbia J Transnational Law 47:451–490
Gélinas F, Camion C, Bates K, Anstis S, Piché C, Khan M, Grant E (2015) Foundations of civil justice: toward a value-based framework for reform. Springer, Dordrecht
Genn H (1999) Paths to justice: what people do and think about going to law. Hart Publishing, Oxford
Genn H, Paterson A (1999) Paths to justice Scotland. Hart Publishing, Oxford
Goldberg S (2011) Problem-solving in Canada's courtrooms: a guide to therapeutic justice. National Judicial Institute. https://www.nji-inm.ca/index.cfm/publications/?langSwitch=en. Accessed 4 Oct 2017
Goldberg JCP (2015) Judging responsibility, responsible judging. DePaul Law Rev 64:475–494
Graff G (2012) Courts are conversations: an argument for increased engagement by court leaders. National Center for State Courts. http://www.ncsc.org/services-and-experts/court-leadership/harvard-executive-session/courts-are-conversations-an-argument-for-increased-engagement-by-court-leaders.aspx. Accessed 4 Oct 2017
Greenberg EE (2017) Bridging our justice gap with empathic processes that change hearts, expand minds about implicit discrimination. Ohio State J Dispute Resolut 32:441–486
Guthrie C, Rachlinski JJ, Wistrich AJ (2001) Inside the judicial mind. Cornell Law Rev 86:777–830
Haavisto V (2002) Court work in transition: an activity-theoretical study of changing work practices in a Finnish district court. Ph.D. dissertation, Department of Education, University of Helsinki. https://helda.helsinki.fi/handle/10138/19754. Accessed 26 Aug 2012
Hansford J (2014) Cause judging. Georgetown J Legal Ethics 27:1–54
Hazard GC, Dondi A (2006) Responsibilities of judges and advocates in civil and common law: some lingering misconceptions concerning civil lawsuits. Cornell Int Law J 39:59–70
Henderson L (1988) The dialogue of heart and head. Cardozo Law Rev 10:123–148
Herz R (2012) The art of justice: the judge's perspective. Hart Publishing, Oxford
Hoffman M (2000) The drug court scandal. N C Law Rev 78:1437–1534
Holmes OW Jr (1897) The path of the law. Harvard Law Rev 10:457–478
Hughes J, Bryden P (2017) Implications of case management and active adjudication for judicial disqualification. Alberta Law Rev 54(4):849–870
Hunter R, Anleu SR, Mack K (2016) Judging in lower courts: conventional, procedural, therapeutic and feminist approaches. Int J Law Context 12(3):337–360
Hutchinson AC (1979) Book review: Law and society in transition: toward responsive law. By Nonet P, Selznick P. Harper and Row, New York
Hutchinson AC (2003) Heydon' seek: looking for law in all the wrong places, 29 Monash UL Rev 85, 103

In re Agent Orange Product Liability Litigation (1984) 597 F. Supp. 740 (E.D.N.Y. 1984). Justia. http://law.justia.com/cases/federal/district-courts/FSupp/597/740/1437287/. Accessed 11 Feb 2018
Indermaur D, Roberts L (2003) Drug courts in Australia: the first generation. Curr Crim Issues Crim Justice 15(2):136–154
Infante EA (1997) Judicial case management in the federal trial courts of the United States of America. World Bank. http://www1.worldbank.org/publicsector/LearningProgram/Judicial/CASEMGMT%20Infante%20paper.doc. Accessed 10 Oct 2017
International Commission of Jurists (2017) International Commission of Jurists. https://www.icj.org/. Accessed 5 Oct 2017
Ipp D (1995) Judicial intervention in the trial process. Aust Law J 69:365–384
Jones v National Coal Board (1957) 2 QB 55
Justice Heydon D (2003) Judicial Activism and the Death of the Rule of Law 47(1) Quadrant 9
Kaiser KA, Holtfreter K (2016) An integrated theory of specialized court programs: using procedural justice and therapeutic jurisprudence to promote offender compliance and rehabilitation. Crim Justice Behav 43(1):45–62
Kaufman IR (1990) Reform for a system in crisis: alternative dispute resolution in the federal courts. Fordham Law Rev 59:1–38
Kessler G, Finkelstein LJ (1988) The evolution of a multi-door courthouse. Catholic Univ Law Rev 37(3):577–590
King M, Wager J (2005) Therapeutic jurisprudence and problem-solving judicial case management. Judicial J Adm 15:28–36
Kirby M (1997) Judicial activism, 27 U.W. Aust Law Rev 1, 20
Kirby M (2017) The Hon. Michael Kirby AC CMG. https://www.michaelkirby.com.au/. Accessed 5 Oct 2017
Kmiec KD (2004) The origin and current meanings of 'judicial activism'. Calif Law Rev 92:1441–1478
Kourlis RL, Singer JM (2007) Using judicial performance evaluations to promote judicial accountability. Judicature 90:200–207. http://iaals.du.edu/sites/default/files/documents/publications/using_jpc_to_promote_judicial_accountability2007.pdf. Accessed 11 Feb 2018
Kourlis RL, Singer JM (2010) Managing toward the goals of rule 1. Federal Courts Law Rev 4:1–17. http://iaals.du.edu/sites/default/files/documents/publications/managing_toward_the_goals_of_rule_1_2009.pdf. Accessed 11 Feb 2018
Kouroutakis AE (2014) Judges and policy making authority in the United States and the European Union. Vienna J Int Const Law 8:186–200
Labarga J, Richardson NA, Knox T (2016) Should I tweet that? Court communications in the 21st century. National Center for State Courts. www.ncsc.org/~/media/microsites/files/trends%202016/trends-2016-low.ashx. Accessed 4 Oct 2017
LaGratta E (ed) (2017) To be fair: conversations about procedural justice. Center for Court Innovation. http://www.courtinnovation.org/topic/procedural-justice. Accessed 4 Oct 2017
Langbein JH (1985) The German advantage in civil procedure. Univ Chicago Law Rev 52:823–866
Langbein JH (2012) The disappearance of civil trial in the United States. Yale Law J 122:522–573
Legal Services Agency New Zealand (2006) Report on the 2006 national survey of unmet legal needs and access to services. Legal Services Agency, Wellington
Lind EA, Tyler TR (1988) The social psychology of procedural justice. Plenum Press, New York
Lippman J (2014) The judiciary as the leader of the access-to-justice revolution. N Y Univ Law Rev 89(5):1569–1588
Livesey v New South Wales Bar Association (1983) 151 CLR 288
Llewellyn K (1930) The bramble bush: on our law and its study. Author, New York
Llewellyn K (1950) Remarks on the theory of appellate decision and the rules or canons about how statutes are to be construed. Vanderbilt Law Rev 3:395–406
Luban D (1997) Heroic judging in an antiheroic age. Columbia Law Rev 97:2064–2090

Mack K, Roach Anleu S (2011) Opportunities for new approaches to judging in a conventional context: attitudes, skills and practices. Monash Univ Law Rev 37:187–215
Marcus RL (1987) Apocalypse now? Mich Law Rev 85:1267–1296
Mate M (2014) Elite institutionalism and judicial assertiveness in the Supreme Court of India. Temple Int Comp Law J 28:361–430
McGuire SC, Macdonald RA (1996) Judicial scripts in the dramaturgy of the small claims court. Can J Law Soc 11:63–98
McLoughlin K (2017) Feminism, women judges, judicial diversity and the High Court of Australia. feminists@law 7(2). http://journals.kent.ac.uk/index.php/feministsatlaw/article/view/417. Accessed 4 Oct 2017
Moore M (2003) Judges as Mediators: a Chapter III prohibition or accommodation? Aust Dispute Resolut J 14:188–204
Morris JB (2015) Jack Weinstein: judicial strategist. DePaul Law Rev 64:279–316
Nejelski P (1977) Judging in a democracy: the tension of popular participation. Judicature 61(4):166–175
Nolan J (2003) Redefining criminal courts: problem-solving and the meaning of justice. Am Crim Law Rev 40:1541–1565
Parker S (1998) Courts and the public. Australian Institute of Judicial Administration, Carlton South
Phelan A (2004) Solving human problems or deciding cases? Judicial innovation in New York and its relevance to Australia: Part 3. J Judicial Adm 13:244–258
Pleasence P, Balmer NJ, Sandefur RL (2013) Paths to justice: a past, present and future roadmap. Nuffield Foundation. http://www.nuffieldfoundation.org/sites/default/files/files/PTJ%20Roadmap%20NUFFIELD%20Published.pdf. Accessed 4 Oct 2017
Posner RA (1990) The problems of jurisprudence. Harvard University Press, Cambridge, Mass
Posner RA (2008) How judges think. Harvard University Press, Cambridge
Procedural Fairness (2017) Procedural fairness for judges and courts. http://proceduralfairness.org/. Accessed 4 Oct 2017
Quintanilla VD (2017) Human-centered civil justice design. Penn State Law Rev 121:745–806
R v Watson; ex parte Armstrong (1976) 136 CLR 248
Rabinovich-Einy O, Sagy Y (2016) Courts as organizations: the drive for efficiency and the regulation of class action settlements. Stanford J Complex Litigation 4:1–46
Resnik J (1982) Managerial judges. Harvard Law Rev 96:374–448
Resnik J (1990) Feminism and the language of judging. Ariz State Law J 22:31–38
Rickard E (2017) The agile court: improving state courts in the service of access to justice and the court user experience. West N Engl Law Rev 39:227–250
Roach Anleu S, Rottman D, Mack K (2016) The emotional dimension of judging: issues, evidence, and insights. Court Rev 52:60–71
Rogers A (1993) The managerial or interventionist judge. J Judicial Adm 3:96–110
Rogers CT (2015) Access to justice: new approaches to ensure meaningful participation. N Y Univ Law Rev 90(5):1447–1462
Rottman DB (2007) Procedural fairness as a court reform agenda. Court Rev 44:32–35. University of Nebraska. http://digitalcommons.unl.edu/ajacourtreview/219/. Accessed 4 Oct 2017
Rowe TD Jr (2007) Authorized managerialism under the federal rules—and the extent of convergence with civil-law judging. Southwest Univ Law Rev 36:191–213
Sander FEA (1976) 70 F.R.D. 111. Varieties of dispute processing. Global Pound Conference. http://baltimore2017.globalpoundconference.org/Documents/1976%20Addresses%20Delivered%20at%201976%20Pound%20Conference.pdf. Accessed 15 Sept 2017
Selznick P (1980) Jurisprudence and social policy: aspirations and perspectives. Calif Law Rev 68:206–220
Selznick P (2003) 'Law in context' revisited. J Law Soc 30(2):177–186
Senft LP, Savage CA (2003) ADR in the courts: progress, problems, and possibilities. Penn State Law Rev 108(1):327–348
Shetreet S (1980) On assessing the role of courts in society. Manitoba Law J 10:357–414

Sinai Y, Alberstein M (2016) Expanding judicial discretion: between legal and conflict considerations. Harvard Negot Law Rev 21:221–278

Sivasubramaniam D, Heuer L (2007) Decision makers and decision recipients: understanding disparities in the meaning of fairness. Court Rev 44:62–71. University of Nebraska. http://digitalcommons.unl.edu/ajacourtreview/222/. Accessed 4 Oct 2017

Sossin L (2010) Listening to Ontarians: report of the Ontario civil legal needs project. Law Society of Upper Canada. http://www.lsuc.on.ca/media/may3110_oclnreport_final.pdf. Accessed 11 Feb 2018

Sourdin TM (2014) Why judges should not meet privately with parties in mediation but should be involved in settlement conference work. J Arbit Mediat 4:99–109

Sourdin T (2016a) A broader view of justice? In: Legg M (ed) Resolving civil disputes. LexisNexis Australia, Chatswood, pp 19–36

Sourdin T (2016b) Alternative dispute resolution, 5th edn. Thomson Reuters, Pyrmont

Sourdin T, Zariski A (eds) (2014) The multi-tasking judge: comparative judicial dispute resolution. Thomson Reuters, Sydney, pp 87–102

Steinberg JK (2016) Adversary breakdown and judicial role confusion in 'small case' civil justice. Brigham Young Univ Law Rev 2016:899–970

Stempel JW (1996) Reflections on judicial ADR and the multi-door courthouse at twenty: fait accompli, failed overture, or fledgling adulthood? Ohio State J Dispute Resolut 11:297–396

Stępień M (2013) The three stages of judges' self-development. In: Amaya A, Ho HL (eds) Law, virtue and justice. Hart Publishing, Oxford, pp 137–155

Stobbs N (2017) Therapeutic jurisprudence and due process—consistent in principle and in practice. J Judicial Adm 26(4):248–264

Tahiri X (2016) 'Judicial activism' or constitutional interpretation?: an analysis of the workings of the constitutional court of Kosovo. Ohio Northern Univ Law Rev 42:799–820

Tamanaha BZ (2015) The third pillar of jurisprudence: social legal theory. William and Mary Law Rev 56(6):2235–2277

Thibaut J, Walker L (1975) Procedural justice: a psychological analysis. Lawrence Erlbaum Associates, Hillsdale

Thornburg EG (2010) The managerial judge goes to trial. Univ Richmond Law Rev 44:1261–1326

Tousek v Bernat (1959) SR (NSW) 203

Tyler TR (2007) Procedural justice and the courts. Court Rev 44:4–26–31. University of Nebraska. http://digitalcommons.unl.edu/ajacourtreview/217/. Accessed 4 Oct 2017

Tyler TR, Sevier J (2013) How do the courts create popular legitimacy?: the role of establishing the truth, punishing justly, and/or acting through just procedures. Albany Law Rev 77:1095–1138

Uzelac A (ed) (2014) Goals of civil justice and civil procedure in contemporary judicial systems. Springer, Dordrecht

Vakauta v Kelly (1989) 167 CLR 568

van Velthoven BCJ, ter Voert M (2004) Paths to justice in the Netherlands: looking for patterns of social exclusion. Leiden University. http://media.leidenuniv.nl/legacy/bvv-2004-04.pdf. Accessed 11 Feb 2018

Wanger P (1994) The political and economic roots of the 'adversary system' of justice and 'alternative dispute resolution'. Ohio State J Dispute Resolut 9(2):203–242

Weinstein JB (1994a) Limits on judges learning, speaking and acting—part I—tentative first thoughts: how may judges learn? Arizona Law Rev 36:539–565

Weinstein JB (1994b) Limits on judges' learning, speaking, and acting: part II speaking and part III acting. Univ Dayton Law Rev 20:1–41

Weinstein JB (1995) Individual justice in mass tort litigation: the effect of class actions, consolidations, and other multiparty devices. Northwestern University Press, Evanston

Weinstein JB (2000) Three gates to justice. Litigation 26(2):3–4–70

Weinstein JB (2011) The roles of a federal district court judge. Brooklyn Law Rev 76:439–454

Weinstein JB (2015) Notes on uniformity and individuality in mass litigation. DePaul Law Rev 64:251–277

Wexler D (1995) Robes and rehabilitation: how judges can help offenders make good. Court Rev 38(1):18–23

Wexler DB (2007) Adding color to the white paper: time for a robust reciprocal relationship between procedural justice and therapeutic jurisprudence. Court Rev 44:78–81. University of Nebraska. http://digitalcommons.unl.edu/ajacourtreview/276/. Accessed 4 Oct 2017

Wexler DB (2016) Guiding court conversations along pathways conducive to rehabilitation: integrating procedural justice and therapeutic jurisprudence. Int J Ther Jurisprud 1:367–372

Wistrich AJ, Rachlinski JJ, Guthrie C (2015) Heart versus head: do judges follow the law or follow their feelings? Texas Law Rev 93:855–924

Yung CR (2013) A typology of judging styles. Northwest Univ Law Rev 107:1757–1820

Zimmerman AS (2017) The bellwether settlement. Fordham Law Rev 85:2275–2298

Tania Sourdin is the Dean of the University of Newcastle Law School and was previously the Foundation Chair and Director of the Australian Centre for Justice Innovation (ACJI) at Monash University in Australia. Professor Sourdin has led national research projects and produced important recommendations for ADR and justice reform. In the past two decades, she has conducted qualitative and quantitative research projects into aspects of the dispute resolution and justice system systems in 12 Courts and Tribunals and six external dispute resolution schemes. Other research has focussed on justice innovation, technology, delay and systemic reforms. Professor Sourdin is the author of a number of books (the 5th Edition of her book 'Alternative Dispute Resolution' was released in February 2016), articles and papers, and has published and presented widely on a range of topics including ADR, justice innovation, justice issues, mediation, conflict resolution, collaborative law, artificial intelligence, technology and organisational change.

Archie Zariski is Professor of Legal Studies at Athabasca University, Canada, a lawyer and an experienced mediator. He has created and taught courses in ADR, negotiation and mediation at Athabasca and at Murdoch Law School, Australia. His research includes exploring the roles of lawyers and judges in dispute resolution processes. Archie is co-editor of the book *The Multi-Tasking Judge: Judicial Dispute Resolution in Comparative Perspective* and the author of *Legal Literacy: An Introduction to Legal Studies*. He is a member of the ADR Institute of Canada, and the Resolution Institute (Australia).

Part I
Theoretical and Conceptual Contributions to Responsive Judging

The Responsive Tribunal: Robust Processes; Fair and Timely Outcomes

Helen Shurven and Clair Berman-Robinson

Abstract Tribunals resolve millions of disputes each year, using final binding decision-making, and dispute resolution processes such as mediation. This chapter explores practical ways in which tribunals can be responsive to participants in the process. This includes being responsive to the materials presented by participants. Strategies are canvassed, such as appropriately using discretion; weighing and balancing information; encouraging agreement; and empowering participants without prejudicing others. Process design is discussed as an important aspect of responsiveness, as well as the effects of good communication, exploring participant interests, and clarifying facts and the law. Providing opportunities for participants to resolve their dispute by agreement and the factors to consider in dispute resolution processes are outlined. Case studies are provided that illustrate real world examples. The authors argue a tribunal can generate a robust process, which is not only fair and delivers timely outcomes but also satisfies participants' needs by paying attention to the factors discussed.

1 Introduction

Tribunals resolve, manage and determine issues which affect the rights and interests of many individuals every day, in jurisdictions all over the world. It is estimated that, in the United Kingdom alone, tribunals resolve over one million disputes per year (Genn and Thomas 2013). The influence and impact of tribunal services is significant. The way a tribunal responds to participants in a dispute, and to the information provided to it, has an impact not only on the substantive outcome (see Genn and Thomas 2013) but also on the satisfaction of the participants involved, as well as the broader community's perception of the tribunal's ability to provide

H. Shurven (✉) · C. Berman-Robinson
National Native Title Tribunal, Brisbane, Australia
e-mail: helen.shurven@nntt.gov.au

C. Berman-Robinson
e-mail: clair.berman-robinson@nntt.gov.au

© Springer Nature Singapore Pte Ltd. 2018

T. Sourdin and A. Zariski (eds.), *The Responsive Judge*, Ius Gentium: Comparative Perspectives on Law and Justice 67, https://doi.org/10.1007/978-981-13-1023-2_2

access to justice. In our view, it is essential that tribunals are responsive in order to provide high quality processes and fair and timely outcomes for participants and for the community as a whole. Being a responsive decision-maker in a tribunal context is to ensure justice is delivered in a variety of ways. Being responsive will help ensure distributive justice (that is, justice to groups or individuals in society), procedural justice (that the process itself is just and fair) and interaction justice (that the people participating in the process have been treated with respect and fairness) (Nisbet and Syme 2017). Inconsistent decisions affect the trust that the community has in government and tribunal decision-making processes, and it is important to ensure there are no incidental inequalities in an outcome from the decision-maker's process.

In this chapter we focus on practical strategies tribunals can use in their service delivery to be responsive to participants in the process. This is in contrast to broader applications and concepts of responsiveness such as in relation to public policy and societal needs. However, we note responsiveness on an individual scale feeds into and impacts these broader concepts. Consistent participant satisfaction and access to justice, especially across many organisations and agencies, builds a society where individuals are confident of their ability to successfully engage with processes to resolve disputes as well as to protect and exercise their rights.

So what does it mean to be responsive in this way? The Oxford Dictionary defines 'responsive' as 'reacting quickly and positively'. It is easy to understand what a quick decision means - in terms of a final binding decision-making process, the decision should be made in a timely manner. Knowing the outcome quickly will usually, though not always, benefit all participants. The aim to proceed 'quickly' should apply not just to the decision-making end of the process, but also to a tribunal's engagement with participants. That is, tribunals might employ case-management procedures such as early and ongoing written communication, telephone contact or interim hearings to efficiently engage participants. Similarly, if tribunals use alternative dispute resolution methods the process should be designed and conducted as quickly as is appropriate in the context of the dispute.

As to the reference to reacting 'positively' in the definition of 'responsive', this does not necessarily mean a tribunal can ensure all participants will greet a final decision with positivity. At least one of the participants to a tribunal process is likely to be unhappy with the outcome, as it may confine, restrict or curtail their rights or interests in some way. What we mean by reacting 'positively' is that a tribunal should have clear processes and make decisions with certainty so that participants, and the broader community, can see what legal and factual positions the tribunal has agreed with, and which it has not accepted, in making its decision. Responding 'positively' also refers to how a tribunal can enhance participants' satisfaction with the process. For example, by ensuring participants have adequate opportunity to present their case. Likewise, in terms of acting 'positively' in a dispute resolution process, a tribunal cannot ensure all participants will be positive about the strategies used during that process, the design of a process or the outcome. However, if participants understand why the tribunal is using certain strategies, or why it has designed the process in a certain way, they are more likely to engage meaningfully, towards an agreed outcome they can live with, and which will endure.

So how can tribunals reach final binding decisions and conduct dispute resolution quickly and positively? How can they be properly responsive to the participants and to the materials provided by participants? We argue in this chapter that tribunals can be responsive by: appropriately using discretion; fairly weighing and balancing information; encouraging participants to engage with each other; empowering all participants to engage with the process; designing decision-making processes for the circumstances of each dispute; communicating effectively with participants; exploring the interests of participants; clarifying the facts and the law; and providing appropriately designed opportunities for participants to resolve disputes by agreement. We show that incorporating these aspects for responsive practice can help ensure decisions reached and dispute resolution conducted is fair and effective. The authors have extensive experience with the arbitral decision-making processes and mediations conducted at the Commonwealth National Native Title Tribunal (NNTT) in Australia. At the NNTT, final binding decisions affect the rights and interests of Aboriginal and Torres Strait Islander groups, state governments, local councils, miners, explorers and others who want to deal with land where native title rights and interests have been asserted. At the NNTT, mediations lead to agreements, which commonly include commercial terms and heritage protection relating to rights and responsibilities associated with land use. While the authors have drawn on their knowledge and experience of this particular context and their wider dispute resolution experience, this chapter poses questions and proffers comments and analysis that are useful to consider and apply beyond the NNTT, to the ways a broad range of tribunals can be responsive in making any final binding decisions or conducting dispute resolution processes such as mediation.

2 Strategies for Responsiveness in Decision-Making Processes

2.1 Using Discretion

A tribunal's jurisdiction is usually enlivened through legislation, which confers decision-making powers and may provide the ability to conduct dispute resolution processes. The relevant legislation may outline the mode of operation of the tribunal, which is often prescribed to be less formal than a court. Tribunals generally have, or endeavour to have, simple, accessible and flexible decision-making processes, including an informal or relaxed approach to the rules of evidence. They also may have broad scope to design dispute resolution processes, unless the method is prescribed by legislation. For example, the NNTT is established under the Native Title Act 1993 (Cth), section 109 of which provides it: must pursue the objective of carrying out its functions in a fair, just, economical and prompt way; may take account of the cultural and customary concerns of Aboriginal and Torres Strait Islander People; and is not bound by technicalities, legal forms or rules of evidence.

Where a statute uses words such as 'shall' or 'must', there is usually no discretion for the decision-maker or dispute resolver. However, where the legislation uses the word 'may', the decision-maker or dispute resolver will have scope to use their discretion. The flexibility and informality of tribunals means their decision-makers and dispute resolvers will often have substantial discretion. This discretion may include choices about whether to act or not to act in a certain way, whether to include or reject certain information or evidence, and so on. In order to be responsive to the needs of each participant and ensure procedural fairness in each particular matter, a tribunal decision-maker or dispute resolver must exercise their discretion appropriately at all stages of a process—from the outset right through to a final decision or other resolution, such as a mediated agreement. Because tribunal decisions and processes affect the rights, interests and/or the responsibilities of participants, the exercise of such discretion can have a powerful impact on those participants and their future conduct, and sometimes impact on the wider society and other stakeholders.

Some tribunals develop policies or guidelines to assist decision-makers and dispute resolvers in their exercise of discretionary powers. However, each matter and process is unique and such guidelines are unlikely to give the decision-maker or dispute resolver a definitive answer in all cases. Decisions must be made consistently and fairly, and decision-makers and dispute resolvers must act reasonably and impartially. Some tribunal decision-makers make many hundreds of decisions each year, and/or conduct a similar number of dispute resolution processes such as mediations or conciliations. It can, therefore, be a challenge to maintain their responsiveness in every single matter, some of which may be highly emotionally charged and have far-reaching and long term consequences for one or more of the participants (for example, immigration and social security decisions).

2.2 *Weighing and Balancing*

Decision-makers operating in a tribunal context must make decisions on reasonable grounds, only considering supporting information and evidence that is relevant. Tribunal decision-makers are also challenged to be responsive in terms of the weight they give to material a participant wishes to include in their submissions. All participants need the opportunity to present their case, but not in a way that may unduly prejudice others.

To be responsive to participants and their interests, and to the requirements of the law, the decision-maker must weigh many factors throughout a single process. For example, in NNTT arbitral inquiries, the decision-maker must take into account factors such as: the effect of certain issues on the interests of participants; the wishes of certain participants; the intentions of other participants; economic factors; existing interests; and existing laws. Even where the legislation provides a list of issues which must be taken into account, a responsive decision-maker will need to weigh up a variety of considerations within each of those issues, such as what type of material is needed and will be accepted, how much material they will accept, whether there will be any compliance deadlines, the consequences of such deadlines and so on. In addition, tribunal legislation may require the decision-maker to take into account any 'other factors' that are relevant, which again means the decision-maker must be responsive to the material which has been provided by participants in order to properly determine what 'other factors' might be relevant in that particular inquiry.

2.3 *Encouraging Responsiveness Between Participants*

It is important that participants themselves are responsive to the submissions and materials of other participants in a timely manner. Many tribunals will have planned or systematic case management processes which are used to endeavour to finalise each matter within a certain timeframe. Tribunals may also employ a system whereby the decision-maker issues directions to participants so they must provide certain materials within a given timeframe, usually with liberty to apply for extensions of time. If a participant makes a request to alter standard case management processes, or for an extension of compliance dates, the tribunal must respond quickly and may need to consult all participants where significant extensions or decisions are to be made that will affect the timing of an outcome, or which may prejudice another participant. Participants should be informed of their responsibilities before and during the decision-making process, and be provided with reasons for case management decisions throughout, and for the final decision at the end of the process.

2.4 *Empowering Participants to Engage Meaningfully*

Tribunals are often structured to enable individuals to represent themselves. In some tribunals, participants may not be allowed to have legal representation without special permission. In jurisdictions where legal representation is not generally allowed, tribunals must be careful to equip participants with information to empower them in preparing and arguing their case. Such information may include: instructions for filling in forms; what to expect during a process; where to get legal advice; procedures for hearings; statements of the law; what evidence is acceptable; and an accessible contact for asking questions.

One of the biggest challenges to being responsive for a tribunal decision-maker operating in a final binding decision-making process is where one or more participants are self-represented. By self-represented, we mean the participant does not have a lawyer, or other skilled person acting as their agent or negotiating on their behalf. Self-represented participants will often take up a significant amount of a tribunal's time and staffing resources. The tribunal decision-maker must endeavour to ensure their responsiveness does not cause undue delays. In our experience, if there are one or more self-represented participants in a dispute, this will usually lead to a slower process than where participants are all represented. In addition, complex pre-existing relationships can affect a participants' responsiveness to the tribunal and to each other.

As outlined in detail in the seminal book *Negotiating on Behalf of Others* (Mnookin and Susskind 1999), the issue of representation is a complex, many layered concept. Participants may choose to be self-represented because they feel they can do it better themselves as they have an actual or perceived understanding of the particular jurisdiction or issue, or because they feel they lack the resources to obtain appropriate representation. What is important in the context of this chapter, is that the decision-maker or dispute resolver must clearly understand and respond to any agents or representatives, and must also respond to, and communicate with, those who are not represented, without prejudicing the process or the outcome. Alternatively, at the very least, those responsible in the tribunal must not respond to what may be an imbalance between participants in such a way so that the imbalance is reflected unfairly in any final binding decision or agreement. The authors, in considering power imbalances between participants in their publications relating to design of mediation processes (Shurven and Berman-Robinson 2016), note disproportionate power may be the result of various differences between participants, such as financial resources, legal arguments and representation, negotiation skills and emotional dependence (see also Sander and Rozdeiczer 2006, 29–31).

Self-represented participants may not understand tribunal processes, the impact of a particular outcome or other nuances and complexities throughout the process, such as confidentiality or particular language, including commercial or legal terminology. To be responsive, a tribunal decision-maker must balance the needs of self-represented participants with those of participants who may be better resourced. The decision-maker must be sure they do not unduly prejudice the other participants in the way they are being responsive to the self-represented participant/s. Decision-makers also need to be careful to avoid actual bias and perceptions of bias. At the same time, decision-makers should maintain awareness of whether self-represented participants have knowledge or information that is key to be considered in making a decision—more on this in the case studies at Sect. 2.5 of this chapter. An example of an action that may undermine impartiality is repeatedly pushing out timelines for submission of materials in favour of a self-represented participant. There is a complex interrelationship between the case management of a tribunal process and the power of the decision-maker to make certain discretionary decisions. For example, self-represented participants may assert that lack of funding and resources means they could not meet a compliance date. As Mortimer J recently stated in Agius v State of South Australia (No. 4) (2017) FCA 361, 'determining where to draw lines in case management processes is not an exact science'. This applies equally to court and tribunal processes.

2.5 *Designing the Process for the Circumstances*

As noted above, tribunals usually have some discretion in choosing how to run particular decision-making or dispute resolution processes. Each matter will have different participant needs and circumstances. To be truly responsive, the decision-maker or dispute resolver should consider these needs and circumstances and, where possible, design the process to address those. In this section we consider design of decision making processes and in a later section we look at designing dispute resolution processes.

It may be appropriate to seek the input of the participants in designing the process, and this can be done through correspondence, telephone, or a meeting between the tribunal and participants. Depending on the jurisdiction, there may even be scope to give one or more participants responsibility for organising part of the process. Participants may also be able to assist in providing resources, such as a venue for a hearing, particularly in regional or remote areas where there are limited options. By regional or remote, the authors refer broadly to those areas which are far away from populated city centres or services. This is a consideration in many countries where tribunals operate, including Australia, the United States of America, Canada, South America and so on.

In this way, aspects of the process can be collaborative and mean participants work together to solve the problem, being tough on the issue and soft on each other. Although participant input may increase participant satisfaction and assist in sharing the workload, the decision-maker must be careful to maintain impartiality and ensure that ownership of the process is not compromised—it is a delicate balancing act.

Examples of variables to be considered in designing decision making processes include:

- The number of opportunities participants are given to present their submissions and evidence, and to reply to the submissions and evidence of other participants
- Whether a decision is made on the papers or following a hearing, or a combination of these approaches (for example, particular issues addressed on the papers and others in a hearing)
- If there is a hearing:
  - Where it is held?
  - Who attends?
  - Whether it is public or private
  - Whether participants attend in person or via phone, video conference or a combination (for example, one or more participants in person and others on the phone, etc.)
  - How evidence is delivered (orally, by affidavit or some other means)
  - If evidence is given orally, whether it is given on oath
  - Whether the rules of evidence apply, do not apply, partially apply or there is some other standard

   - Whether the proceedings are recorded or not, and if recorded, whether a transcript is made

- Whether the decision-maker decides the issues in one or more decisions (for example, if there are preliminary matters, these may be dealt with separately or together with the substantial question)
- Whether reasons for the decision are provided, and, if they are, how (for example, in person or in writing)
- Whether decisions are publicly available.

Tribunals may find a particular structure works best in their jurisdiction. We argue that decision-makers, even within an established structure for a decision-making process, must be given some autonomy to further refine the process to suit the circumstances of each individual matter. For example, having the ability to decide when and where a hearing is held, who attends it, and what evidence and submissions are heard. To be truly responsive, tribunals should be flexible in their approach to participants and the process.

The case studies below are examples of flexible approaches to designing a final binding decision-making process which fits the particular dispute and the needs of the participants, while keeping the ownership of the process and its impartiality firmly within the remit of the tribunal and the decision-maker.

Case study examples

1. *Allowing time to obtain information*
   Participant A and B were both unrepresented in a final binding decision-making process. Participant A clearly misunderstood the commercial nature of operations which were proposed by Participant B. Participant C was silent on the matter. The decision-maker did not, strictly speaking, need to explore that misunderstanding, before making a final binding decision. Participants were content to proceed, however, the decision-maker wanted to ensure there were no incidental inequalities in the outcome of the process which could arise from the misunderstanding. Participant A was given some further time to seek clarifying information, which was brought back to the decision-making process, and Participant B and C had the opportunity to respond. The decision was then able to incorporate a number of conditions which met the needs of all participants, and which would not have been possible without allowing that additional information to be sought. Participant B and C were not prejudiced in terms of the additional time taken. The case flow of all other matters on the decision-makers list was not disturbed as a firm date was provided to participants by which time a decision would be made if the additional information was not forthcoming from Participant A.

2. *Where evidence is in issue, procedural fairness may require the issue to be resolved by oral testimony and cross examination*
   Participants were locked into a deeply distrustful and harmful values conflict. Participant E had asked the tribunal to make a final binding decision. Generally, a decision on the papers would be made. However, it was clear in this matter the decision-maker would be presented with many thousands of pages of material, together with hard biting written contentions, which would only inflame participants' differences, and be of little assistance to the decision-maker as to the outcome. Participants were directed to provide oral contentions, and such contentions could be supported only by materials that were already in existence (for example, letters, maps, memos, contracts and emails). Three hours was set aside for Participant F to present their contentions as to why the decision should be in their favour, with Participants E and G to listen and ask clarifying questions as needed. Time was also set for Participants E and G to present their reply the following week, with Participant F to listen and ask clarifying questions as needed. However, at the first three-hour hearing, having heard the arguments orally, Participant E subsequently withdrew their application for a final binding decision and the matter was concluded. Using the strategy of an oral hearing instead of the usual approach of receiving submissions and evidence in writing saved the tribunal and participant's significant time and resources that would have been spent collating, producing and reading material. It also forced participants to engage with each other's arguments and gave them an opportunity to assess the strength of their own cases.

3. *Clear communication on old messages*
   Many tribunals have existed for a number of years, and are often time poor due to workloads, with little opportunity to review their paperwork and messages to participants. As a result of attending the Law and Courts in an Online World Conference in 2016, and hearing from the Civil Resolution Tribunal in British Columbia, the world's first online Tribunal (which had done a great deal of work on communicating clearly with participants), the NNTT updated a selection of relevant communications to participants so participants now receive clear and short emails/letters with headings such as:

   - 'Reason for this message'
   - 'What you must do'
   - 'What happens if this is not done?'

   Participants are provided with contact details of tribunal staff so they may ask any clarifying questions, and are in no doubt as to what they need to do in response to the communication and what will happen if they do not respond.

4. *Strict compliance versus substantial compliance*
A self-represented participant lodged eight applications for binding decisions. The applicant had no available telephone communication, limited computer access, and lived and travelled remotely. The tribunal needed to tread the fine line between assisting that participant, without providing advice to him on how to proceed. Assistance was provided by printing hard copy forms and relevant information sheets (which were available online). The applications for the arbitral decisions were difficult to follow, and this raised the issue of whether there were defects such that the tribunal could not accept the applications. The decision-maker needed to exercise responsiveness and careful judgement as to whether substantial compliance with the statutory basis for the applications had been met, and whether strict compliance was necessary. Part of this was weighing up whether injustice would be caused to other participants in accepting the applications and whether the tribunal was complying with legislative requirements that it proceed informally and effectively. The applications were ultimately accepted. The tribunal decision-maker convened a number of status conferences, where discussion was encouraged between participants to draw out their underlying interests. The purpose of the status conferences were to provide an opportunity for the participants to resolve the applications by agreement. The sessions were audio recorded, and a copy of the recording was provided to all participants on request (as transcript services are too costly and time consuming). Through the process of status conferences, participants were able to reach agreement on these eight applications, together with a further 5 applications that were pending, saving considerable tribunal time and resources that would have been spent on deciding the applications and providing reasons. In circumstances like this, if participants are likely to have or need an ongoing relationship, assisting them to reach agreement may mean they are diverted from the tribunal process in the future, as they may be better equipped to successfully negotiate future disputes between themselves.

5. *Dealing with a history of non-compliance*
Responsiveness does not always mean a final decision upholding a participant's rights or interests will be made. In some cases, being appropriately responsive will mean taking steps to dismiss or discontinue an application unless a participant takes certain action. For example, where there is a history of non-compliance from one participant during a decision-making process, arguably this prejudices the rights and interests of other participants. It may be that dismissing the application for a decision, or terminating the decision-making process, is a quick and positive response to such non-compliance. Techniques such as 'springing', 'guillotine' or 'pre-emptory' orders can be used, which automatically terminate a process

by a certain date in the absence of particular action from a participant, such as submitting material, which parties are made aware of. These orders are not made lightly and usually only after a pattern of non-compliance with directions. The principle underlying them is that tribunal directions must be complied with, and a participant who persistently or deliberately and without proper excuse fails to comply with them, must be called to account for that action or course of conduct—see Re Jokai Tea Holdings Ltd. (1993) 1 All ER 630. Using these techniques puts the non-compliant participant on notice that their matter is at risk of being dismissed, and provides them with a final chance to progress their application in a timely manner. Giving this opportunity means the participant may be able to avoid having their matter dismissed, and so avoid losing the opportunity to have their rights and interests determined.

6. *Using hearings*
   Part of a dispute had already been decided on the papers. In relation to the main outstanding issue, it became apparent to the decision-maker that a hearing was required in order to make an informed decision. Because the decision was in relation to a particular geographical remote location, and features of that location were central in deciding the outcome, the hearing was held at that location. Participants were actively consulted and engaged in organising the hearing, and were given an opportunity to have input and provide feedback on the design of the process. As the logistics for the hearing were detailed, it was important for the tribunal to clearly establish the roles and responsibilities of everyone participating, at each stage. Written material comprising legal arguments and evidence was submitted at various stages, in accordance with directions made by the decision-maker.
   The main hearing comprised a site visit with evidence given orally, as well as legal argument and evidence in a more traditional tribunal environment at a hired venue in the remote town. The participants who were familiar with the area provided information to the tribunal and other participants, relating to travel and logistics.
   The decision-maker and participants agreed on the dates for the hearing, in accordance with everyone's availability. As the site visit would provide evidence in support of a particular participant's case, they organised that part of the hearing, including catering lunch, and provided a detailed itinerary. For the rest of the process, participants met their own costs, and the tribunal paid for the venue and catering for the part of the hearing in the hired venue.
   At the conclusion of the hearing on location, participants expressed their wish to further consider and reply to the submissions and evidence given. The decision-maker and participants agreed to a further oral hearing held at the tribunal's office in a metropolitan area, with only legal representatives

in attendance. This hearing was limited to replying to matters raised and was not to introduce anything new.
During the hearing process, the decision-maker explored with participants briefly whether there might be an opportunity to resolve the matter by agreement. Stemming from this, a dispute resolution process, overseen by a different tribunal member, ran concurrently with the final binding decision-making process. Participants were unable to reach agreement through dispute resolution and the matter was ultimately resolved by written decision. Reasons were provided addressing the various arguments and evidence presented.

2.6 *Communicating Effectively*

Courts and tribunals traditionally operate in a relatively formal manner, as compared to participants negotiating between themselves. There is increasing movement towards using online platforms for the lodgement of applications and materials and for providing orders and compliance directions. Tribunals are usually able to be less formal than courts in their approach to decision-making, by virtue of their statutory framework. The authors argue this flexibility should be exercised to make communication with participants accessible, clear and frequent in order for tribunals to be responsive.

The NNTT allocates one case manager to each matter and this person communicates with participants by phone, email or letter (depending on each participant's location and availability) in clear language using concise messages. Email is the most common method of communicating with participants. There are several benefits to using email as a communication method, including: it is low cost; it may be more environmentally friendly than paper communication; it is relatively instant; most people have an email address; the same message can easily be sent to several participants; everyone receives the information at the same time (postal timeframes can vary depending on the location of the person); information can be easily forwarded on; it is easy to reply; attachments can be saved electronically; and previous communication can be shown in the one email chain for ease of reference. All participants are included in all email communications (particularly in final binding decision-making) so everyone has access to the same information at the same time. This also allows participants to 'reply all' and easily communicate their views to the tribunal and other participants at the same time. If a participant does not have email, copies of email communications are mailed to them. We have found email communication to be a valuable tool in case management of tribunal matters because it allows information to be sought from participants or communicated to participants quickly, easily and cost effectively. We have also found participants are satisfied with this mode of communication where they have it available to them. This also applies to dispute resolution processes, such as mediation, unless there is an issue with confidentiality or a participant wishes to have a confidential communication, and the process can be tailored accordingly (Shurven and Berman-Robinson 2016, 146).

At the NNTT, the direct phone number of the case manager is provided so participants can ask questions or have a discussion as needed. For email communication, headings are used that immediately communicate the purpose of the email, options open to participants are listed and the consequences of certain actions, or failure to do them, are outlined (see the case study 3 *Clear communication on old messages*).

2.7 Exploring Interests

If a participant, particularly a self-represented participant, comes from a principled or values based position, it is going to be difficult for the decision-maker to get any movement towards discussing that person's interests. By 'values' and 'interests' we are referring to concepts such as those outlined by Moore early in the development of the mediation process (see Moore 2003). These concepts also apply more broadly to dispute resolution processes such as conciliation and settlement conferences. For example, Moore states in relation to 'interests' that each participant may have numerous types of interests that could be used to satisfy the outcome of a dispute, so it is possible for participants to trade on these interests to reach an acceptable agreement. In relation to 'values', Moore outlines that values disputes focus more on right and wrong, or on beliefs about who is correct or what principles should guide each party, or the decision-maker. While these concepts are more commonly associated with facilitative dispute resolution, in the authors' experience, a successful final binding decision-making process will also have elements of addressing both interests and values. There may be less room for emotions and concerns to be aired, as the final binding decision-making process in a tribunal context generally follows a timetabled and rigorous approach. Emotions are explored in more detail by the authors in another paper (Berman-Robinson and Shurven 2017). For this chapter, we argue tribunals should consider that the expression of values which underlie strongly felt emotions might contribute to a successful process (Douglas and Coburn 2014, 112). In addition, 'Emotions may communicate a lot about a participant's values' (Randolph 2016, 49). Quite often, 'there are facts in the feelings' (Douglas and Coburn 2014, 119).

We argue that exploring and responding to participants' underlying interests can assist to bring matters to a fair resolution that is palatable to all participants. This approach may even lead to an appropriate withdrawal of all participants from the tribunal's final binding decision-making process. In a tribunal context, exploration of interests might be carried out, for example, in an oral hearing or conference, which assists participants to reach an agreement between themselves (see Genn and Thomas 2013).

If a tribunal decision-maker who may be dealing with many matters has the jurisdiction and power to make a decision, and is able to provide proper reasons for that decision having heard each participants' case in a matter, why would they spend time unearthing participants' interests during the decision-making process? We argue that even where participants may not agree with the outcome, if they understand the outcome, if their interests have been fully ventilated in the process and the outcome responds to their interests (albeit not supporting them), then the decision is more likely to achieve distributive justice, procedural justice and interaction justice. Fisher and Shapiro (2005) refer to this as addressing the core concerns of the participants, which will more likely lead to participants feeling satisfied with the process, even if the outcome is not in their favour.

2.8 Clarifying Facts and the Law

It may be appropriate for the tribunal, in the same or a concurrent process, to work with participants to settle the facts and the applicable law. This may be done through participants drawing up a schedule of agreed facts and agreeing on the legislative provisions and applicable case law. This may be more difficult to do with self-represented participants, or might take longer, but it is likely to assist participants get to the underlying interests of the matter in a way that opens up the decision-maker to a more nuanced approach.

In this sense, everyone is being 'tough on the problem' in that the issues are narrowed to focus attention on those that are the most difficult and contentious. Calloway (2010, 357–60) outlines several helpful techniques which can be used to assist in focusing attention appropriately. Such may also save all participants time and resources in not having to address unnecessary issues. The decision-maker is relieved of the burden of having to read and analyse additional yet unnecessary pages of evidence and information. It does mean devoting time to the beginning of the process, which may be difficult to do where tribunals are dealing with large case volumes, but in the authors' experience, it saves time in the overall process, provides a more robust outcome and increases participant satisfaction (which may be reflected in fewer appeals or judicial reviews).

3 Providing Opportunities to Resolve by Agreement

Many tribunals have the ability, through legislation or other means, to offer participants the opportunity to resolve their dispute by agreement, prior to a binding decision being made. The use of dispute resolution can be an essential part of tribunals being responsive, as it may reduce costs for the community by providing efficient and timely outcomes, increase participant satisfaction and empower participants to resolve their own disputes. There are many options as to how and when dispute resolution may be used. Mediation is often used by tribunals, and there are many kinds of mediation models which may be used. This section explores the options and different factors for consideration by tribunals in using dispute resolution processes within decision-making. Tribunals may select features for their own dispute resolution processes which best suit their jurisdiction and the needs of their stakeholders. Within an established model, a dispute resolver should also have some leeway to tailor a process for particular participants. The discretion given to the dispute resolver may be set out in legislation, regulations or the tribunal's internal procedures.

3.1 *Timing*

There are many options open to tribunals in terms of the timing of offering or imposing dispute resolution on participants, and tribunals should determine what works best in their jurisdiction. As Sebenius (2017) notes, it is important to focus participants on 'what set of possibilities is likely to unfold' if they cannot reach agreement. Some of the possibilities are discussed here. Dispute resolution will usually occur prior to, or concurrently with, the decision-making process. Participants may be required to attend a dispute resolution process following lodgement of an application for a binding decision, or there may be pathways to dispute resolution during the decision-making process, such as if a decision-maker identifies opportunity for agreement or a participant requests dispute resolution (for example, conciliation or mediation). In some cases, it may be effective to have dispute resolution following a decision-making process. For example, in arbitration-mediation (often called arb-med), mediation follows a hearing where the participants present their arguments and evidence, and the decision-maker drafts a decision. Instead of communicating the decision to the participants, the decision-maker puts the decision in a sealed envelope only to be opened if agreement is not reached in mediation.

3.2 *Compulsory or Optional Processes*

Dispute resolution processes may be compulsory or optional, either because of legislative requirements or policy. Even if attendance at dispute resolution is compulsory, participation in the process may be voluntary, to avoid participants feeling forced into agreements not in their best interests. The value of participants having control over the outcome of the process may be lost where they feel they 'have' to settle. There is some evidence that in commercial matters, participants may prefer a compulsory order to participate in dispute resolution such as mediation or conciliation where one participant does not want to lose face or appear to have a weak case by requesting such a process. Where applications are automatically referred to a compulsory dispute resolution process following lodgement of an application for a binding decision, a broad screening process may assist to exclude matters clearly inappropriate for dispute resolution—for example, if there is a court order such as a domestic violence order on file that would be breached by having participants attend.

In some jurisdictions, such as the Queensland Civil and Administrative Tribunal in Australia, if the respondent participant does not attend a mediation, the applicant participant may be able to have a decision made immediately in the respondent's absence.

3.3 The Mediation Model and Broader Dispute Resolution Principles

The need to design final binding decision-making processes in order for tribunals to be responsive is discussed above. The design principles for dispute resolution are equally important. The nuances of the particular jurisdiction of any tribunal will mean some dispute resolution models or processes are more suitable than others.

In her article, 'The Mediation Meta-Model—The Realities of Mediation Practice', Alexander (2011) identifies six different mediation approaches. The approaches described can be employed broadly across a range of dispute resolution processes. The different approaches are:

1. *Expert advisory*
   Involves a predominantly positional bargaining approach and dispute resolvers give advice on the merits of each participant's case. Settlements are legally or technically oriented and often fall within the range of outcomes that a court could have ordered.
2. *Settlement*
   Also adopts a predominantly positional bargaining approach with settlement negotiations between the participants.
3. *Facilitative*
   Involves an interest-based approach to bargaining. Participants are encouraged to reveal their needs and interests in relation to the conflict and to acknowledge the dispute from the other participant's perspective.
4. *Wise counsel*
   Combines a problem-oriented dispute resolver intervention with the participants engaging in interest-based negotiation. Dispute resolvers evaluate the merits of the case based on the interests and concerns of the participants. Dispute resolvers provide advice in terms of identifying interests, options, walk-away alternatives and solutions.
5. *Tradition-based*
   The primary aim is restorative justice—the restoration of stability and harmony to the community, industry or group. Dispute resolvers regard the values of the community as having priority.
6. *Transformative*
   The primary goals include transforming how participants relate to each other, healing and reconciliation of relationships and restorative justice. Participants are

empowered to articulate their own feelings, needs and interests and to recognise and acknowledge those of the other participant.

Expert advisory and settlement processes are most suited to disputes about legal principles and money, and the other models are more suited where relationships are important.

Tribunals may adopt one of the models described above, or other dispute resolution processes or models, depending on what best suits the circumstances of the dispute, the participants within the particular jurisdiction, and the subject matter in dispute. Aspects of different dispute resolution process can also be blended together. In the NNTT, mediation is used. The mediator often facilitates exploration of participant interests and options for resolution, gives information on tribunal processes and may explain what decisions have been made in similar matters. The mediator maintains impartiality because the information provided is not advice or an opinion on how the particular matter would be decided, but rather information to assist participants to make informed decisions in their own best interests.

Aside from the kind of model to be used, other variables to consider in constructing a dispute resolution process include:

- The time allocated to each meeting
- Where the process is held (in terms of the geographical location, and the venue or room/s available)
- Whether the process comprises one or more meetings of the participants, within a certain timeframe
- Whether the process is done face to face, by phone or video conference, or a combination
- Whether participants can have support people
- Whether participants can be represented.

3.4 Process Design

While tribunals may adopt an overarching approach to dispute resolution in their jurisdiction and be likely to construct or rely on a standard model, flexibility within that approach and model will assist the dispute resolver to be responsive to the needs of the particular participants and circumstances of the dispute. This responsiveness is improved if the person conducting the dispute resolution process has some discretion to make decisions to tailor the process further. This may include, for example, the ability to:

- Decide not to proceed if, in the dispute resolver's view, the matter is unsuitable or terminate the process part way through if it becomes unsuitable
- Decide who may be in the room and their respective roles, for example, if participants bring support people with them
- Determine who sits where in the room

- Allocate extra time for the process, particularly if agreement is within reach
- Separate the participants in order to shuttle between them if necessary/appropriate
- Apply aspects of different model approaches
- Within reason, use their own style with respect to dispute resolution and explain information in their own words.

3.5 Choice of Dispute Resolver

A dispute resolution process may be convened by a tribunal member, employee of the organisation, or an external person. In relation to tribunal members carrying out dispute resolution, they might be the same member as the one appointed to the final binding decision-making process, or a different person. Legislation may state the same member is not to be appointed to both processes, unless the participants agree. In any case, if a tribunal member is to oversee the decision-making process as well as a dispute resolution process, procedural fairness may require seeking participant permission, as information may be disclosed in dispute resolution that is relevant to the binding decision-making process. The benefits of using the same person for dispute resolution and final binding decision-making can include: the whole process may be shorter than having two different people who would each need to understand the information and circumstances; participants may be encouraged to settle if information disadvantageous to their case comes out in dispute resolution; and providing time for rapport and trust to be built between participants, leading to satisfaction with the final outcome. One disadvantage of using the same person is that participants may be reluctant to disclose information in dispute resolution that they perceive may affect or be relevant to a decision-making process.

In considering whether the dispute resolver should be an internal or external person, tribunals should determine how familiar they want that person to be with organisational procedures and how much information they wish participants to receive about these factors. For example, on a sliding scale, on the high end of information and advice disclosure, tribunal members may be able to tell participants about the likely outcome, should their matter proceed to a binding decision, or outline what the tribunal has decided previously in similar matters. Employees may be able to tell participants about usual practice and what is involved in decision-making processes. Dispute resolvers external to the organisation may only be able to give very general procedural information, unless they are well informed in that particular jurisdiction. Using an internal tribunal person to provide participants with information about what to expect in a decision-making process may mean participants are better informed and encouraged to settle. However, it may also mean participants are less trusting of the dispute resolution process, as it is not perceived to be independent, and they may be reluctant to participate meaningfully. Using an external person may mean the tribunal gains the benefit of using a specialist dispute resolution practitioner, rather than a subject matter expert employee with dispute resolution training. An external dispute resolution specialist, with varied experience across a range of subject matter types, may be better able to assist participants explore the dispute from a number of different viewpoints, perhaps even setting aside legal principles, and thereby be more likely to assist participants to reach agreement. This is in contrast to someone internal to the organisation who may view the issue mainly in the context of the tribunal's processes and the applicable law.

4 Conclusion

Paying attention to aspects of responsive practice can help ensure decisions reached and dispute resolution processes conducted in a tribunal context are fair and effective. Distributive, procedural and interaction justice can be achieved and it is less likely that any inequalities which arise throughout a process will flow on to adversely affect the outcome. We have argued that acting in a timely and positive manner means being responsive to the needs of each participant and ensuring procedural fairness in each particular matter. We have also outlined that a tribunal decision-maker or dispute resolver must exercise their discretion appropriately through all stages of a process, and be aware that their exercise of such discretion can have a great impact on the outcome of the process, as well as on participants, other stakeholders and society in general.

If a final binding decision-maker is not appropriately responsive to participants, the decision can be subject to judicial oversight, either through an appeals process, which is usually on a question of law, or through a judicial review process. If a dispute resolver is not appropriately responsive, participants may disengage from the resolution process, or have little faith in any agreement which arises from such a process. If either of these situations occur, participants may avoid using the tribunal altogether and find other ways of resolving their disputes. How a tribunal decision-maker or dispute resolver goes about designing and conducting processes is also important. By ensuring responsive and consistent decisions are made, and that there are no incidental inequalities in tribunal outcomes, participants and the community can maintain confidence in tribunal processes.

References

Agius v State of South Australia (No. 4) (2017) FCA 361

Alexander N (2011) The Mediation Meta-Model—the realities of mediation practice. Altern Dispute Resolut Bull 12(6):126–131

Berman-Robinson C, Shurven H (2017) Working with strong negative emotions in dispute resolution processes: boiling blood and frozen fear. Altern Dispute Resolut Law Bull 4:59

Calloway D (2010) Using mindfulness practice to work with emotions. Nevada Law J 10:338–364

Douglas K, Coburn C (2014) Attitude and response to emotion in dispute resolution: the experience of mediators. Flinders Law J 16:111–144

Fisher R, Shapiro D (2005) Beyond reason: using emotions as you negotiate. Viking Penguin, USA

Genn H, Thomas C (2013) Tribunal decision-making: an empirical study. Nuffield Foundation. http://www.nuffieldfoundation.org/tribunal-decision-making. Accessed 1 Sept 2017

Mnookin RM, Susskind LE (eds) (1999) Negotiating on behalf of others. Sage Publications, California

Moore C (2003) The mediation process: practical strategies for resolving conflict. Jossey-Bass, San Francisco

Native Title Act 1993 (Cth)

Nisbet T, Syme GJ (2017) No way to build a highway: law, social justice research and the Beeliar Wetlands. Environ Plann Law J 34:162–175

Randolph P (2016) The psychology of conflict: mediating in a diverse world. Bloomsbury, Place

Re Jokai Tea Holdings Ltd. (1993) 1 All ER 630

Sander F, Rozdeiczer L (2006) Matching cases and dispute resolution procedures: detailed analysis leading to a mediation-centered approach. Harvard Negot Law Rev 11:1–41

Sebenius J (2017) BATNAs in negotiation: common errors and three kinds of "no". Negot J 33(2):89–99

Shurven H, Berman-Robinson C (2016) ADR process design: considerations for ADR practitioners and party advisors. Australas Dispute Resolut J 27:140–149

Helen Shurven is a Member of the National Native Title Tribunal, appointed by the Governor General of Australia. She is a nationally accredited mediator and, since 1994, has mediated many hundreds of disputes, including complex multi-party matters. Helen has also made over 400 arbitration decisions between three or more parties. Helen has many articles in peer reviewed publications, and holds a Master of Education, a LLB and a BA with Honours in Psychology. Helen has previously practiced law, researched and lectured at universities, worked in Government and practiced as a mediator and mediation supervisor in the community sector.

Clair Berman-Robinson is a Practice Manager at the National Native Title Tribunal and an accredited mediator. She has a Bachelor of Laws and a Graduate Certificate of Dispute Resolution and is admitted to legal practice in Queensland. Clair is currently undertaking a Master of Dispute Resolution.

Settlement Adjudication and Judicial Responsiveness: The Choice Between a Wide and a Narrow Model

Karni Perlman

Abstract The chapter describes a range of judicial roles that have developed in Anglo-American law countries and Israel. These roles are implemented in a variety of judicial processes, commencing with traditional adversarial adjudication through settlement adjudication in which significant judicial efforts are made to conclude the case in an agreed solution, and up to judicial processes with therapeutic objectives. The chapter links the collaborative approach towards dispute resolution to changes that have impacted the judicial role and the manner in which that role is performed. It asserts that settlement judging may be pursued along a gradual continuum between a narrow model and a wide model. Each of these models presents a different measure of judicial responsiveness to considerations that go far beyond legal rights and duties in an attempt to address the underlying strata of the conflict. The narrow model expresses judicial responsiveness which is primarily limited to considerations of efficiency whereas the wide model relates to additional needs and interests, such as those involving personal relationships and community welfare. The chapter describes the characteristics of settlement adjudication in terms of both models and argues for the application of the wide model. It suggests that the wide model expresses a more comprehensive conception of the judge as a settler of disputes who displays a greater degree of judicial responsiveness and of judicial proceedings as having the potential to yield a variety of benefits.

1 Introduction

The essence of the judicial role—the perception of the role of the judge and the proper ways to fill this role—is dynamic and changing (Sourdin and Zariski 2013).

The content of the judge's role has been shaped and developed in recent decades in response to ideological, systemic, legislative and other changes in a way which

K. Perlman (✉)
College of Management Academic Studies, Rishon Lezion, Israel
e-mail: karnip1@netvision.net.il

© Springer Nature Singapore Pte Ltd. 2018

T. Sourdin and A. Zariski (eds.), *The Responsive Judge*, Ius Gentium: Comparative Perspectives on Law and Justice 67, https://doi.org/10.1007/978-981-13-1023-2_3

makes it possible to discern significant shifts in the content of this role in the legal system (Perlman 2009; Sourdin and Zariski 2013).

The role of a contemporary judge in the Anglo-American and Israeli jurisdictions is varied and often contradictory.[1] It is possible to point to an entire arc of legitimate judicial court conduct that encompasses a variety of judicial roles, each of which is distinguishable from the other in terms of the perception of the judge's role, the purpose of the procedure, and the way in which the judicial proceeding is being managed (Sourdin and Zariski 2013; Alberstein 2015).

The judge's role is constantly changing and developing and is affected by several factors. These factors include conceptual changes that are reflected in the development of various legal theories[2] and practical-philosophical movements that offer a perception of a judicial role that suits their approach.[3] Systemic factors that include various organizational programs aimed at dealing with the court system's needs and the attempt to supply a qualitative and efficient judicial service. Legislative changes which enable the judicial system to absorb new processes, as well as broaden the various type of proceedings that a judge is authorized to conduct.[4] Among the relevant factors,[5] this chapter will focus on conceptual changes that have occurred in the perception of proper conflict management and the expansion of the impact of the collaborative approach to conflict resolution.

Towards the end of the twentieth century, real changes began to take place in the legal systems of the United States, other Anglo-American countries and Israel. One principal change involved the transition from a dominant adversarial approach to dispute management, to a trend that systematically encouraged a non-adversarial approach to conflict resolution.[6] The collaborative approach to conflict resolution, as explained below, conceives of the conflict as being composed of several layers. Deep within the conflict it perceives a layer of needs and interests that underlie the demands and claims. An in-depth clarification of the conflict and identifying a suitable solution requires attention to this dimension. The collaborative approach contributes to the perception of the conflict brought before the court as a complex problem that goes

---

[1]For further analysis of the points raised in this chapter as applied in Israeli Law see Perlman (2015a).

[2]For example, the Legal Realism movement, which challenged the formalist world view and the judicial role derived from it. This movement which found expression in the 1920s and 1930s influenced the growth of various legal theories including the Therapeutic Jurisprudence movement described below in this chapter. For a discussion of Legal Realism see, for example, Fisher et al. (1993). For Legal Realism and its connection to the role of the therapeutic judge, see Perlman (2010).

[3]For example, the ADR and the TJ movements that will be described below in this chapter.

[4]For example, in the United States, various amendments to Rule 16 of the Federal Rules of Civil Procedure, which enable the judge to hold preliminary hearings in order to examine whether the parties are willing to settle the dispute by way of compromise or should be referred to alternative means of dispute resolution.

[5]One of the factors contributing to shaping the judge's role relates to technological developments, see Tidmarch (1992), Katsh and Rabinovich-Einy (2017, 149–169).

[6]For a comprehensive survey of the non-adversarial approach and its implementation in the legal system, see King et al. (2014).

beyond the discourse of rights and obligations embodied in the pleadings. Elements such as the relationship between the parties, their interests, even their emotions, which have been given different definitions such as "rights plus" (Daicoff 2006, 9, 2011, 18–21) or "conflict considerations" (Sinai and Alberstein 2016) have become relevant to decision-making process of the judge.

The weakening power of the adversarial approach and the rise in status of the collaborative vision were manifested in substantive changes to the law,[7] the court systems,[8] and the role of lawyers in the legal system.[9] These changes testify to the existence of competing theories and reflect a process of paradigmatic change in the sense proposed by Kuhn (1962).[10] The adversarial paradigm in court processes has given way to one that is more cooperative in nature and at times even therapeutic; a trend producing a concept that now contemplates a variety of judicial roles and a broad range of corresponding functions.

This chapter will deal with the function of the judge who engages in significant efforts to end the conflict in a settlement. It will be suggested that the role of the settlement judge may be performed in one of two models each of which reflects a different degree of judicial responsiveness to conflict or extra-legal considerations. The first model is described here as the narrow model, since the judicial response in this framework is propelled by concerns limited primarily to considerations of efficiency. The second is described as the wide model, since underpinning the judicial approach to the conflict and the manner in which it is managed, is a broader concept that embraces quality considerations. The latter are attributable to the collaborative approach to conflict resolution, in which it is possible to speak of more comprehensive and inclusive responsive adjudication.

The first section of the chapter describes the range and development of the different forms of judicial conduct currently prevalent in the court systems; starting with a description of developments in the United States and proceeding with a brief reference to the approach taken by the Israeli legal system. This section emphasizes the settlement role of the judge who manages the judicial process and routinely seeks to formulate an agreed solution to the conflict rather than impose a decision. It suggests that this form of adjudication may be conceived of as either a narrow model, or a wide model. The scope of the phenomenon of settlement adjudication in the court systems has given rise to widespread concern about its potential outcomes. In the last part of this section the chapter briefly reviews some of these concerns. In a separate section, consideration is given to the way in which the wide model, in contrast to its narrow counterpart, may allay anxieties.

---

[7]See, for example, the Alternative Dispute Resolution Act of 1998 (ADR) 28 U.S.C.

[8]For an example of how proceedings adopting the collaborative approach have become entrenched in the court system, see Brazil (1990).

[9]For the shifting role of lawyers who have adopted the collaborative approach to resolving problems when representing their clients, see, for example, Menkel-Meadow (1999), Macfarlane (2008).

[10]A paradigm in the sense of a full complex of opinions, values and techniques shared by the members of a known community: See Kuhn (1962).

The second section of the chapter presents the narrow model; describing its characteristics, advantages and disadvantages. The third section focuses on the wide model. Initially, the chapter discusses its characteristics compared to those of the narrow model and subsequently engages in a broader analysis of its advantages and disadvantages. It is noted that the wide model facilitates more responsive judging. It contemplates a more comprehensive function for the judge as a problem solver and sees the judicial proceedings as an opportunity to address the interests and needs of the disputants as well as their well-being. The advantages inherent in the use of the wide model, and in particular, the practice of interpersonal communication based on empathy and care, may mitigate some of the concerns raised regarding the expansive use of settlement adjudication. Accordingly, the fourth section of the chapter puts forward a number of suggestions that may contribute to the broader use of this form of adjudication.

2 The Range and Development of the Judicial Role

2.1 The Range and Development of the Judicial Role in the United States

During the twentieth century, significant changes occurred in the Anglo-American legal systems in terms of the perception of the judicial role and the manner in which that judicial role would be performed. These changes have led to the situation where judges in the United States now engage in a wide spectrum of roles. The range of judicial conduct currently prevalent in court systems is described in Fig. 1. The range marks the options for legitimate judicial conduct and indicates the direction of development; it shifts along a timeline from a dominant adversarial approach towards extensive use of collaborative measures aimed at conflict resolution achieved by consent of the parties. Judicial conduct has evolved from formalism and judicial distance to judicial engagement supported by empathic and respectful interpersonal communication.

During the first half of the twentieth century, it was the "adversarial judge", managing traditional judicial proceedings, who fulfilled the prevalent role within the court systems in the United States. The perception of the judge's role was impacted by the formalist theory that prevailed during that period. The formalist school viewed the judicial role as management of a technical process involving the uncovering of judicial norms available in law. The main role of the judge was understood to be that of an authority who stated the law and applied it by means of a compulsory judgment (Horwitz 1975; Kronman 1995, 179–199).

The judicial proceeding was administered on a rules oriented basis. This meant that the legitimacy of judicial comportment relied on the existence of rules of legal procedures and laws of evidence that were supposed to ensure procedural fairness, as well as on the identification of universal legal rules and their application to the cir-

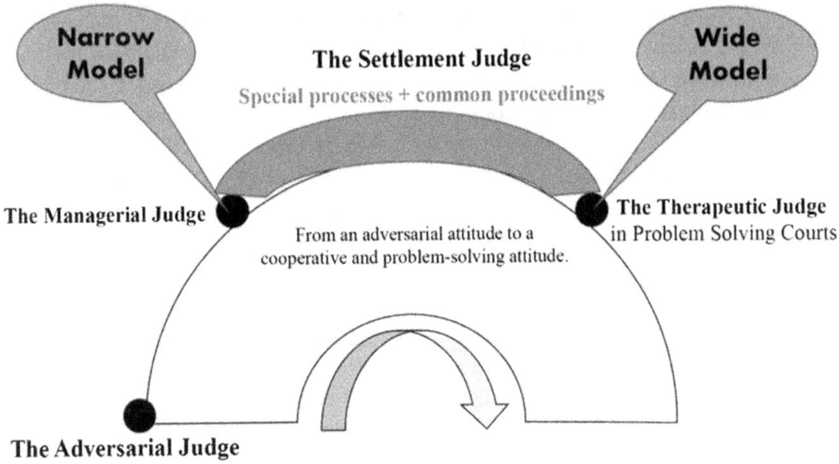

Fig. 1 Settlement adjudication spectrum

cumstances of the case (Fuller 1978; Lehman 1984). The judicial process applied an adversarial approach to conflict resolution. The adversarial approach views disputes as a struggle between parties competing over limited resources. Thus, the entitlement of one party to part of these resources entails a loss for the second party (Hazard 1985, 4–8; Menkel-Meadow 1996).

In the traditional adversarial judging procedure, discussion focuses on an examination of the rights and obligations asserted by the parties to the dispute, and the disagreement is resolved by a judicial decision based on the skilled exercise of the judge's discretion (Fuller 1978, 269). Due process is conceived as being dependent upon judicial neutrality which in turn relies on judicial passivity and creating a distance from the parties when managing the process.[11] This approach steers the development of the adversarial judicial model under which the judge manages the process of clarifying the parties' dispute and settles it by handing down a reasoned binding judgment, albeit while acting passively and at a distance from the litigants. The classic judicial adversarial proceeding is based on the assumption of a judicial truth that must be uncovered (Finkelstein 2011).

During the twentieth century, the basic assumptions of the formalist school were shaken by a number of legal theories that objected to the formalist position and its conception of the nature of the judge's role and the purpose of the judicial proceeding.[12] The adversarial approach to dispute settlement also became the focus of critical

[11]Maintaining distance and judicial passivity are designed to ensure the control element of the parties to an adversarial process and allow each party an equal opportunity to raise arguments, be heard and influence the decision of the judge. Martin Shapiro asserted that judicial neutrality resembles an isosceles triangle in which the judge stands at the apex of the triangle and the parties are equidistant from him in terms of the issue at hand and the judicial treatment thereof, see: Shapiro (1986, 1–2).

[12]Starting from the Legal Realism movement: Shapiro (1986, 2).

discourse. It was claimed that using an adversarial approach to dispute management could be inefficient, was capable of becoming abusive, encouraged the escalation of disputes and presented the judge with a partial and erroneous picture of the conflict which did not take into account complex human reality. All these assertions are still being voiced today (Menkel-Meadow 1996; Wexler 1999; Menkel-Meadow 2000).

In the second half of the twentieth century, certain theoretical-practical movements began to develop in the United States, which called for the implementation of a different approach to conflict resolution—the collaborative approach. A major force advocating the new concept was the Alternative/Adequate Dispute Resolution (ADR) movement (Goldberg et al. 1992; Sourdin 2002; Menkel-Meadow et al. 2004). The ADR movement promoted the development of a variety of proceedings for settling disputes using a non-adversarial approach that strove to achieve a pragmatic solution with an optimistic orientation toward the future.[13] It emphasized the importance of the proceeding and not just its results, as well as the concept of matching the type of process to the type of dispute (Sander and Goldberg 1994).

According to the collaborative approach, all disputes have several layers that should be addressed and examined. The top-most, overt layer, consists of the positions of the parties. A deeper layer, necessitating exposure, is formed by their interests, needs, emotions, and desires. Often, uncovering the layer of needs and interests reveals that the positions of the parties to the dispute may be disparate, yet their needs and interests are not contradictory but actually complementary or even mutual. According to this non-adversarial approach, a discourse that deals with all layers of the dispute enables a deeper discussion of the disagreement and opens the door to settling the dispute by way of a consensual solution that is mutually profitable (Menkel-Meadow 2000; Fisher et al. 2011). The collaborative approach therefore emphasized the need to address the dispute before the court as being composed of more than merely claims to legal rights and obligations entailing legal considerations—those perceived as belonging to the upper stratum of the opposing positions. Under the collaborative approach, a deeper and more appropriate handling of the dispute, involves an examination of aspirations, emotions, the relationship between the parties and between them and the communities to which they belong and other extra-legal considerations informing the dispute.

The collaborative approach is regarded as being highly advantageous, both on a personal level for the litigants and in terms of its public aspect. With regard to the parties to the dispute, a collaborative approach, when examining contentious issues, enables the parties to engage in an in-depth discussion, and identify a creative solution that matches their interests. Such a solution is forward-looking, stable, mutually beneficial, encourages future cooperation and more (Menkel-Meadow 1995, 1999). On the public and social level, pursuing the collaborative approach, which includes listening to the opposing party and giving him due consideration, contributes to strengthening the pillars of tolerance and democracy in society (Barak 2002; Welsh 2014).

---

[13]For a proposal as to six organizing principles for conflict resolution, relevant also to the ADR movement, see Alberstein (2015, 887–892).

A major process promoted by the ADR movement that implemented the collaborative approach, was mediation. As part of the mediation process under the pragmatic model, the needs and interests of the parties to the conflict were clarified, and the parties were encouraged to formulate an agreed solution that met the maximum needs and interests of each side and yielded a mutual profit (Kovach 2004; Fisher et al. 2011). The ideas of the ADR movement, accompanied by practical means of implementation, percolated into the American legal system. The movement promised change regarding both the quality and the effectiveness of the dispute resolution process in the legal system and society (Brazil 1990; Menkel-Meadow 1995).

In parallel, the American judiciary was required to cope with significant administrative difficulties, including the problem of onerous caseloads and long delays in supporting an effective judicial solution. A further problem was the considerable burden of expenses involved in managing claims, which limited litigants' access to the courts. These problems and others gave rise to dissatisfaction with the management of the system and a decline in public trust (Levin and Wheeler 1976).

The failures of the court system were linked to its conduct, which was widely characterized by the presentation of a single central procedure for dispute management adopting an adversarial approach. The promise of greater efficiency and better quality in the management of disputes using alternative processes to conflict resolution and the need to cope with the functional difficulties of the court system led to the assimilation of ADR processes in the judiciary in general and the mediation process in particular (Plapinger and Shaw 1997; Brazil 1991). The combination of a conceptual change regarding the proper way to handle disputes and the possibility of using practical tools to apply the collaborative approach, learned from the mediation process, impacted the perception of the judicial role and the techniques for its fulfillment.

Even though the ADR movement did not attempt to make changes to the judicial process but only suggested an alternative, in practice it influenced the conception of the judge's role and reshaped the judicial process. The support given to the collaborative approach to conflict management and the assimilation of processes that illustrated that approach in the court system contributed to shaping an innovative conception of a responsive judge. It impacted the feasibility of the judge's role as a problem solver addressing various types of conflict considerations.

In addition to the assimilation of alternatives processes, the court systems began to adopt a "case management" approach. According to this managerial approach, judges were responsible for managing the timetable, hearings and progression of the case. This perception led to the creation of a new judicial role that Professor Resnik described as that of the "managerial judge" (Resnik 1982). Resnik claimed that judges invested a considerable amount of time in managing the case and adopting informal techniques aimed at concluding the hearing of the case in the most expedient way possible. A commonly accepted judicial technique for ending a dispute was to focus efforts on causing the parties to settle (Resnik 1982; Kritzer 1982). This type of adjudication promoting settlement on the basis of a case-management approach reliant mainly on considerations of efficiency is described here as the narrow model. This definition seeks to emphasize that the degree of consideration given to the conflict and the perspective employed by the judge in response to the conflict considerations are more limited.[14] In this form of judicial responsiveness that goes beyond merely adjudicating legal rights and responsibilities, the main concerns reflect the economic impact of litigation on the parties, as well as the court, and attempts to respond to the parties' desire for time-saving, cost-effective solutions and proportionality in achieving justice.

The role of the managerial judge became dominant in the 1980s and was especially suited to judges who dealt with pre-trial proceedings. The end of the twentieth century witnessed a significant trend towards judicial efforts to bring disputes to an agreed solution in all judicial processes and all instances. Prominence was given to an innovative role that is described here as that of the "settlement judge".

The settlement judge refers to an adjudicator who makes repeated efforts to formulate an agreed solution between the parties, including by way of compromise. The settlement judge is active and involved. The adjudication proceedings that he administers include judicial efforts to find a pragmatic solution that is acceptable to the parties, rather than attempt to discover some legal or factual truth. The proceeding takes place at a reduced level of formality, cutting short the accepted stages of judicial hearings (for example, by refraining from hearing evidence) and concludes with a short judgment, usually foregoing judicial reasoning.

Settlement adjudication is comprehensively expressed in the judicial systems and may be identified in two areas of activity. The first is as part of a unique process in the court system designed to settle disputes by consensual solution. A case in point is the settlement conference in the United States.[15] The second area of activity is part of a general trend which encourages the parties to arrive at a consensual solution within the framework of "regular" judicial processes designed to end in a judicial determination (Alfini 1999; Robinson 2006). The frequency and scope of these judicial settlement efforts to create an agreed solution, including by obtaining the consent of the parties to a ruling by way of compromise, indicate the development of a new organizational culture —"a settlement culture" (Alfini 1999, 11).

The existence of this settlement culture may be discerned in a variety of arenas. One is an analysis of judgments containing various utterances by judges to the effect that an agreed solution is preferable to a solution imposed by judicial decision (Resnik 2000). Another is studies examining the judges' perception of the judicial role.[16]

---

[14]Riskin used the terms "narrow" and "broad" to describe a mediator's orientation when framing the problem presented by the parties. The term "narrow" is comparative reference to a possible solution within a multi-stage adversarial judicial process whereas "broad" refers to other issues that are taken into account such as a business interest in maintaining reputation. Therefore, the broad orientation of a mediator can lead to a mediation process similar to the judicial settlement process using the wide model with its reference to personal and social interests: see Riskin (1996, 19, 22).

[15]In this special procedure the judge holds meetings with the parties in order to clarify the dispute and tries to settle it by means of an agreed solution. The content of the hearings is confidential. The judicial proceeding in fact emulates a mediation proceeding under the pragmatic model and strives to enjoy the advantages of dispute resolution using this collaborative process: Parness (2006), Robinson (2009).

[16]Studies performed in 1970 revealed different judicial approaches to the functions entailed by the judge's role which included determination of conflicts, offering interpretations, supervision of the

It may also be seen in data indicating the unequivocal decline in the number of judgments issued at the end of a multistage adversarial adjudication proceeding. This phenomenon, which has become known as the "vanishing trial phenomenon" (Galanter 2004), is widespread in all of the aforementioned judiciaries.[17]

Settlement adjudication, whether conducted in special proceedings or in the regular proceedings, may be pursued out of an understanding of the advantages of the collaborative approach and ensuing desire to utilize the applicable judicial processes. Settlement adjudication that promotes settlements for reasons of quality, as advanced by the collaborative approach, is a form of settlement judging typical of the wide model. The term "wide model" seeks to emphasize that in this form of judicial responsiveness that goes beyond merely adjudicating legal rights and responsibilities, an attempt is made to respond to a broad number of additional considerations. These considerations include recognition of the non-economic needs and interests of the litigants, the legal system and society. For example, the parties' relationships, or the desire to achieve a high level of satisfaction and trust in the judicial system based on procedural justice relying on components that establish fairness in the litigants' eyes and strengthen the psychological welfare of the litigants. This perception of wide responsiveness has been reinforced by the formation of the role of the therapeutic judge. In the beginning of the twenty-first century, an additional development has affected the settlement role of the judge, transforming him into what may be described as the "therapeutic judge". The therapeutic judge manages judicial proceedings with the goal of attaining positive emotional and behavioral results for the litigants (Wexler 2001; Winick and Wexler 2003).

This type of adjudication implements some of the ideas of the Therapeutic Jurisprudence (TJ) Movement (Wexler and Winick 1991; Winick and Wexler 2003). This theoretical-practical movement that developed at the end of the twentieth century studies the role of law as a therapeutic agent. It focuses on the law's impact on emotional life and psychological well-being (Wexler and Winick 1996, XVII). The movement examines legal rules and procedures and the roles of legal actors involved in the administration of procedures. It proposes ways to increase their implementation in a manner that takes into account emotional repercussions and aspires to positive, constructive and rehabilitative outcomes (Perlin 2000; Wexler 2014). These outcomes refer to conflict considerations or extra-legal concerns and go far beyond rights and duties.

Therapeutic judging is most evident in the framework of special courts, the "'problem-solving'" courts. These courts which have only developed in recent decades possess educational, rehabilitative and therapeutic goals. They mainly deal with criminal issues related to chronic social problems such as drug violations

---

courts and more: Glick (1971). Only two decades later did it become apparent that the perception of the judicial role included a new function, namely, bringing the dispute to an end through agreement. Numerous judges state that one of their chief tasks is to act as catalysts for the creation of agreements between the parties and note their preference to perform their functions using a settlement-oriented approach: Edgar (1995), Robinson (2006).

[17]For example, in Australia, see Scott (2008); for data relating to the United States, see Langbein (2012).

(Berman and Feinblatt 2001; Hora 2011). Problem-solving courts deploy multidisciplinary teams of professionals with whom the judges consult and collaborate when making decisions. The judicial proceedings in these courts adopt a collaborative approach that applies to all the parties involved in the conflict management, including the prosecution and defense.

The judicial process strives to find a response that may bring about relief for all parties involved in the dispute, including the litigant and the community where the violation has occurred. This response is usually formulated as an agreed solution reflected in a "therapeutic contract" that is adapted to the needs of the defendant and aspires to provide him with the tools and a road map for escaping the vicious cycle of recidivism (Hora 2011, 46). These tools include repeat appearances by the litigant before a judge over a period of time in which his compliance with the therapeutic contract is examined; these repeated appearances create a lengthy process in which the judge fulfills the significant role of assisting in the rehabilitation of the litigant (Wexler 2001; King 2008).

The emphasis in the administration of the proceedings is on a problem-solving approach based on a relational orientation. The relational orientation emphasizes the existence, importance and influence of relationships and interpersonal relationships on individual human behavior and regards them as designers of consciousness, forms of expression and ways of behavior.[18]

In our context, it accentuates the creation of interpersonal communication and a respectful attitude of the judge, as the manager of the conflict resolution process, towards all those taking part in the process, including the litigants, their lawyers, family members or invited community representatives. A direct dialogue takes place between the judge and the litigant. The judicial process is conducted using elements of active listening, positive focus, linguistic clarity, the provision of explanations about the proceedings and more (King 2009; Goldberg 2011).

The judge in the problem-solving court views her role not only as a source of authority capable of exerting force and meting out punishment, but also as a source of education and guidance that may help the litigant break free from the cycle of crime and social ostracism. This is achieved by using judicial power to impose punishments in combination with sensitivity, persuasiveness, encouragement and support. The quality of a judge is no longer merely a function of her ability to provide a legal solution to an issue in a rational and methodical manner, but also of her ability to relate to psychological and social aspects of an act and the person performing it. Therapeutic judging in these courts has established a new professional paradigm for the judge's role. It has replaced the formalistic, adversarial and distanced judicial role with an active, involved, collaborative and less formal administration that displays judicial care and empathy.[19]

---

[18]For the relational concept and its characteristics, see for example, Bush and Folger (2005, 59–62). For the relational concept which is supported by therapeutic jurisprudence in so far as concerns the shaping of the functions of the contemporary lawyer, see Steir (1992). For rules oriented conduct compared to relational oriented conduct of litigants, see Conley and O'Barr (1990).

[19]For the change in paradigm offered by therapeutic jurisprudence, see Perlman (2010, 419–421), Stobbs (2013).

Alongside these special courts, settlement judging with a therapeutic emphasis finds expression in the regular courts. The formulation of a settlement is achieved in the context of the wide model which also considers the well-being of the litigants. Usually the dispute clarification process and the formulation of an agreed solution are attained by insisting on the principles of listening to the litigant ("giving voice"), neutrality that is interpreted by applying legal principles and transparency about how decisions are made, treating the litigants with dignity, and judicial expressions of interest and empathy. These components establish a sense of procedural fairness in the eyes of the litigants (Tyler 1983; Burke and Leben 2008).

Settlement-therapeutic judging is also reflected in such judicial activities as writing the judicial decision in a manner that displays respect towards the claimant's arguments even if these are ultimately rejected ("letter to the losing party", Jones 2012; Wexler 2014) and through judicial gestures such as giving the litigant an opportunity to be heard by reading a letter and so forth (King 2011; Spencer 2017; Perlman 2017).

The search for therapeutic outcomes, which refer to extra-legal outcomes, can be described as a form of judicial responsiveness which treats the litigants as whole persons, not just as legal categories. It promotes judicial attempts to respond to the complexity of the conflict in all its layers, and address values, relationships, emotions, human development, personal wellbeing and community welfare. The therapeutic role and other means of facilitating the judicial function as described in relation to the American legal system, are relevant to other legal systems as well. The next section shall briefly describe the situation prevailing in the Israeli legal system.

The dominance of the settlement role and the scope of its application in various legal systems have given rise to important concerns. Some of these concerns will be described at the end of this part of the chapter, so as to allow a discussion in the second part of the chapter as to how the different models can fulfill their function in light of these concerns and the degree of judicial responsiveness to the fears raised.

2.2 *The Range and Development of the Judicial Role in Israel*

The description of the development of the judicial role in Fig. 1 is also relevant to the legal system in Israel. In the early decades following the establishment of the State of Israel, the judicial role primarily took an adversarial form (Mautner 2011). Beginning in the 1990s, with the integration of the ADR movement into the Israeli legal system, a change occurred in the nature of the judicial role (Perlman 2015b, 221–236).

Concurrently, as in the United States, difficulties in the legal system and particularly heavy caseloads (Sulitzeanu-Kenan et al. 2008), spurred the Israeli judiciary to adopt a case-management approach. The court system has since developed an array of pre-trial procedures aimed at speeding the clarification of disputes and handling them more efficiently. Israeli managerial judges who administer pre-trial proceedings make a considerable effort to end cases at the interlocutory stage. They do so in a variety of ways which include asking the parties for their consent to conclude the case through a compromise ruling—a brief ruling without reasoning that does not require evidentiary hearings; referring the dispute to alternative non-judicial proceedings such as a mediation process; and encouraging the litigants to reach an agreement with judicial assistance.[20]

In addition, due to the fact that there is no explicit statutory provision in Israel that allows a settlement conference procedure, the judiciary has developed and implemented various projects over the past decade which have been defined as "judicial mediation". In the context of these projects, which are implemented in both civil and criminal disputes, settlement judges conduct a confidential judicial proceeding with the aim of bringing the parties to an agreed solution. If the case is not resolved by consensual solution, it is transferred to another judge to conduct a traditional adversarial process that ends by an imposed decision (Perlman 2015a, 404–407).

Settlement adjudication in Israel is presently the foremost process used. The data shows that about 90% of all motions filed in Israeli courts are neither heard nor adjudicated in a multi-stage adversarial proceeding that ends with a detailed judgment (Weinshall-Margel et al. 2015). A number of community courts have been established in Israel in recent years. These courts operate in the format of problem-solving courts and accord prominence to the role of the therapeutic judge. Settlement-therapeutic judging may be found in many other courts in the Israeli court system, particularly in juvenile courts and family courts (Perlman 2008, 353–356; Segev 2013).

2.3 *Concerns and Criticisms of Settlement Adjudication*

The comprehensive use of settlement adjudication within the judiciary has given rise to important concerns. Some of these concerns are linked to the possibility that the functions of the law will be undermined, in particular the educational function of adjudication in shaping society and its function in directing rules of conduct.[21] Other concerns relate to the manner of managing the judicial process and ensuring its fairness. A few of these issues are briefly described below in order to allow a subsequent examination of how each model treats them and the advantages and disadvantages of their respective approach.

One issue relates to confidentiality and absence of public awareness. Settlement adjudication proceedings, such as the settlement conference procedure, are usually confidential. A standard of concealment is created that could lead to the silencing of vital public discussion. Moreover, settlement adjudication usually ends with a brief decision rather than a detailed and well-reasoned judgment. The fact that judicial decisions are not publicized precludes analysis and critique; prevents the publication of guiding standards; foils the creation of binding precedents and arrests the

---

[20] Section 79 A–D of the Israeli Courts [Consolidated Version] Law 1984.

[21] This in addition to the function of dispute resolution in accordance with the screening proposed by Smith (1991).

development of common law (Resnik 2006). Settlement adjudication may also harm the educational role of adjudication and its function in directing the future behavior of people in society and establishing boundaries and relationships (Friedman and Wickelgren 2008).

Another widely voiced criticism of settlement adjudication ensues from a stance that generally opposes promoting a collaborative approach that aspires to achieve consent as part of the judicial process. Opponents believe that setting a goal of compromise and harmony may lead to social conservatism and regression. Such adjudication would be unable to advance rights or long term public interests (Fiss 1984; Resnik 2003). Some claim that settlement adjudication undermines democracy and that proceedings without juries violate the public's right to participate in the judicial process. Indeed, there are those who assert that refraining from decision-making damages the principle of the three way separation of powers and endangers constitutional rights (Young 2006; Ackerman 2006).

Another problem relates to assuring procedural fairness. Minimizing the formality of the proceedings, the lack of insistence on proper procedure and rules of evidence, and holding proceedings without maintaining records raise concerns. These processes are deemed capable of prejudicing the neutrality and unbiased stance of the judge, as well as creating coercive pressure to end the case in a settlement (Resnik 1982). In the absence of procedural transparency and documentation it becomes a challenge to assure judicial accountability (Brody 2008). An extensive discussion and response to these concerns falls outside the scope of this chapter[22]; however, this chapter will try to show that, given the current use of settlement adjudication and the accompanying fears outlined above, application of the wide model of responsive judging, that takes into account a broader range of extra-legal concerns offers a more successful response and greater help in ameliorating these fears than would the narrow model.

3 Settlement Adjudication According to the Narrow Model

3.1 *Characteristics of the Narrow Model*

Settlement adjudication based on the narrow model is motivated by considerations of efficiency which are relevant both to the judiciary and to the parties. From a system perspective, increased efficiency means that the caseload with which the system contends is decreased when case management is swift, with a corresponding reduction in judicial time used. From the parties' point of view, efficiency equates to a quick end to the dispute, necessitating less time and a concomitant reduction in the costs involved in managing the dispute over a long period. Accordingly, the management of a judicial proceeding using the narrow model is characterized by judicial tactics that emphasize the strengths and weaknesses of the parties' arguments.

[22] See, for example, Sourdin (2011).

The judicial hearing focuses on the risks and opportunities for each of the parties inherent in continuing the management of the proceeding. The emphasis is placed on the resources of time and costs and the advantages that the parties may gain from the savings achieved (Robinson 2009, 126–127).

The settlement adjudication proceeding within the narrow model emphasizes the role of the judge as a specialist in the management of disputes and as more knowledgeable than the parties, making him capable of leading the dispute to an appropriate agreed solution. Emphasis is placed on the results of the proceeding. Prominence is also given to the role of the lawyer as the client's representative, as one who is authorized to guide the discussion and agree to a solution on the client's behalf. The judicial dialogue is held mainly with the lawyer.[23]

3.2 *Advantages and Disadvantages*

The narrow model of settlement adjudication expresses a limited degree of judicial responsiveness. It responds to the respective needs of litigants and the system but on a scale that can be interpreted as restricted to efficiency considerations. A successful judicial procedure using the narrow model will supply the litigant with a quick, reasonable and affordable solution to the conflict. It responds to the litigant's desire for a cost-effective solution and proportionality in achieving justice. Likewise, the system gains when efficient use is made of judicial time and resources, and the dispute is handled swiftly. It has also been argued that these proceedings sharpen the parties' understanding of the issues in contention and those that are agreed even if the case is not concluded by way of a settlement. Ultimately, this development enables a concise and well-defined dispute to be brought for decision within the adversarial process (Kritzer 1982). Thus, increased efficiency can lead to long term gains by avoiding unnecessary activity in the clarification of disputes, accelerating the handling of files and more.

Nonetheless, efficiency considerations, according to the collaborative approach, form only part of the spectrum of needs and interests preoccupying litigants and the court system. Thus, common to most litigants is the need to be heard and engage in a process that invests time and effort to solve their conflict. Arguably, a disadvantage of using the narrow model is that conducting the judicial process using this approach may be seen as a form of bartering that precludes the disputing parties from having their day in court. The quick process does not allow a multitude of other needs and interests to be addressed which might go to the root of the dispute. In addition, the

---

[23]This conclusion ensues from a number of studies prepared on the basis of observations of judicial proceedings in Israel. For example, a 2008 study within the framework of a mediation clinic operated by Bar Ilan University, see the study report of the therapeutic jurisprudence team under the guidance of Karni Perlman, Clinic Supervisor Dr. Michal Alberstein; and the observation study within the framework of the Non-adversarial and Therapeutic Justice Center in the College of Management Academic Studies 2017.

narrow model places key emphasis on financial aspects and accordingly encourages the proposal of limited solutions.

With regard to the concerns relating to settlement adjudication, this model per se does not offer a comprehensive response. Its legitimacy is generally based on the efficacy of the process and degree of satisfaction of the parties and their counsel, which is in turn based on their assessment of the particular case rather than an evaluation of the process as a social and legal phenomenon.[24] General support for settlement adjudication may be voiced here, for example, to the effect that judicial intervention in a settlement process reduces the influence of extra-legal factors which sometimes sway the outcome of the adversarial dispute management process. One such factor might be the economic ability of one of the parties to bear the cost of conducting a prolonged trial (Elliot 1986).

Likewise, the status of the judge earns him the trust and respect of the parties to the settlement process. A judge is deemed neutral, knowledgeable about the law and able to assess the prospective outcome of an adversarial process. There is a presumption that the judge will examine whether informed consent has been given to an agreed resolution and will assist in formulating a solution that does not violate binding rules of law (Schuck 1986). The presumption of non-coercion and the existence of informed consent does not necessarily reflect reality. It has often been suggested that to achieve accountability it is essential to determine guidelines for obtaining informed consent to settlement adjudication and its outcome.[25]

4 Settlement Adjudication According to the Wide Model

4.1 Characteristics of the Wide Model

In contradistinction to the above, settlement adjudication according to the wide model is motivated by considerations of quality forming part of the collaborative approach to dispute resolution. Therefore the judicial process includes a discourse focused on clarifying the wide range of needs and interests underlying the statements of claim submitted by the parties. An attempt is made to identify a forward-looking solution that offers mutual profit to both parties. The adjudication techniques used to promote a settlement include addressing non pecuniary losses and the possibility of maintaining good relationships or improving communications between the parties.

Settlement adjudication according to the wide model is also characterized by a different power allocation in attorney-client relations and the empowerment of the client in dispute management. The appropriate framework for representing clients in this context is "problem-solving advocacy" that accords greater prominence to the client and allows him the ability to take a meaningful part in the process (Macfarlane

[24]For lawyers' preferences and satisfaction with the process, see Resnik (2002), Wissler (2011).

[25]This for example, was the recommendation put forward by the Ombudsman of the Israeli Judiciary in an opinion dealing with settlement judging, See Ombudsman of the Israeli Judiciary (2004).

2008, 110; Bush 2013). Settlement adjudication according to the wide model is conducted within the context of interpersonal judicial communication characterized by empathy and respect. It accords importance to the process and not just to the result. The communication between the litigants is also promoted through practices that encourage the parties to express emotions and help each side understand the concerns and emotions of the other.[26]

4.2 *Advantages and Disadvantages*

Settlement adjudication based on the wide model expresses a broad approach to the judge's role as a settler of disputes. The wide model carries the promise of a judicial proceeding that maximizes gains rather than one that merely realizes rights and duties. These gains may be obtained as a result of the consideration given to needs and interests in relationships as well as psychological welfare. This role extends beyond the concrete judicial issue facing the judge and expresses broad notions of judicial responsiveness to the litigants (an individual aspect of responsiveness), the court system (a systemic aspect) and societal considerations. It views the court not only as an arena for determining and implementing legal rights but also as a forum for treating the problems underlying legal disputes and helping to solve them. Consequently, this type of adjudication reinforces the importance of the judiciary and the role of the judge in the modern world.

The wide model strives to formulate a pragmatic solution to disputes giving consideration to the human aspect involved and understanding that the person involved in a dispute is an individual with his or her own needs and abilities. Settlement adjudication based on the wide model gives adjudication a human face and extends judicial influence from the mere exertion of corrective power and the fear of authority to a source of empowerment for attaining positive and rehabilitative results.[27] It strengthens the perception of the judge as a "human being"[28] who administers "ethics of care" (Gilligan 1982).

Settlement adjudication based on the wide model makes it possible to minimize concerns regarding the assurance of procedural fairness in the judicial process. The concern about maintaining procedural fairness in the collaborative process arises from an examination of the proceeding from a rules oriented perspective. Many of the opponents of the settlement conference, for example, examine it according to the

---

[26]This practice was described by Robinson (2012a, 130). Robinson drew a distinction between one adjudicative style which he defined as "problem solving" and another adjudicative style which he called the "directive approach". The former style is consistent with the wide model of settlement adjudication whereas the latter is more compatible with the narrow model of settlement adjudication: Robinson (2009, 129). Moreover the problem solving approach is consistent with a facilitative mediation style whereas the directive approach is more compatible with an evaluative mediation approach, according to the types proposed by Riskin (1996).

[27]This conception accords the therapeutic judge the importance of a social leader: See King (2008).

[28]Relating to the famous question posed by Jerome Frank (1931): "Are Judges Human?".

degree of compliance with the rules of procedure and the laws of evidence. They fear, for instance, that it is not possible for one side to respond to the other side's arguments if the arguments are voiced in separate meetings. Application of the wide model offers an alternative method that applies a conception of fairness within a relational orientation. In this perspective procedural fairness is measured by the litigants' point of view which encompasses voice, neutrality, respectful treatment and trustworthiness, within the framework of interpersonal communications characterized by judicial respect and empathy (Tyler 2006, 22; Burke and Leben 2008, 6).

Indeed, it has been found that, in practice, attorneys do evaluate the procedural fairness of a settlement conference within a relational orientation. Lawyers report that in cases where they feel that the judge has put some thought into solving the dispute, where the parties and attorneys have been addressed with empathy and respect, and where the judge refrains from exerting pressure and clarifies her viewpoint by conducting a clear dialogue with the parties, a sense of neutrality and absence of judicial bias is produced. According to this interpretation, judicial conduct not only underpins procedural fairness but also legitimizes the very existence of the proceeding, thereby increasing trust in the judiciary (Wissler 2011). Settlement judging, using the wide model, can also be regarded as combining the benefits of managing disputes in a non-adversarial framework with the benefits attributable to the clarification of disputes by a judge. Apart from the general advantages attributed to this form of adjudication, as set out in relation to the narrow model, adjudication according to the wide model, which digs deep into the root causes of the dispute, enables the discrepancy in power between the parties to be treated in an appropriate and effective manner. Such adjudication can better prevent improper exploitation of the legal process by the "strong players' in society or "repeat players" who are active in dispute management.[29]

Compared to the narrow model, settlement adjudication pursuant to the wide model, better implements the function of the law in dispute settlement, guiding conduct, and educating and shaping society. Certainly, managing and concluding a dispute out of the public eye, for example, in a settlement conference, precludes the public from becoming aware of judicial rules that may direct future behavior and enable appropriate planning. Nonetheless, settlements reached between the parties, and particularly those concluded with various institutions and authorities, also include rules of desirable behavior that may affect the entire public in the future. A solution that is reached through voluntary agreement is usually respected by the parties and implemented in an organization in a more comprehensive fashion than a coercive solution. Thus, settlement adjudication using the wide model may also contribute to fulfilling the judicial function of coordinating and directing social relationships.[30]

---

[29] This power discrepancy was discussed by Galanter (1974).

[30] Tyler's studies have shown that the more the parties experience the decision making process as being fair, the more the results are considered just and the greater the sense of obligation to uphold and implement the results: Tyler (2006). For the success in implementing rules formulated by agreement, in contrast to rules forced on medical institutions, see Dubler and Liebman (2004, 217–218).

Also in education terms, the collaborative approach which underlies the wide model addresses both the individual aspect of the needs and interests of the parties, and the interpersonal aspect of respecting others, taking care of relationships and the community in general. For this reason, even though settlement adjudication pursuant to the wide model deals with needs and interests and does not necessarily advance rights in a public manner, it does promote considerate and appropriate social behavior and thereby implements an important educational function. Such education (Barak 2002; Welsh 2014) strengthens the foundations of democratic society and does not undermine it. Further, interpersonal communication that displays judicial involvement and concern increases public satisfaction with the way in which the dispute is managed and augments public trust in the judiciary as an efficient and appropriate system for clarifying disputes (Warren 2000; Burke and Leben 2008, 12–15).

The in-depth handling of the dispute and the involvement of the parties in its solution usually give rise to a solution that settles the conflict in its entirety, thereby preventing the submission of additional claims by these parties. Thus, settlement adjudication based on the wide model also contributes to the efficiency of the judicial system and the proper performance of the function of dispute resolution.[31]

Adjudication that promotes agreements through considerations of both quality and efficiency, constitutes an important systemic response to the concerns regarding the privatization of justice that takes place when the management of disputes is transferred to private settlers of disputes, such as mediators. It mitigates the concerns that have been raised with regard to the promotion of non-formal justice within the court system.[32] The concern over an informal, confidential proceeding that allows suspension of norms and that is carried out under the administration of a mediator who is not part of the court team,[33] is thereby addressed by the system, which offers another option. That option is to administer the dispute in a collaborative proceeding carried out by a judge who is subject to the judiciary's rules of selection, training and auditing.

Accordingly, managing a process of settlement adjudication in accordance with the wide model may be regarded, from a gender perspective, as enjoying the advantages attributed to managing a dispute by way of collaboration. The latter is compatible with the cultural feminism approach to justice and dispute resolution (Alberstein 2009, 12–14), on the one hand, and ameliorating the concerns regarding harm to

---

[31]With regard to the concern relating to the potential decline of common law, it would seem that this issue does not impact the question of the substance of the settlement adjudication model but only its actual application and scope within the system. This concern may be met, inter alia, by the establishment of a mechanism for channeling disputes within the court system that would have the necessary time resources and knowledge to distinguish between disputes of legal and social significance best dealt with in an open public process and decided in a detailed judgment that would be published and possibly form a binding precedent, and other types of disputes conducted in a more confidential manner. This issue falls outside the scope of this chapter which deals with the choice of settlement adjudication models.

[32]For some of these concerns, see Auerbach (1983).

[33]The concerns raised, for example, in relation to possible harm to women's rights in the event of a forced mediation in custody proceedings: See Grillo (1991).

women's rights in a consensual process conducted outside the court, on the other hand (Grillo 1991).

Adjudication according to the wide model also has some disadvantages. The principal difficulty is that from the point of view of the court system, this type of adjudication is liable to be lengthier than adjudication according to the narrow model and may therefore be deemed less efficient. Additionally, due to its emphasis on the individual concrete aspects of the case at hand, it may lead to inequality compared to the outcome of similar cases. Further, it involves active participation of the litigants—something that neither they nor their attorneys always find desirable.

Finally, in the absence of suitable regulatory tools or appropriate training, this model of adjudication may be perceived as an overly soft exercise of power, or as one that competes with the mediation process performed outside the court.[34] Although these disadvantages are significant, once weighed in light of the advantages inherent in the use of this model, it is evident that settlement adjudication based on the wide model achieves comprehensive and worthy judicial and social ends within the legal system. Today, judiciaries present a "multi-option model" (Sourdin 2011, 148) for the clarification and settlement of disputes. In fact, a pre-defined proceeding adopting a settlement adjudication approach, such as the settlement conference, currently constitutes one of many options for clarifying disputes as an alternative to adversarial adjudication. Settlement adjudication based on the wide model, in contradistinction to the narrow model, is dedicated to the judicial option and endows it with valueable signficance.

5 Proposals for Increasing the Use of the Wide Model

In practice, judicial proceedings are handled using a variety of judicial management styles that range from the adoption of the narrow model of settlement adjudication to the wide model. Thus, a judge may manage a proceeding clarifying the parties' needs and interests but do so in a limited fashion, confining the dialogue to the parties' attorneys. In view of the advantages noted above and bearing in mind the considerable use of settlement adjudication in judiciaries, it is appropriate to take steps to increase the use of the wide model format.

A number of factors may underlie a judge's choice to adopt a wide or narrow model. This choice may derive from the perception of the content of the judicial role and the degree of responsiveness that should be applied in general or specifically in light of the circumstances of the case at hand. A change may occur depending on the subject of the dispute and the type of process or judicial instance. Other factors may be ascribed to the judge's judicial background, such as his legal education, knowledge, training and skills in dispute management. In addition, the selection of model type

[34] Although there are those who consider that it is the very knowledge that most judicial proceedings are not conducted in a full multi-stage adjudication process that may actually lead to increased demand for mediation or other alternative proceedings outside the courts: Kovach (2005).

may be influenced by the legal rules that provide the framework for the management of this form of adjudication and determine which judicial rules of conduct may be deemed appropriate or otherwise. The ability to conduct a judicial proceeding in accordance with the wide model also depends on the attitude of lawyers and their ability to participate in that framework (Perlman 2008).

It therefore seems that in order to increase the use of settlement adjudication in accordance with the wide model, the following measures should be implemented:

1. Steps to bring about a change in legal education. Anglo-American and Israeli legal education are still based on an adversarial approach to conflict resolution (O'Brien 2011). The inclusion of a compulsory course on dispute resolution that would explicate the collaborative approach, its advantages, and the variety of processes available for implementing this approach is vital (Lande and Sternlight 2010; Kloppenberg 2013). This may help open new horizons of thought in the minds of future lawyers and judges regarding the appropriate way to administer disputes and create a preference for the use of the wide model.
2. Continuing legal education and promotion of courses and training for jurists that would provide them with practical professional tools to pursue the collaborative approach. The skills and qualifications that are required for applying a collaborative approach are different from those required for the management of conflicts applying an adversarial and formalistic approach (Daicoff 2006, 52–55). For example, training is required to improve active listening and the ability to engage in team work with experts. It is unnecessary to improve the ability to cross-examine witnesses.
3. Provision of rules governing settlement adjudication during the conduct of judicial processes. These might include outlining permitted or prohibited practices, such as the possibility of meeting parties individually or holding telephone conversations in order to promote a settlement, or the stages of the judicial process during which it is acceptable to engage in an effort at settlement adjudication. It would be appropriate to determine guidelines to ensure informed consent to a judicial process which is based on consent and the results thereof.[35]
4. Updating the judicial rules of ethics so as to apply to judicial conduct within the collaborative framework. The current judicial rules of ethics are designed to regulate behavior relevant to the clarification of disputes pursuant to the adversarial approach which ends in a judgment. The rules do not afford an adequate solution to issues relevant to judicial conduct directed at achieving an agreed solution. Consideration must be given to formulating a separate system of rules or updating those in force (Cratsley 2006; Deason 2017, 137–143).
5. Examining and assessing the judges' work according to more than mere indices of quantitative efficiency that count the number of disputes submitted to a judge and the time it takes to conclude them. Instead, the indices should also examine the extent of the parties' satisfaction with the process, their opinion as to its fairness and other issues of quality.

[35] For common judicial techniques designed to ensure compliance with judicial ethics when conducting settlement processes, see Robinson (2012b).

6. Establishing an organizational infrastructure for learning and deriving knowledge from the experience of incumbent judges. Such an infrastructure may be established through data collection and research. It could help shape the appropriate tools and be used for purposes of comparison and critique. The concentration of knowledge in the hands of an internal body specializing in professional analysis will make it possible to identify and distribute practices that have been successfully implemented within the framework of the wide model.[36]
7. Expanding the academic discourse, as performed in the framework of this book, which examines the content of the judicial role and proposes updated models that are compatible with the needs of society at the beginning of the twenty-first century. Deepening the links between academia and practice so that mutual information is exchanged that will enable an accurate picture to be obtained of the current situation and allow suitable improvements to be fashioned.

6 Conclusion

The conception of the judge's role has changed and developed over time. Today, it is possible to describe a range of judicial functions in Anglo-American law countries as well as in Israel. Accordingly, various types of judicial proceedings are currently being conducted in the legal systems, from traditional adversarial adjudication through a judicial process in which significant judicial efforts are made to conclude the case in a settlement, and up to a judicial process with rehabilitative and therapeutic objectives.

In recent decades the rise in status of the collaborative approach to conflict resolution and its support by the ADR and the TJ movements have been among the factors that have changed the perception of the judicial role and the manner in which that judicial role is performed.

In the beginning of the twenty-first century it is a commonly held assumption that potentially judicial proceedings are capable of yielding profits that pertain to more than mere legal rights and duties, which the collaborative approach describes as the upper level of a conflict. The judicial proceeding can and should also care for the needs and interests of the assorted parties involved in the conflict and address the underlying strata of the conflict. Consequently, judicial responsiveness and its manifestations in courts are diverse. Judges take into account a broad range of considerations that go far beyond legal issues. These considerations embrace individual aspects such as emotions, relationships and the psychological well-being of the litigants, social aspects such as the welfare of the community and institutional considerations such as efficiency.

The judicial settlement role has developed and found expression in the court system. The fulfillment of this role can be carried out through the use of different

---

[36]For the importance of gathering and processing information and using technology within the framework of the court system, see Katsh and Rabinovich-Einy (2017, 149–169).

models in which different levels of judicial responsiveness are expressed. Settlement adjudication applying the narrow model places a central emphasis on addressing needs and interests connected with considerations of efficiency. Settlement adjudication applying the wide model includes responsiveness to additional considerations, such as maintaining a proper future relationship between the parties, enhancing the parties' satisfaction with the way the conflict is managed in the judicial system, and strengthening social values of listening and consideration for others. The wide model envisages a more comprehensive function for the judge as a settler of disputes. It combines the benefits of managing disputes using a non-adversarial approach with the advantages attributed to the clarification of conflicts by a judge.

Application of the wide model may allay the concerns that have been raised regarding settlement adjudication within the judiciary and accord such adjudication a unique value. Therefore, use of the wide model should be extensive. To this end, it is recommended that emphasis be placed on studying the collaborative approach and providing tools in various training programs for its operation in a qualitative and efficient manner. It is also desirable to examine judicial work through the application of more than merely quantitative standards and determine rules that will influence the choice to use the wide model.

References

Ackerman RM (2006) Vanishing trial, vanishing community? The potential effect of the vanishing trial on America's social capital. J Dispute Resolut 1:165–180

Alberstein M (2009) The jurisprudence of mediation: between formalism, feminism and identity conversations. Cardozo J Conflict Resolut 11:1–28

Alberstein M (2015) Judicial Conflict Resolution (JCR) a new jurisprudence for an emerging judicial practice. Cardozo J Conflict Resolut 16:879–965

Alfini J (1999) Risk of coercion too great, judges should not mediate cases assigned to them for trial. Dispute Resolut Mag 6:11–14

Auerbach JS (1983) Justice without law?. Oxford University Press, New-York and Oxford

Barak A (2002) On mediation. Shaarey Mishpat Law Rev 3:9–11 (In Hebrew)

Berman G, Feinblatt J (2001) Problem solving courts: a brief primer. Law Policy 23:125–140

Brazil WD (1990) A close look at three court-sponsored ADR programs: why they exist, how they operate, what they deliver, and whether they threaten important values. Univ Chicago Legal Forum 1:303–397

Brazil WD (1991) Comparing structures for the delivery of ADR services by courts: critical values and concerns. Ohio State Dispute Resolut 14:715–811

Brody DC (2008) Use of judicial performance evaluation to enhance judicial accountability, judicial independence, and public trust. Denver Univ Law Rev 86:1–42

Burke K, Leben S (2008) Procedural fairness: a key ingredient in public satisfaction. Court Rev 44:4–25

Bush RBA (2013) Mediation skills and client-centered lawyering, a new view of the partnership. Clin Law Rev 19:429–488

Bush RBA, Folger JP (2005) The promise of mediation. Jossey-Bass, San-Francisco

Colney JM, O'Barr WM (1990) Rules versus relationships: the ethnography of legal discourse. The University of Chicago Press, Chicago

Cratsley JC (2006) Judicial ethics and judicial settlement practices: time for two strangers to meet. Ohio State Dispute Resolut 21:569–596
Daicoff S (2006) Law as a healing profession: the “comprehensive law movement”. Pepperdine Dispute Resolut Law J 6:1–61
Daicoff S (2011) The future of the legal profession. Monash Univ Law Rev 37:7–32
Deason EE (2017) Beyond “managerial judges”: appropriate roles in settlement. Ohio State Law J 78(1):73–144
Dubler NN, Liebman CB (2004) Bioethics mediation: a guide to shaping shared solutions. United Hospital Fund of New-York, New-York
Edgar AR (1995) A judge’s view—ADR and the federal courts—The eastern district of Tennessee. Univ Memphis Law Rev 26:995–1005
Elliot D (1986) Managerial judging and the evolution of procedure. Univ Chicago Law Rev 53:306–336
Finkelstein R (2011) The adversarial system and the search for truth. Monash Univ Law Rev 37(1):135–145
Fisher WW, Horwitz MJ, Reed TA (eds) (1993) Philosophy of law American legal realism. Oxford University Press, New-York
Fisher R, Ury W, Patton B (2011) Getting to yes: negotiating agreement without giving in (Revised Edition). Penguin Books, New-York
Fiss O (1984) Against settlement. Yale Law J 93:1073–1090
Frank J (1931) Are judges human? Univ Pennsylvania Law Rev 80:17–53
Friedman S, Wickelgren A (2008) No free lunch: how settlement can reduce the ability to induce efficient behavior. SMU Law Rev 61:1355–1376
Fuller LL (1978) The forms and limits of adjudication. Harvard Law Rev 92:353–409
Galanter M (1974) Why the “haves” come out ahead: speculations on the limits of legal change. Law Soc Rev 9:95–160
Galanter M (2004) The vanishing trial: an examination of trials and related matters in federal and state courts. J Empirical Legal Stud 1:459–570
Gilligan C (1982) In a different voice: psychological theory and women’s development. Harvard University Press, Cambridge
Glick HR (1971) Supreme courts in state politics: an investigation of the judicial role. Basic Books, New-York
Goldberg S (2011) Problem solving in Canada’s courtrooms: a guide to therapeutic justice. http://www.civiljustice.info/cgi/viewcontent.cgi?article=1002&context=tj. Accessed 24 Sept 2017
Goldberg S, Sander F, Nancy R (1992) Dispute resolution: negotiation, mediation and other processes, 2nd edn. Little Brown and Company, Boston
Grillo T (1991) The mediation alternative: process dangers for women. Yale Law J 100:1545–1610
Hazard J (1985) Civil procedure, 3rd edn. Little Brown and Company, Boston
Hora PF (2011) Courting new solutions using problem-solving justice: key components, guiding principles, strategies, responses, models, approaches, blueprints and tool kits. Chapman J Crim Justice 2:7–52
Horwitz FMJ (1975) The rise of legal formalism. Am J Legal Hist 19:251–264
Jones M (2012) Mainstreaming therapeutic jurisprudence into the traditional courts: suggestions for judges and practitioners. Phoenix Law Rev 5(4):753–775
Katsh E, Rabinovich-Einy O (2017) Digital justice, technology and the internet of disputes. Oxford University Press, New-York
King MS (2008) Problem-Solving Court Judging, Therapeutic jurisprudence and transformational leadership. J Judicial Adm 17:155–177
King MS (2009) Solution-focused judging bench book. https://aija.org.au/wp-content/uploads/2017/07/Solution-Focused-Judging-Bench-Book.pdf. Accessed 24 Sept 2017
King MS (2011) Realising the potential of judging. Monash Univ Law Rev 37(1):171–186
King M, Freiberg A, Batagol B, Hyamas R (2014) Non adversarial justice. Federation Press, Sydney

Kloppenberg LA (2013) Training the heads, hands and hearts of tomorrow's lawyers: a problem-solving approach. J Dispute Resolut 103:103–142
Kovach KK (2004) Mediation: principles and practice, 3rd edn. Thomson West, Saint-Paul
Kovach KK (2005) The vanishing trial: land mind on the mediation landscape or opportunity for evolution: ruminations on the future of mediation practice. Cardozo J Conflict Resolut 7:27–75
Kritzer HM (1982) The judge's role in pretrial case processing: assessing the need for change. Judicature 66:28–38
Kronman AT (1995) The lost lawyer. Harvard University Press, Cambridge
Kuhn TS (1962) The structure of scientific revolutions. University of Chicago Press, Chicago
Lande J, Sternlight JR (2010) The potential contribution of adr to an integrated curriculum: preparing law students for real law lawyering. Ohio State J Dispute Resolut 25:247–298
Langbein J (2012) The disappearance of civil trial in the United States. Yale Law J 122: 522–572
Lehman W (1984) Rules in law. George Washington Law J 72:1571–1603
Levin LA, Wheeler RR (eds) (1976) The pound conference: perspectives on justice in the future. West. Pub. Co., Saint-Paul
Macfarlane J (2008) The new lawyer: how settlement is transforming the practice of law. UBC Press, Vancouver
Mautner M (2011) The decline of formalism and the rise of values. In: Law and the culture of Israel. Oxford University Press, Oxford
Menkel-Meadow C (1995) Whose dispute is it anyway?: a philosophical and democratic defense of settlement (in some cases). George Washington Law J 83:2663–2696
Menkel-Meadow C (1996) The trouble with the adversary system in a postmodern, multicultural world. William Mary Law Rev 38:5–44
Menkel-Meadow C (1999) The lawyer as problem-solver and third party neutral: creativity and non-partisanship in lawyering. Temple Law Rev 72:785–809
Menkel-Meadow C (2000) When winning isn't everything: the lawyer as problem solver. Hofstra Law Rev 28:905–924
Menkel-Meadow C, Love LP, Schneider AK, Sternlight JR (2004) Dispute resolution beyond the adversarial model. Aspen Publishers, New-York
O'Brien MT (2011) Facing down the gladiators: addressing law school's hidden adversarial curriculum. Monash Univ Law Rev 37:43–56
Ombudsman of the Israeli Judiciary (2004) Opinion No. 8/04 Settling disputes through compromise or a verdict by way of compromise. http://www.justice.gov.il/Units/NezivutShoftim/MainDocs/804.pdf. Accessed 24 Sept 2017 (In Hebrew)
Parness JA (2006) Improving judicial settlement conferences. Univ Calif Davis Law Rev 39:1891–1909
Perlin M (2000) A law of healing. Univ Cincinnati Law Rev 68:407–433
Perlman K (2008) It takes two for TJ: correlation between bench and bar attitudes toward therapeutic jurisprudence—an Israeli perspective. Thomas Jefferson Law Rev 30(2):351–365
Perlman K (2009) The new judge? Challenges and transformations of the judicial role in the beginning of the 21st century in view of the ADR (Alternative Dispute Resolution) and the TJ (Therapeutic Jurisprudence) Movements. Ph.D Thesis (In Hebrew)
Perlman K (2010) The role of the therapeutic judge and its reference to ideas derived from the legal realism school. Mhekari Mishpat 26(2):415–461 (In Hebrew)
Perlman K (2015a) A settlement judge? On judicial dispute resolution and a proposal for Israeli law. Mishpat Veasakim 19:365–414 (In Hebrew)
Perlman K (2015b) Dispute resolution: applying non-adversarial and therapeutic justice. Bursi publications, Tel-Aviv (In Hebrew)
Perlman K (2017) The promise of therapeutic judging in cases involving a high level of sensitivity. Lecture presented at IALMH Conference, Prague, 11 July 2017
Plapinger E, Shaw M (1997) Court ADR: element of program design. Center for Public Resources, New York
Resnik J (1982) Managerial judges. Harvard Law Rev 96:376–448

Resnik J (2000) Trial as error, jurisdiction as injury: transforming the meaning of Article III. Harvard Law Rev 113:924–1037
Resnik J (2002) Mediating preferences: litigant preferences for process and judicial preferences for settlement. J Dispute Resolut 1:154–169
Resnik J (2003) For Owen M. Fiss: some reflections on the triumph and the death of adjudication. Univ Miami Law Rev 58:173–200
Resnik J (2006) Uncovering, disclosing, and discovering how the public dimensions of court-based processes are at risk. Chicago-Kent Law Rev 81:521–570
Riskin LL (1996) Understanding mediators' orientations, strategies, and techniques: a grid for the perplexed. Harvard Negot Law Rev 1:7–51
Robinson P (2006) Adding judicial mediation to the debate about judges attempting to settle cases assigned to them for trial. J Dispute Resolut 2:335–385
Robinson P (2009) Settlement conference judge—Legal lion or problem solving lamb: an empirical documentation of judicial settlement conference practices and techniques. Am J Trial Advocacy 33:113–165
Robinson P (2012a) An empirical study of settlement conference nuts and bolts: settlement judges facilitating communication, compromise, and fear. Harvard Negot Law Rev 17:97–149
Robinson P (2012b) Opening Pandora's Box: an empirical exploration of judicial settlement ethics and techniques. Ohio State J Dispute Resolut 27:53–108
Sander Frank EA, Goldberg SB (1994) Fitting the forum to the fuss: a user-friendly guide to selecting an ADR procedure. Negot J 10:49–68
Schuck PH (1986) The role of the judge in settling complex cases: the agent orange example. Univ Chicago Law Rev 53:337–365
Scott M (2008) Collaborative law: dispute resolution competencies for the new advocacy. Queensland Univ Law Justice J 8(1):213–237
Segev D (2013) The TJ mainstreaming project: an evaluation of the Israeli Youth Act. Arizona Summit Law Rev 7(3):527–538
Shapiro MM (1986) Courts: a comparative and political analysis. University of Chicago Press, Chicago
Sinai Y, Alberstein M (2016) Expanding judicial discretion: between legal and conflict considerations. Harvard Negot Law Rev 21:221–278
Smith SD (1991) Reductionism in legal thought. Columbia Law Rev 91:68–109
Sourdin T (2002) ADR in Australia. Lawbook Company, Sydney
Sourdin T (2011) Five reasons why judges should conduct settlement conferences. Monash Univ Law Rev 37(1):145–170
Sourdin T, Zariski A (2013) The multi-tasking judge, comparative judicial dispute resolution. Thompson Reuters, Pyrmont
Spencer P (2017) Trauma informed court craft for judges. Lecture presented at IALMH Conference, Prague, 11 July 2017
Steir S (1992) Essay review: reframing legal skills: relational lawyering. J Legal Educ 42:303–323
Stobbs N (2013) Mainstreaming therapeutic jurisprudence and the adversarial paradigm—Incommensurability and the possibility of a shared disciplinary matrix. https://papers.ssrn.com/sol3/papers.cfm?abstract_id=2347810. Accessed 24 Sept 2017
Sulitzeanu-Kenan R, Reichman A, Vigoda-Gadot E (2008) The burden on the judicial system—-comparative caseload analysis of 17 states. http://elyon1.court.gov.il/heb/haba/Courts_burden_Final_report_5.07.pdf. Accessed 24 Sept 2017 (In Hebrew)
Tidmarch J (1992) Unattainable justice: the form of complex litigation and the limits of judicial power. George Washington Law Rev 60:1683–1817
Tyler TR (1983) What is procedural justice?: criteria used by citizens to assess the fairness of legal procedures. Law Soc Rev 22:103–136
Tyler TR (2006) Why people obey the law?. Yale University Press, New-Haven
Warren KR (2000) Public trust and procedural justice. Court Review 37:12–16

Weinshall-Margel K, Galon I, Ifat Taraboulos I (2015) Creating a case weight index for measuring judicial workload. Mishpatim 44:769–834 (In Hebrew)
Welsh NA (2014) The place of court-connected mediation in a democratic system. Cardozo J Conflict Resolut 5:117–145
Wexler DB (1999) Therapeutic jurisprudence and the culture of critique. J Contemp Legal Issues 10:263–277
Wexler DB (2001) Robes and rehabilitation: how judges can help offenders "make good". Court Rev 38:18–26
Wexler DB (2014) New wine in new bottles: the need to sketch a therapeutic jurisprudence 'code' of proposed criminal processes and practices. Arizona Summit Law Rev 7:463–479
Wexler DB, Winick BJ (1991) Essays in therapeutic jurisprudence. Carolina Academic Press, North Carolina
Wexler DB, Winick BJ (1996) Law in a therapeutic key: developments in therapeutic jurisprudence. Carolina Academic Press, North Carolina
Winick BJ, Wexler DB (eds) (2003) Judging in a therapeutic key: therapeutic jurisprudence and the courts. Carolina Academic Press, North Carolina
Wissler RL (2011) Court-connected settlement procedures: mediation and judicial settlement conferences. Ohio State J Dispute Resolut 26:271–325
Young WG (2006) Vanishing trials, vanishing juries, vanishing constitution. Suffolk Univ Law Rev 40:67–94

Karni Perlman is a researcher and lecturer in the field of law and conflict resolution. She is the founder and head of the Non-Adversarial and Therapeutic Justice Center at the Sriks School of Law, College of Management Academic Studies. She is also an adjunct lecturer at the Evens Program in Mediation and Conflict Resolution, Tel-Aviv University. Dr. Perlman is the author of various academic articles and a book entitled "Conflict Resolution—Applying Non-Adversarial and Therapeutic Justice".

Do Judges Need to Be Human? The Implications of Technology for Responsive Judging

Tania Sourdin and Richard Cornes

Abstract Judicial responsiveness requires judges to act from the perspective of conscious legal rationality and also with intuition, empathy and compassion. To what extent will the judicial role change in terms of responsiveness as many aspects of human activity, including aspects of the work of lawyers and judges, are not only augmented, but even taken over entirely by replacement technologies? Such technologies are already reshaping the way the legal profession operates, with implications for judges by virtue of how cases are prepared and presented. In relation to courts, the judicial role is also being augmented, and modified, by technological advances, including the growth of online adjudication. There has even been speculation that the role of the judge not only could be taken online, but as computing techniques become more sophisticated, be fully automated. The role of the human judge though is not merely that of a data processor. To reduce judging to such a definition would be to reject not only the humanity of the judge, but also that of all those who come before them. A better understanding of the essential humanity of the judge will help ensure that technology plays a principled and appropriate role in advancing a responsive justice system. Insights from psychoanalytical thought will aid in that understanding, and in developing the code that drives future applications of artificial intelligence in judicial processes.

This Chapter also draws upon material in T. Sourdin (2018) forthcoming.

T. Sourdin (✉)
University of Newcastle, Newcastle, Australia
e-mail: tania.sourdin@newcastle.edu.au

R. Cornes
University of Essex, Colchester, UK
e-mail: r.cornes@essex.ac.uk

© Springer Nature Singapore Pte Ltd. 2018

T. Sourdin and A. Zariski (eds.), *The Responsive Judge*, Ius Gentium: Comparative Perspectives on Law and Justice 67, https://doi.org/10.1007/978-981-13-1023-2_4

1 Introduction

The role of a judge is multifaceted. It can incorporate activism, complex interactions with people, dispute settlement, case management, public and specific education activities, social commentary as well the core adjudicatory functions which might be conducted with other judges, or less commonly in some jurisdictions with lay people (juries).[1] These varying functions are relevant when considering how technology will impact on the role of judges within our society. Alongside technological developments, modern trends in judicial approaches are leading some judges to be more "responsive" and to embrace the realization that judging requires not only knowledge of the law and the surface facts of a case, but also the empathic ability to understand the emotions underlying the matters which come before their court; "emotion not alone but in combination with the law, logic, and reason—helps the judges get it right" (Chin 2012, 1581; see also Sinai and Alberstein 2016, esp. 225; Colby 2012, esp. 1946). The reasons for this are discussed in chapter one of this book.

Also noted in Sourdin and Zariski's introduction: innovations in responsive judging raise the debate between formalist and realist approaches to the law.[2] Judicial awareness of underlying emotions per se should not be of concern to either side of the realism/formalism debate. The rule of law, while demanding that cases be decided according to the law, has never required judges to be blind to the non-rational motives which may drive litigants coming before them. Indeed, the ability to comprehend, and where appropriate, respond to such motives, will assist the judge in application of the law and just resolution of disputes.

In this context, increased judicial responsiveness will require a better understanding of emotional intelligence, as judges engage court participants with varying levels of emotion and compassion, consider therapeutic justice interventions, or pursue procedural justice approaches. The work of Thibaut and Walker suggests that if people consider that they have been treated fairly they are more likely to accept a decision and outcome (Thibaut 1978; Thibaut and Walker 1975; Lind and Tyler 1988; Van den Bos et al. 2014). Their work also suggests that dignity, voice and participation factors, that are linked to a range of judicial interventions, can have a significant impact on all court participants. The extent to which judges engage with this research, and their respective judicial styles, varies across jurisdictions and between judges. These variations and innovations in judicial approach present one of a number of challenges to

[1] For a helpful discussion of this issue see Sourdin and Zariski (2013).

[2] See 'Responsiveness and the jurisprudence of judging' in Chapter "What is Responsive Judging?" of this book. For an overview see also Leiter (2010). Our concern in this chapter is primarily with the challenge of coding legal rules and reasoning, and how that touches on the formalism/realism debate. A further chapter would be required to engage in detail with the question of fact finding by Judge AI. On the essential relationship between facts and law Frank (1949, 14) noted that, "a legal rule… is a conditional statement referring to facts". Facts may be even more uncertain than legal rules (see also Frank 1930, viii–xiii), and are arguably even less amenable to Judge AI. Our argument in this chapter about the limits of Judge AI in relation to coding legal reasoning must apply with even greater force regarding facts. From a computer science perspective see also MacCrimmon and Tillers (2002).

determining how technological developments will, and should, reshape the judicial role, emphasising as they do the degree to which the judicial role will in significant part be modeled according to the distinct socio-legal norms of different jurisdictions.

As with many other fields of contemporary life, one of the most significant challenges to how judges deal with and determine disputes is linked to current and future developments in Artificial Intelligence or "AI". AI is an umbrella term which encompasses many branches of science and technology and will often involve the creation of complex algorithms to enable decisions to be made, and outcomes determined. As such, much AI is focused on evaluating and decision-making of the type which is often perceived to be the primary activity undertaken by judges.

AI can include machine learning, natural language processing, expert systems, vision, speech, planning, cognitive computing and robotics (Mills 2016). Schatsky et al. (2014, 3; emphasis in original) offer a practical definition of AI, stating that it "is the theory and development of computer systems *able to perform tasks that normally require human intelligence*." AI is an evolving concept. It can also include "affective processing" a field that is linked to understanding emotion and extends to the creation of human like avatars (Picard 1997). However, at its simplest, AI and other technological advances mean that computer programs and systems will become more capable of performing tasks and functions that previously have been undertaken by humans. Of AI in law, Ashley (2017, 3) notes that it is a "research field… about to experience a revolution."

What we will call "Judge AI" are developments in the various branches of AI specifically concerned with contributing to judicial tasks. As currently discussed in the literature, Judge AI covers a range of possibilities from the increasing use of technology in legal and judicial processes prior to trial, through to playing some role in court and decision-making processes. Even before a case comes before a judge, AI may already be having an impact on the judicial task by virtue of AI's impact on the legal profession and how cases are prepared and presented to the court (Lopez 2016).[3] Impacts here may even include influencing which cases get before a judge, as predictive coding developments enable predictions to be made as to the outcome of litigation (Schubarth 2016). Finally, once cases *are* before courts, Judge AI is now playing some role in aspects of judicial decision-making, though not without controversy. In Mexico, the Expertius system is advising judges and clerks "upon the determination of whether the plaintiff is or is not eligible for granting him/her a pension" (Carniero et al. 2014, 227). In the United States, predictive coding has been used to help determine whether recidivism is more likely in criminal matters and to assist in making decisions about sentencing (Liptak 2017). A due process challenge by a Wisconsin inmate to the use of one such program was rejected by the state's Supreme Court, even though the inmate was unable to examine the detail of the

[3]See also, for example, Tamburro (2012) for an analysis of computer-assisted document coding and review, often referred to as "predictive coding" with implications for the discovery process. The analysis of large sets of data is likely to have a "game-changing" impact. The technology collapses the time (and costs) needed to review millions of pages of discovered material, to identify relevant aspects without devoting massively costly person hours.

software being used against him (it being protected proprietary information).[4] This would appear to be a breach of Principle 8 of the Asimov AI Principles (endorsed by the likes of Stephen Hawking and Elon Musk, among many more), that "any involvement by an autonomous system in judicial decision-making should provide a satisfactory explanation auditable by a competent human authority" (see Future of Life Institute, n.d.-b). The need for such scrutiny became clear in relation to *Loomis*, when the investigative journalism organization ProPublica carried out an analysis of "Compas" (the program in question) and found that it was prone to overestimate likelihood of recidivism by black defendants, and underestimate that of white (see Angwin et al. 2016).

In New Zealand, Alistair Knott of the University of Otago's AI and Law project has raised concerns about the use of a computer-based prediction model to handle claims and profile claimants under the country's state accident compensation scheme (the Accident Compensation Corporation, "ACC") (see University of Otago, n.d.). While the ACC is a state corporation and may appear to be akin to say a welfare department, it should be recalled that the introduction of no fault compensation under the scheme commencing in 1974 was premised on the bargain that the right to sue in court for the tort of personal injury was abolished. With that in mind ACC claim handlers are carrying out what was previously a judicial task. The program now raising questions, rather sinisterly named the "Survival Analysis Model", is defended by the ACC as leading to cost efficiencies (an aspect of concern here is also the general advance of managerialism into "the justice sector" raising separation of power concerns).[5] On one view the Survival Analysis Model reduces human claimants to a matter of data processing, analysis and dry statistical prediction. Questions are now being raised as to its fairness, humanity, and accountability (see Nine to Noon 2017; Chiang 2017).

While we acknowledge that many of the developments in Judge AI thus far have merit, and while we will make the argument for the expansion of Judge AI alongside human judges, our purpose in this chapter is also to sound a note of caution as to how far AI *should* go in relation to the judicial function. In what follows we discuss—in Part 1—the range of beneficial contributions AI can make to judicial processes, from supportive developments, appropriate replacement technologies, through to constructively disruptive reforms. In Part 2 we make the case for principled limits to the use of AI in relation to the work of judges, concluding that the role of the judge, and certainly the developing role of the responsive judge, requires at its heart, a human mind. The existential core of that argument is based on insights into the judicial mind drawn from psychoanalytical concepts.

---

[4] State v Loomis (2016). See critique in State v Loomis (2017) and Brooks (2017). The US Supreme Court declined to take the issue up: see Loomis v Wisconsin (2017).

[5] We do not have space here to pursue this in detail. The essence of the critique is that executives (governments), for possibly quite innocent concerns of managerial efficiency can tend to view the work of the courts as merely part of the overall justice sector, including the police and prisons, and not as the operating of a distinct branch of the state. See discussion in Elias (2017).

2 Part 1—How AI Can Beneficially Contribute to the Work of Courts and Judges

2.1 *Technology and Dispute Resolution*

As Sourdin (2015a) has noted, there are three main ways in which technology is already reshaping the justice system. First, and at the most basic level, technology is assisting to inform, support and advise people involved in the justice system (supportive technology). Many people now locate and obtain legal support and services online and the growth of online legal firms who may provide "unbundled" legal services has been significant over the past three years (see, e.g., Lawyal Solicitors 2016).

Second, technology can replace functions and activities that were previously carried out by humans (replacement technologies). Some web-based information (including digital video), video-conferencing (including internet-based group video calls), teleconferencing and email can supplement, support and replace many face-to-face in court interactions. At this second level, justice is supported by technology and in some circumstances, this can alter the environment in which court hearings takes place (see, e.g., Soars 2016). In this regard, there has been a growing focus on online courts and what they may provide (see Ministry of Justice 2016). These pressures are partly a response to growing evidence of unmet legal needs including that for legal assistance, concerns about access to justice more generally, and the growth in large scale online dispute resolution systems which are already being used to support some court and tribunal systems (see, e.g., Tyler Technologies 2017; Civil Resolution Tribunal 2018). The creation of an online court involves replacing a physical court and litigation process with an online alternative that encourages the resolution of a dispute but retains the stature and powers of a physical court of law (Harvey 2016).

Chief Justice Warren of the Supreme Court of Victoria has suggested another model where technology is supportive: the distributed courtroom (Warren 2015). A physical courtroom remains central in this model, but the participants are replaced by life-size screens or holographic projections to enable judges, lawyers, jury members and parties to *appear* in court from any location of convenience. This model is facilitated through online videoconferencing technology, such as Skype, but still preserves the option of a physical space for the court, and the option of physically attending court. Essentially such technologies enable judges to be more responsive by enabling remote participation in court proceedings and by meeting communication preferences of court users.

Finally, at a third level, technology can change the way that judges work and provide for very different forms of justice (disruptive technology), particularly where processes change significantly (Sourdin 2015a). Technologies may enable people to access more sophisticated online "advice" that is supported by AI or to consider options and alternatives or engage in different ways. In contrast to the traditional rational decision-making approaches, some of these more sophisticated technological programs are designed to encourage the development and refinement of a number of options (rather than producing one outcome) (see, e.g., Smartsettle One+ 2017).[6] These areas of technological innovation have the capacity to be more disruptive than previous innovations that supported a "graft and grow" approach and assumed that adjudicative processes would not change in the context of their basic procedural stages (Sourdin 2015a, 97).

Legal information and AI systems can already use sophisticated "branching" and data searching technology to create elaborate decision trees that can suggest outcomes to disputes. This is done by a system which emulates human intelligence (neural networks) (see, e.g., Chaphalkar et al. 2015). Essentially, what takes place is that the system asks the user a number of questions or uses existing data about the user and poses questions about the dispute to enable an accurate description of the dispute to be built. The computer then arrives at a conclusion by applying the law to the dispute description. It does this by applying rules for specific sets of facts. Finally, the computer can perform tasks based on the description given. New developments in AI enable machines to learn from existing data and in effect create their own decision trees. These processes could provide indicative decisions, or, as we will argue below, be used as a quality control mechanism to look for, inter alia, signs of unconscious bias. Such systems can be continuously updated and are reflexive in that machine learning enables systems to improve and be constantly revised with new data sets.

Similarly, developments in Online Dispute Resolution (ODR), a form of alternative dispute resolution (ADR) where parties use the internet and technology to help resolve their dispute cheaply and efficiently, also support and enable the development of AI by creating the structure and context within which it can flourish. In ODR, disputants are not required to meet in person, as the ODR process can happen remotely through an internet connection. AI decision-making is already being used within the field of ODR. These systems are labelled expert systems, which are programmed by experts in the field and integrate rule-based algorithms to assist the program to make decisions based on information received from the parties (Legg 2016). Legg explains that these processes "collect facts from users through interview-style questions and produce answers based on a decision-tree analysis" (2016, 228). More sophisticated technologies can now do more than this and Susskind and Susskind (2015, 45) have noted "massive data-storage capacity and brute-force processing" do not require a replication of a human expert system and a fundamentally different way of thinking.

In the Netherlands, an advanced ADR program called Rechtwijzer had ODR components that were used to assist couples in the separation or divorce process. Rechtwijzer asked questions about the parties and their relationship and provided options based on this input information (Bickel et al. 2015). The program also provided "information, tools, links to other websites and personal advice" which encouraged the parties to resolve their dispute between themselves (2015, 4). If resolution was not reached, the final step involved Rechtwijzer providing the parties

[6]It has been said that collaborative platforms, such as GroupMindExpress.com, are likely to be used more frequently in large multi-party disputes where information and participants are plentiful (Gaitenby 2004).

with information and contact details of professional third parties, such as mediators, legal representatives, and other dispute resolution processes. Whilst Rechwijzer will largely be replaced by a new system and online arrangements, its creators have noted that the primary obstacle in terms of the success of such ODR arrangements relate to the incapacity of courts, lawyers and government to fully embrace these types of innovations (see, e.g., Barendrecht 2017).

If these techniques can be used effectively within the field of ADR, then it follows that the introduction of AI programs into the court system is also feasible. Designers and implementers may draw on the experiences of these ADR programs to help inform any AI judge programs, or alternatively AIs more specifically designed to assist judicial officers. Although Rechtwijzer has been the subject of some recent criticism particularly in respect of security and safeguards, the primary concern appears to relate to the lack of societal infrastructure to support a more online court-based model (see, e.g., Barendrecht 2017). The experience of AI in ODR and ADR does however, suggest that there is room to blend more disruptive technologies and platforms with court processes that can support judicial work.

2.2 *Technology Supporting Human Judges and Court Processes*

If technologies can support non-judicial decision-making (by for example, enabling more accurate potential outcome identification by participants) they may play an increasing role in some forms of judicial dispute resolution.[7] In Australia, non-rule-based branching technology has been used in a project of the Intelligent Computing Systems Research conducted by La Trobe University and Victoria University (called "Split-Up"). The project, led by Professor John Zeleznikow, determined that there are 94 factors relevant for a distributive decision, and was directed at applying AI to assist in calculating the division of property in family law proceedings (see Victoria University, n.d.). Split-Up, a hybrid rule-based neutral network system that grew out of this research, offers advice on how property is likely to be distributed if the matter were to be determined by a court. It has been trialed by some judges, judicial registrars and registrars of the Family Court of Australia as well as legal practitioners, mediators and counsellors. A more advanced approach, which is oriented at supporting negotiation, is called FamilyWinner (Zeleznikow and Bellucci, n.d.; Zeleznikow et al. 2007).

Further examples of technology now aiding courts and tribunals can be found in British Columbia, Northern Ireland, and possibly soon, England & Wales. In British Columbia, Canada, the Civil Dispute Tribunal uses an online platform to guide disputants (Civil Resolution Tribunal 2018). Online-supported negotiation and informal dispute resolution are features of the system, together with adjudication,

[7]For an example of one mechanism supporting disputants, see MyLawBC (n.d.), available at: http://mylawbc.com/info/about.php.

with most cases decided "... on evidence and arguments submitted through the tribunal's online tools. However, when necessary, the adjudicator will have discretion to conduct a telephone or video hearing" (see Benyekhlef and Vermeys 2017). In Northern Ireland, the Northern Ireland Courts and Tribunal Service now offers an online process in respect of small claims, although final adjudication remains a face-to-face option (Northern Ireland Courts and Tribunals Service 2011). In England and Wales plans to introduce Judge AI in relation to some categories of dispute were dropped in 2017 (less controversial, but significant, aspects associated with the introduction of online dispute resolution are proceeding) (Hyde 2017; for current developments see Johnstone 2016).[8]

2.3 All Rise for Judge "Co-bot"?

The issues associated with the total replacement of human judges, which we turn to below in Part 2, lead us to argue that the focus should continue to be on using technological advances to support human judges in their judicial work. Judge AI systems, we argue, should complement current human work, allowing for greater efficiencies (Surden 2014). This approach suggests that assistant "co-bots" rather than replacement robot judges could play a more important role in the future.

Already there is precedent for programs to predict likely outcomes based on previous cases. In relation to the European Court of Human Rights (ECtHR), Aletras et al. (2016) have developed a program that textually analysed that Court's decisions relating to breaches of human rights to discover patterns in judgments. The program learnt these patterns and was able to predict the outcome of cases presented to it in textual form with 79% accuracy on average (Aletras et al. 2016). This is an example of machine learning, where the computer system was able to "analyze past data to develop rules that are generalizable going forward" (Surden 2014, 105). Machine learning allows computer programs to learn complex tasks through experience, rather than through hand-crafted computer functions (see Silver et al. 2016, 489; Surden 2014, 89).

We noted above though that the distinct norms of different jurisdictions present a challenge to Judge AI development. Of note here in relation to Aletras' and colleagues work is the fact that the form of ECtHR judgments (following the decision template outlined) are heavily influenced by the distinct legal reasoning style of the civil law jurisdictions covered by the Court. The ECtHR's relatively standard form of judgment contrasts with the rather more open textured and at times idiosyncratic styles of judgments often found in common law courts. It may well be that one disruptive effect of use of such software in common law jurisdictions could be a change in judgment writing styles, as judges adapt to better work with such technology.

AI programs that can not only predict outcomes, but also produce a suggested reasoned decision based on the information input, could be used to assist human

[8] The reforms fell because of the snap election called in 2017.

judges in judgment preparation. These systems could produce a draft judgment based on the system's determined outcome (Sourdin 2015a, 102). A human judge could then use this draft (much as many judges, especially in appeal courts, make use of drafts from legal assistants) to produce their own reasons for judgment. This use of AI would allow for human oversight over the computer program and enable discretionary or social considerations to be taken into account by the human judge that may be beyond the capacity, or authority, of the computer program. Such developments are not without significant risk and the capacity for AI decisions to be appealed or reviewed by human decision-makers is often cited as a necessary component of any automated decision-making system (Perry 2017). Evaluations of Rechtwijzer, the ADR program outlined above, similarly found that although participants were satisfied with their experiences (Bickel et al. 2015), a majority still felt the need to have a third party check over the agreement made through the system (Bickel et al. 2015).

2.4 *Judge Co-bot: Human Unconscious Bias and Quality Control?*

While the value of increased judicial diversity is now widely accepted, and with that, the reality that different judges will legitimately reach different decisions applying the same law to the same facts, unconscious biases affecting a human judge's decision (for example, racism or sexism) are clearly a concern. In a decision concerning the alleged bias of a judicial officer the psychoanalytically informed Judge Jerome Frank said:

> Every judge, … unavoidably has many "idiosyncratic "leanings of the mind," uniquely personal prejudices, which may interfere with his fairness at trial. He may be stimulated by unconscious sympathies for, or antipathies to, some of the witnesses, lawyers or parties in a case before him (In Re JP Linaham 1943, 652).

As those in the access to justice movement have noted, the outcome of court adjudication can clearly be influenced by many factors, including the quality of representation, the resources available to the litigant and the quality of the decision-making and surrounding rights-based framework.[9] In addition, adjudicative decision-making can be influenced by a range of factors that can influence substantive justice (Sourdin 2012). As Sourdin (2016) has noted, these include a range of impacts on the decision-maker that include:

- when and what a person has eaten (Tierney 2011)[10];
- the time of day (see Tierney 2011);

[9] For further discussion, see Sourdin (2015b).

[10] Tierney (2011) refers to a study of parole board decision-making reported in Danziger et al. (2011).

- how many other decisions a person has made that day (decision fatigue) (Tierney 2011);
- personal values (Chisholm 2009; see also Quintanilla 2012);
- unconscious assumptions (Mason 2001, 680);
- reliance on intuition (Kirby 1999b, 4);
- the attractiveness of the individuals involved (Agthe et al. 2011)[11];
- emotion (Bennett and Broe 2007, 84–86).

Judge Frank thought that "the conscientious judge will, as far as possible, make himself aware of his biases of this character, and, by that very self-knowledge, nullify their effect" (In Re JP Linaham 1943, 652). The extent to which these unconscious factors influence judges is unknown, but it is likely that even if Judges become aware of these factors, they are likely to underestimate their impact (Wilson and Gilbert 2008). This is partly because we are more likely to exaggerate information about our own personal qualities that we perceive as positive and less likely to accept information that raises any doubts about our positive characteristics.[12]

Sourdin (2012) has suggested previously that AI could play a role in addressing unconscious judicial bias. A premise of our note of caution about Judge AI in Part 2 below is that it does not allow for the *beneficial* contributions from the human judge's unconscious. It might therefore be argued that a Judge AI—"Judge Co-Bot"—lacking an unconscious, would not be subject to the adverse impacts of negative unconscious bias. One potential benefit from Judge AI could therefore be the use of algorithms to review either individual judicial decisions, or larger sample groups, to exercise a quality control function by identifying evidence of inappropriate biases in decision making (see discussion in Ashley 2017, Chap. 12). The simple application of statistical analysis can do this to some extent presently. Could judicial co-bots using more sophisticated algorithms do so more thoroughly, or in real time, working alongside human judges?

Care will be needed in taking the steps described above. As we have already noted in cases such as *State v Loomis*, some forms of AI currently in use have already demonstrated that there can be significant risks in using AI because programmers and others may embed their own unconscious biases in computer programs without intending to do so. That problem goes beyond the law, with algorithms in other contexts producing unwanted results including promoting racism and inaccurate outcomes (see Levin 2016).[13] In addition, using Judge AI has the potential to reduce the capacity of the justice process to deal with people within courts with dignity and to respond in a human way (which may incorporate emotion and compassion). On this last weakness of Judge AI, developments in affective computing suggest that it may be feasible in the future to develop coded applications able to recognise and respond appropriately to human emotion.[14] While we expect such progress to

---

[11]The researchers in this area suggest that there may be a bias away from attractive same sex individuals and a bias towards attractive other sex individuals.

[12]For an interesting discussion of this phenomenon, see Brooks (2011, 220).

[13]See also Smith (2016) regarding the use of algorithms in relation to recidivism.

[14]For an interesting overview on affective technology, see Wikipedia (2017), quoting Picard (1997).

continue, there will remain limits, some of them of a nature that, we suggest, will place an ultimate limit on the application of AI in judicial systems.

3 Part 2—Limits to Judge AI

3.1 More Than Presiding in Court—the True Extent of the Role of the Modern Judge

A threshold challenge to future developments in Judge AI is linked to inadequate understandings of the nature and extent of the judicial role. The role is often interpreted as being synonymous *only* with judicial decision-making or adjudication at first instance between contesting individuals, and little, if anything, more. Whilst the question of Judge AI is certainly fraught with complex issues when considering decision-making alone, there are other aspects of the judicial role where judicial functions cannot be readily displaced by AI. Most civil and criminal disputes settle before getting to a full hearing. Judges play an important role in both managing and settling cases long before an actual trial. Their curiosity, emotional understanding of parties and their lawyers, their agile questioning and exploration of issues can be decisive in enabling litigants to consensually determine their own outcomes, rather than submitting to a formal judicial decision.

The evolving nature of the judicial role, and a strong rationale for caution in terms of the development of Judge AI, also arises because of the therapeutic influence that judges may have on disputes, through interventions in both criminal and civil contexts that are directed at changing parties' future behaviors as well as determining outcomes in respect of past activities (as discussed more generally in this book). Such interactions require judges to be empathic and understanding and to communicate with a range of people in different and supportive ways to support individual transformation and acceptance.

In addition, apart from their critical adjudicative role, judges also play an educative role, informing litigants and lawyers about approaches to be taken and contributing to civic education at a broader level. While judges must be cautious as to how they express themselves (lest, if expressing themselves too forcefully they open themselves to apparent bias challenges) it is now accepted that they play an important role in public debates.[15] Proponents of the view that judges could be replaced by AI fail to acknowledge the full range of what judges contribute to society beyond adjudication, including important and often unexamined issues relating to compliance and acceptance of the rule of law.

[15]For a successful apparent bias challenge on the basis that a judge so clearly disliked aspects of criminal defendants' rights protected in the European Convention on Human Rights, that a fair trial was not possible before an appellate court containing that judge, see: Hoekstra v. H.M. Advocate (No.2) (2000) S.L.T. 605; discussed in MacQueen and Wortley (1998).

3.2 *The Rule of Law, Judicial Authority, and the Human Judge*

A judge exercisses the judicial power of the state. That may entail an authority to deprive a person of their liberty, determine private rights against other persons, or their rights vis a vis the powers of the executive or legislative branches (and behind them, the wider populace). Access to an independent and impartial judge (hitherto always understood to be a person trained in the law according to the usages of their jurisdiction) is a requirement of any liberal democratic state. Judicial functions under the rule of law entail a complex cocktail of legal rationality and legally trained human judgment. An element of litigants' respect for judicial judgment, and the social legitimacy of the judiciary more broadly, must come from, we think, the fact that it is rendered by a fellow human being. As Harvey (2016, 95) notes, "what is at stake [in developing Judge AI] is continued confidence in and adherence to the rule of law."

On this point, Cornes and Henaghan (forthcoming) argue that individual and community recognition of the authority of "the judge" is not only traceable back to very early infancy, but also primitive desires for the group (society) to be led. Any project for an AI judge must contend with that uniquely human provenance. Discussing the early contest between siblings vis a vis parents Freud reasoned, "there grows up in the troop of children a communal or group feeling, which is then further developed at school. *The first demand made by this reaction formation is for justice, for equal treatment for all*" (1921, 120). We may disagree with our parents, but, in (mostly) functional families we accept our parents' inter alia judicial authority over us because of instinctive early bondings and reactions. The respected authority of those early judicial decisions (over disputes say between us and siblings) is translated later into respect for the human judge who we may later in life encounter in court.

Questions therefore arise as to whether a computer program or automated process could possess both the rational *and emotional* authority to make decisions in place of a human judge. In the context of an automated system delivering administrative decisions, Justice Perry (2017, 31) raises questions such as *who* makes the decision, and who possesses the legal authority to make such a decision. Is it the computer programmer, the policy-maker, the human decision-maker, or the computer or automated system itself?

Legislators have attempted to remove some of the complexities of this issue. For example, a decision made under the Therapeutic Goods Act 1989 (Cth) by a computer program is deemed to have been made by the Secretary.[16] How such a deeming provision would fare in litigation, and whether it would be accepted by litigants remains uncertain.

Justice Kirby, writing in 1999, noted that the need for the public and open nature of adjudication may also present difficulties with the adoption of electronic courts and Judge AI: "[t]he right to see a judicial decision maker struggling conscientiously,

[16]Therapeutic Goods Act 1989 (Cth) s 7C(2).

in public, with the detail of a case is a feature of the court system which cannot be abandoned, at least without risk to the acceptance by the people of courts as part of their form of governance" (Kirby 1999a, 188). Without a public, open forum for the administration of the state's judicial powers, would the exercise of these powers be accepted by the populace? Chief Justice Warren of the Supreme Court of Victoria in Australia (2015) suggests that they would be, at least insofar as justice is linked to public access: few people attend court hearings in person, and information and news is sourced more and more from online media, including social media. It is important to note though that AI is still unable to interact with people with compassion, emotion, or agile or intuitive responsiveness. Also, an AI judge would not be able to meet the need for a party in court to see a decision-maker "grapple conscientiously" with a decision.

3.3 Variation in the Adjudicative Function Within the Judicial Hierarchy

The adjudicative component of the judicial function, in most common law systems, occurs at three levels, each with a distinct function. While first instance judges deal with the raw matter of a dispute, first level appeal court judges work to correct obvious errors at first instance, and to some degree—legal systems vary—to carry out wider legal system supervisory roles. Finally, higher level courts (for the most part second level appellate) have wide ranging responsibilities which necessarily go beyond the concerns of the individuals, organisations and government entities that are directly involved in a court action (as for the most part, upper tier courts hear cases of "general or public importance").[17]

At the initial appellate, and certainly at the secondary appellate level, there is scope for policy making which requires an ability for dealing with polycentric problems and policy questions. At all three levels, decision-making requires consideration of the context of the dispute and the legislation. Simply put, judges at all levels need to be responsive to contextual factors that assist to determine the meaning of legislation and human activities. This is a complex task and where boundaries are overstepped there can be a concern that judges, rather than an elected government, are "making law."

The objections to *human* judges entering this arena may be amplified with AI involvement. If, for example, from a democratic perspective one objects to human judges placing legislative and other material within context and in some circumstances reviewing legislation or executive actions, an AI judge approach must be even more troubling. Furthermore, an AI judge may not be perceived to be independent (it would be the creature of its programmer). Given the limits Surden (2014) notes it is also doubtful it would have the capacity to question beyond the presenting

[17] See discussion in Le Sueur and Cornes (2000, 53–97).

material; that is, to view actions and legislation within a broader and evolving human context.

Also, what would be the relationship between a full AI judge and the human judges in a legal system? The idea that the AI judge would be reviewable by a human judge is unremarkable; though even here questions would arise as to what is reviewed—the decision only? Or also the algorithms which gave rise to the decision? In *State v Loomis* the code was held to be unreviewable, yet as we have seen, the code in question itself was found to be racially biased. In relation to lower tier courts, where Judge AI is currently more likely to gain a foothold for at least filtering purposes, the default availability of a responsive human judge permitted to review all aspects of the AI input, and able to call on a complex array of communication and social skills, remains desirable to support understanding and compliance with the law. The concept of an AI judge authoritatively reviewing a human judge raises even more serious ethical conundrums going to the very heart of the question of what it means to be human.

3.4 The Challenge of Novelty

For the moment, most instances of Judge AI are at the entry level issues of dispute settlement, or with AI playing an assisting role. That is, AI is used to inform or support some initial participant decision-making rather than carrying out the judicial decision-making itself. Judicial decision-making arguably requires more though than algorithmic sophistication, particularly where novel situations exist. As Surden (2014) notes machine learning techniques are only useful where analysed information is similar to new information presented to the AI. Should an AI program be presented with a novel case where no similar precedent exists, it may not be well-suited in making a prediction or coming to an outcome. These issues may arise in Judge AI where the sample size of previous cases is not large enough for the computer program to discover patterns and create effective generalisations (Surden 2014, 105–106). It may also be argued that the exercise by a judge of discretion—the application of principle to novel factual circumstances—to some extent will always require a fresh evaluation of circumstances beyond the capability of machine learning.

AI researchers *have* had a number of clear successes addressing these sorts of issues outside of the legal field. These successes do suggest that predictive analysis, even where there are significant variations in terms of novelty, can be "learned" and that these insights could be extended into Judge AI applications. Google's DeepMind researchers successfully trained an AI program, AlphaGo, to play the complex game of Go at a higher level than the European master of the game by training the neural networks of the program "directly from gameplay purely through general-purpose supervised and reinforcement learning methods" (Silver et al. 2016, 489). There are also many examples in the medical field with AI now increasingly being used for diagnostic purposes and in relation to some human functions (Ramesh et al. 2004; Tirrell 2017; Neill 2013).

Working from the basis of the current state of AI use in courts, Harvey (2016) gives a simplified description of a hypothetical advanced application of Judge AI using the example of algorithms already present in legal databases. These databases employ natural language processing to assist with the sourcing of relevant material based on search terms. The application, Harvey posits, would be able to decide cases. It would be required to go further than existing applications, reducing returned sources to a manageable and relevant sample, and then deploying tools to compare these sources of law to a present case and engaging in analysis to determine the outcome (Harvey 2016, 93).

Harvey (2016, 93) explains that this final step would require "the development of the necessary algorithms that could undertake the comparative and predictive analysis, together with a form of probability analysis to generate an outcome that would be useful and informative." Aside from the question of how the case facts would be determined, as will become clear from our discussion below however, we are concerned that one of the premises Harvey starts from is that the material required to be coded is, "the entire corpus of legal information" (2016, 94). We will argue that while such conscious knowledge is certainly essential to judicial decision-making, so too is the wider influence of the judge's life experience at work in the judge's unconscious and the extent to which that experience enables the judge to be responsive from a human perspective.

3.5 *Translating Law into Code*

Commentators have also raised the issue of how to accurately translate the law into codes, commands and functions that a computer program can understand.[18] Computer programmers and IT professionals rarely have legal qualifications or experience, nor are they policy or administrative experts. However, it is these professionals who are tasked with translating legislation and case law into computer codes and commands to allow an autonomous process to make decisions. These sources of law—whilst complex on their own—also operate within the context of statutory presumptions, and discretionary judgment. Ensuring these intricacies are properly coded into an autonomous process is challenging. Because of these challenges, commentators note that more regulatory areas of the law may be better suited to be transformed into computer code (Bathurst 2015).

Similarly, these codes will need to be constantly updated due to frequent amendments, new case decisions, and complex transitional provisions (Perry 2017). Autonomous systems will also require the capacity to apply the law from various points in time, to ensure that cases are decided on the laws that applied at the relevant time the actions occurred. These challenges can potentially be met by including lawyers and policy-makers in the creation and updating of these computer programs;

[18]See, for example, Perry (2017), which provides a thorough treatment of the issues involved in translating law into computer code.

however, as most legislators will attest, converting human behaviours into legislation is complex and often fraught with uncertainty (Perry 2017). In relation to involving lawyers with such work there may be issues of capacity as despite the now decades of developments in the AI field, only in recent years have some legal academics acknowledged that while lawyers and judges may not need to know how to write computer code, "they will need… an ability to think about legal practice in terms of engineering a cognitive computing process" (Ashley 2017, 36). If AI in the law is to reach its true potential law schools need to be considering now how to prepare their graduates to be conversant in the language of IT professionals.

3.6 Syntax and Semantics

The use of AI in law will be confronted by the philosophical distinction between syntax and semantics. Searle (2002) noted that computer programs possess syntax (a formal structure of operation), but do not possess semantics (meaning behind these operations). Digital technology processes information in the form of abstract symbols, namely ones and zeros. The technology possesses the ability to process and manipulate these symbols, but it does not understand the meaning behind these processes. In other words, the machine does not currently understand the information that it is processing. This can be contrasted with the human mind, which can understand the information that it processes.

Therefore, while computer programs may be able to approximate human ways of thinking, they cannot yet *duplicate* human ways of thinking (Searle 2002). As the information that is required for human decision-making becomes more complex (involving multiple complex data sources),[19] humans, including judicial officers may benefit from some form of AI assistance. Assistance, though, is not replacement. Of all the challenges to advancing Judge AI, this one—capturing in AI form the semantics of judicial thinking—is the most challenging because it raises directly the question not only of the nature of the human judge's psyche, but that of the human psyche generally.

3.7 To Judge Is Human—An Existential Limit to the Development of Judge AI

We may well ask, generally (let alone in relation to Judge AI) whether there are *or should be* any limits to the reach of AI.[20] Harari (2015, 394) writes:

---

[19]It is argued that the information that may be considered by a judge has expanded significantly in recent years. See, for example, Tashea (2016).

[20]Contrast, for example, the views of Musk and Zuckerberg, outlined in Domonoske (2017) and Solon (2017).

> Scholars in the life sciences and social sciences should ask themselves whether we miss anything when we understand life as data processing and decision making. Is there perhaps something in the universe that cannot be reduced to data? Suppose non-conscious algorithms could eventually outperform conscious intelligence in all data-processing tasks – what, if anything, would be lost by replacing conscious intelligence with superior non-conscious algorithms?

Our answer is: humanity. In relation to the life of courts we suggest that there is more complexity in the work of the human judge, and the lives of the litigants before them, than can, or should, be coded for entirely in the most sophisticated of algorithms. Hariri's thesis is that there is a new religion associated with the advance of AI: "Dataism". The premise of Dataism is that the universe "consists of data flows, and the value of any phenomenon or entity is determined by its contribution to data processing. … It collapses the barrier between animals and machines and expects electronic algorithms to eventually decipher and outperform biochemical algorithms" (Harari 2015, 428).[21]

Dataists, he argues, "are skeptical about human knowledge and wisdom, and prefer to put their trust in Big Data and computer algorithms" (Harari 2015, 368). High priests of the new religion, such as Mark Zuckerberg, therefore regard any impediments to the uploading and sharing of information (whether true or not) as heresy.[22] Like Hariri, Lanchester (2017) reaches for another grand analogy: he calls Facebook and Google, "the new colonial powers."[23] Barry Lynn and Matt Stoller of the Open Markets Institute (2017) similarly warn of the monopolistic power of these tech companies as a threat to democracy and the rule of law. Lynn lost his job at the New America Foundation (significantly funded by Google) after publicly endorsing the EU's 2.42 Euro fine of Google for abuse of a dominant position.[24] These are the high stakes contexts in which AI, and Judge AI is being developed.

Not all entrepreneurs of the age of data support Zuckerberg and the dataists. Elon Musk (Domonoske 2017), echoing the concern implicit in Hariri's speculations, has warned of the existential risk general AI advances pose to humankind. As noted above there is also the work of the Future of Life Institute in relation to AI.[25] Those at the forefront of affective computing themselves could not be termed dataists. Rosalind Picard discussed the potential to build a computer which could replicate the human judge—the one we outline from a psychoanalytical perspective below, of rationality harnessed to emotion. In her seminal article she opened with the disclaimer that, "I am *not* proposing the business of building 'emotional computers'" (Picard 1997, 1; emphasis in original).

---

[21] While certainly linked to a number of laudable aims, and noting sensitivity issues in relation to, for example, medical data, see the proposals for "Data Trusts" in the UK to better facilitate data sharing provided by Hall and Pesenti (2017).

[22] For an interesting critique of modern attitudes toward knowledge sharing, see Leith (2017).

[23] See also Foer's (2017) sustained critique of Big Tech; and from fiction, Eggers (2013).

[24] For coverage of this event, see the European Commission (2017) and Vogel (2017).

[25] For news see Future of Life Institute (n.d.-a).

3.8 Responding to Dataism in Relation to Judge AI—A Psychoanalytical Model of the Legal/Judicial Psyche

Discussions concerning the use of AI in the judicial context (theoretical *and even more worryingly contemporary policy proposals*) have so far not pursued an in-depth engagement with just what it is that algorithms are being touted as able to replicate: the legal/judicial psyche (Posner calls it the "judicial mentality"), i.e., the thing which carries out the semantic operations of legal reasoning (Posner 2010, 5). Capturing in code the operation of the conscious, rational side of legal thinking (the "entire corpus of legal knowledge", as Harvey suggests) has not only been to the fore but has been the entire focus of attention. If that were all that needed to be coded, "judges would be well on the road to being superseded by digitized [AI]" (Posner 2010, 5).

However, the legal reasoning of lawyers and judges (as with all human beings) is only partly conscious; the unconscious also plays an essential role. A psychoanalytical understanding of the judicial mind suggests that the judicial function requires at its heart the organic home of a *human* mind, within which contradictions, at the heart of the judicial process—and human life—are managed. These messy, human, contradictions and accommodations are part of the very definition of "the judge", enabling as they do the judge to understand both the law and the people to which it is being applied. The Scottish judge, Lord MacMillan, writing in the late 1930s (the decade Alan Turing was doing foundational work in computer science) made the point that:

> The judicial mind is subject to the laws of psychology like any other mind. When the judge assumes the ermine he does not *divest himself of humanity*. He has sworn to do justice to all men without fear or favour, but the impartiality which is the noble hallmark our bench *does not imply that the judge's mind has become a mere machine to turn out decrees*; the judge's mind remains a *human instrument working as do other minds*, though no doubt on specialised lines and often characterized by individual traits of personality, engaging or the reverse (1937, 202).

The point at which an algorithm matches the abilities, *and just as importantly, the frailties, confusions, perversions, quirkiness, and uncertainties,* of a human mind (enabling for example empathic understanding and reasoning) is the point at which we have managed to replicate that mind, not imitate or approximate it. A society capable of that may very well be beyond the need of something so basic as a judicial process; so advanced would be its sense of understanding, its mastery of thought and emotion, and ability to avoid conflict. Indeed, in a world of such perfect comprehension, conflict itself might become a relic.

Skepticism about the notion that a judge could be replaced entirely by a smart machine is also linked to the rejection of strong legal formalism and a move to more realist understandings of judicial decision-making, including acknowledging that judges make law. As Lord Reid said in 1971:

> There was a time when it was thought almost indecent to suggest that judges make law – they only declare it. Those with a taste for fairy tales seem to have thought that in some Aladdin's

> cave there is hidden the Common Law in all its splendour and that on a judge's appointment there descends on him knowledge of the magic words Open Sesame. Bad decisions are given when the judge has muddled the pass word and the wrong door opens. But we do not believe in fairy tales any more (Reid 1972, 22).

In the context of a discussion of Judge AI, we might substitute Lord Reid's "magic words", for computer code.

Rejecting legal formalism necessarily allowed for two confessions: not only that judges make law, but second, that the legally correct answer is simply the one delivered by the last judge or judges (or majority of them in an appellate court) to hear a matter. As Reid (1972, 22) said, "the practical answer is that *the law is what the judge says it is*" (emphasis added); and therefore the outcomes of cases turn in part on which judges hear them. There is thus legitimate variance in the results of legal and judicial reasoning which may arise from different *human* judges' understanding of the same legal concepts and their application in different ways. Observe, for example, instances of top courts overturning their own precedents, or cases where judges reach different conclusions as they pass through the appellate hierarchy (and quite possibly with an overall majority of judges favouring the side which finally loses).

How can we explain such accepted judicial variance? Clearly judges are not free (under any view of the judicial role, formalist or otherwise), as are politicians, consciously to give rein to personal or ideological convictions. Yet clearly elements of a judge's personal self play a role in their decisions and this truth is well accepted. As the British judge, Sir Terence Etherton notes, whether a judge realises it or not, their decisions will be influenced by "their personal outlook based on personal experience, and their judicial philosophy" (Etherton 2010, 740).

Legal scholars (especially the realist and critical legal studies (CLS) movements), and political scientists have proposed various theories and models to explain judicial decision-making.[26] While some of these approaches have made use of psychological insights, none of the theorising has yet considered directly, comprehensively, how *psychoanalytical* concepts, Freud's vocabulary and grammar of the psyche, might assist.[27]

[26] See, for example: Baum (1998, 2008); and contributors in Klein and Mitchell (2010).

[27] For some reasons as to why psychoanalytic-legal work receded after the 1960s see Weisstub et al. (2016), and in response, Sourdin and Cornes (2016). There is also a long running debate about the value of psychoanalysis and Freud's insights per se. A good place to start for the contentions on either side is Menand (2017). It will be apparent from our discussion that we do see value in psychoanalytical concepts in assisting to better understand the work of judges.

3.9 Legal Training and Practice Builds a Separate "Legal Self" Alongside the "Personal Self"

One of Freud's propositions was the idea that our mind (psyche) has three parts (see Fig. 1).

The id, or in German, es (it),[28] is where our most primal selves are found. It is a zone of want, urges, desire. Were it not controlled we, individually, or as a society, would be in anarchy. Control comes from the operation of the super-ego, in German, über-ich (over-I), and ego, in German, ich (I). The super-ego is what we take from our parents and society as we grow up: the learning which conditions what is regarded as appropriate or inappropriate behaviour. Finally, we have the ego. From this we operate on a daily basis; it is the most personal, to the fore, aspect of our psyches.

We suggest that legal training entails the development of distinct legal super-egos and legal egos from which we learn to approach the world as a lawyer, and for some, as a judge (see Fig. 2).

First year law students will often be told that one of their initial challenges is to start to think about the world in a quite distinct way; that "thinking like a lawyer" requires a very different way of looking at the world to the one they have been used to. Learning, as Schauer (2010, 109) puts it that, "what the law requires to be done may be something other than that which a non-legal decision-maker would decide."[29]

The first year of legal training is the most difficult because during that year not only is one learning the law, one is also building within the additional psychical apparatus of a legal super-ego and ego: one's legal self. This gives rise to the psychic growing pains of the first stage of legal study. One is training one's psyche to be able to think from two distinct points, each aware of the other, but, when operating in "legal mode", regardless of the ordinary self's conscious reactions, allowing this new learnt legal self to prevail, even if its conclusions clash with the personal self's view of the matter.

3.10 The Legal Super-Ego

The legal super-ego is the repository of our legal knowledge, not just learnt legal rules, but also the broader cultural experience of the law. Like the personal super-ego, the legal super-ego, is built up over time by thinking and views which run through generations of legal thinkers. As the United States' jurist Oliver Wendel Holmes (1881, 5) put it: "The life of the law has not been logic: it has been experience…. The law embodies the story of a nation's development through many centuries, and it cannot be dealt with as if it contained only the axioms and corollaries of a book of mathematics."

[28]See discussion in Freud (1923) and Frosh (2012, Chap. 7).

[29]Space does not allow a wider discussion here of the nature of legal education, but for a CLS perspective see Kennedy (1982).

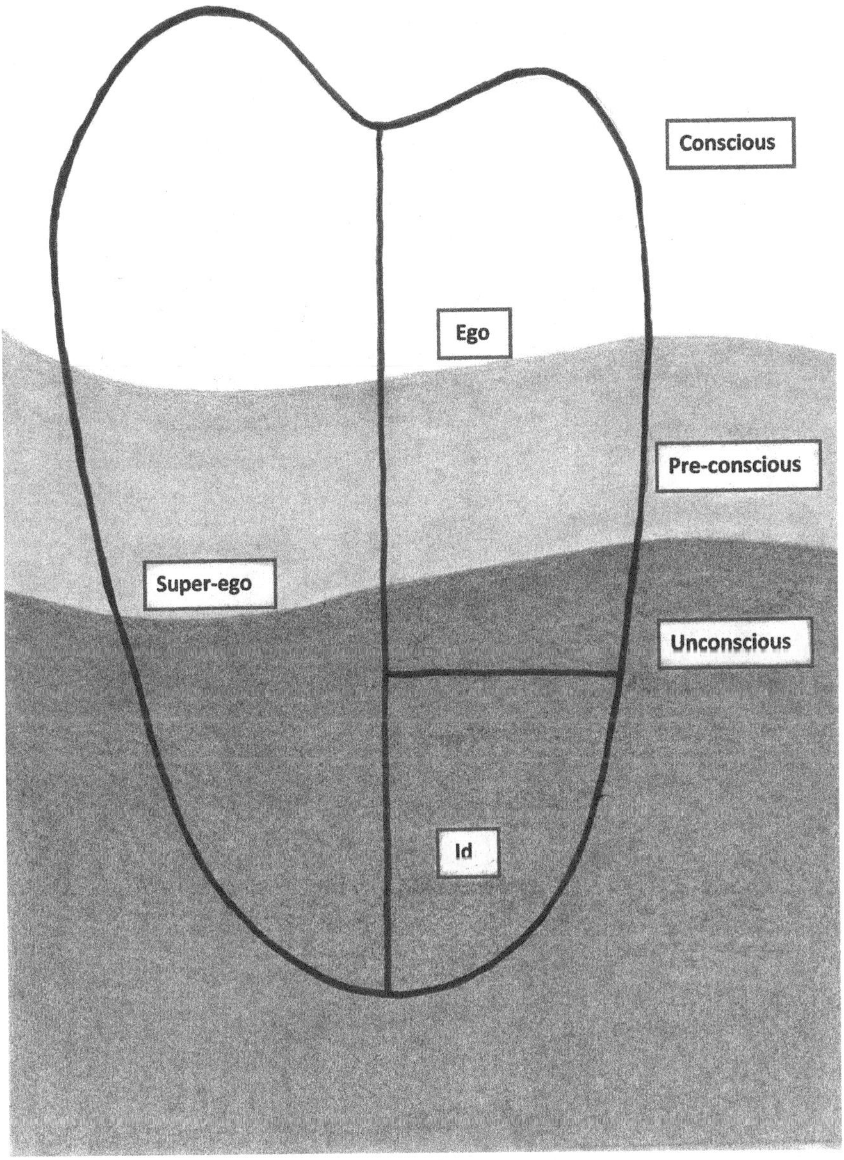

Fig. 1 Freud's topographical/structural model of the mind (artwork, Carole and Richard Cornes)

During legal training, and beyond, the young lawyer will likely come across teachers who become in a sense, the young lawyer's "legal parents." The views of such teachers as to the workings of the law, like the law student's domestic parents' views of moral life, go to building aspects of the legal super-ego. The unique culture of the law school, reflected in its faculty and alumni, will also contribute to molding the new

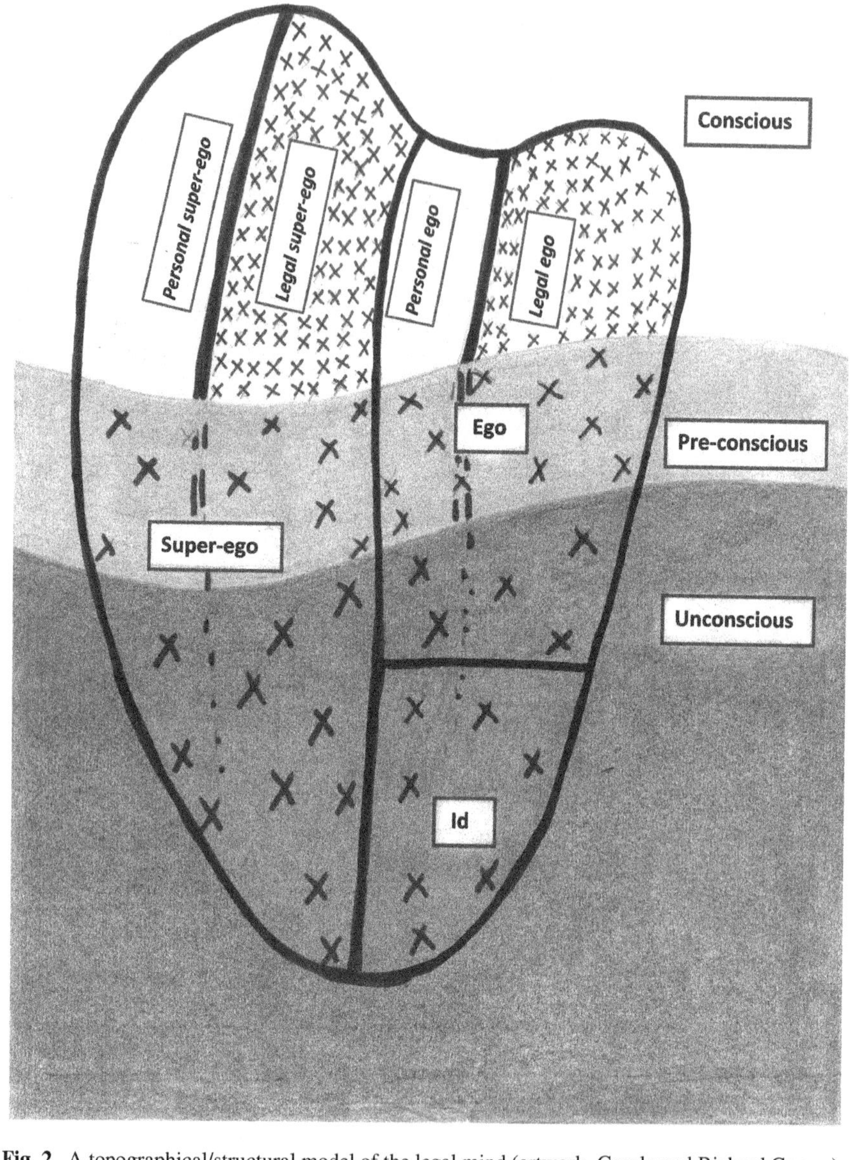

Fig. 2 A topographical/structural model of the legal mind (artwork, Carole and Richard Cornes)

graduate's legal super-ego. The way the legal super-ego comes about (through training and acculturation in the legal world), means it also operates to tie the emerging lawyer's pysche into the social super-ego of the legal world. Concerning the concept of the social super-ego, Wheelis (1959, 66; emphasis added) has argued that it:

> Does not refer to a hypothetical superego of society [for our purposes here: the legal and judicial professions] as a whole. … but only to those *superego elements which are shared by*

> *a significantly large group*. When one views the superego of an individual, one sees it as the incorporated images of parents. … The faces disappear when one views the social superego; for there one sees only the *shared elements—the ideals and faiths which that particular society holds dear, and hence wishes to preserve and perpetuate*.

Once qualified by formal education the young lawyer's psychical growth continues. They are admitted to the profession, and while the culture of jurisdictions will vary, in most common law jurisdictions this entails an application to a court, including the filing of affidavits as to the applicant's character. The process is a sacral one, marking the emergence of a new self, and marking that self as linked, and subject to, a wider set of values. Entering legal practice, the new lawyer will then be taught by the senior lawyers they work with. All these people will contribute, along with the young lawyer's formal studies, to the developing legal super-ego. The influence of some of them will stay with the person throughout their professional life—as when in practice, or academia, we find ourselves wondering what view these early mentors or teachers might take on an issue we confront.

3.11 The Legal Ego

The legal ego: this is the place from which lawyers and judges learn to approach and analyse the world in legal terms, obeying the commands of the legal super-ego. Like the personal ego it is a place from which one speaks as one's self, but in this case, one's legal self. While undergoing legal training at university, and after, the young lawyer will also be developing their own sense of what it is to be a lawyer; what their own legal voice will be. In building this aspect of their psyche there is perhaps more opportunity to draw on their personal self; the natural process of psychical development will, as it were, twin track. Their personal self will help to temper the way they develop their legal ego, under the influence of the factors and people which are building their legal super-ego. In another sense, the legal ego is a child not just of the external factors of law school and "legal parents", but also the person's own super-ego and ego. Clearly this psychical structure could be expected to give rise to a range of tensions and conflicts; it is our argument that the outcomes of those unconscious conflicts is one of the defining features of legal thinking.

3.12 The Place of the Pre-conscious and Unconscious as a Link Between the Legal Psyche and the Personal Psyche

Freud also developed the idea that we think from three levels of the mind: the conscious (what is present in our immediate thoughts), the pre-conscious (the things we are about to bring to conscious as the circumstances require), and the unconscious (the realm of the psyche and thought that we cannot access ordinarily), accessible only through exceptions such as our dream life, or through phenomena such as lapsis linguae, jokes, or when we allow ourselves to free associate.[30] In *The Interpretation of Dreams*, Freud said of *unconscious* thinking that it is a process which "could easily be very different from the one we are aware of in ourselves in the course of purposeful reflection accompanied by consciousness" (Freud 2008, 214).[31] Ian Craib (2001, 21)—a sociologist and psychotherapist—said of the idea of the unconscious generally, "the suggestion that people do not necessarily know what they are doing, that they are driven by forces beyond their consciousness or their control, that they can be mistaken about their own motives, is a scandalous idea."

It is certainly an idea which would have scandalised the legal formalist orthodoxy Lord Reid (1972) rejected in *The Judge as Law Maker*, and it will continue to provoke resistance from more black letter lawyers and any remaining formalists. The implications are significant. While we might control what happens at the conscious level we can only pretend to control what goes on below. As Freud (1991, 139) said, the, "unconsciousness is a regular and inevitable phase in the processes constituting our psychical activity; every psychical act begins as an unconscious one, and it may either remain so or go on developing into consciousness, according to whether it meets resistance or not."

The importance of considering the judicial unconscious (and to an extent, pre-conscious) is this: as much as a judge honestly claims to be operating consciously from the perspective of their legal super-ego and ego, they cannot control for the leakage from their personal super-ego/ego which may occur beneath the membrane of consciousness. Furthermore, in that realm there will also be influences from the judge's id. Judge Benjamin Cardozo (1921, 167) addressed this in explicitly psycho-analytic terms: "deep below consciousness are other forces, the likes and dislikes, the predilections and the prejudices, the complex of instincts and emotions and habits and convictions which make the man, whether he be litigant or judge."

For Schauer (2010, 114), the question, "do judges think like human beings, or like lawyers, or like judges?… should be one of the central items on a research agenda for the psychology of judging, but it is, surprisingly, an item that up to now has been almost completely absent." What then are the functional implications, from a psychoanalytical perspective, (including for any AI designer) of the inevitable influence of a judge's unconscious on how they think? We are not concerned now with conscious legal reasoning (which possibly may be well expressed in a sophisticated algorithm). Here, we are concerned with the unconscious processes which play a part in all human judicial reasoning - how, in the unconscious mind the personal self can affect the conclusions of the legal self.

The psychoanalytic concept of use here is that of "phantasy," spelt within the discipline of psychoanalysis with a "ph" rather than "f". The novel English spelling

---

[30] See discussion in Freud (2002, 2008).

[31] For a neuro-psychoanalytical view of the unconscious see Solms (2013).

arises from a translation compromise—Freud's term in German is "phantasie."[32] Along with the interplay between legal and personal super-egos and egos, discussed previously, phantasy, not only as a way of thinking, but also through the interplay of different phantasies of "justice", plays a role in how judges think. Freud thought phantastic reasoning part of the "phylogenetically inherited capacity of the human mind" (Spillius et al. 2011, 3). Isaacs (1948, 80–95) characterised phantasy as, "the primary content of unconscious mental processes", implicitly identifying it as of fundamental importance: "phantasy is (in the first instance) the mental corollary, the psychic representative, of instinct. There is no impulse, no instinctual urge or response which is not experienced as unconscious phantasy."

Every judge's phantasies, in Isaac's terms, *instincts*, of justice, shaped by their life experiences, *from the moment of birth*, will play a role at the unconscious level, influencing how they consciously apply legal rules. Phantastic reasoning will operate to meld the inclinations of the judge's legal super-ego and ego with that of their personal super-ego and ego, producing a synthesis which ultimately emerges to consciousness. This mental product - the conclusion on the problem before the judge—is then filtered through conscious judicial reasoning and articulated consistently with learnt legal rules. This "internal [i.e., unconscious] dialogue of reason and passion, does not taint the judicial process, but is in fact central to its vitality" (Brennan 1988, 3). United States Supreme Court Justice Brennan's references to the importance of passion in judicial decision-making echoes the concept of phantastic reasoning. He goes on: "by 'passion' I mean the range of emotional and intuitive responses to a given set of facts or arguments, responses which often speed into our consciousness far ahead of the lumbering syllogisms of reason" (1988, 9). Foreshadowing the need for the Judge AI project to take care not to revert to the fairy tales of formalism he also notes that, "an appreciation for the dialogue between head and heart is precisely what was missing from the formalist conception of judging" (1988, 9).

The unconscious, and unavoidable (because it is innately human), reality of phantastic reasoning means that the judge will still honestly be able to say they consciously put their personal preferences to one side and simply followed the law. They cannot, however, control for what happens in their unconscious where phantasies, instincts, of justice, phantastic and instinctual reasoning, play a role. Phantastic mixing in the unconscious ensures that legal reasoning is tethered to a judge's humanity; it ensures that the "quality of mercy is not strained", and that the application of legal rules is seasoned by the judge's life experience.[33] Lord Kerr of the UK Supreme Court comes close to acknowledging this: "In the course of one's legal career, although one has to maintain a certain professional detachment, occasions arise where you feel strongly that a particular person's interests requires to be vindicated" (BBC4 2011, ~17').

The fact that personal experiences do influence the law as enunciated by judges via the operation of phantasy raises a practical point for the legal system and any Judge AI project: a more diverse bench (in terms of judicial backgrounds and experience;

---

[32]For further elucidation see discussion of the concepts of "fantasy" and "phantasy" in Brenner (2003).

[33]See Portia's speech on mercy in Shakespeare's, *The Merchant of Venice*, Act IV, Sc1, ll2125-46.

the bench in the UK is still remarkably homogeneous), should increase confidence in the judicial process as a wider range of concepts and phantasies of justice are given expression to. Further, we might get substantively "better" law with a more diverse bench, because the decisions which make up the common law would be based on a richer range of experience. As Cardozo (1921, 177) argued, "The eccentricities of judges balance one another. …[O]ut of the attrition of diverse minds there is beaten something which has a constancy and uniformity and average value greater than its component elements."

Finally, as Cornes and Henaghan (forthcoming) argue, the concept of the judge is not exemplified solely by the individuals who fulfill that role. The notion of the independent and impartial judge is one collectively agreed to and understood via the mechanisms of the social unconscious. That psychic system operates to co-construct (as between the legal profession and wider society) our collective understanding of the judge we trust in the courtroom. The implication here for the Judge AI project is that "a judge" is not a single data processing unit to be adequately represented in code. Judges are intimately and psychically linked to the wider social system within which they operate.[34]

For any Judge AI project the problem thus arises: how to code to allow for the influence of a similar range of varying *personal, human, and societal* inputs in addition to reflecting legal rules and principles? The problem is especially difficult because such personal inputs, emanating from human judges', and society's unconscious, are by definition not consciously knowable and therefore not translatable into code. As Lord Phillips has said of judgment writing: "I sometimes start writing a judgment and I don't know where I'm going to get to at the end of it" (BBC4 2011, ~50').

While, therefore, many aspects of the judicial task may ultimately be captured in code, the human heart of the judicial process, being a combination of conscious and currently unknowable unconscious thought, remains quite literally beyond the comprehension of the most talented programmer. And, as we suggest above, the point at which technology and society is so sophisticated as to allow a complete understanding of all aspects of the human psyche is likely to be a point at which conflict itself, arising as it does in part because of clashes of understanding (of ourselves *and* others), is a spent force in human history.

4 Conclusion

The roles of those involved in the delivery of justice and judging are changing rapidly. Newer more disruptive technologies have already reshaped some aspects of the justice system and the business of litigation. We expect courts will continue to build and

[34]The role of the social unconscious and confidence in "the judge" is set out in detail in Cornes and Henaghan (forthcoming).

extend online platforms and systems that support filing, referral and other activities.[35] Further, we may see judicial passions (always reasoned), being monitored by trusted dispassionate Judge Co-Bots.

However, developments thus far do not lead inevitably to technology entirely taking over the judicial function or role. Whilst AI can contribute to some adjudicative functions, the issues that emerge are whether this is appropriate per se, and under what circumstances human judges should hand over aspects of their adjudicative functions to AI. Whilst some conjecture that AI may one day completely replace human judges, such suggestions could only be credible if the automation were able to replicate a human mind. We have argued that at no point soon does it appear that AI will be able to replace the necessary and essential humanity of a human judge, and we suggest further that to do so would be undesirable.

It is important to understand that judges do far more than render judgments. They manage cases, provide a responsive and human framework within which conflict is contained, settle cases, and manage court systems and processes as well as playing an important public and educative function. Further, clearly the contributions of a judge's unconscious mind, the exercise of discretion, and constructive judicial variance are three of the factors which make human judicial decision-making acceptable to litigants and legitimate within society. Issues also arise about whether AI processes possess the legal authority to make judicial decisions in place of a human judge.

Policy approaches that increasingly result in the transfer of lower value matters or categories of disputes (such as insurance disputes) to administrative tribunals and commissions suggest that judicial work is likely to continue to change over the next twenty years. It is equally probable that AI will play a more prominent role in administrative and other decision-making contexts before being used in courts. This all means that the impact in respect of Judge AI is more likely to be significant, at least initially, in relation to smaller civil claims as AI support spreads throughout the administrative decision-making arena.

Drawing the boundaries of acceptable Judge AI (should it be extended for use in larger claims than it is currently used for?) requires consideration of ethical questions as well as questions about who produces the algorithms of Judge AI and the extent to which discretion and oversight will be maintained within the judiciary.[36] It is unhelpful to conceive of Judge AI as disconnected from the work of human judges. Rather, as for example Autor argues, while humans may not be replaced by AI, human intelligence may be supplemented by technological advances (Autor 2015). The requirement for interaction between judges and AI systems will in turn give raise to issues about judicial appointment, workload, and retention, as well as broader questions about how judges contribute to society and the importance of humanly responsive judging. There is a need to better understand and explore the impact on

---

[35]See e.g., New South Wales Department of Justice (n.d.) and Whitbourn (2015) for further detail on the new online court websites in New South Wales. The Federal Court of Australia has had an e-courtroom and expanding online lodgement services for some years, see Federal Court of Australia (n.d).

[36]Issues about robot ethics are currently the subject of some limited discussion. See Devlin (2016).

people of a human judge who deals sensitively with their concerns. Whilst Judge AI may not be able to replicate the human judicial mind, clearly technology will continue to influence the evolving role of the responsive human judge in legal systems worldwide.

References

Agthe M, Spörrle M, Maner J (2011) Does being attractive always help? Positive and negative effects of attractiveness on social decision making. Pers Soc Psychol Bull 37:1042–1054

Aletras N, Tsarapatsanis D, Preotiuc-Pietro D, Lampos V (2016) Predicting judicial decisions of the European Court of Human Rights: a natural language processing perspective. Peer J Comput Sci 2:e93. https://doi.org/10.7717/peerj-cs.93. Accessed 30 May 2017

Angwin J, Larson J, Mattu S, Kirchner L (2016) Machine bias. Propublica, May 23. https://www.propublica.org/article/machine-bias-risk-assessments-in-criminal-sentencing. Accessed 30 Nov 2017

Ashley KD (2017) Artificial intelligence and legal analytics—new tools for the digital age. Cambridge University Press, Cambridge

Autor DH (2015) Why are there still so many jobs? The history and future of workplace automation. J Econ Perspect 29(3):3–30

Barendrecht M (2017) Rechtwijzer: why online supported dispute resolution is hard to implement. HIIL Innovating Justice. http://www.hiil.org/insight/rechtwijzer-why-online-supporte-dispute-resolution-is-hard-to-implement. Accessed 13 July 2017

Bathurst T (2015) iAdvocate v Rumpole: who will survive? An analysis of advocates' ongoing relevance in the age of technology. Paper presented at 2015 Australian Bar Association Conference, Boston, 9 July 2015

Baum L (1998) The puzzle of judicial behaviour. University Michigan Press, Ann Arbor

Baum L (2008) Judges and their audiences—perspectives on judicial behaviour. Princeton University Press, Princeton

BBC4 (2011) The highest court in the land: justice makers. https://www.youtube.com/watch?v=PZtYENfNa7k. Accessed 3 Feb 2018

Bennett H, Broe GA (2007) Judicial neurobiology, Markarian synthesis and emotion: how can the human brain make sentencing decisions? Crim Law J 31(2):75–90

Benyekhlef K, Vermeys N (2017) ODR and the (BC) courts. Slaw. http://www.slaw.ca/2012/05/28/odr-and-the-bc-courts/. Accessed 19 June 2017

Bickel E, van Dijk M, Giebels E (2015) Online legal advice and conflict support: a Dutch experience. Report, University of Twente, March 2015

Brennan (1988) Reason, passion, and the progress of the law. Cardozo Law Rev 10:3–23

Brenner A (2003) Fantasy. University of Chicago. http://csmt.uchicago.edu/glossary2004/fantasy.htm. Accessed 4 Dec 2017

Brooks D (2011) The social animal. Random House, New York

Brooks M (2017) Artificial ignorance. New Scientist, 7 October

Cardozo B (1921) The nature of the judicial process. Yale University Press, Connecticut

Carniero D, Novais P, Andrade F, Zeleznikow J, Neves J (2014) Online dispute resolution: an artificial intelligence perspective. Artif Intell Rev 41(2):211–240

Chaphalkar NB, Iyer KC, Patil SK (2015) Prediction of outcome of construction dispute claims using multilayer perceptron neural network model. Int J Project Manage 33(8):1827–1835

Chiang J (2017) ACC accused of using model to get people off its books. Radio New Zealand, 15 September. http://www.radionz.co.nz/news/political/339513/acc-accused-of-using-model-to-get-people-off-its-books. Accessed 30 Nov 2017

Chin D (2012) Sentencing: a role for empathy. Univ Penn Law Rev 160(6):1561–1584

Chisholm R (2009) Values and assumptions in judicial cases. Paper presented at the National Judicial College Conference, Judicial Reasoning—Art or Science, Canberra, 7–8 February 2009. https://njca.com.au/wp-content/uploads/2013/07/Values-and-Assumptions-in-Judicial-Decisions-Chisholm.pdf. Accessed 30 May 2017

Civil Resolution Tribunal (2018) How the CRT works. https://civilresolutionbc.ca/how-the-crt-works/. Accessed 4 Feb 2018

Colby TB (2012) In defense of judicial empathy. Minn Law Rev 96:1944–2015

Cornes R, Henaghan M (forthcoming) Believing in the judge—understanding and defending the role of the fair minded and informed observer in bias jurisprudence from a psychodynamic perspective. Otago Law Rev

Craib I (2001) Psychoanalysis—a critical introduction. Polity, Cambridge

Danziger S, Levav J, Avnaim-Pesso L (2011) Extraneous factors in judicial decisions. Proc Natl Acad Sci USA 108(17):6889–6892

Devlin H (2016) Do no harm, don't discriminate: official guidance issued on robot ethics. The Guardian (online), 18 September. https://www.theguardian.com/technology/2016/sep/18/official-guidance-robot-ethics-british-standards-institute?CMP=share_btn_tw. Accessed 30 May 2017

Domonoske C (2017) Elon Musk warns governors: artificial intelligence poses 'existential risk'. The Two Way, 17 July. http://www.npr.org/sections/thetwo-way/2017/07/17/537686649/elon-musk-warns-governors-artificial-intelligence-poses-existential-risk. Accessed 4 Dec 2017

Eggers D (2013) The circle. Penguin, UK

Elias S (2017) Managing criminal justice. Address given at Criminal Bar Association Conference, University of Auckland Business School, Auckland, 5 August 2017. https://www.criminalbar.org.nz/cba_conference_2017. Accessed 30 Nov 2017

Etherton T (2010). Liberty, the archetype and diversity: a philosophy of judging. Public Law 727

European Commission (2017) Antitrust: commission fines Google €2.42 billion for abusing dominance as search engine by giving illegal advantage to own comparison shopping service. Press Release (27 June 2017). http://europa.eu/rapid/press-release_IP-17-1784_en.htm. Accessed 4 Dec 2017

Federal Court of Australia (n.d.) eCourtroom. http://www.fedcourt.gov.au/online-services/ecourtroom. Accessed 30 May 2017

Foer F (2017) World without mind—the existential threat of big tech. Jonathan Cape, London

Frank J (1930) Law and the modern mind. Brentano's, New York

Frank J (1949) Courts on trial—myth and reality in American justice. Princeton University Press, Princeton

Freud S (1921) Mass psychology and analysis of the "I". In: Mass psychology and other writings (2004). Penguin, London

Freud S (1923) The ego and the id. In: Standard edition of the complete psychological works of Sigmund Freud, vol XIX. Hogarth Press, London

Freud S (1991) A note on the unconscious. In The essentials of psycho-analysis—the definitive collection of Sigmund Freud's writing, selected by Anna Freud. Penguin, London

Freud S (2002) The psychopathology of everyday life (Penguin Modern Classics). Penguin Classics, London

Freud S (2008) The interpretation of dreams (Oxford World's Classics). Oxford University Press, Oxford

Frosh S (2012) A brief introduction to psychoanalytic theory. Palgrave, Basingstoke

Future of Life Institute (n.d.-a) Artificial intelligence news. https://futureoflife.org/ai-news/. Accessed 4 Dec 2017

Future of Life Institute (n.d.-b) Asilomar AI principles. https://futureoflife.org/ai-principles/. Accessed 30 Nov 2017

Gaitenby A (2004) Online dispute resolution. The Internet Encyclopaedia. https://doi.org/10.1002/047148296X.tie129

Hall W, Pesenti J (2017). Growing the artificial intelligence industry in the UK, a report for the UK Government. https://www.gov.uk/government/publications/growing-the-artificial-intelligence-industry-in-the-uk. Accessed 4 Dec 2017
Harari YN (2015) Homo Deus: a brief history of tomorrow. Harvill Secker, London
Harvey D (2016) From Susskind to Briggs: online court approaches. J Civil Litigation Pract 5(2):84–93
Hoekstra v. H.M. Advocate (No.2) (2000) S.L.T. 605
Holmes OW (1881) The common law. http://www.general-intelligence.com/library/commonlaw.pdf. Accessed 4 Dec 2017
Hyde J (2017). Prison and courts bill scrapped. Law Soc Gazette, 20 April. https://www.lawgazette.co.uk/news/breaking-prisons-and-courts-bill-scrapped/5060715.article. Accessed 13 July 2017
In Re JP Linaham (1943) 138 F.2d 650 (2d Cir). Justia. https://law.justia.com/cases/federal/appellate-courts/F2/138/650/1481751/. Accessed 4 Feb 2018
Isaacs S (1948) The nature and function of phantasy. Int J Psychoanal 73–93
Johnstone R (2016) HM Courts and Tribunals Service's Susan Acland-Hood on digital courts, making big changes and her Whitehall hammock. Civil Service World, 6 October. https://www.civilserviceworld.com/articles/interview/hm-courts-and-tribunals-service%E2%80%99s-susan-acland-hood-digital-courts-making-big. Accessed 4 Dec 2017
Kennedy D (1982) Legal education and the reproduction of hierarchy. J Leg Educ 32:591–615
Kirby M (1999a) The future of courts—do they have one? J Judicial Adm 8:383–391
Kirby M (1999b) Judging: reflections on the moment of decision. Aust Bar Rev 18:4–22
Klein DE, Mitchell G (eds) (2010) The psychology of judicial decision making. Oxford University Press, Oxford
Lanchester J (2017) You are the product. Lond Rev Books 39:3–10
Lawyal Solicitors (2016) About us. https://lawyal.com.au/about-us. Accessed 31 Oct 2017
Le Sueur A, Cornes R (2000) What do the top courts do? Curr Leg Probl 53(1):53–97
Legg M (2016) The future of dispute resolution: online ADR and online courts. Australas Dispute Resolut J 27:227–235
Leiter B (2010) Legal formalism and legal realism: what is the issue? Leg Theory 16(2):111–133
Leith S (2017) Nothing like the truth. TLS, 18 August. https://www.the-tls.co.uk/articles/public/post-truth-sam-leith/. Accessed 25 Aug 2017
Levin S (2016) A beauty contest was judged by AI and the robots didn't like dark skin. The Guardian (online), 9 September. https://www.theguardian.com/technology/2016/sep/08/artificial-intelligence-beauty-contest-doesnt-like-black-people?CMP=share_btn_tw. Accessed 30 May 2017
Lind EA, Tyler TR (1988) The social psychology of procedural justice. Plenum Press, New York
Liptak A (2017) Sent to prison by a software program's secret algorithms. New York Times (online), May 1. https://www.nytimes.com/2017/05/01/us/politics/sent-to-prison-by-a-software-programs-secret-algorithms.html?smid=tw-share&_r=0. Accessed 30 May 2017
Loomis v Wisconsion (2017) *SCOTUSblog*. http://www.scotusblog.com/case-files/cases/loomis-v-wisconsin/. Accessed 30 Nov 2017
Lopez I (2016) The early years begin for AI's transformation of law. Legaltech News, 5 October. http://www.legaltechnews.com/id=1202769286334/The-Early-Years-Begin-for-AIs-Transformation-of-Law?cmp=share_twitter&slreturn=20160912054113. Accessed 29 May 2017
Lynn B, Stoller M (2017). How to stop Google and Facebook from becoming even more powerful. The Guardian, 2 November. https://www.theguardian.com/commentisfree/2017/nov/02/facebook-google-monopoly-companies. Accessed 6 Feb 2018
MacCrimmon M, Tillers P (eds) (2002) The dynamics of judicial proof: computation, logic, and common sense. Physica-Verlag, Heidelberg
MacMillan L (1937) Law and other things. Cambridge University Press, Cambridge
MacQueen HL, Wortley S (1998) Human rights, the judges and the new Scotland. Scots Law News, 18 October. http://www.sln.law.ed.ac.uk/1998/10/18/78-human-rights-the-judges-and-the-new-scotland/. Accessed 4 Dec 2017
Mason K (2001) Unconscious judicial prejudice. Aust Law J 75:676–687

Menand L (2017) The stone guest: can Sigmund Freud ever be killed? The New Yorker, 28 August, 75

Mills M (2016) Artificial intelligence in law: the state of play 2016 (Part 1). Legal Executive Institute, 23 February. http://legalexecutiveinstitute.com/artificial-intelligence-in-law-the-state-of-play-2016-part-1/. Accessed 29 May 2017

Ministry of Justice of the Government of the United Kingdom and Her Majesty's Courts and Tribunal Service (2016) Transforming our justice system. https://www.gov.uk/government/uploads/system/uploads/attachment_data/file/553261/joint-vision-statement.pdf. Accessed 30 May 2017

MyLawBC (n.d.) Separation, divorce & family matters. http://mylawbc.com/paths/family/. Accessed 29 May 2017

Neill D (2013) Using artificial intelligence to improve hospital inpatient care. IEEE Intell Syst 28(2):92–95

New South Wales Department of Justice (n.d.) NSW online registry—courts and tribunals. https://onlineregistry.lawlink.nsw.gov.au/content/nsw-supreme-district-local-courts-online-registry. Accessed 29 May 2017

Nine to Noon (2017) Is ACC "passing the buck" with prediction based evaluations? Radio New Zealand, 26 September. http://www.radionz.co.nz/national/programmes/ninetonoon/audio/201859974/is-acc-passing-the-buck-with-prediction-based-evaluations. Accessed 30 Nov 2017

Northern Ireland Courts and Tribunals Service (2011) Small claims online: a users guide. http://www.courtsni.gov.uk/SiteCollectionDocuments/Northern%20Ireland%20Courts%20Gallery/Online%20Services%20User%20Guides/Small%20Claims%20Online%20User%20Guide.pdf. Accessed 30 May 2017

Perry M (2017) iDecide: administrative decision-making in the digital world. Aust Law J 91:29–34

Picard R (1997) Affective computing. MIT Media Lab, Massachusetts

Posner R (2010) How judges think. Harvard University Press, Harvard

Quintanilla V (2012) Different voices: the role of gender when reasoning about the letter versus spirit of the law. Presentation at the Law and Society Conference, Honolulu, June 2012

Ramesh AN, Kambhampati C, Monson JRT, Drew PJ (2004) Artificial intelligence in medicine. Ann R Coll Surg Engl 84:334–338

Reid L (1972) The judge as lawmaker. J Soc Public Teachers Law 12(1):22–29

Schatsky D, Muraskin C, Gurumurthy R (2014) Demystifying artificial intelligence: what business leaders need to know about cognitive technologies. University Press, Deloitte

Schauer F (2010) Is there a psychology of judging? In: Klein DE, Mitchell G (eds) The psychology of judicial decision-making. Oxford: Oxford University Press, pp 103–121

Schubarth C (2016) Y combinator startup uses big data to invest in civil lawsuits. Silicon Valley Bus J, 24 August. http://www.bizjournals.com/sanjose/blog/techflash/2016/08/y-combinator-startup-uses-big-data-to-invest-in.html. Accessed 29 May 2017

Searle J (2002) Can computers think? In: Chalmers D (ed) Philosophy of mind: classical and contemporary readings. Oxford University Press, Oxford, pp 669–675

Shakespeare W (16th Century) The merchant of Venice, Act IV, Sc1, ll2125-46

Silver D, Huang A, Maddison C, Guez A, Sifre L, Van Den Driessche G, Schrittweiser J (2016) Mastering the game of Go with deep neural networks and tree search. Nature 529(7587):484–489

Sinai Y, Alberstein M (2016) Expanding judicial discretion: between legal and conflict considerations. Harvard Negot Law Rev 21:221–277

Smartsettle One+ (2017) Smartsettle. http://www.smartsettle.com/home/products/smartsettle-one/. Accessed 31 Oct 2017

Smith M (2016). In wisconsin, a backlash against using data to foretell defendant's futures. New York Times (online), 22 June. http://www.nytimes.com/2016/06/23/us/backlash-in-wisconsin-against-using-data-to-foretell-defendants-futures.html?_r=0. Accessed 30 May 2017

Soars J (2016) Draft procedural order for use of online dispute resolution technologies in ACICA rules arbitrations. The Australian Centre for International Commercial Arbitration. https://acica.org.au/wp-content/uploads/2016/08/ACICA-online-ADR-procedural-order.pdf. Accessed 31 Oct 2017

Solms M (2013) "The unconscious" in psychoanalysis and neuropsychology. In: Akhtar S, O'Neill MK (eds) On Freud's "The unconscious". Karnac Books, London, pp 101–118

Solon O (2017) Killer robots? Musk and Zuckerberg escalate row over dangers of AI. The Guardian Australia, July 2017. https://www.theguardian.com/technology/2017/jul/25/elon-musk-mark-zuckerberg-artificial-intelligence-facebook-tesla. Accessed 30 Nov 2017

Sourdin T (2012) Decision making in ADR: science, sense and sensibility. Arbitrat Mediat 31(1):1–14

Sourdin T (2015a) Justice and technological innovation. J Judicial Adm 25:96–105

Sourdin T (2015b) The role of the courts in the new justice system. Yearb Arbitrat Mediat 7:95–116

Sourdin T (2016) Alternative dispute resolution, 5th edn. Thomson Reuters, Pyrmont

Sourdin T (2018, forthcoming) Judge v Robot? Artificial intelligence and judicial decision making. U New South Wales Law J 41(4)

Sourdin T, Cornes R (2016) Implications for therapeutic judging (TJ) of a psychoanalytical perspective to the judicial role. Int J Law Psychiatry 48:8–14

Sourdin T, Zariski A (eds) (2013) The multi-tasking judge: comparative judicial dispute resolution. Thomson Reuters

Spillius EB, Milton J, Garvey P, Couve C, Steiner D (2011) The new dictionary of Kleinian thought. Taylor & Francis, East Sussex

State v Loomis (2016) 881 N.W.2d 749. Leagle. https://www.leagle.com/decision/inwico20160713i48. Accessed 4 Feb 2018

State v Loomis (2017) Docket for 16-6387. Supreme Court of the United States. https://www.supremecourt.gov/docketfiles/16-6387.htm. Accessed 4 Feb 2018

Surden H (2014) Machine learning and law. Wash Law Rev 89:87–115

Susskind D, Susskind R (2015) The future of the professions. Oxford University Press, Oxford

Tamburro M (2012) The future of predictive coding—rise of the evidentiary expert. IMS ExpertServices. http://technology.findlaw.com/electronic-discovery/the-future-of-predictive-coding-rise-of-the-evidentiary-expert-.html. Accessed 30 May 2017

Tashea J (2016) New York considers "Textalyzer" bill to allow police to see if drivers were texting behind the wheel. ABA J, 1 October. http://www.abajournal.com/magazine/article/newyork_distracted_driving_textalyzer_bill/. Accessed 30 May 2017

Therapeutic Goods Act 1989 (Cth)

Thibaut J (1978) Procedural justice: a psychological analysis. Duke Law J 6:1289–1296

Thibaut J, Walker L (1975) Procedural justice: a psychological analysis. Erlbaum, New Jersey

Tierney J (2011) Do you suffer from decision fatigue? New York Times (online), 17 August. http://www.nytimes.com/2011/08/21/magazine/do-you-suffer-from-decision-fatigue.html?_r=2&pagewanted=1. Accessed 30 May 2017

Tirrell M (2017) From coding to cancer: how AI is changing medicine. CNBC, 11 May. http://www.cnbc.com/2017/05/11/from-coding-to-cancer-how-ai-is-changing-medicine.html. Accessed 30 May 2017

Tyler Technologies (2017) Modria. https://www.tylertech.com/solutions-products/modria. Accessed 31 Oct 2017

University of Otago (n.d.) Artificial intelligence and law in New Zealand. http://www.cs.otago.ac.nz/research/ai/AI-Law/index.html. Accessed 30 Nov 2017

Van den Bos K, Van der Velden L, Lind A (2014) On the role of perceived procedural justice in citizens' reactions to government decisions and the handling of conflicts. Utrecht Law Rev 10(4):1–26

Victoria University (n.d.) Professor John Zeleznikow. http://www.vu.edu.au/contact-us/john-zeleznikow. Accessed 30 May 2017

Vogel K (2017) Google critic ousted from think tank funded by the Tech Giant. New York Times (online), August 2017. https://www.nytimes.com/2017/08/30/us/politics/eric-schmidt-google-new-america.html. Accessed 4 Dec 2017

Warren M (2015) Embracing technology: the way forward for the courts. J Judicial Adm 24:227–235

Weisstub DN, Pitz A, Burt RA (2016) Introduction—Robert A. Burt. Int J Law Psychiatry 48:1–7

Wheelis A (1959) Psychoanalysis and identity. Psychoanal Rev 46A:65–74

Whitbourn M (2015) NSW government trials online court for civil cases in Sydney. Sydney Morning Herald (online), 10 August. http://www.smh.com.au/nsw/nsw-government-trials-online-court-for-civil-cases-in-sydney-20150807-giuig2.html. Accessed 30 May 2017

Wikipedia (2017) Rosalind Picard. https://en.wikipedia.org/wiki/Rosalind_Picard. Accessed 14 July 2017

Wilson T, Gilbert D (2008) Explaining away: a model of affective adaptation. Perspect Psychol Sci 3(5):370–386

Zeleznikow J, Bellucci E (n.d.) Family Winner: integrating game theory and heuristics to provide negotiation support. http://www.jurix.nl/pdf/j03-03.pdf. Accessed 30 May 2017

Zeleznikow J, Bellucci E, Schild UJ, Mackenzie G (2007) Bargaining in the shadow of the law—using utility functions to support legal negotiation. Paper presented at the 11th International Conference on Artificial Intelligence, Stanford, California, 4–8 June 2007

Tania Sourdin is the Dean of the University of Newcastle Law School and was previously the Foundation Chair and Director of the Australian Centre for Justice Innovation (ACJI) at Monash University in Australia. Professor Sourdin has led national research projects and produced important recommendations for ADR and justice reform. In the past two decades, she has conducted qualitative and quantitative research projects into aspects of the dispute resolution and justice system systems in 12 Courts and Tribunals and six external dispute resolution schemes. Other research has focussed on justice innovation, technology, delay and systemic reforms. Professor Sourdin is the author of a number of books (the 5th Edition of her book 'Alternative Dispute Resolution' was released in February 2016), articles and papers, and has published and presented widely on a range of topics including ADR, justice innovation, justice issues, mediation, conflict resolution, collaborative law, artificial intelligence, technology and organisational change.

Richard Cornes is a Senior Lecturer in Public Law at the University of Essex, England. He is also a Visiting Fellow at the University of Otago, New Zealand, Centre for Legal Issues, and an Associate Member of Landmark Chambers, London. Dr. Cornes graduated BA/LLB(Hons) from Auckland University (English and Law) in 1992 and the following year was admitted as a Barrister and Solicitor of the High Court of New Zealand. After practicing at Simpson Grierson, Auckland, and studying at the University of Melbourne (Grad Dip International Law), he moved to the UK in 1997 where he worked on aspects of the new Labour Government's constitutional reforms as a Senior Research Fellow at UCL's Constitution Unit. Since 2000 has been on faculty at Essex Law School where he runs the core modules in public law. His research and consultancy interests are focused on judicial branch matters, with a specific focus on the application of psycho-social and organisational dynamic approaches.

The High Court and the Cocktail Party from Hell: Can Social Media Improve Community Engagement with the Courts?

Andrew Henderson

Abstract

> Everybody is continuously connected ... with the flood of information jeopardizing meaning. Everybody's talking at once in a hypnotic, hyper din: the cocktail party from hell. (Dowd 2013)

Our understanding of the world around us is increasingly connected to the smartphone in our pocket. Twitter, Facebook and Instagram all deliver information to us in the gym or on the bus. Courts in Australia have often lamented the lack of understanding of their work and have begun to turn to social media as a potential means of becoming more responsive to the views of the wider community. But social media management is time consuming, especially if the Courts' message is to be heard above the "hyper-din" of other simultaneous exchanges. The user-generated content also means that it can be unpredictable and active engagement by Courts with litigants also raises significant issues. Despite these risks, there has been little research done about the extent to which Courts' engagement with social media will deliver any benefit. As a means of testing this idea in the "real world", this chapter collects and examines the volume and content of Twitter commentary concerning a recent decision of the High Court of Australia to assess the depth and breadth of community discussion. It finds that as a platform for community engagement, Twitter would appear to be neither well used nor persuasive. In light of the potential costs and risks, further research is required before opening the Courts to this medium generally.

1 Introduction

In light of the increasing prevalence of the use of social media, courts and judges both in Australia and the United States have begun to adopt a more flexible approach

A. Henderson (✉)
Australian National University, Canberra, Australia
e-mail: Andrew.Henderson@canberra.edu.au

A. Henderson
University of Canberra, Canberra, Australia

© Springer Nature Singapore Pte Ltd. 2018

T. Sourdin and A. Zariski (eds.), *The Responsive Judge*, Ius Gentium: Comparative Perspectives on Law and Justice 67, https://doi.org/10.1007/978-981-13-1023-2_5

to the use of social media. A number of State Courts in the United States have Facebook, Twitter and even Instagram accounts (National Center for State Courts n.d.). In Australia, only a handful of courts have established a social media presence, there is no uniform practice and all are at different stages of adoption. A number of courts have no presence whatsoever. South Australia is managed collectively by the South Australian Courts Administration (@CourtsinSA). Others have energetically adopted social media including the Supreme Court of Victoria (@SCVSupreme-Court), County Court (@CountyCourtVic) and Magistrates Court (@MagCourtVic). The Family Court of Australia and the Federal Circuit Court of Australia use social media predominately as a notification service of publications and changes in the law (@FamilyCourtAU, @FedCctCourtAU)).

Academics and judges in Australia have enthusiastically encouraged more courts to establish a social media presence principally on two grounds: as a means of improving public confidence through transparency; and as a means of protecting judicial independence by providing the opportunity to explain judicial decision-making (Blackham and Williams 2014, 2016, 2017; Krawitz 2014a, b; Warren 2014). That is, rather than as a means of communicating with parties to proceedings, social media could be used as a mass communication vehicle to place judging in "context" (Goldberg 2015; Weinstein 1995; Fuller 1978)—both for judges and the community.

1.1 Social Media and Responsive Judging: An Australian Context

Contemporary Australian commentary shares some of what is referred to elsewhere in this volume as "classic" responsive judging.[1] For example, Weinstein's call for judges to use their discretion to communicate with the public to avoid them being "left in the dark" is an alternative method of expressing a desire for transparency (Weinstein 1995, 95). It also shares some common characteristics with concerns about a perceived loss of trust in judges among other public officers (Fortunato 1999; McKenzie 2012)—although in Australia public confidence in Judges would appear to have traditionally remained high or increased (Roy Morgan 2017).

However, Australian commentary has tended to focus to a greater extent on the role of social media as a platform for courts to advocate for themselves, rather than as a means of engaging in conversation with lawyers, litigants or the community. For example, Blackham and Williams maintain that the traditional isolation of judges remains an important consideration:

> [W]hile judges must be accountable to the public, they are not expected or supposed to be responsive to popular will or sentiment. The task is to strike an appropriate balance. (Blackham and Williams 2017)

---

[1] See Sourdin and Zariski's discussion in 'Introduction' in Chapter "What is Responsive Judging?" of this book.

Former Chief Justice of Victoria, Marilyn Warren, argued that "open justice" with the consequent benefits of confidence and accountability should underpin courts' and judges' engagement with social media (Warren 2014, 47).

Where Australian courts have adopted a policy with regard to social media, it has tended to reinforce the "one way" nature of communications. For example, the Family Court of Australia and the Federal Circuit Court of Australia (which adopted identical policies) explicitly identify the objectives and use of their social media accounts as "notification of: judgments; registry closures; legislation and rules changes; selected job vacancies; new publications and forms and changes to existing ones; and media releases" (Federal Circuit Court of Australia 2016; Family Court of Australia 2016). However, what the Family Court in particular is able to publish, and the Federal Circuit Court in its family law jurisdiction, is heavily circumscribed by restrictions contained in s 121 of the *Family Law Act 1974* (Cth).

Courts in Victoria, which have more actively adopted communications through Twitter and Facebook, have also tended to adopt the same "open justice" motif that was advanced by the former Chief Justice. The Supreme Court's *Media Policies and Practices* notes that it is intended to "facilitate full and accurate reporting of what the Court does"—an objective consistent with that jurisdiction's *Open Courts Act 2013* (Vic). However, it also takes the additional step of identifying as the other objective to "further the community's understanding of the Court's function and its work" (Supreme Court of Victoria 2016), although it is silent on how that objective might be *actively* achieved.

Where Australian commentary or courts have, therefore, addressed the issue of engagement with social media, they have consistently identified the public as the principal audience. This is consistent with the "mass communication" nature of the medium. While there are some Australian judges who are known to have social media accounts (Blackham and Williams 2016), it is difficult to argue that social media might be the best or most direct manner in which judges might attempt to influence or "self-present" to one another or the executive (Baum 2008).

No Australian court has identified social media as a means of communicating with individual litigants. This is unsurprising since most courts already have a direct line of communication to litigants and their lawyers without the need to trawl through thousands of social media messages.

If one accepts that Weinstein's "passive" to "passionate" judging (Weinstein Weinstein 1995, 102) might represent a spectrum, what tends to be advocated in Australia is an approach to the use of social media as a form of announcement or pronouncement of the business of the courts—a position closer to Weinstein's "passive" judge than to a "passionate" role. This is somewhat at odds with the more advanced or active role that Oliver Wendell Holmes and others have advocated (Holmes 1881; Goldberg 2015). That is, in an Australian context, social media is less about the "conversation" (Graff 2012)—the two way exchange of information between the judge and the community—and closer to a one way form of communication. It is not about "responsive judging" but closer to a traditional or passive use of media to communicate *to* (and not *with*) the community.

1.2 Active Use of Social Media and Responsive Judging

Social media nevertheless carries with it the possibility of opening a conversation with the wider community and allowing judges to make themselves more open to direct engagement with the individuals who their decisions affect, both directly and indirectly. That is, to judge with an understanding of the polycentric nature of a dispute (Fuller 1978) or the "networked" context within which judging happens in both its conceptual and, now, technological meanings.

Engaging directly with the community through social media, rather than relying on the traditional media, carries with it some concerns. From a practical perspective, Court staff have expressed their concerns with the time consuming nature of maintaining "conversations" with litigants, practitioners and the public. They have also expressed concern at their lack of expertise in what is perceived to be a specialised form of communication (Krawitz 2014a; Keyzer et al. 2013). From a more traditional perspective, the avoidance of bias and partiality, has also been identified as an issue where a judge were to step directly into the defence or discussion of a decision that she has published (Krawitz 2014b; Blackham and Williams 2017; Jackson and Shelly 2016).

Advocacy for a more "passionate" approach to the use of social media to open a conversation with the community also carries with it a number of assumptions—two of which this chapter seeks to assess. The first is that in an environment where the public is presented with an enormously diverse range of topics and sources available, they will pay attention to information being published by the courts themselves. The second is the implicit belief that social media can influence public perceptions. Despite the lengthy history of advocacy on behalf of responsive judging, there appears to be little empirical data to suggest that where it is deployed, it can affect change in either the judge or the judged.

As a means of establishing an initial assessment of the effect of opening communication through social media with the community, this chapter seeks to examine the breadth and depth of commentary on the High Court of Australia's decision in *Plaintiff M68-2015 v Minister for Immigration and Border Protection* [2016] HCA 1 through one common social media platform—Twitter. As a means of providing context, comparison and counterpoint, this paper also draws on data from concurrent social media events, earlier research on Twitter and the High Court (Henderson 2016) and the United States Court of Appeals for the Ninth Circuit decision in *State of Washington v Trump* United States Court of Appeals for the Ninth Circuit, No. 17-35105, 9 February 2017.

Twitter has been referred to as a 'micro-blogging' social media platform. Users publish messages—tweets—of up to 280 characters in length and may include pictures, hyperlinks and video. Users may also choose to subscribe to other users' accounts—referred to as 'following'—to automatically receive messages from that account. Users are also able to on forward—referred to as 'retweeting'—messages they receive to their own followers, thereby sharing those messages with others. Twitter, and social media generally, is a short term, instantaneous means of sharing information and ideas. Accordingly, this case study can only ever assess a moment in time rather than long-term engagement or changes in opinion among users. However, by drawing on research around earlier High Court decisions, potential changes or trends can also be sketched.

This case study is also focused on a single jurisdiction—the High Court of Australia. Its role as the apex Australian appellate court means that the matters that come before it set precedent nationally. In its capacity as the principal jurisdiction for constitutional law, its decisions also have a significant effect on the community and its governance.

The chapter does not consider the effect or impact of more limited objectives to social media use, for example, its use as a means of notification to individual parties or practitioners, or to groups that might directly affected by a decision, which Weinstein's model of passionate judging incorporates (Weinstein 1995). That is simply not a purpose to which Australian courts have put their social media accounts and therefore there is no available data. What it does, however, is attempt to assess whether the broader concepts of "network" and "context", to include judging as a public act (Fuller 1978), can stand out among the hyper-din of social media and affect how individuals perceived or understand that act.

What this study finds is that there is limited evidence from the case study that communication about the High Court is either widely disseminated or affective. Given the concerns that have been expressed about the dangers of judges stepping into discussions about their own judgments, the chapter argues that there is substantially more research required to by undertaken as to whether those risks are outweighed by the perceived rewards.

2 Breaking Through the Din: Publishing Information on the Courts

Encouraging Courts to be active social media players is in part advanced on the basis that it provides a further measure of transparency to the justice system and judicial decision making with a consequential benefit to public confidence. The manner in which the community gets access to current affairs generally, and judicial proceedings specifically, has definitely changed, raising important questions about whether the courts themselves should also change. However, in proposing that social media may provide an answer, there are two assumptions made: there is the opportunity to cut through the diverse array of subjects discussed daily on social media; and a desire among users to learn more about the justice system through that medium.

2.1 *Open Justice and Empty Galleries*

The idea that Courts operate in public has been a feature of common law justice systems since at least the 17th century. In *Raybos Australia Pty Ltd. & Anor v Jones* (1985) 2 NSWLR 47, Kirby P identifies references to public trials as early as 1649 while Nettheim refers to Sir Edward Coke's *Institutes of the Laws of England* published in 1642 (Nettheim 1984). In *Hogan v Hinch* (2011) 243 CLR 506, then Chief Justice French tied open justice to notions of a fair trial, judicial impartiality, judicial independence and the maintenance of public confidence in the courts.

In the United States, the Supreme Court in *Richmond Newspapers Inc v Virginia* 448 US 555 (1980) found that the arbitrary exclusion of the public and the media from a courtroom is "an abridgement of the freedoms of speech and of the press protected by the First Amendment [of the US Constitution]". The guarantee that Courts will be open appears in different forms in the constitutions of 40 of the United States (Abram 2000).

In Australia, the conduct of courts in public has been identified as a fundamental element of the judicial process, progressively transforming it from an "attribute" in *Dickason v Dickason* (1913) 17 CLR 50 to a "rule" in *Russell v Russell* (1976) 134 CLR 495 subject only to limited exceptions that former Chief Justice French found in *Hogan* will not "lightly be extended". However, it is neither embodied in an explicit constitutional guarantee nor has it been elevated to the status of an implied right.

While the conduct of courts in public is cast as a principal means of ensuring transparency, individuals now rarely visit courts or have the time available to sit through hours or even days of hearings. The advent of more extensive media and more universally consistent levels of literacy has meant that the traditional model of the public visiting the courts to see justice 'being done' is outmoded (Gamble and Mohr 1996; Keyzer 1999).

The role of the media as a proxy for the public has been more formally recognised by the United States Supreme Court in *Richmond Newspapers*. In Australia then Chief Justice Brennan of the High Court has gone as far as to suggest that the function of the courts and the media are "interlocking" in the maintenance of the rule of law (Brennan 1997). As a result of the recognition of the role of the media as an intermediary in communicating the work of the courts to the public, Australian courts have placed a greater emphasis on improving media access to information about judicial proceedings (Davies and Then 2004). For example, every Australian Commonwealth Court now has a position designated as a Public Information Officer (or PIO) whose role is to liaise with members of the media and the wider public concerning current proceedings (Johnstone 2008; Nelson 1995). However, with the advent of the internet and social media, the role of traditional media is perceived to have come increasingly under pressure.

2.2 Social Media: Killing the Messenger?

The use of social media is endemic. In 2016 there were an estimated 2.34 billion social media accounts across all platforms, projected to rise to 2.95 billion in 2020 (Statista 2017). Facebook is by far the most popular social media platform globally with 1.94 billion active users using the platform each month (Facebook 2017) with Twitter reporting 328 million active users monthly (Twitter 2017l). In 2016, a survey of 800 Australians found that 87% used the internet daily, more than two thirds (69%) of which visited social media sites (Sensis 2016). Research in the United States has found a similar proportion of adults using social media (Perrin 2015). Some Australian users have reported accessing social media five or more times each day with half reporting that it was the first thing that they did each morning.

The ubiquitous nature of social media has changed the manner in which people now access information about a diverse range of topics. While social media platforms generally began as personal communications or what have been referred to as 'micro-blogs', they have become a much more frequent means of accessing information. Recent studies have suggested that social networks are being used for health information (Fox 2011), recommendations on social outings (Rainie et al. 2011) tracking current topics in academic research (Gruzd and Goertzen 2013) and undertaking undergraduate research (Kim et al. 2011).

Social media has also become a popular source for information on current affairs (Kwak et al. 2010), particularly for younger users. Reuters has found that 53% of a sample of users from 26 countries used social media to access news with 12% reporting it was their main source of news (Newman et al. 2016). In Australia and the United States it was higher with 18 and 14% using social media as their principal news source respectively (Newman et al. 2016).

Media organisations who now find their legacy activities such as print and cable news challenged have been quick to adopt electronic platforms, including social media, as a means of distributing their content (Nielsen et al. 2016). Even then, they are perceived to be struggling to maintain their unique role. Reuters found that users were not reliant on or loyal to one particular media brand or publisher. Users generally reported an increased use of news 'aggregators' or apps that collect headlines and breaking news from several sources based on user preferences. As a result, a larger proportion of users were taken to articles selected for them, rather than making their own selection from a website (Newman et al. 2016).

On its face, this would tend to suggest social media platforms may provide a significant means of publishing information about the justice system generally. There is arguably the opportunity for the courts to step outside traditional media channels and communicate directly with the community—to (re)create virtual public galleries. Examples of where proceedings have been the subject of social media commentary would tend to reinforce this view. For example, the day on which Oscar Pistorius' evidence in his trial for the murder of his partner was reported, there were 168,000 Twitter posts from 58,000 users—representing more than 80% of all online content published in connection with the trial at that time (Granger 2014). His sentencing in October 2014 generated a little less than half of that interest.

However, leaving aside the number of users, it is important to understand not only the size of the potential audience for the courts, but both the volume of information that is already being produced into which the courts are being encouraged to insert themselves and the competition that they face in making themselves heard.

2.3 *Of Judges, Rock Stars and Judicial Rock Stars: Cutting Through the Hyper Din*

The most current statistics published by Facebook in 2013 disclosed that 4.75 billion pieces of content are shared daily on its platform (Facebook 2013). Given the rise in the number Facebook users, that statistic can only have increased. Twitter also estimated that in 2013 there is on average 500 million tweets sent each day (Krikorian 2013).

In the context of competition for users' attention, some individual accounts have an overwhelming reach. In Australia, the popular band Five Seconds of Summer is the most popular account on Twitter with almost 11 million 'followers' (Twitter Twitter 2017a)—that is, users who have subscribed to messages from that account. In the United States, those numbers are dwarfed by the most popular Twitter account in that country. For example, Katy Perry has 99.5 million followers (Twitter 2017h). On 1 February 2016, former One Direction band member Harry Styles tweeted a lyric written by his ex-girlfriend Taylor Swift. The tweet went to Styles' more than 30 million followers and was retweeted more than 710,000 times making it the second most retweeted message of 2016 (Twitter 2016).

Despite allegations that traditional media brands have lost their appeal, the number of followers reported by media organisations is also much more substantial than the courts. In Australia, ABC News (the public broadcaster) has more than 1.3 million followers (Twitter 2017b) which increases to 1.8 million followers if ABC's News 24 account is included (Twitter 2017c). Daily newspapers *The Age* and *The Sydney Morning Herald* also have 1.5 million followers between them (Twitter 2017k, j). All four media accounts rank within the top 100 Twitter accounts in Australia (Twitter Counter 2017). Globally, Associated Press has more than 10 million followers (Twitter 2017d), the BBC's News Breaking account has more than 32 million followers (Twitter 2017e) and CNN more than 35 million followers (Twitter 2017f). The reports of the messenger's death may have been grossly exaggerated—or at least premature.

By comparison, the number of Twitter followers that Australian courts can muster is minuscule—the Supreme Court of Victoria that has most enthusiastically embraced social media claims only 8200 followers (Twitter 2017i). Even so-called judicial "rock stars" (Giles 2015) like former High Court Justice Michael Kirby do not reach the same number of users (Twitter 2017g).

2.4 A Case Study: #Letthemstay

In order to explore the potential for information about specific decisions to cut through or gain an audience in the existing hyper din and the role of existing Twitter accounts, Twitter activity around a particular decision in the High Court of Australia was examined in more detail.

On 3 February 2016, the High Court of Australia published orders and reasons in *Plaintiff M68-2015 v Minister for Immigration and Border Protection. Plaintiff M68* concerned an application by a Bangladeshi woman who had sought asylum in Australia. The boat aboard which she and other asylum seekers had attempted to gain entry to Australia was intercepted by Australian authorities and the applicant was removed to an immigration detention centre on Nauru.

Under a memorandum of understanding between the Governments of Australia and Nauru, a regional processing centre for asylum seekers has been established on Nauru where asylum seekers are detained until their status as refugees has been determined. In August 2014, the applicant was transferred to Australia for medical care which could not be provided on Nauru. Before she could be returned, an application was made under the High Court's original jurisdiction seeking a determination that her detention on Nauru and the operation of the detention centre were *ultra vires* of the Commonwealth's legislative power under the Australian *Constitution*.

The application received widespread media attention in large part because, if the application were successful, a number of other asylum seekers and their children who were temporarily in Australia would also be unable to be transferred to Nauru—including 37 infants and 50 older children (Gordon et al. 2016). The decision also received significant attention on Twitter with the hashtag #letthemstay 'trending' (i.e. being included with a greater frequency in Twitter messages) in Australia.

Earlier research found that Twitter messages about judicial decisions or court events tended to increase in volume 24–48 h before the day on which the event was to occur and fall away 24–48 h after the event (Henderson 2016). The focus of this research is on testing the extent to which courts may be able to take advantage of social media to explain or defend decisions (Warren 2014; Blackham and Williams 2016, 2017). Only Twitter messages for the period after the decision was published were examined.

Based on an initial survey of Twitter messages around the event to determine what form of search would produce the most relevant and accurate results, all Twitter messages including tweets and retweets and using the words or phrases 'High Court', #letthemstay, 'nauru', 'M28' and 'offshore detention', either alone or together, were retrieved and examined for 3, 4 and 5 February 2016. From the initial search set of approximately 129,000 messages retrieved, duplicates and messages not relevant to the proceedings were removed leaving a sample of 70,198 messages (Table 1).

Consistent with previous research, the volume of Twitter messages dropped in the period immediately following the decision. Given that the discussion of asylum seekers was also not specifically related to the High Court, the sample was also coded for mentions of the Court and the decision (Table 2).

Table 1 Number of Twitter Messages

		Frequency	Percent	Valid percent	Cumulative percent
Valid	03-FEB-16	33,362	47.5	47.5	47.5
	04-FEB-16	28,770	41.0	41.0	88.5
	05-FEB-16	8066	11.5	11.5	100.0
	Total	70,198	100.0	100.0	

Table 2 Number and % of Court mentions each day

			Court mention		Total
			No	Yes	
Time	03-FEB-16	Count	21,267	12,095	33,362
		%	63.7	36.3	100.0
	04-FEB-16	Count	25,685	3085	28,770
		%	89.3	10.7	100.0
	05-FEB-16	Count	7167	899	8066
		%	88.9	11.1	100.0
Total		Count	54,119	16079	70,198
		% within time	77.1	22.9	100.0

Consistent with the overall fall in Twitter messages, mentions of the Court and the decision also fall the more time elapses, dropping to only 899 within 48 h of the decision.

In the context of the potential for the courts to adopt a commentary role outside the scope of media commentary, the messages were further coded based on their origin: media; advocate organisation; popular celebrity; academic commentary; or no apparent affiliation (Table 3).

Advocacy for a more active role for courts in social media based on the assumption that there is a waiting audience is a difficult argument to make. As noted earlier, the total number of messages (70,198) or the total number of messages mentioning the decision (16,079) is substantially dwarfed by the number of messages being sent each day (500,000) or one pop star's break up with an ex-girlfriend occurring at the same time (710,000). The issue is also not necessarily associated with the size of the potential audience either. The decision in *Washington v Trump* attracted only 143,000 messages.

Public attention also wanes quickly after the decision—similar to the public gallery, it is full when the court is sitting but empties quickly once proceedings end. However, there are some emerging issues within this sample that are notable.

Table 3 Court mentions by source

			Court mention		Total
			No	Yes	
Source	Academic	Count	4	1	5
		%	0.0	0.0	0.0
	Celebrity	Count	81	22	103
		%	0.1	0.1	0.1
	Media	Count	290	151	441
		%	0.5	0.9	0.6
	None	Count	53,434	15,818	69,252
		%	98.7	98.4	98.7
	Organisation	Count	310	87	397
		%	0.6	0.5	0.6
Total		Count	54,119	16,079	70,198
		% within court mention	100.0	100.0	100.0

3 Role of Traditional Media

Data on the number of accounts to which each message was delivered was also gathered. Collectively, 499 million accounts received one or more of the messages from the sample. That number does not represent individual users but the total number of deliveries to accounts. Some accounts may have received 2 or more messages from the sample and in fact some senders may have also received other messages from within the sample. However, the metric does give a broad indication of the potential audience.

Although messages directly from media sources represented a small proportion of all messages on the decision, as discussed earlier, they also distribute that information to substantial audiences. Messages sent by media represent deliveries to more than 250 million accounts, That is, less than 1% of all Twitter messages in relation to the decision were seen by a little more than 50% of the potential audience for Twitter messages whereas 98% of all messages that were sent by individuals were seen by 44% of the potential audience. This would tend to suggest that while there is a perception that more active engagement by courts *directly* in social media may somehow provide a more accurate picture of proceedings, Twitter users are still substantial users of media as a means of gathering information—an outcome consistent with the discussion of media "aggregators" earlier in this chapter.

What this suggests is that perhaps rather than courts seeking to circumvent or develop a direct channel of communication to the public as has been suggested by Warren, Blackham and Williams, and others (Warren 2014; Blackham and Williams 2017), courts should examine the extent to which traditional media might remain the best available means of disseminating information.

4 Role of Advocacy Organisations

In earlier research concerning two High Court decisions in September and October 2014, the total number of Twitter messages was only 1448. *M68* was the subject of a substantially greater amount of Twitter attention.

It is arguable that there is an increasingly large (virtual) public gallery for the High Court. However, one difference between this event and the earlier research is the role of advocacy organisations. In the earlier research one of the decisions examined was *CPCF v Minister for Immigration and Border Protection* [2015] HCA 1 which also involved the diversion and detention of asylum seekers. The hearing attracted 851 Twitter messages, the largest proportion of which came directly from media and advocacy organisations. In *M68*, advocacy organisations were much more active. Despite less than 1% of all Twitter messages coming from that source, messages by advocacy organisations were rapidly retweeted. Messages from the Human Rights Law Centre, in tweets and retweets, represented 6% of all activity while messages from the Asylum Seekers Resource Centre (including its CEO) represented another 5%.

A further difference between the proceedings is the subject matter. *CPCF* dealt with adult asylum seekers. A particular rallying point in *M68* was the effect of the decision on infants and children. There were 16,629 (23.6%) messages from all sources making reference to babies and children.

4.1 Is There a (Virtual) Public Gallery?

What this collected data suggests is that advocacy for a more active role for courts in social media based on the assumption that there is a waiting audience who are no longer reliant on traditional media brands is a difficult argument to make. Media organisations, while representing a small proportion of that traffic still commanded a large audience through followers and retweeted messages. The competition which courts face, the hyper din that they need to break through, is therefore significant.

Nevertheless, there is still a potential audience where action is taken in a timely fashion. If it is the intention to use social media to defend or explain the process, it needs to occur almost immediately on the decision being published—which raises a further question of the purpose of publishing reasons or the manner in which they need to be published.

This data also suggests that where a court does choose to actively engage in discussions on social media, it need not do so for every decision. The subject matter, role of third parties and media interest may provide an indicator for where there is a need to take a greater role.

However, this still assumes that there is a purpose and benefit to engaging actively with social media. That is, that the reasonable user's opinions or beliefs may be affected by what they see on their smartphones as they wait for the Clapham omnibus.

5 Can Social Media Be Influential?

In 2012, a strange epidemic caught the attention of people across North America. Individuals would appear on social media videos and, as a result of a dare by friends, would unceremoniously dump buckets of iced water on their heads before naming others to attempt the same behaviour. By mid-2014, the epidemic had become so widespread that even a former President of the United States (Steel 2014) as well as the then President (CBS DC 2014) had been affected.

The amyotrophic lateral sclerosis (or ALS) Ice Bucket Challenge is one of a number of examples of so called "viral" social media events. They range from the frivolous, such as the Harlem Shake meme, which at its peak in early 2013 saw as many as 4000 different versions of the meme uploaded by users to Youtube every day (almost 3 every minute) (McCarthy 2014), to the destructive such as the "Blue Whale" social media "game" which has allegedly been linked to the deaths of a series of Russian teenagers and prompted the arrest of its creator (Bershidskky 2017).[2]

Empirically, the potential for social media to influence, persuade or motivate is difficult to ignore. Anecdotally, these types of viral events or memes suggest that there is a substantial capacity for social media to affect individuals' behaviour, even for the few short minutes needed to dump iced water or don a horse costume and dance badly in front of a camera (Heyden 2013).

In a more practical or observable sense, there is even some empirical evidence of the capacity of social media to have either ongoing or consequential effects albeit for brief periods. For example, the ALS Association in the United States reported that between July and August 2014 it had received double the value of donations from the Ice Bucket challenge than it had reported for the whole of the financial year (Steel 2014). The potential for long term changes to behaviour are more questionable (van der Linden 2017).

While the inclination of the current President of the United States to use social media as a means of communicating with the voting public is notorious (Bender and Nicholas 2017), empirical evidence of social media affecting beliefs about government and politics is much more challenging to identify, often inconclusive and sometimes contradictory.

The role of social media as an alternative to traditional media in influencing voters in the most recent United States and even the French presidential elections has begun to generate discussion and analysis (Hine et al. 2017). There is research to suggest that social media is a platform for communicating with potential voters. For example, in 2015 60% of 18–29 year olds in the United States reported accessing political news through Facebook (Mitchell et al. 2015). More than a third of 18–29 year old respondents to a recent survey also reported that social media was the most "helpful"

---

[2]See Chapter "The #BlueWhale Challenge to the Indian judiciary: A Critical Analysis of the Response of the Indian Higher Judiciary to Risky Online Contents with Special Reference to the BlueWhale Suicide Game" of this book in which Dr. Debarati Halder provides an in-depth discussion of the Blue Whale game.

source of information about the 2016 United States presidential election (Gottfried et al. 2016).

Of greater interest is the influence of social media sources other than those directly associated with the candidates. The most recent United States presidential election has prompted a body of work into the extent to which social media accounts associated with what has come to be referred to as the "alt-right" attracted, marshalled or motivated the American voting public. What had been dubbed by users themselves as "the Great Meme War" and the role of some forms of social media to motivate supporters achieved a degree of public notoriety following a shooting in a Washington DC pizza restaurant allegedly prompted by stories about members of the Clinton campaign and human trafficking (Tate 2016). Some studies have suggested that the use of various social media platforms may have had the effect of galvanising or motivating voters (Masip et al. 2017; Sáez-Mateu 2017).

5.1 *Echo Chambers or Accidental Exposure?*

To the extent that advocacy for courts' engagement in social media assumes that there is a tangible benefit in terms of taking the opportunity to engage with public opinions or perceptions and potentially influence them, the jury is still out.

Despite the attention that has been given by researchers to the effect of social media in mobilising, persuading or motivating users, particularly in relation to politics, there would appear to be no clear position on what that effect is. The tight knit nature of social networks has been identified as resulting in echo chambers where users self-select into online communities that confirm and reconfirm ideas and beliefs (Canini et al. 2011; Jonas et al. 2001). Alternatively, the sheer volume of online information means that even casual users are likely to happen across information without even actively seeking it out, leading to some research linking online access to increased political motivation Rojas and Puig-i-Abril 2009; Xenos et al. 2014).

More recently, two meta-analyses of research articles have attempted to identify trends or common characteristics which would tend to indicate influence, effect or changes in intention around political participation based on social media use (Boulianne 2015; Skoric et al. 2016). Both find that there is generally a positive correlation between participants' social media use and political participation. However, neither is able to identify trends in research that establish a causal link between them, leading one to conclude that "we do not know the causal effects of social media use on participation" and that "correlations of social media use and political participation could be spurious" (Boulianne 2015, 534).

There is a body of research to suggest that where the community is given more information about judicial proceedings, it can alter initial perceptions. Studies conducted in Australia (Indemaur et al. 2012) and overseas (de Keijser et al. 2007) have found that where individuals are provided with more information about a criminal offender, it can result in changes in the group's view of what is an appropriate sentence. However, these are panel studies based on providing more than the Twitter limit of 280 characters worth of additional information to participants.

Determining the influential nature of social media is therefore notoriously difficult and inconclusive. However, as a starting point, we are able to review the content of Twitter messages to determine to what extent there is any discussion about the High Court's decision and whether that discussion suggests a positive or negative perception of the Court or its decision. In doing so, we can gain a very simple indication of the extent to which users are already influenced based on what they have already seen.

5.2 *"The High Court Is High", the "Nutty Ninth" and Other Epithets*

The sample of Twitter messages in respect of the High Court's decision in *M68* was coded for mentions of the Court and then again for whether the message expressed a positive, negative or neutral view of the decision (Table 4).

As a proportion of Twitter messages that mention the Court, those that express any opinion at all is very low. As a proportion of all messages in the sample, it is less than 1%. The source of opinion can also be determined by source (Table 5).

Table 4 Court mentions—positive, negative or neutral

	Negative	Neutral	Positive	Total
Court mention	391	15,686	2	16,079
%	2.4	97.6	0.0	100.0

Table 5 Expression of opinion by source

		Negative	Neutral	Positive	Total
Academic	Count	0	1	0	5
	%	0.0	20.0	0.0	100.0
Celebrity	Count	1	21	0	103
	%	1.0	20.4	0.0	100.0
Media	Count	1	150	0	441
	%	0.2	34.0	0.0	100.0
None	Count	389	15,427	2	69,252
	%	0.6	22.3	0.0	100.0
Organisation	Count	0	87	0	397
	%	0.0	21.9	0.0	100.0
Total	Count	391	15,686	2	70,198
	%	0.6	22.3	0.0	100.0

The largest proportion of Twitter messages expressing an opinion come from accounts with no apparent affiliation. However, the proportion of all messages is still very small.

This is a substantial difference compared to earlier research and the High Court's decision in *CPCF* with only 1 message from the more than 800 reviewed expressing any opinion of the Court—which was neutral.

Some of the messages were quite strident in their criticism, including alleging that "the high court is high" (sic) (1), the Court was racist (17), the Court had confirmed "rendition" was lawful (14) or the Court and law lacked a sense of "morality" (147). Some users did attempt to counter criticism by pointing out the need for adherence to the law and the role of the Parliament in agreeing to the legislative framework that underpinned the arrangement with Nauru. However, there was no apparent engagement between the two groups.

It is arguable that the large proportion of neutral tweets is not indicative of a lack of engagement but in fact may be the reservation of a position or an acknowledgement of the authority of the High Court to make a determination without criticism or endorsement. However, the extent to which the High Court is held in such regard by the community as to avoid criticism is not something into which any research is immediately available. In that sense it reinforces the idea that before any court embarks on active engagement with social media, there needs to be some research into the extent to which any engagement at all is required as a means of addressing a perceived loss of faith or confidence—either to determine the extent to which the silent majority requires influencing or perhaps whether active engagement with them may in fact erode pre-existing confidence.

6 The Ninth Circuit and the Media

There is also an arguably unique cultural distinction between the discussion of the Australian High Court and the Ninth Circuit decision in *State of Washington v Trump*. Of the 143,000 Twitter messages concerning the travel ban which was the subject of the proceedings, a little more than 20,000 (13%) mentioned the Court. Among the 20,000 mentions, one fifth was negative, a larger volume of criticism than that directed at the High Court. However, unlike the discussion of the Australian Court, 14% of all negative mentions came from media accounts.

An interesting feature of the commentary on the Court's decision was the propensity for the President and his staff to comment directly on the merits of the decision and on the members of the Court itself. For example, President Trump was reported as: expressing the opinion that the Court had put national security "at risk"; comparing the Court to "bad high school students"; and arguing that the Courts were "so political". Many of these observations were republished by media accounts. While the media arguably was doing no more than publishing a quote, given the substantial audience to which media accounts publish, it becomes reflected in Twitter activity.

7 Addressing the (Virtual) Gallery

As discussed earlier, the nature of the proceedings in *M68* were highly emotive which is also likely to produce strong views. The virtual public gallery of the High Court clearly had some rowdy members. If one accepts for the moment that there is the potential to influence opinion, there is arguably the opportunity for the Court or someone on its behalf to correct misconceptions where they arise.

However, the proportion of opinions being expressed is very small. Further, and as was discussed earlier, the number of court mentions also falls dramatically shortly after the decision is published. Unless there was almost immediate action to address or correct discussions, the utility of engaging in the online debate is questionable. There is also the question, outside the scope of this paper, about whose role it is to engage in that discussion. Is it the role of individual judges? If it is the role of a media officer, what authority do they have to speak on the Court's behalf? And at what point does it become pointless or even foolish to attempt to explain in 280 characters or less distinctions between law and morality or that High Court Justices are not impaired by a hallucinogen?

8 Breaking Through the Hyper-din?

Every day on social media, users exchange billions of items of information. They like, share, tweet, poke and retweet to audiences of hundreds, thousands or even millions. This exchange happens simultaneously, 24 h each day, 7 days each week.

Advocating for courts to become actively involved in this "cocktail party from hell" as a means of becoming more responsive in its broader sense assumes that there is a waiting audience open to differing points of view on the work of the courts. This may, in part, be true. As a surrogate of the packed public galleries of bygone age, social media offers a potentially vast audience. However, the overwhelming choice of material available to users means that breaking through the background noise is challenging.

Identifying the merits of engaging in social media is also difficult to discern both on the basis of current large scale research and the samples used here. The attention span in which to achieve meaningful communication is very limited as is the physical and temporal space into which the courts can insert themselves.

In light of the concerns expressed about the practical and perceived effects on the courts and the justice system, and to the extent that courts choose to purse social media a vehicle to communicate *with* (not just *to*) the public, there is substantially more research required to determine whether there are in fact tangible benefits. What this survey is also unable to determine is to what extent if courts were to step into the public debate and respond to allegations of being "high" or "nutty" what consequent effect that may have on the attention and perception of social media users. On its face, the short attention span of users might also tend to suggest that it could be very little.

Alternatively, the ongoing popularity of media outlets, despite the move to alternative platforms, means that arguably direct communication with the public is neither useful nor necessary. Instead, courts should examine their relationship with media organisations to leverage their current followers as a means of disseminating information about their work.

One of the clearest and perhaps superficially simplest barriers to overcome is what exactly is the objective and therefore benefit that the courts seek to achieve? Policy statements by Australian courts on the objectives of their engagement with media are, as this chapter notes, sparse both in terms of their number and content. This objective is superficially simple though, since moving to a truly responsive judiciary means confronting the change from "passive" to "passionate" and overcoming the "self-enforced silence" (McKenzie 2012) about the nature of judging.

References

Abram S (2000) Problems of contemporaneous construction in state constitutional interpretation. Brandeis Law J 28:613–642

Baum L (2008) Judges and their audiences: a perspective on judicial behavior. Princeton University Press, Princeton

Bender M, Nicholas P (2017) Trump pushing Big White House changes as Russia crisis grows. Wall Street J, 27 May. http://www.wsj.com/articles/trump-eyeing-white-house-shakeup-1495831679

Bershidskky L (2017) Why the Russian suicide game went global. Bloomberg. Accessed 12 May 2017

Blackham A, Williams G (2014) Social media and the courts. Law Inst J 88:31–33

Blackham A, Williams G (2016) Social media and the judiciary: a challenge to judicial independence. In: Annian-Welsh R, Crowe J (eds) Judicial independence in Australia: contemporary challenges, future directions. The Federation Press, Sydney, pp 223–240

Blackham A, Williams G (2017) A balancing act. Law Inst J (May 2017). Accessed 12 May 2017

Boulianne S (2015) Social media use and participation: a meta-analysis of current research. Inf Commun Soc 18(5):524–538

Brennan G (1997) The third branch and the fourth estate. Broadcasting, Society and the Law, University College, Dublin, 22 April 1997

Canini K, Suh B, Pirolli P (2011) Finding credible information sources in social networks based on content and social structure. Third IEEE International Conference on Privacy, Security, Risk, and Trust, Boston, 9 October 2011

CBS DC (2014) Obama rejects ALS ice bucket challenge, will donate to charity instead. CBSDC, 12 May 2017. http://washington.cbslocal.com/2014/08/13/obama-rejects-als-ice-bucket-challenge-will-donate-to-charity-instead/

Davies GL, Then S-N (2004) Why the public needs a Court Information Officer. Aust Law Reform Comm Reform J 85:9–11

de Keijser JW, van Koppen PJ, Elffers H (2007) Bridging the gap between judges and the public? A multi-method study. J Exp Criminol 3(2):131–161

Dowd M (2013) Lost in space. New York Times, 23 April 2013. http://tinyurl.com/p3t3j2p

Facebook (2013) Did you know that… Facebook. https://www.facebook.com/FacebookSingapore/posts/563468333703369. Accessed 11 Dec 2017

Facebook (2017) Facebook reports first quarter 2017 results. Facebook. https://s21.q4cdn.com/399680738/files/doc_financials/2017/Facebook-Reports-First-Quarter-2017-Results.pdf. Accessed 11 Dec 2017

Family Court of Australia (2016) Official use of Twitter by the Family Court. Family Court of Australia. http://www.familycourt.gov.au/wps/wcm/connect/fcoaweb/about/about-social-media/. Accessed 11 Dec 2017

Federal Circuit Court of Australia (2016) Official use of Twitter by the Federal Circuit Court. http://www.federalcircuitcourt.gov.au/wps/wcm/connect/fccweb/about/about-social-media/. Accessed 11 Dec 2017

Fortunato S (1999) On a judge's duty to speak extrajudicially: rethinking the strategy of silence. Georgetown J Legal Ethics 12:679–716

Fox S (2011) The social life of health information. Pew Research Center. http://www.pewinternet.org/files/oldmedia//Files/Reports/2011/PIP_Social_Life_of_Health_Info.pdf

Fuller L (1978) The forms and limits of adjudication. Harvard Law Rev 92:353–409

Gamble H, Mohr R (1996) Courts and communities: tensions and accommodations. In: Mohr R, Lloyd S (eds) Delivering with diversity. University of Woolongong, Woolongong, NSW

Giles K (2015) The Honourable Justice Michael Kirby: witnessing the birth of a creative spirit. Arts Law Centre of Australia. http://www.artslaw.com.au/articles/entry/the-honourable-justice-michael-kirby-witnessing-the-birth-of-a-creative-spi. Accessed 11 Dec 2017

Goldberg J (2015) Judging responsibility, responsible judging. DePaul Law Rev 64:475–494

Gordon M, McKenzie N, Baker R (2016) The faces of the babies Australia wants to send back to 'hell' on Nauru. The Sydney Morning Herald, 2 February 2016. http://www.smh.com.au/federal-politics/political-news/the-faces-of-the-babies-australia-wants-to-send-back-to-hell-on-nauru-20160201-g[illegible].html

Gottfried J, Barthel M, Shearer E, Mitchell A (2016) The 2016 presidential campaign – a news event that's hard to miss. Pew Research Center. http://www.journalism.org/2016/02/04/the-2016-presidential-campaign-a-news-event-thats-hard-to-miss/

Graff G (2012) Courts are conversations: an argument for increased engagement by court leaders. Harvard Kennedy School

Granger L (2014) #OscarTrial: the social media stats the week Pistorius testified. http://tinyurl.com/qhg2yhr. Accessed 11 Dec 2017

Gruzd A, Goertzen M (2013) Wired academia: why social science scholars are using social media. 46th International Conference on System Sciences, Hawaii, 7 January 2013

Henderson A (2016) The High Court and the cocktail party from hell: can social media improve community engagement with the courts? J Judicial Adm 25(3):175–192

Heyden T (2013) Harlem Shake: tracking a meme over a month. BBC News Magazine. Accessed 12 May 2017

Hine GE, Onaolapo J, De Cristofaro E, Kourtellis N, Leontiadis I, Samaras R, Stringhini G, Blackburn J (2017) Kek, Cucks, and God Emperor Trump: a measurement study of 4chan's politically incorrect forum and its effects on the web. 11th International Conference on Web and Social Media, Montreal, Canada, 15–18 May 2017

Holmes OW (1881) The common law. American Bar Association, Chicago

Indemaur D, Roberts L, Spiranovic C, Mackenzie G, Gelb K (2012) A matter of judgment: the effect of information and deliberation on public attitudes to punishment. Punishment Soc 14:147–165

Jackson M, Shelly M (2016) The use of social media by Australian courts. Lexis Nexis. https://www.lexisnexis.com.au/en/insights-and-analysis/practice-intelligence/2017/30jan2017-the-use-of-social-media-by-australian-courts. Accessed 11 Nov 2017

Johnstone J (2008) The court media interface: bridging the divide. Aust Journalism Rev 30:27

Jonas E, Shultz-Hardt S, Frey D, Thelen N (2001) Confirmation bias in sequential information search after preliminary decisions: An expansion of dissonance theoretical research on selective exposure to information. J Pers Soc Psychol 80:557–571

Keyzer P (1999) What the courts and the media can do to improve the standard of media reporting of the work of the courts. Univ Technol Sydney Law Rev 1(1):50–158

Keyzer P, Johnston J, Pearson M, Rodrick S, Wallace A (2013) The courts and social media: what do judges and court workers think? Judicial Officers' Bull 25:47–51
Kim K-SK, Yoo-Lee E, Sin S-CJ (2011) Social media as information source: undergraduates' use and evaluation behavior. Proc the Am Soc Inf Sci Technol 48:1–3
Krawitz M (2014a) An examination of social media's impact on the courts in Australia. Doctor of Philosophy, School of Law, Murdoch University
Krawitz M (2014b) Summoned by social media: why Australian Courts should have social media accounts. J Judicial Adm 23:182–199
Krikorian R (2013) New Tweets per second record, and how!. Twitter Official Blog. https://blog.twitter.com/engineering/en_us/a/2013/new-tweets-per-second-record-and-how.html
Kwak H, Lee C, Park H, Moon S (2010) What is Twitter, A Social Network or News Media? 19th International Conference on the World Wide Web, Raleigh NC, 26 April 2010
Masip P, Suau-Martínez J, Ruiz-Caballero C (2017) Questioning the selective exposure to news: understanding the impact of social networks on political news consumption. Am Behav Sci (online)
McCarthy N (2014) Ice bucket challenge: ALS wikipedia page views increase 18-fold. Forbes, 8 September. https://www.forbes.com/sites/niallmccarthy/2014/09/08/ice-bucket-challenge-als-wikipedia-page-views-increase-18-fold-infographic/?utm_campaign=techtwittersf&utm_source=twitter&utm_medium=social#b9c0af55358c
McKenzie B (2012) Extrajudicial speech: judicial ethics in the new media age. Reynolds Court Media Law J 2:185–210
Mitchell A, Gottfried J, Matsa KE (2015) Millenials and political news: social media—the local TV for the next generation? Pew Research Center. http://www.journalism.org/2015/06/01/millennials-political-news/
National Center for State Courts (n.d.) Social Media and the Courts: State Links. National Center for State Courts. http://www.ncsc.org/Topics/Media/Social-Media-and-the-Courts/State-Links.aspx?cat=Social%20Media%20and%20the%20Courts#Puerto%20Rico. Accessed 30 May 2017
Nelson J (1995) The role of the public information officer in New South Wales courts. Judicial Officers Bull 7:33–38
Nettheim G (1984) The principle of open justice. Univ Tas Law Rev 8:25–45
Newman N, Fletcher R, Levy D, Nielsen RK (2016) Digital news report 2016. Reuters Institute for the Study of Journalism, Oxford
Nielsen RK, Cornia A, Kalogeropoulos A (2016) Challenges and opportunities for news media and journalism in an increasingly digital, mobile and social media environment. Reuters Institute for the Study of Journalism, Oxford
Perrin A (2015) Social media usage 2005–2015. Pew Research Centre. http://www.pewinternet.org/files/2015/10/PI_2015-10-08_Social-Networking-Usage-2005-2015_FINAL.pdf
Rainie L, Purcell K, Mitchell A, Rosenstiel T (2011) Where people get information about restaurants and other local businesses. Pew Research Center. http://www.pewinternet.org/files/old-media//Files/Reports/2011/PIP-Local-business.pdf
Rojas H, Puig-i-Abril E (2009) Mobilizers mobilized: information, expression, mobilization and participation in the digital age. J Comput-Mediated Commun 14(4):902–927
Roy Morgan (2017) Roy Morgan image of professions survey 2017. Roy Morgan, Sydney
Sáez-Mateu F (2017) Democracy, screens, identity, and social networks: the case of Donald Trump's election. Am Behav Sci (online)
Sensis (2016) Sensis social media report 2016. Accessed 1 June 2016
Skoric MM, Zhu Q, Goh D, Pang N (2016) Social media and citizen engagement: a meta-analytic review. New Media Soc 18(9):1817–1839
Statista (2017) Number of social media users worldwide from 2010 to 2020 (in billions). https://www.statista.com/statistics/278414/number-of-worldwide-social-network-users/. Accessed 6 June 2017
Steel E (2014) 'Ice bucket challenge' donations for A.L.S. research top $41 million. New York Times, 21 August 2014. https://nyti.ms/1oVFnn7

Supreme Court of Victoria (2016) Media policies and practices. Supreme Court of Victoria, Melbourne

Tate A (2016) Pizzagate: how a 4chan conspiracy went mainstream. The New Statesman. http://www.newstatesman.com/science-tech/internet/2016/12/pizzagate-how-4chan-conspiracy-went-mainstream. Accessed 11 Dec 2017

Twitter (2016) @HarryStyles. Twitter. https://twitter.com/Harry_Styles/status/694229236677120000. Accessed 11 Dec 2017

Twitter (2017a) @5SOS. Twitter. https://twitter.com/5SOS. Accessed 11 Dec 2017

Twitter (2017b) @ABCNews. Twitter. https://twitter.com/abcnews. Accessed 11 Dec 2017

Twitter (2017c) @ABCNews24. Twitter. https://twitter.com/ABCNews24. Accessed 11 Dec 2017

Twitter (2017d) @ap. Twitter. https://twitter.com/AP. Accessed 11 Dec 2017

Twitter (2017e) @BBCBreaking. Twitter. https://twitter.com/BBCBreaking. Accessed 11 Dec 2017

Twitter (2017f) @CNN. Twitter. https://twitter.com/CNN. Accessed 11 Dec 2017

Twitter (2017g) @HonMichaelKirby. Twitter. https://twitter.com/HonMichaelKirby?lang=en. Accessed 11 Dec 2017

Twitter (2017h) @KatyPerry. Twitter. https://twitter.com/katyperry. Accessed 11 Dec 2017

Twitter (2017i) @SCVSupremeCourt. Twitter. https://twitter.com/SCVSupremeCourt?lang=en. Accessed 11 Dec 2017

Twitter (2017j) @smh. Twitter. https://twitter.com/smh. Accessed 11 Dec 2017

Twitter (2017k) @theage. Twitter. https://twitter.com/theage. Accessed 11 Dec 2017

Twitter (2017l) Twitter announces first quarter 2017 results. Twitter. http://files.shareholder.com/downloads/AMDA-2F526X/4592846641x0x939178/F2518C3F-B4E7-48F9-A787-65A384693C16/TWTR_Q1_17_Earnings_Press_Release.pdf. Accessed 11 Dec 2017

Twitter Counter (2017) Top 100 followers in Australia. Twitter Counter. https://twittercounter.com/pages/100/australia. Accessed 11 Dec 2017

van der Linden S (2017) The nature of viral altruism and how to make it stick. Nat Hum Behav 41(1). Accessed 12 May 2017

Warren M (2014) Open justice in the technological age. Monash Univ Law Rev 40(1):45–58

Weinstein J (1995) Individual justice in mass tort litigation. Northwest Univ Press, Evanston

Xenos M, Vromen A, Loader BD (2014) The great equalizer? Patterns of social media use and youth political engagement in three advanced democracies. Inf Commun Soc 17(2):151–167

Andrew Henderson (LLB, BA, BEd, LLM (ANU)) is a Sessional Academic at the University of Canberra and a PhD candidate at the Australian National University. He spent 15 years working in and with Australian courts in the development of policy and practice. He has researched and published on legal education, legal professional conduct, legal history and the use of social media as a form of commentary on the work of the courts.

Sustainable Justice, A Social Responsible Focus on Innovation in Justice

Alexander F. de Savornin Lohman and Jaap van Straalen

Abstract Following the UN Conference on the Human Environment of 1972 and *The Limits to Growth* report published in the same year, an internationally coordinated, planned approach has ensured that thinking in terms of sustainability has penetrated all sectors of society. Social Responsibility, which is based on sustainable development, has become a determining factor for international companies and international organisations alike throughout the world. This change process has taken place relatively quickly and successfully, especially in business and international organisations and it is also beginning to take a hold in the judiciary. This Chapter discusses the substantive and organisational aspects of this development process. We have formulated universal core principles of Social Sustainability for the judiciary. These principles were derived from various Declarations and Development Goals by the United Nations, the Earth Charter, the OECD Guidelines, the ICC Business Charter, and the ISO 26000 Guidance on Social Responsibility. The Sustainable Justice Charter 1.0, which is co-signed by scientists and professionals with international influence from many parts of the world, is based on these principles. The authors have also examined the way in which the increasing complexity of social issues call for both a top-down and bottom-up organisation of the legal system to ensure that it functions successfully and in a sustainable manner. This Chapter highlights examples of socially sustainable justice system projects that have already been realised and also provides directions for successful mainstreaming of these and other sustainable justice innovations.

A. F. de Savornin Lohman (✉) · J. van Straalen
Center for Sustainable Justice, Utrecht, The Netherlands
e-mail: alexlohman@me.com

J. van Straalen
e-mail: jaapvanstraalen@live.com

© Springer Nature Singapore Pte Ltd. 2018

T. Sourdin and A. Zariski (eds.), *The Responsive Judge*, Ius Gentium: Comparative Perspectives on Law and Justice 67, https://doi.org/10.1007/978-981-13-1023-2_6

1 From Stockholm 1972 and Limits to Growth to the 2030 Agenda for Sustainable Development of the UN and the Earth Charter

Development of the sustainability movement

The first international environmental conference of the United Nations was held in Stockholm in 1972. In that same year, the Club of Rome[1] published the report *The Limits to Growth* (Meadows et al. 1972) which confronted the world with the fact that there is only a finite amount of fossil fuels, while there is an ever-increasing need for energy through exponential growth of the economy and global population. The report struck like a bomb. It was translated into 30 languages and more than 16 million copies were sold.

Environmental awareness, and the realisation that active and targeted policies are required to achieve sustainable development, came about at the turn of the 20th century. Russia, the United Kingdom, Japan and the United States concluded a treaty in 1911, for instance, to prevent eradication due to fur poaching. This realisation only truly came through in the 1970s in the private sector due to confrontations with raw material scarcity and pressure from increasing environmental awareness. Numerous action programmes and conventions were also established, e.g. on global pollution (Paris 1974), cross-border air pollution, ozone depletion (Vienna Convention of 1985 and the Montreal Protocol of 1987), the convention on the control of transboundary movements of hazardous wastes and their disposal (Basel 1989) and the UN Environment and Climate Conferences. Developing countries had already started organising themselves (G77), because they did not want to be crippled in the development of their own economies due to environmental problems caused by richer countries.

The Stockholm conference was a great success in linking the importance of environmental protection, the importance of poverty reduction, and economic growth in developing countries. Environmental issues were placed in a global socioeconomic perspective, and attention was drawn to the potential for sustainable growth, which included environmental protection, human rights, poverty alleviation and development issues.

In 1983, the United Nations invited Gro Harlem Brundtland, Norway's former prime minister, to lead the World Commission on Environment and Development to provide advice on sustainable growth (Wikipedia 2017a). The Brundtland Commission defined sustainable development as "*development which meets the needs of current generations without compromising the ability of future generations to meet their own needs*" and published the report *Our Common Future* in 1987 that became the foundation of a global-based sustainability policy, which is widely supported by international organisations such as the United Nations, the OECD and the European Union (World Commission on Environment and Development 1987). The

[1] A group founded in 1968 that consists of leading scientists, economists, industrialists and former politicians from all over the world who are engaged in global developments, conducting scientific research into future expectations.

Brundtland commission also made a strong appeal to the United Nations to draw up an action programme for sustainable development. The United Nations heeded this call, through the United Nations Conference on Environment and Development in Rio de Janeiro in 1992, where Agenda 21[2] for the 21st century was established with an action plan for environmental issues, human rights, labour rights, poverty alleviation and development of Third World countries. This conference also gave rise to the Earth Charter, which was established 8 years later (Earth Charter Initiative 2016): "The drafting was done during a six-year worldwide consultation process, overseen by an independent commission, which was convened by Maurice Strong and Mikhail Gorbachev and chaired by Steven Clark Rockefeller with the purpose of developing a global consensus on values and principles for a sustainable future. The official launch of the Earth Charter was on 29 June 2000 in a ceremony at The Peace Palace in The Hague, Netherlands. The Earth Charter's ethical vision proposes that environmental protection, human rights, equitable human development, and peace are interdependent and indivisible. The Charter attempts to provide a new framework for thinking about and addressing these issues. The Earth Charter Initiative organisation exists to promote the Charter" (Wikipedia 2017b).

The Earth Charter expresses the core of the United Nations' sustainable development policy, such as the UN Millennium Development Goals (United Nations 2015a) and the UN 2030 Agenda for Sustainable Development, *Transforming our World*, which was adopted unanimously by 193 member states (United Nations 2015b). The Copenhagen climate treaty of 2009, the Paris climate agreement of 2015, the Rio +10 summit in Johannesburg of 2002 and the successful Rio +20 conference in Rio de Janeiro of 2012 are all in line with this.

The Earth Charter is the principle statement for social responsibility and sustainable development. It carries a vision of hope, but also a call for action: sustainable development does not simply appear out of the blue. The Earth Charter also identifies the non-material aspects of sustainable development, which is also relevant to justice.

Sustainable development and careful and responsible handling of the planet Earth for future generations as well, has since become widely accepted. It is shared by international institutions, national governments, national and international companies, interest groups and consumers. The consciousness of sustainability has given society a different face, and it has changed people's intentions. Such changes cannot be achieved solely through law or regulations. National legislation has become increasingly inadequate, while international agreements are often insufficiently binding on sovereign states. There is a visible shift from legislation and tolerance to conferences, charters, intentions and non-binding rules of conduct and recommendations. Sustainability conferences can attract participants en masse from all sectors of society. Inspirational goals and agendas, innovations and charters are being established with great involvement and they are becoming increasingly ambitious. Non-enforceable guidelines and recommendations are often voluntarily observed. The influence of

[2]An ambitious plan to resolve urgent issues before the end of the millennium and to prepare the world for the 21st century: See United Nations (1992).

interest groups and NGOs are also on the increase as they establish civil initiatives. Through the use of media and social media, they are also gaining increasing influence over governments and business.

Innumerable initiatives, plans, policies and intentions have been created by governments, government organisations, business, society, and citizens.

Initiatives for change and renewal are increasingly starting from the bottom. Governments follow these initiatives by looking into how legislation needs to be adjusted to honour initiatives. Business and governments are increasingly expected to focus on a broad social debate and for initiatives to be focussed from the bottom up.

The international business community, as well as other interest groups, prepared very thoroughly for the UN Rio Summit in 1992. This led to the formation of the World Business Council for Sustainable Development, which created a vision for sustainable development of business. In 1991, the International Chamber of Commerce (ICC) also established a Business Charter for Sustainable Development. In 2008, the Organisation for Economic Co-operation and Development (OECD) came up with new guidelines for multinational companies (OECD Guidelines for Multinational Enterprises 2008), in part with a view on sustainable development which they improved in 2011 (OECD Guidelines for Multinational Enterprises 2011).

In 2015, the ICC continued to update its Business Charter from a more holistic viewpoint (ICC Sustainable Business Charter 2015). This emphasises that business is also committed to closely following developments related to sustainable policy. Corporate Social Responsibility (CSR) greatly influences the internal policies of organisations and the manner in which they should deal with external factors such as the environment, human rights, working conditions, public health. This has led to issues that people deal with becoming more complex, which also applies to the solutions found. The introduction of CSR and sustainable development has since become a specialty as large consultancies and audit offices have set up special advisory departments for this purpose. The increasing complexity of society and the consequences thereof have penetrated organisations that are affiliated with governments. This also applies to justice. The question is how organisations, such as the justice system, can rely on changes that bring increase complexity with it.

The International Organisation for Standardisation published ISO 26000 in 2010 to help organisations with the integration of social responsibility and sustainable development. The purpose of this standard is not certification, which is usually the case with ISO. The great importance of ISO 26000 (2010) standard is that, as opposed to OECD Guidelines and the ICC Business Charter, it is very extensive, detailed and thorough in all aspects of social responsibility and sustainable development.

The impact of the sustainability movement on justice

In addition to CSR and the sustainability movement, there is also a changing mentality. Citizens are becoming more vocal and they set more and higher demands. Justice is also confronted with the increasing complexity of cases and the consequences of judicial decisions. There is also criticism of justice, which could be an indication that justice has not yet been adequately adapted on a number of points.

In the Netherlands this was recently expressed through public criticism. In a 2015 memorandum, 24 leading Dutch people from the legal field expressed their concern about the functioning of justice (Brenninkmeijer et al. 2015), and in 2017 The Hague Institute for the Innovation of Law (HiiL) published a comprehensive and alarming report *Menselijk en rechtvaardig—Is de rechtsstaat er voor de burger?* (Humane and justified—Does the rule of law work for citizens?) (Barendrecht et al. 2017) which criticises the functioning of the legal system. It is stated that justice is stuck in its own systematic thinking. The report signals perverse incentives, established interests and funding systems that hold development and innovation back. People often do not recognise their own problems in a legal diagnoses and questions are asked in the form of a precious tournament, which is also the premise in the Netherlands, which is often not the most successful way to resolve a conflict, according to the HiiL report.

Justice is therefore coming under increasing pressure. Citizens, governments and journalists find that they are insufficiently familiar with justice. More transparency and explanation is required. More stringent requirements must be set for the reasoning behind decisions. There is an increasing tendency to withdraw more and more issues from the decision-making authority of the court, through measures such as administrative handling of cases outside of the courts. Politicians are increasingly less likely to question disparaging legal decisions or even question the authority of an independent judge and it seems that the legal systems in Turkey and Poland are no longer independent. Justice has also experienced increasing pressure from citizens and politicians to hand out harsher punishments. It is up to justice to respond in a transparent manner while actually listening to issues, without being enthralled by emotional pressure and without compromising its own values and integrity. The added value of justice is no longer accepted without question.

2 Implementing Sustainability in Organisations

The concepts of social responsibility and sustainable development are defined in descriptions contained in OECD Guidelines and the ICC Business Charter and are expanded in more detail in the ISO 26000 standard.

In ISO 26000 (2010) and the ISO Sustainability Brochure (2012), social responsibility is defined as follows:

> [R]esponsibility of an organisation for the impacts of its decision and activities on society and the environment, through transparency and ethical behaviour that:
>
> - Contribute to sustainable development, including health and welfare of society
> - Takes into account the expectation of stakeholders
> - Is in compliance with applicable law and consistent with international norms of behaviour
> - Is integrated throughout the organisation and practices in its relationship.

Sustainable development is defined, according to the Brundtland definition, in ISO 26000 (2010), and in the OECD Guidelines and the ICC Business Charter, as follows:

> [D]evelopment that meets the needs of the present without compromising the ability of future generations to meet their own needs. ISO 26000 (2010) also adds: Sustainable development is about integrating the goals of a high quality of life, health and prosperity with social justice and maintaining the earth's capacity to support life in all its diversity.[3]

In ISO 26000 (2010), social responsibility and sustainable development are seen as related concepts that are extensions of each other. When social sustainability is discussed in this Chapter, it is understood to refer to both concepts.

Basic principles of social responsibility and sustainable development

Concrete environmental regulations and recommendations from the OECD Guidelines, the ICC Business Charter and the ISO26000 standard were initially written for dealing with nature and for protection of the natural environment (material sustainability). These rules of care, integrity and openness are also excellent for application to intangible sustainability and interpersonal relations, the social environment. These principles thereby form valuable starting points for the development of a vision for justice.

Social sustainability focuses on sustainable development. ISO 26000 (2010) is a tool for organisations to add goals that focus on social justice, high quality of life, health and prosperity, good relations in society and security.

For justice and judiciary, this means that it must be verified whether all methods and activities of justice are aimed at improving the social environment through effective and beneficial use of jurisdiction.

Table V of ISO 26000 (2010) summarises the positive effects of social sustainability.[4] For justice, the following can be expected:

- The reputation of justice will improve, and public confidence will increase if courts explain better how legal requirements relate to social expectations and existing views about the risks of non-socially responsible behaviour.
- Justice has a special position because its legitimacy is based in law. But by making the balance between legal frameworks and social expectations transparent, social agreement with the decisions made will increase. Decisions will not be doubted as often.
- This approach will lead to more emphasis on innovation, both in the way in which justice functions and in the manner in which it cooperates with others.
- By emphasising cooperation with others, the relationship with stakeholders will improve.
- The loyalty, involvement, participation and morale of employees will improve, thereby increasing the ability of the organisation to recruit, motivate and retain employees and increase the effectiveness of the work organisation.

---

[3]This addition was derived from the Dutch version of ISO 26000. The English version of ISO 26000 may be formulated differently.

[4]Note: The authors worked on the Dutch version of ISO 26000. It is therefore possible that there may be deviations from the English text of ISO 26000.

Social sustainability in the judiciary

While ISO 26000 (2010) assists with the implementation of a new policy that is focused on social sustainability, the topics covered by this policy can be derived from the OECD guidelines.

But before these topics are discussed, it would be helpful to realise that it is not immediately clear for many experts, including lawyers, where the relationship lies between sustainability and justice. The reasoning that follows is that the judiciary does not have an adverse impact on the natural environment. This is correct if a limited environmental description is applied, but if the environment is viewed as a broader concept to also include the social environment, then jurisdiction includes the environment. An adverse impact can result in such case through the implementation of judicial coercion, which changes relationships between those involved. Coercion works well in some instances, but it can also easily cause an adverse impact if special care is not taken: people could lose respect for each other, with the negative consequences that has on family ties and social networks. In the judiciary environmental policy and protection should focus on the social environment, with the question of whether its decisions and interventions have social (intangible) positive or negative effects on parties and their stakeholders, their living environments and society as a whole.

The subjects of social sustainability policies that are of importance for justice, as discussed below, are derived from the OECD Directive. The most important ones are: prevention of an adverse impact, encouragement and promotion of social sustainability, investment in human capital, stakeholder involvement, transparency and supervision, self-control and openness about findings and environmental impact assessment.

Preventing adverse impact[5]

Prevent damage! is the most important premise for sustainability and environmental protection. With non-material sustainability, it is all about preventing negative effects on relationships between people, security and quality of life in society.

This raises the question of which judiciary interventions are effective when minimising intervention. For example, parties involved in a dispute can be given the opportunity to resolve the matter themselves, rather than being placed in a situation where a court decision decreases their responsibility. Should Judicial Mediation not be given preference when turning to jurisdiction?

Think about the occurrence of an adverse impact; question the policy of retribution. It is clear that the effect and side effect of retribution is that there is an adverse impact on those involved, stakeholders and society as a whole. Can this adverse impact be prevented through a different approach? Are there any penalties that would have a lower adverse impact or none at all, which are aimed at restoring relationships and improving society? An effective punishment could be seen as more sustainable if its overall burden on society is reduced.

[5]Based on and derived from OECD Guidelines II. A.11., A.12., OECD Guidelines II. Commentary on General Policies ad 14., ad 17., ad 18., ad 19., ad 20., OECD Guidelines VI. 6., OECD Guidelines VI. Explanation of the Environment 61, 62. 71.

Encourage and promote social sustainability[6]

Social sustainability does not occur naturally, but must be encouraged and promoted. Enterprises and organisations can exercise moral and legal pressure within their spheres of influence to promote socially responsible behaviour among their suppliers, their industry partners and their customers.

What does this mean for justice and the judiciary? What is the sphere of influence of the court and the judiciary to promote social sustainability? Here, there are various possibilities.

First of all, judges, prosecutors and other judicial officers hold power and authority. This allows them to have a positive influence on the behaviour of parties, suspects and victims, in part due to the fast access they have to agencies that can provide assistance and support. Within the judicial chain, officials can encourage each other and organisations in the judicial chain to join forces to strive for a high quality of life, health and prosperity for the parties involved, perpetrators and victims, and their living environment. This has a positive impact on society and social justice.

The current final result of justice still requires attention. A decision that favours one party at the expense of another, is contrary to the call of the Earth Charter: "We must join together to bring forth a sustainable global society founded on … a culture of peace. This requires a change of mind and heart. … We must imaginatively develop and apply the vision of a sustainable way of life locally, nationally, regionally, and globally." There is an interest in many parts of the world in judicial settlement practices and Judicial Mediation, which is in line with the Earth Charter and ISO 26000 (2010).

Investing in human capital[7]

An important part of social sustainability and social progress is investment in human capital. Initially, the OECD sustainability policy involved activities in developing countries, but it can also be seen as a general starting point for social sustainability. Development is good for everyone, as it makes people happy and helps them to become better persons. This also contributes to the quality of society and sustainable development. Special attention is paid to vulnerable groups internationally, and at a national level.

For the judiciary this would mean that those who come into contact with the judiciary should have become better people when the court withdraws its reach from them. The court has the authority to make this positive difference. A means of achieving this could, for example, be a neighbourhood justice centre which, in the application of jurisdiction, focuses on promoting social progress in a problematic or disadvantaged neighbourhood. Strengthening human capital is essential, to ensure

---

[6]Based on and derived from OECD Guidelines II. A.13., A.14., OECD Guidelines II. Commentary on General Policies ad 11., ad 12., ad 18., ad 19, ad 20., ad 22.

[7]Based on and derived from OECD Guidelines II. Commentary on General Policies ad 2., ad 3., ad 5., ad 12., ad 23., ad 24., ad 25., OECD Guidelines V. Commentary on Employment and Industrial Relations ad 58. (among others), OECD Guidelines VI. 6. 7.

that a better person returns to society. Interventions and decisions of the judiciary or court can play an important role in this regard.

The involvement of stakeholders on the effects of justice[8]

The involvement of local and other stakeholders affected by the activities of organisations, and the conduct of open dialogue with them, are essential aspects of social sustainability. Confidence can be gained, and stakeholder interests can be taken into account. Sometimes better, more effective and innovative solutions can be found.

In justice this could have a threshold-reducing effect for society and chain partners alike. An effective approach in many cases can be a neighbourhood justice or peace law with a judge who knows the neighbourhood, who enjoys trust and who thinks in terms of solutions that are embedded in the environment. Many disputes involve stakeholders, in addition to the parties to the trial, who are interested in a good conclusion. By involving these stakeholders in the solution, there is a better chance of integrating the solution into the social environment and to contribute to sustainable development. Sometimes chain partners are also important stakeholders with these solutions. Collaboration with chain partners will, where necessary, lead to a method in which structural problems can be addressed better and more effectively or solved in a sustainable manner.

Supervision, monitoring of own actions and transparency[9]

The importance for organisations to monitor and control the consequences of their own actions to prevent damage is self-explanatory. The independence of the judge complicates such control when it comes to an individual ruling, even if there is prior consultation on the frameworks within which certain decisions should be made. In most cases the judge is not responsible for the execution of his/her decisions.

However, it is possible to investigate the impact and consequences of judicial decisions and subsequent interventions. The court could use the results of such an investigation to see if the decisions could have a better and more effective social impact. This type of investigation also fits in with sustainable actions that organisations should provide open and timely information on the expected adverse effects or side-effects of their policies and activities. Transparency and openness about positive effects naturally also contribute to levels of trust attributed to that organisation.

Courts and the judiciary publish the results achieved in their annual reports. The emphasis is on some information that is easy to quantify, such as a report on an administrative and organisational efficiency and about the chances of recidivism. However, little or no information is given about the effects, both of the decisions taken and of the administrative and organisational goals that have been unsuccessful, of stakeholders and other stakeholders, or of the underlying causes of recurrence. No

[8]Based on and derived from OECD Guidelines II. B.2., OECD Guidelines II. Commentary on General Policies ad 23., ad 24., ad 25.

[9]Based on and derived from OECD Guidelines II. A.10., II. Commentary on General Policies ad 14., III. 1.–4. Commentary on Disclosure 28. (and next), and VI. 1., 2., Commentary on the Environment 65.

report exists on the effects of civil law. Whether and to what extent justice contributes to an improvement in the quality of the social environment has not been sufficiently examined from a sustainability perspective.

Applying Environmental Impact Reporting (EIR)[10]

With large investments it has become a habit to estimate the environmental impact of the investment (EIR) in advance. Companies that are confronted with this perform environmental impact reports. The establishment of an environmental management system, which maps the environmental impacts of policies and activities, has become standard practice for business. The knowledge gathered in this manner has become an important driving force behind innovation. Such a system requires years of intensive focus, and it is in constant development.

A similar system for courts and justice systems would map the effects of justice on the social environment. It is an important question which social effects should be included in such a system. The developments in justice, which we will discuss in Part 4, show that, when courts intend to make justice more meaningful to those who voluntarily or forcefully come in contact with the court, they need information and knowledge about other aspects than what is traditionally discussed in court litigation. The question is which kind of data should be recorded in an environmental management system to be kept by courts to enable them to justify as a legal system what the influence of decisions and practices on process parties is, as well as on others such as family members and the social network.

In the first chapter of this book, *What is Responsive Judging?*, Sourdin and Zariski extend the concept of judicial responsiveness to a more "progressive" or "active" form which also incorporates (1) responsiveness to accountability for public investment in the legal system and the demand for justice; (2) responsiveness to the problems of interdependent, network society; (3) responsiveness to litigants' experiences of the legal system and courts; and (4) active responsiveness in the context of public attention. In Table 1.1 of their chapter, *Potential Responsive Judging Elements,* they provided a valuable overview of relevant elements of responsive judging, distinguishing between *In Court Engagement* (individual and social responsiveness), *Decision Making* (individual, social and legal system responsiveness) and *External Court Engagement* (social and legal system responsiveness). All these elements are closely linked to the principles of Sustainable Justice. It would be interesting to examine how these potential elements of responsive judging relate to the principles of social sustainability, described in Part 2 of this chapter: preventing adverse impact, encouragement of socially sustainable behaviour, investment in human capital, involvement of stakeholders, monitoring of one's own behaviour and impact and transparency about this, and a continuous mood to innovate and improve one's own societal impact.

[10]Based on and derived from OECD Guidelines II. A 10., VI. 1., and VI. Commentary on the Environment 61., 62., 64.

3 Organisational Tools for Designing Judicial Organisations in a Complex Society

Introduction

Judicial matters have become more complex in the last decades. In this Part we will discuss how the judicial system may respond to this. In the last decades in the judicial system, several organisational forms have been chosen to tackle societal problems with which they were confronted. They will be described in the next Part. Although many excellent projects have been launched through a common-sense approach, the choice of their organisational form was done merely on a trial and error base. In this Part will we argue that the choice of an organisational form can be done systematically using knowledge of how organisations in general respond to complexity.

Organisations reacting to an increasingly complex environment

The interest in complex problems arose in the 1970s, which is the same period during which the sustainability movement started: at first problems like the limits of growth and the oil crisis of 1973 made it clear that we needed more than traditional reasoning to solve problems and to make decisions in naturalistic complex and dynamic situations. Later, the organisational forms and management techniques that were developed proved to be very useful in general. So, companies that were not directly involved in sustainability also adopted these organisational forms and management techniques to solve complex problems. Complexity arises when there is interaction between a desired situation and the actions to reach that situation. Often these actions may result in something other than the desired situation, or there is a reaction of some other actor which frustrates the reach of the desired situation. This possibility makes the relation between a decision and the desired outcome of the situation not transparent. Such a situation with a lack of transparency is often the case in the judicial system. This is experienced as an unsatisfying situation by judges and is one of the main reasons why innovative projects have been started in the judicial system, which will be described in the next Part.

We will describe first some general results of studies in the organisational field on how to deal with complexity. From these studies we will discuss what could be learned from this in the judicial field.

The interest in how to solve complex problems coincides with many studies in the psychological and management field on making organisations and decision-making more effective. The effectiveness of the sole application of autocratic leadership was questioned. It turned out not to be the best way to handle questions arising from societal changes and the growth of companies and organisations through mergers and centralisation. This tendency to centralise is also current in the judicial field where organisations which support prosecutors, judges, prison keepers, and probation staff members, have grown over time. Alternatives were formulated and tested. Advantages and improvements were reached by making use of skills and knowledge on the work floor. Many problems were solved this way, which was the former competence of staff. From this arose for instance the question on the size of staff support where the staff should be positioned in the organisation.

Of the many questions that were asked and the answers that were given, we will focus on one of the themes in those discussions: what are the advantages and disadvantages of top-down and bottom-up management? This might be a relevant topic for the judicial field, and can be of help in the organisational design of the individual offices where judicial professionals work. This knowledge can also help to better understand how these organisations, which might be seen as the top, interact with society, which might be seen as the bottom. This latter interaction is useful to solve complex problems which will arise when courts set themselves a goal to increase the social effectiveness of their interventions and decisions, in pursuit of sustainable development. Sustainable justice sees this interaction between society and the judicial system as a cyclical one: starting from identical observed individual cases with its solutions, the judicial system may detect a wider societal problem, which can be addressed. In solving these problems, new problems will occur, on which the judicial system will react in return.

First, we will discuss the characteristics of top-down organisations with autocratic leadership, and secondly the reaction on this, the bottom-up approach, to see in the end why a combination of both leads to successful organisations. In the end we will discuss how this might be applied in the judicial system.

Top-down organisation

In his article *Top-down versus bottom-up management styles*, Harper (2015) deals with the question in which way effective behaviour of organisations is affected by the way hierarchy is used. The traditional style is top-down, followed by an upheaval of bottom-up initiatives during the last decades. Focus on either one of these styles doesn't seem to be the solution, according to Harper. And for the judicial system we will here argue in line with this article that a combination of these styles will have the best results in terms of effectivity. Top-down management is also called autocratic leadership, especially in the context of psychology. Autocratic leadership is the process of upper management reaching independent decisions that will change or improve the workplace or the organisation. These decisions are handed down to employees. They will work to accomplish the goals on their own or with other employees. Although lower-level managers may have input on how to accomplish the final goal, they cannot change policies without approval from the upper management. These top-down decisions allow leaders to be clear on goals and expectations. Autocratic leadership has the potency to give an organisation a strong drive. Autocratic leadership can easily be viewed as bossy or dictatorial. Employees are more likely to dispute decisions taken by the upper management. When an organisation wants to implement change effectively, this can be viewed as a disadvantage of the top-down style.

Bottom-up action plans

In some situations, a top-down management style is impractical. For instance when the upper management needs information, knowledge or skills from their employees. After World War II, the bottom-up approach to increase the effectiveness of organisations has been subject of systematic study. Bottom-up management can be described as a process where team members are invited to participate in every step of the management process. Team members are encouraged to come up with the steps needed to reach milestones in a decision process on their own. How tasks are performed is up to the teams, and they feel involved in project development. Every employee has the best knowledge of the circumstances under which his work must be done. When all levels of an organisation are involved in the decision-making process, employees feel part of the whole. Employees are more open to work and strive harder to reach goals and objectives in ways that work best for them. Building morale in this way can stimulate the improvement of productivity and effectiveness. The bottom-up management style can also have possible pitfalls. Employees might be confused by too much information or too many unproven ideas. And managers might have a harder time finding an effective plan for reaching goals.

The popularity of (also using) the bottom-up approach is growing. Researchers in industrial and organisational psychology found that common hierarchies are not as conducive for productivity and employee happiness. The upswing of a kinder and gentler employer has been in the middle of the 20th century as Harvard Business School professor Elton Mayo started the human relations movement, focusing on improving the social aspects of the workplace. This movement helped to inspire the first iterations of bottom-up management.

The best of both worlds

Deep down, the proponents of a top-down structure believe that if there isn't an appropriate level of centralised control, 'chaos will reign'. And proponents of the bottom-up style hold the view that a top-down hierarchy separates authority from those doing the work. So which style is to be chosen? We will show the answer is in the middle. The bottom-up style is closely connected with the term "self-managed organisation". In his book *Reinventing Organizations*, Laloux (2014) discusses some of the elements of self-managed organisations and references companies like AES, Buurtzorg, FAVI, Holacracy, MorningStar, Patagonia, Semco, Steam, W.L. Gore & Associates, Whole Foods, and Zappos. Laloux explains that the leading edge of global consciousness is partly connected with the global interest in sustainable ways of operating. An increase in sustainable ways of operating will, according to Laloux, supported by new forms of self-managed organisational design.

When we take a close look into a high-performing, bottom-up, self-managed company, one will find out that it is in fact a well-run top-down hierarchal organisation: the best self-managed organisations turn out to be top-down hierarchies in disguise.

One should realise that it is a purpose of an organisation to delegate or decentralise authority to meet organisational goals, whether the organisation is top-down or bottom-up structured. When organisations are growing, the upper management needs to delegate authority and decision-making. In a top-down structured organisation organisational structure is often seen as a way to effectively control all operations. In bottom up organisations, that also use a top-down strategy, structure is seen as a means to delegate. The upper management will foster the organisation to thrive to be self-managed. An interesting example from the military field, known for a classic top-down hierarchy, can nicely illustrate this. Four-star General Stanley McChrystal describes the fight of the Joint Special Operations Command in Iraq against Al Qaeda (McChrystal et al. 2015). At the start of his command in 2003, the Joint Special Operations Command Forces were not successful, despite having superior training, weapons, support, and satellite intelligence. Al Qaeda was just too agile, nebulous, and rapidly evolving for the traditional top-down military command-and-control paradigm. McChrystal had to evolve how the military had traditionally operated. He created autonomous, cross-functional teams of soldiers, analysts, and support personnel. Instead of the command-and-control dictatorship, which was originally used, the team adopted a structure, almost exclusively relying on communication and influence. A culture of secrecy and need-to-know intelligence had been changed into a new culture based on transparency and decentralised decision-making. Ultimately, this change turned the tide against Al Qaeda in Iraq.

Team of Teams (McChrystal et al. 2015) makes the strong case that for a top-down hierarchy to survive and thrive in a fast-paced, unpredictable environment, it must transform its organisational structure and design from Command-and-Control to a "Team of Teams." There seems to be no more hierarchy and things magically happen within the teams. But this is common misconception of self-managed systems. General McChrystal did not change the hierarchy. What he changed was the information exchange, transparency, and delegation of authority within the structure, more than the structure itself.

This scenario is not unique to the military. How can we use the above knowledge to improve the judicial system as an organisation? And how can we improve the relationship between the judicial system and society to improve the way societal problems will be solved? How we can make the judicial system more effective which is not necessarily more efficient, considering that the judicial system is a partner in a process of solving complex societal issues?

What kind of leadership will be needed in an organisation that combines top-down strategies with bottom-up actions to become a high performing organisation? The upper management takes ownership to steward the on-going alignment between the organisation and its environment. This includes vision, strategy, culture, functional structure, and collaborative processes. Just about everything else will be delegated in the organisation. In general, the upper management is constantly observing and listening to feedback signals from within and outside the organisation. They are monitoring how the current vision, strategy, culture, functional structure, and team-based collaborative processes are performing. If adjustments need to be made, they rely mostly on communication and influence (vs. command and control) to accomplish a shift. The upper management will rarely pull out its authority card, for if they appear to be in charge, then the organisation will lose its advantages acting like a self-managed organisation. Rather than relying on authority, the design-centric leader almost exclusively depends on feedback, communication, relationships and influence to sense and respond to environmental signals occurring from within and outside the organisation.

There are three challenges to build a high performing organisation. Firstly, is the mindset of the upper management. They must focus on the whole. Instead of applying their own knowledge, being the smartest persons in the room, the will have to stir all the knowledge of their organisation. Secondly, successful organisations have a practice of complete transparency. They make key information available, along with the education to go with it, to everyone in the company. Thirdly they manage the balance between effectiveness and efficiency. Efficiency will, if left unchecked, soon 'grow' to destroy organisational effectiveness. This shift in organisation and leadership style is also advocated by Scharmer and Kaufer (2013). Working in Massachusetts Institute of Technology (MIT), they are tributary to *The Limits to Growth* (Meadows et al. 1972).

One of their arguments is that knowledge gained from extensive studies, like that in *The Limits to Growth*, is not easily transformed into action. Experts have great trouble to convince leaders in the public field and in business. This stems mainly from the general impression that academic knowledge is presented in a top-down atmosphere. In their work, Scharmer and Kaufer (2013) stress the importance of recognising problems and their solutions bottom-up. Academic solutions are likely to be opposed, if the necessity of them is not felt by those who have the problems. Further, in coping with societal problems, there is an increasing tendency to have solutions accepted by working bottom-up, although solutions from academic studies are presented in a top-down setting. Scharmer and Kaufer (2013) expect a development from an ego-oriented way of working to an eco-orientation. So, they position the development in organisational style right in the middle of the sustainability movement.

Possible implications for the judicial system

So, what can we learn in the case of the judicial system? First of all, it can be established that the judicial system consists of several organisations that have a shared social responsibility. All of these organisations have traditionally a top-down leadership style. Although some changes are noticeable, many features are still present, like long periods of in-house training transferring the existing culture to newcomers. The top-down approach is not in itself illogical, considering that legislation is also top-down. But when you consider the legal field of work with mainly highly educated, often specialist lawyers, you should actually expect a bottom-up style. For such a system would gain the most from each lawyer's individual knowledge. Exception to this are the court and the judge. The judge functions independently, and in a court the question is how a unit of policy can be achieved, in spite of the independence of the individual judge.

At many law firms, the top-down approach is actually reinforced by appointing a CEO instead of a COO, while the bottom-up process is given more space at the same time. For example, concepts such as 'lean and mean' and 'agile' are linked to the increasingly complex issues facing the offices. Although this complexity often goes further than resolving legal conflict and is focused on underlying problems, law firms have to deal with a complexity that is simpler than the judicial system, which is designed to impose measures that should have a social impact, e.g. in criminal law and family law.

Throughout the world, courts and prosecutors have responded to this complex situation, in particular by attempting a different approach to revolving door justice, family law justice and indigenous justice (see the next Part for a more detailed description). This is a response to the inadequate functioning of the top-down functioning judicial system, in response to the increasing complexity of problems in society. Not only do the problems encountered in the judiciary resemble those of the 4-star General McChrystal, but also the solutions that have been found for them, which is to organise case law as an interdisciplinary team, in which officials from successive organisations in the legal chain cooperate with each other and share as much information as possible.

In practice, these developments have proven to be very slow among prosecutors and the courts. This can be attributed to a number of factors, and some of the more important issues are discussed here:

- Many of the institutions in the judicial system, such as prosecutors and courts, are taking a closer look at their organisations, in order to improve the balance between top-down and bottom-up, utilising knowledge and innovation. New employees start to gain influence slowly by becoming more involved, thereby initiating a bottom-up approach. The influence of ICT also plays a role: in the judicial system, the transfer of paper from one location to another and the associated planning of legal officials have traditionally played a dominant role. The need for central planning of this paper stream will decrease through developments in automation. These developments will make these organisations stronger if the top-down and bottom-up approaches are both strengthened and linked to each other.
- An important issue is who exactly is the client of the judicial system? There is a reason why nothing has been stated yet about the place of people who are the centre of the issue. Although the factual situation has in fact diminished somewhat by giving persons a more central place in the law, a shift to society as the customer will require further adaptation of the process. It would be nice to focus that change on a judicial system that acts as a driving force behind social change for those directly involved and for their environment and society as a whole.
- Independence, especially of the judiciary, is an important premise in justice. New ways must be found to keep working together in teams, while still guaranteeing independence. This applies to the authority and to transparency in information sharing.
- Although participating organisations in the judicial chains may have opposing functional interests, even they ultimately serve the same social interest. With regard to civil law, the judicial chain is the simplest with a legislator, parties, lawyers and judges, but in criminal law the chain is more complex as it involves lawyers, police, prosecutor, judge, prison, institutions for behavioural improvement and mental health care, and probation. But also in family law and administrative law the chains can be complicated. Working together in the chains is a special skill, for

which purpose the Dutch government has formed a separate team.[11] An important issue with chains is determining how to develop cooperation with independent organisations to achieve a common goal.

From the discussion of the factors stated above, it is clear that it is possible for the judicial system to cater more effectively for increasing complexity. Within the organisations themselves, including prosecutors, courts and prisons, we can work on anchoring a strong top-down process, in combination with as much use of bottom-up knowledge as possible. The effectiveness of these organisations will increase as a result.

A number of questions must be answered for effective cooperation of the links in the judicial chains, which are aimed at a more effective contribution to social issues. Who does the judicial system serve? How can independence be combined with cooperation? And what skills are needed to direct the justice chain?

4 Response of the Judicial System to Societal Problems

Summary

Since the 1980s there have been several responses of the judicial system to urgent societal matters. In this Part, we will describe some bottom-up court initiatives developed in response to social urgencies. These bottom-up courts led to quite new ways of judicial intervention and decision-making. These initiatives have in common that the judiciary cooperates with social service providers within the judicial system. Worldwide, there are many other examples of initiatives in judicial renewal and innovation, like judicial mediation, restorative justice and transitional justice, like truth commissions. Those developments are beyond the scope of this Chapter.

Drug courts (problem solving courts)

Stricter anti-drug laws in the United States in the 1980s led to an unmanageable overload of the criminal chambers at courts (Winick 2002, 1056; Berman and Feinblatt 2005, 23). Judges noted that drug criminals constantly reoffended and they then started to realise that the legal system simply acted as a link in the chain of a persisting problem, instead of acting as a solution.[12] In 1989, the court in Miami took a radical new course as they created the first drug court, which was aimed at resolving the problem in a structural manner (Winick 2002, 1056–7). In the drug court addicted repeat offenders who have plead guilty are given the option to undergo rehabilitation and training programs under the supervision of the drug court judge, whereby they

[11]The Dutch Ministry of the Interior and Kingdom Relations (BZK) is responsible for the *Nederlandse Overheid Referentie Architectuur* (NORA) [Dutch Government Reference Architecture]. The management of NORA has been delegated to the ICTU Foundation.

[12]This expression was used by one of the pioneers of the Problem Solving Court movement interviewed by A.F. de Savornin Lohman in 2009.

can receive help for all the issues that have contributed to their criminal behaviour. The drug court closely collaborates with addiction clinics, social emergency services, the police, and lawyers. On average the drug court judge monitors the progress of each participant for a period of 1½ years by having him or her appear regularly in person. The drug court judge closely cooperates with social chain partners that are involved in the process. His or her decisions coordinate and structure their cooperation. When regression is noted on the part of a participant the judge immediately puts measures in place to get the participant back on the straight and narrow. The judge can also regularly reward participants when they seem to be trying their best. At the completion of each treatment phase the judge awards a graduation certificate and congratulates the participant in person. This strengthens the participant's commitment to continue the program. When everything goes well the frequency of urine tests can be reduced and participants do not need to appear so frequently. Sanctions in the event of a relapse are often therapeutic, such as requiring the participant to write an essay on how to prevent a relapse again in future. When there is serious doubt about the commitment of a participant, the judge can impose detention for a short period of time (a few hours to several days) to give the participant the opportunity to think about whether he or she wants to continue with the drug court program. The ultimate sanction is expulsion from the rehabilitation program, after which the matter is referred to an ordinary criminal court. Upon successful completion of the entire program the participant will have his or her life back on track and the drug addiction will be over or at least manageable. The person will then again be an integrated part of society, live independently and have a job, instead of having a criminal record. Final graduation certificates are awarded to participants under a festive atmosphere and in the presence of other participants. This is accompanied by heart-warming congratulations from the judge, who will have kept a close eye on the participants during the entire course of the program, including good and bad times.

Drug courts work without a delay: immediately after a suspect has been arrested it is verified whether the person is eligible for the drug court program. Treatment commences immediately when the suspect agrees to that.

The drug court system is obviously more expensive than a regular criminal court, but on balance it leads to major savings on the long term due to reduced recidivism and a much faster and more effective rehabilitation and treatment program because judicial pressure serves as an extra motivational tool for participants (Berman and Feinblatt 2005, 155–158; King et al. 2009, 147–148). The success of the drug court system has led to the establishment of other types of specialised courts based on the same system, which are known as problem solving courts. Mental health courts, driving while impaired courts, homeless courts, re-entry courts, veteran courts, family violence courts, family treatment courts and juvenile courts have all since been established.

There are currently around 4000 problem solving courts operational in the United States, 2734 of which are drug courts (National Association of Drug Court Professionals 2017). The problem-solving court system has been expanded to places such as Canada, Ireland, Scotland, England, Australia and Belgium (King et al. 2009, 143).

Community courts

The success of specialised problem-solving courts raised awareness that justice can find solutions to social problems. This awareness inspired creative thinking about the ways justice can be employed in different ways to find solutions to social problems. During the early 1990s, the Times Square area, the theatre district of Manhattan, was severely plagued by petty crime, so stakeholders and the authorities decided to establish a community court to resolve the problem (Berman and Feinblatt 2005). In 1993 the Midtown Community Court was established (Berman and Feinblatt 2005). One judge was appointed to head this court and she was tasked with making the neighbourhood safe again in as short a timeframe as possible. She was given a high degree of freedom and authority, in consultation with stakeholders from the community, police, and social chain partners, to develop a prosecuting and sanctioning policy that would achieve the desired objective of making the neighbourhood safe again. The result was a court that could immediately prosecute and punish minor misdemeanours and crimes. A person who is arrested for an offence such as shoplifting, graffiti, or street prostitution, for instance, is immediately prosecuted and the person often starts serving community service on the same day, which is aimed at enhancing the appearance of the neighbourhood (e.g. graffiti removal or cleaning of parks). The Midtown Community Court proved to be so successful that four community courts are currently located in New York City (Midtown Manhattan, Red Hook in Brooklyn, Harlem and the Bronx). There are also currently more than 40 neighbourhood justice courts active in the United States. Community courts based on this system have been developed outside of the United States in Melbourne (Australia), Liverpool (England) and Vancouver (Canada) (Center for Court Innovation 2017). The Centre for Court Innovation in New York contains full information about community courts, provides support with the establishment of such a court, and provides training for professionals. A. F. de Savornin Lohman has visited several of these courts in New York, New Jersey, California and Australia and was surprised at the extent to which these courts are interwoven with society, to the extent that it is right in the centre of life and society.

Indigenous Sentencing Courts

These courts essentially serve to improve relations between the Aborigines and the Western population (Auty and Briggs 2004). There has been a deep cultural gap between the native Aboriginal population and Western domination ever since the colonisation of Australia. Until recently, justice was aimed at punishing all persons in accordance with Western standards, irrespective of the background of the person. The result was an overwhelming over-representation of Aboriginal people in the prison population, with no real prospect of any improvement. The effect of the policy of punishing and imprisonment was rather worsening than beneficial socially. A key federal report from the Royal Commission into Aboriginal Deaths in Custody in 1991 concluded that the Western justice system was culturally unfit to be applied to Aborigines. Recommendations of this committee led to the establishment of indigenous sentencing courts in all the Australian states (except for Tasmania where almost no Aborigines live anymore). The first indigenous sentencing court was established in 1999 and there are currently about fifty operational in Australia.[13] This is quite a large number considering that there are only about 650,000 Aborigines living in Australia at present (Australian Bureau of Statistics 2017). Indigenous sentencing courts were established in consultation with the leaders of the Aboriginal communities in which they are set. Because there are significant cultural differences between Aboriginal communities', various forms of indigenous sentencing courts have also been developed. A common feature of all the forms is that the judge cooperates in one form or another with respected elders from the Aboriginal communities to which the Aboriginal perpetrators belong. The independence of the court is guaranteed, because Aboriginal elders refuse to share any responsibility for the decisions that the judges make. The reason for this is that it would put the position of trust that the elders enjoy in the community at risk. Many indigenous sentencing courts have integrated restorative justice elements and the way in which restorative justice is intertwined in the various systems varies greatly. Sometimes restorative justice meetings are held prior to court sessions and the results are presented as recommendations to the judge. In Nowra NSW the judge participates with four elders, the perpetrator, the victim, the police prosecutor, probation services, and family and supporters of the perpetrator and of the victim in a circle sentencing conference where the judge can enforce the outcome of the consultation. The Koori courts in Victoria work more based on a problem-solving court system (Auty and Briggs 2004; Harris 2006; Marchetti and Daly 2004; Marchetti and Daly 2007; Potas et al. 2003; Fryer-Smith 2008).

This type of court has a considerable and symbolic meaning for the Aborigines. "We got our self-respect back again and we can now create order within our communities in a way that is consistent with our cultural traditions. Our Western leaders hardly realise how important these courts are for the welfare of our communities and how much we need that."[14]

Sessions of indigenous sentencing courts are informal and approachable. They are usually attended by many relatives, friends and supporters of the accused and, depending on the system, there is similar attendance for the victim. Sessions are held around a table or in a circle, but sometimes also partly in the formal setting of a courtroom which is also decorated with symbolic objects from Aboriginal heritage. During sessions everyone can join in the discussions, even from the public gallery. This helps the judge to obtain all sorts of background information that would normally not be obtained during a standard trial, which can sometimes be very useful. The procedure enables the judge or magistrate to identify opportunities for reintegration and rehabilitation and to avoid imprisonment. The involvement of the elders ensures that the influence of the court remains in place between the court sessions as well. Their authority within the community ensures that suspects better comply with

[13]See Marchetti (2009) for an explanation of Indigenous Sentencing Courts.

[14]These and similar statements were often expressed by Aboriginal Elders, Aboriginal Justice Coordinators and Aboriginal Liaison Officers, during informal discussions taking place after the Indigenous Sentencing Courts sessions that Alexander de Savornin Lohman attended in 2010 in Port Adelaide (SA), Shepparton (Vic), Rockhampton (Qld) and Nowra (NSW).

court orders that are imposed, and suspects respond better to notices from the court. As a result, treatment and rehabilitation programs are more successful. Through their cooperation with elders, the judges obtain a better understanding of Aboriginal culture and they are better able to improve conditions in those communities.

Sustainable justice: a global development

Problem solving courts, community courts and indigenous sentencing courts are 'founded on respect for (nature) universal human rights, economic justice, and a culture of peace' as recommended by the Earth Charter (Earth Charter Initiative 2016). They are excellent manifestations of the fundamental "change of mind and heart and the new sense of global interdependence and universal responsibility", expressed by the Earth Charter, which is required to achieve social sustainable development. "This requires a change of mind and heart. … We must imaginatively develop and apply the vision of a sustainable way of life locally, nationally, regionally, and globally." They function in line with most of the principles described in the second Part of this Chapter as they aim to achieve sustainable development, and to prevent doing harm as much as possible, they invest in human capital, cooperate with stakeholders and social service providers, and stimulate others to adopt socially sustainable standards.

The fundamental innovation of these courts is the shift in focus of the application of judicial power: It is not again used to punish of another, but to foster behavioural change and to create a better world for the participant and his or her family, and for society as a whole. By doing this they contribute effectively to the solution of individual and social problems. Mutual relations are improved in a sustainable manner, thereby ensuring that society becomes more liveable and safer. In these forms of justice, the courts have taken on a catalyst function for the overall improvement of mutual relations in society. Social sustainability is thereby entwined in the legal structure. This makes these types of courts particularly interesting from the perspective of sustainable development.

The appearance of these forms of sustainable justice does not stand alone. Across the world developments can be identified in justice systems that clearly show a search for forms of problem solving and conflict resolution that have a constructive influence on mutual relations in society.

These practical solutions found in different countries are supported by scientific studies. Two important ones should be mentioned here.

First Procedural Justice (or Procedural Fairness), an interesting study emphasising the importance of a fair procedure as studies revealed that judicial decisions are much better accepted and followed when the parties have perceived the procedure as fair, even when the outcome was negative for them (Thibaut and Walker 1975; Tyler 2006; Burke and Leben 2007).

The other important field is Therapeutic Jurisprudence (International Network on Therapeutic Jurisprudence 2017), studying therapeutic and anti-therapeutic effects of justice, and trying to achieve better and more therapeutic outcomes of judicial interference through the application of findings from other disciplines, like psychology, criminology, and social work (Wexler 2000; Winick 2002; International Network on Therapeutic Jurisprudence 2017).

5 Sustainable Justice Charter 1.0 (Dd. 2015, December 10)[15]

Improving social harmony, quality of life, and transparency, through integration of values of social sustainability into justice

Introduction

Sustainable justice is the approach to justice that aims to improve social harmony, wellbeing, the general feeling of safety within society, and furthers personal and societal development, within a framework of human rights and principles securing legal uniformity and equality.

In order to enable justice to intervene effectively, justice is vested with power and independence and acts in the pursuit of social sustainability of society and its members.

Consciousness of sustainability is rapidly spreading around the world and gradually improving every sector of society. Social sustainability is nowadays interconnected with ideas like love, empathy and compassion.

In the recent decades, criticism has been growing that existing justice systems do not appropriately and effectively meet societal needs. Many innovations have developed in justice and legal practice and theory aiming at serving values of social sustainability, like different forms of Problem Solving Courts, Restorative Justice, Intercultural Justice, Procedural Justice and Therapeutic Jurisprudence. These innovations have proven to be effective contributors to solving societal problems and seemingly unbridgeable intercultural gaps. A justice system which acts on principles of social sustainability to guide its remedies for conflict resolution, will have a positive impact on conflict resolution outside the legal system.

Context of Sustainable Justice

Social sustainability

The main goal of Sustainable Justice is increasing the quality of life by improving the quality of relationships and social networks. This cannot be enforced by coercion, punishment or deterrence. Mature inter-humane relationships, mutual respect, empathy and understanding, and an ability to transform negative emotions into creativity and constructive behaviour are essential requirements to improve the level of social sustainability. Values of social sustainability complement judicial values and contribute to the effectiveness of judicial systems.

[15] Sustainable Justice Charter 1.0 is an initiative of the Center for Sustainable Justice by Alexander F. de Savornin Lohman and Jaap van Straalen in close cooperation with Dr. Andrew Cannon: See Center for Sustainable Justice (2015).

Conflicts, criminal acts, and social networks

Sustainable justice sees conflicts and criminal acts as opportunities to restore and improve social harmony. These incidents can occur easily as people and society develop and are seen in the broader context of an individual or societal problem, abuse or wrong. Conflicts and criminal acts not only affect the people directly involved, but also their relatives. They pervert and destroy more than one relationship and social network.

Socially sustainable conflict resolution solves the problem of the people directly involved in a way that benefits all the other stakeholders involved. The individual case is seen as a vehicle to reduce the individual and societal burden of these problems.

Sustainable judicial toolbox

Judicial power is given by society to justice on the assumption that this is beneficial to society. Judicial officers using judicial power are societal change agents, who can act as a catalyst for a better society.

Prestige, independence, and the position as ultimate decision-maker drapes judges with a kind of magic that enables them to accomplish outcomes that others cannot achieve. Judges have the potency to change mindsets and behaviours that were interfering with the resolution of problems. Postponement of the judicial decision opens a rich array of opportunities for sustainable intervention by judges to effectively make use of their transformational magic. This quality grants to judges a key position to procure socially sustainable outcomes.

Socially sustainable outcomes are achieved by using a minimal, but effective, dose of power. Any unsolicited exercise of power breaks down the balance in social relationships and networks, but a well-chosen and well-directed slight corrective impulse of power can restore and heal the harmony that has been disturbed.

Judicial systems and regulations, including budgeting rules can either support or impede the opportunities for the justice system and for judicial officers to achieve socially sustainable outcomes.

Application of Sustainable Justice

The general principle of sustainable judging is to turn bad into good, contributing to social harmony and personal and societal development. This asks for reconsideration of some basic principles of law and justice concerning the function of judicial decision-making and punishment.

Sustainable intervention and decision-making

Judicial decision-making often removes responsibility from a person, which does not support social sustainability. The passive decision-making judge focusing on what went wrong in the past gives perverse incentives to the litigants to play games with their responsibilities.

From the perspective of social sustainability people should not escape responsibility but rather accept personal responsibility and learn from that process. Societal wellbeing and sustainable interests of the parties are served if the judge actively confirms the parties' responsibilities, strokes up mutual respect, enhances mature behaviour and the parties' capacity to deal with their problems constructively, focusing on the best sustainable future for all, including society. Sometimes it can be useful to involve other stakeholders and social service providers in the process of conflict resolution in order to achieve socially sustainable outcomes. Restorative practices can be applied which bring the parties and other stakeholders together into a collaborative process that aims to restore harmony in affected social networks.

Sustainable punishment

Sustainable punishment aims to bring or restore harmony in socially valuable networks, including those of victims, offenders and their relatives. It enables offenders to become valuable members of society, stimulating and supporting them to develop constructive pro-social behaviour, and to reduce unhealthy and anti-social behaviour.

Punishments that include a form of social isolation are breaking down social networks which often causes severe, sometimes lifelong irreparable harm to relatives of the offenders who are innocent. Punishment that harms socially valuable networks should be avoided whenever possible.

Social sustainability does not reject the principles of retribution and deterrence if the results of the application of these principles support values of social sustainability for society and those involved. Great difficulties that ex-prisoners and people with a criminal record experience in getting socially accepted again contribute to their return to criminal behaviour.

Judicial officers using therapeutic techniques and assisting other stakeholders to bring about constructive behavioural change in the offender make use of judicial power as a catalyst to build a socially sustainable society. This method of 'punishing' is sometimes honoured with the nickname 'Smart sentencing' (Hora 2011).[16]

Accountability and Transparency

The contribution of the justice system to the quality of life and social sustainability of society should be clear, transparent and measurable from a material, social, and psychological point of view. A system for measurement with solid parameters should be scientific developed, concerning the structure of the justice system and the contribution of individual judicial officers.

The changing perspective of Justice

Social sustainability provides valuable guiding principles to justice systems encouraging them to gradual change so that they contribute to social harmony more effectively. Conflicts about material interests and criminal behaviour should be used as a vehicle to foster improvement of relationships and social networks, realising the best sustainable future for everybody involved. This can be realised by enhancing

---

[16]See also the Smarter Sentencing Acts of 2013 and 2015 in the USA.

responsibility and accountability of those involved, improving their capacity to manage conflicts and problems in socially constructive ways. This way of working avoids legalisation of conflicts and an adversarial attitude.

A starting point for the whole of the system should be an indissoluble interconnectedness between law and interpersonal respect. This will result in less victimisation and less escalation of conflict, less imprisonment and less bankruptcy.

Justice systems based on principles of social sustainability are role models guiding people in the best ways to manage conflicts and other challenges constructively without harming others.

Initial main co-signers

The Sustainable Justice Charter 1.0 has been initially co-signed by influential leaders in the legal field from all over the world: Hon. Andrew Cannon (Australia), Prof. Martine E. Evans (France), Hon. Ginger Lerner-Wren (USA), Prof. Tania Sourdin (Australia), Jeremy Travis (USA), Prof. Tom R. Tyler (USA), Prof. David B. Wexler (USA) and J. Kim Wright (USA).

6 Conclusion: The Charter and Its Place in the Sustainability Movement

The Sustainable Justice Charter 1.0 and the basic principles of social sustainability, as described in Part 2 of this Chapter, could initiate a structured discussion on integrating CSR principles and sustainable development into justice and the judiciary.

In Part 2 we noted that it is often asked what sustainability and justice have to do with each other. We stated in this Chapter from different perspectives what the position of the judiciary and the justice system are in relation to the sustainability movement. Over time, more and more attention has been paid to intangible sustainability and the quality of the social living environment. Organisations make the effort when it comes to material sustainability, and additional elements of sustainability are being introduced in their way of working and in their approach to fellow human beings, employees and customers. This was also stimulated by legislation and by the attention it had received, e.g. from interest groups and consumer initiatives. By paying more attention to material and social sustainability, it is generally assumed that "society" has become more complex. Disagreements and conflict of interests can therefore also arise much easier. These differences in opinion and conflicts of interests are becoming increasingly complex, which must also be recognised in the judicial system.

Changes have even been introduced in the administration of justice in various parts of the world as a result, also separate from the ideas of the sustainability movement. It has been found for various reasons that the existing methodology in the case law is simply insufficient. Judges have often found solutions through intensive cooperation with other criminal justice partners. This cooperation is mainly focused on two topics: Is it possible to delve deeper into the underlying problems of conflict to thereby find better solutions for both civil law and family problems, and how can people who come into contact with criminal law be prevented at an earlier stage from continuing down the wrong path? Some of these developments and their scientific sources of inspiration, Procedural Justice and Therapeutic Jurisprudence are described in Part 4 of this chapter.

An important question that can also be asked based on these developments is, to what extent should the existing legal system adapt to be better equipped to play its social role?

In this Chapter, we outline two ways to look at this question.

In the first place, the sustainability movement has given a strong impetus to the pursuit of social responsibility and sustainable development. This has led to the need of giving a clear outline to the objectives of sustainability which are often perceived as abstract. The OECD Guidelines and ISO 26000 give substance to this question, as described in Part 2.

Secondly, Part 3 contained a description of how organisations have reacted in general to the increasing complexity of their environment and the more complex issues that arise with that, which is in part caused by an increased need for outcomes which are related to the pursuit of sustainable development. How have they adjusted their organisational structure in response to the increasing complexity?

From the descriptions given in Parts 2, 3 and 4, it appears that there are many similarities between the two perspectives and the reaction in the legal world with innovation initiatives. There appears to be much agreement between the three descriptions about how organisations should adapt to the more complex environment in which they are located. It is important with this adjustment to pay attention to existing knowledge at the basis of the organisation and to increase transparency in the process and information exchange. In Part 3 we described that attention to these two points in particular should lead to successful organisations. These organisations also appear to have a clear objective and policy and they have a clear definition of who their customers or clients are.

This knowledge can be of interest in two ways. Firstly, judicial organisations can benefit from this knowledge by adapting their own organisation and processes in such a way that a clear and unambiguous policy (top-down style) creates balanced use of knowledge within the organisation (bottom-up).

This knowledge is also important for the manner in which the legal system functions within society. If we propose interaction between the judicial system and society as an organisation (legal system) with customers (citizens of society), then the question becomes how the legal system can serve society and its citizens as well as possible. What potential cooperation between parties in the judicial chain would lead to better solutions for society and its citizens, which is currently not fully included with the current justice system?

It is also important that clear information will be available on the degree of perceived satisfaction among people with the solutions. The way in which related registration will take place requires further research. Examples from the sustainability movement can be used, such as environmental impact reports.

The Sustainable Justice Charter 1.0 sets out the way in which officials, and especially judges, can contribute to better solutions, and thereby to a sustainable justice system. The practical initiatives in justice that we described in Part 4 indicate that justice is strenuously attempting to find out which method and organisational form better suits citizen issues to be resolved. The Sustainable Justice Charter therefore provides substantive pointers, while frameworks are outlined in Parts 2 and 3 on how adequate organisational forms can be established in a systematic manner. This applies both to individual organisations in the judicial chain and to the way in which these individual organisations should cooperate.

References

Australian Bureau of Statistics (2017) 2016 Census shows growing Aboriginal and Torres Strait Islander population (Media release 075/2017, 27 June). http://www.abs.gov.au/ausstats/abs@.nsf/mediareleasesbyReleaseDate/02D50FAA9987D6B7CA25814800087E03?OpenDocument. Accessed 26 Feb 2018

Auty K, Briggs D (2004) Koori Court Victoria: Magistrates Court (Koori Court) Act 2002. Law Text Cult 8. http://ro.uow.edu.au/cgi/viewcontent.cgi?article=1113&context=ltc. Accessed 8 Jan 2018

Barendrecht M, ter Beek K, Muller S (2017) Menselijk en Rechtvaardig, Is de rechtsstaat er voor de burger? The Hague (HiiL). http://www.hiil.org/data/sitemanagement/media/HiiL%20Menselijk%20en%20rechtvaardig%20Launch%203%20mei%202017%20def.pdf. Accessed 14 Oct 2017

Berman G, Feinblatt J (2005) Good courts: the case for problem-solving justice. The New Press, New York

Brenninkmeijer A et al (2015). Zes Suggesties voor de Verbetering van de Toegang tot het Recht. The Hague (HiiL). http://www.hiil.org/data/sitemanagement/media/Zes%20Suggesties%20voor%20Verbetering%20van%20de%20Toegang%20tot%20Recht.pdf. Accessed 18 Oct 2017

Burke K, Leben S (2007) Procedural fairness: a key ingredient in public satisfaction (A white paper of the American Judges Association). Court Rev 44(1/2):4–24

Center for Court Innovation (2017). http://www.courtinnovation.org/research/community-courts-around-world?mode=4&url=research%2F4%2Farticle. Accessed 15 Oct 2017

Center for Sustainable Justice (2015) Sustainable justice charter 1.0. www.sustainablejusticecharter.com. Accessed 17 Oct 2017

Earth Charter Initiative (2016) Earth charter around the world. www.earthcharter.org. Accessed 13 Aug 2017

Fryer-Smith S (2008) Aboriginal Benchbook for Western Australian Courts, 2nd edn. Australasian Institute of Judicial Administration, Melbourne. https://aija.org.au/wp-content/uploads/2017/07/Aboriginal-Benchbook-for-WA-Courts-2nd-Ed.pdf. Accessed 6 Jan 2008

Harper M (2015) Top-down versus bottom-up management styles. Business Administration and Management Touro University Worldwide. http://www.tuw.edu/content/business/top-down-bottom-up-management/. Accessed 6 Jan 2018

Harris M (2006) "A Sentencing Conversation": Evaluation of the Koori Courts Pilot Program: October 2002–October 2004. Department of Justice, Melbourne. https://www.indigenousjustice.gov.au/resources/a-sentencing-conversation-evaluation-of-the-koori-courts-pilot-program-october-2002-october-2004/. Accessed 6 Jan 2018

Hora PF (2011) Smart justice: building safer communities, increasing access to courts, and elevating trust and confidence in the justice system. Adelaide Thinker in Residence, Department of the Premier and Cabinet, South Australia

ICC Sustainable Business Charter (2015) Inspire and grow your business. International Chamber of Commerce. http://www.icc.nl/docman-standpunten/docman-commissies/docman-commisies-klimaat-energie/83-icc-business-charter-sustainable-development/file. Accessed 5 Oct 2017

International Network on Therapeutic Jurisprudence (2017) www.therapeuticjurisprudence.org. Accessed 18 Oct 2017

ISO 26000 (2010) Guidance on social responsibility. International Organisation for Standardisation, Geneva. https://www.iso.org/iso-26000-social-responsibility.html. Accessed 21 Sept 2017

ISO Sustainability Brochure (2012) Sustainability, sustainable development and social responsibility: ISO definitions and terminology. http://iso26000.info/wp-content/uploads/2016/03/ISO_Sustainability_brochure.pdf

King M, Freiberg A, Batagol B, Hyams R (2009) Non-adversarial justice. Federation Press, Sydney

Laloux F (2014) Reinventing organisations, a guide to creating organizations inspired by the new stage of consciousness. Nelson Parker, Brussels

Marchetti E (2009) Indigenous sentencing courts. Indigenous Justice Clearinghouse, December 2009. http://www.indigenousjustice.gov.au/briefs/brief005.pdf. Accessed 17 Oct 2017

Marchetti E, Daly K (2004) Indigenous courts and justice practices in Australia. Trends & Issues in Crime and Criminal Justice 277. Australian Institute of Criminology. http://www.aic.gov.au/media_library/publications/tandi_pdf/tandi277.pdf. Accessed 6 Jan 2018

Marchetti E, Daly K (2007) Indigenous courts: towards a theoretical and jurisprudential model. Sydney Law Rev 29:415–443

McChrystal S, Collins T, Silverman D, Fussell C (2015) Team of teams: new rules of engagement in a complex world. Penguin Books, London

Meadows DH, Meadows DL, Randers J, Behrens WW III (1972) The limits to growth: a report for the Club of Rome's project on the predicament of mankind. Potomac Associates, Washington DC

National Association of Drug Court Professionals (2017) http://www.courtinnovation.org/research/community-courts-around-world?mode=4&url=research%2F4%2Farticle. Accessed 15 Oct 2017

OECD Guidelines for Multinational Enterprises (2008) Organisation for economic co-operation and development, Paris. http://www.oecd.org/corporate/mne/1922428.pdf. Accessed 18 Oct 2017

OECD Guidelines for Multinational Enterprises (2011) organisation for economic co-operation and development, Paris. https://www.oecd.org/corporate/mne/48004323.pdf. Accessed 18 Oct 2017

Potas I, Smart J, Brignell G, Thomas B, Lawrie R (2003) Circle sentencing in New South Wales: a review and evaluation. NSW Aboriginal Justice Advisory Board, Judicial Commission of New South Wales, Sydney. https://www.judcom.nsw.gov.au/wp-content/uploads/2016/07/research-monograph-22.pdf. Accessed 6 Jan 2018

Scharmer O, Kaufer K (2013) Leading from the emerging future, from ego system to eco system economics. Barrett-Koehler Publishers, San Francisco

Thibaut J, Walker L (1975) Procedural justice: a psychological analysis. Larence Erlbaum Associates, Hillsdale

Tyler TR (2006) Why people obey the law. Princeton University Press, Princeton

United Nations (1992) United Nations Conference on Environment & Development Rio de Janerio, Brazil, 3–14 June 1992: Agenda 21. https://sustainabledevelopment.un.org/content/documents/Agenda21.pdf. Accessed 13 Aug 2017

United Nations (2015a) Millennium objectives. http://www.unmillenniumproject.org/goals/. Accessed 13 Aug 2017

United Nations (2015b) Transforming our world: the 2030 agenda for sustainable development. https://sustainabledevelopment.un.org/post2015/transformingourworld. Accessed 17 Oct 2017

Wexler DB (2000) Therapeutic jurisprudence: an overview. Thomas M. Cooley Law Rev 17:125–134

Wikipedia (2017a) Brundtland Commission. https://en.wikipedia.org/wiki/Brundtland_Commission. Accessed 4 Oct 2017

Wikipedia (2017b) Earth Charter. https://en.wikipedia.org/wiki/Earth_Charter. Accessed 5 Oct 2017

Winick BJ (2002) Therapeutic jurisprudence and problem solving courts. Fordham Urban Law J 20:1090–1155

World Commission on Environment and Development (1987) Our common future (also known as the Brundtland Report). UN Documents. http://www.un-documents.net/wced-ocf.htm. Accessed 13 Aug 2017

Alexander F. de Savornin Lohman has practiced as a civil legal attorney in the Netherlands, integrating principles of sustainable development and social responsibility into legal practice. He developed sustainable lawyering and sustainable justice and has published, inter alia, about sustainable justice, end of life medical treatment and victim's rights. He is co-founder of the Centre for Sustainable Justice and co-author of the Sustainable Justice Charter 1.0.

Jaap van Straalen is sustainability entrepreneur and advisor. He is an experienced director, advisor and interim manager in medium-sized companies, and an expert in making strategic choices and shaping a more effective organisation in which new technical resources may also be involved. He is co-founder of the Centre for Sustainable Justice and co-author of the Sustainable Justice Charter 1.0.

Part II
Comparative Approaches to Responsive Judging

Inside Out or Outside In?: Looking at Judges' Relations with the Public in Canada and China

Archie Zariski and Changqing Shi

Abstract This chapter presents comparative case studies of relations between members of the judiciary in Canada and China with the public in general in those countries. It adopts a conceptual and theoretical framework centered on comparing internal (participants) and external (observers) perspectives on the judicial institution specifically as they relate to questions of social legitimacy of courts and their judges. The actions of several prominent judges in both countries concerning high profile cases and issues are described and analyzed within this framework. The responses of the judiciaries of Canada and China to the challenge they share of securing and protecting their legitimacy in the eyes of the public are thus compared and contrasted. Two types of counter-intuitive results of this comparison are found: those where the two judiciaries appear to be following the same steps, but when examined closely, for different purposes, and the opposite situation where actions differ but purposes accord. These situations occur respectively in the areas of regulation of judicial activity in local matters, and actions intended to enhance the sociological legitimacy of the judiciary.

1 Introduction

To be called "Judge" sets a person apart in society, but does it also entail taking no part in the ordinary life of that society? In this chapter we tackle that question through a comparison of judges and judging in Canada and China. Judges may be responsive to those around them in many ways. Here we focus on judges' interactions with the public at large rather than with litigants in particular cases before the courts.

A. Zariski (✉)
Athabasca University, Athabasca, Canada
e-mail: archiez@athabascau.ca

C. Shi
Shanghai University, Shanghai, People's Republic of China
e-mail: shchq1127@126.com

© Springer Nature Singapore Pte Ltd. 2018

T. Sourdin and A. Zariski (eds.), *The Responsive Judge*, Ius Gentium: Comparative Perspectives on Law and Justice 67, https://doi.org/10.1007/978-981-13-1023-2_7

Our study explores three questions regarding relations between judges and the public in which we believe the "internal/external distinction"[1] in socio-legal studies is implicated:

1. How are boundaries set for the proper conduct for judges when they interact with the public?
2. What is the role of judges in relation to the interchange between a legal system and the society in which it exists?
3. Should comparative studies of judges in different legal systems focus on norms or facts (or both)?

Barzun (2015) has recently provided a helpful restatement of the modern meaning and application of the internal/external dichotomy as applied to law. In general terms, it may be understood as drawing a distinction between describing and understanding the content of law (as opposed to "non-law") and the work of law in a society either from the subjective (internal) perspective of an actor within the legal system, or as an objective (external) observer without a stake in the action. As Barzun notes, the idea has been adapted and modified since being advanced in the mid twentieth century for a variety of methodological and rhetorical purposes. Unlike Professor Barzun, we believe that the concept of a (perhaps blurry) line (even if not a boundary) between what is considered internal and external to a legal system remains useful when considering the kinds of questions set out above.

We employ the internal/external concept (henceforth "I/E") both in its substantive and its methodological variants as identified by Barzun.[2] Thus, we adopt I/E as encompassing not only a substantive normative distinction between "what counts" in legal practice and what does not, but also a methodological stance which permits taking different perspectives on a legal system, based on whether they are those of "participants" or "outsiders".[3] Here is a brief outline of our arguments in response to the questions raised above.

First, we suggest that I/E may help to clarify the setting of boundaries for judicial behavior through contrasting legal rules with social norms and expectations. Many judiciaries today are either subject to legislation which governs the conduct of judges, or have adopted rules, guidelines or principles of their own. For example, judges are prohibited from accepting bribes from litigants, or using confidential information acquired in judging for personal financial gain. Such rules are intended to prevent corruption and ensure that adjudication is fair to all parties. These are internal controls that legal systems impose on themselves, but they are supplemented by concern for how the public views the actions of judges both when they are engaged in cases

---

[1] For a helpful description and analysis of the use of this concept in socio-legal studies see Tamanaha (1996, 2006).

[2] We acknowledge the difficulties that can arise from using both perspectives in one study as described by Posner and Vermeule (2013) and hope we have avoided the traps through adopting what has been called a "detached viewpoint": see Rodriguez-Blanco (2007).

[3] As Martha Minow puts it: "observers have a different understanding than do participants in a particular activity." (Minow 1990, 795).

and when they are not. This concern is often expressed in terms of maintaining the independence, impartiality and integrity of the judiciary so that the public has trust and confidence in their judges. Once public opinion is considered relevant it is our argument that we have moved to an external perspective that is best understood as a question of the public perception of the legitimacy of the judicial establishment.[4] Thus, in cases of questionable judicial behavior that does not offend clear internal rules of conduct it becomes necessary to consider how an external perspective may assist in judging judges.

Second, we argue that I/E helps to describe and analyze the porous boundary between law and society as exemplified in the person of the judge who is both always a judge and always an ordinary citizen. Today it is now widely accepted that law and legal systems should play an instrumental role in society. That is, law does not exist in and for itself, but is one way amongst others for a society to govern itself peacefully and productively. To accomplish that goal a legal system must be both responsive to the needs and interests of society, and also at the same time what has been described as "semi-autonomous" within the society with a distinct culture, norms, and process of its own. If a legal system did not enjoy such autonomy it would be hard to distinguish it from everyday politics. The question then becomes how does a legal system remain responsive while maintaining a degree of autonomy? We believe that judges may be part of the answer to that question because they can play dual roles in society—both as internal actors within a legal system as well as external "ambassadors" interacting with other social systems. In this sense, judges can be considered as forming part of a permeable "membrane" separating law from other social forces. I/E therefore contributes a useful perspective in describing and evaluating the responsiveness of legal systems.

Third, we propose that I/E is a helpful conceptual framework when making a comparative analysis of a universally recognized legal role ("judge") in its concrete manifestation in different societies. It follows from the functional view of law that different societies may place different demands on their legal systems. To the extent these interests are integrated in law they become part of the internal meaning and reasoning of legal actors within those systems. When comparing systems we believe that it is best to attempt to describe both the practices that may be observed from an external viewpoint, and the meanings attached to that behavior by legal actors such as judges understood from an internal perspective. Fairer and more accurate comparisons may thus be made in a way that does not privilege the internal perspective of one of the legal systems in question as an evaluative lens.

Concerning the first two questions above we adopt a case study approach to illustrate their importance in the careers of several judges in both countries. The third question is responded to by the comparative nature of this chapter.

The chapter is organized as follows: next we provide a fuller explanation of our conceptual and theoretical framework with I/E at its core; then we apply that

---

[4]The Supreme Court of Canada seems to have recognized this in an important constitutional case by stating that "law's claim to legitimacy also rests on an appeal to moral values"—presumably those of the community it serves. (Reference re Secession of Quebec 1998).

analytical lens to observations of Canadian and Chinese judges; this is followed by comparisons between them and finally we offer some conclusions.

2 Internal and External Aspects of the Judicial Role

Judges play a unique role in all legal systems, but they are also social actors bearing the hopes and expectations of justice of the communities in which they live and work. What judges do may therefore be usefully described and analyzed in two aspects: as internal participants in legal processes, or as citizens engaged in social life external to the legal system. Although this may be a useful distinction it must also be kept in mind that the judge is always and everywhere both just a member of society like others and at the same time the living embodiment of the search for justice of that society.[5]

2.1 Legitimacy

"Legitimacy" is a term with many usages both internally to law and externally in society generally. Fallon (2005) has analyzed and described what he calls three concepts of legitimacy: as a legal concept, as a sociological concept, and as a moral concept. We collapse the latter two concepts into a category we will call "external legitimacy" while the legal concept will be considered as "internal legitimacy".

Legitimacy from an internal perspective has a variety of usages and meanings. Perhaps the most familiar is as the traditional description of a child born to parents who are married ("legitimate"), as distinguished from one whose parents are not ("illegitimate"). The common law also has a doctrine of "legitimate expectations"[6] in which legitimate means something like "reasonable and justifiable". Thus, if a party is found to have a legitimate expectation that an authority will follow due process by allowing them to respond to factual allegations or legal arguments, then the law will require that opportunity to be given by such authority. The word legitimate may also be used to describe recognized rights in law, such as those granted by contractual obligations. These are examples of forms of legitimacy that are internal to legal systems and are part of positive law.

External (sociological and moral) legitimacy as applied to law is a matter of opinion based upon perceptions of the legal system by members of the public. It is an evaluation that may be reached in relation to a discrete act such as the judgment in a single case, or it may be applied to an entire legal system or one of its institutional

[5]For discussion of public influence on judging from an American perspective see Nagel (1990) and Delgado (1990).

[6]The leading Canadian case on this principle is Mavis Baker v. Minister of Citizenship and Immigration (1999).

components such as the judiciary.[7] One measure of external legitimacy is public opinion gauged through surveys or other methodologies.[8]

Judicial behavior is subjected to the test of both internal and external legitimacy, although this terminology is not often used. When considering questionable actions by judges it is usually asked whether they transgressed ethical rules or offended the principles of judicial conduct. These are internal tests especially when applied to actions clearly within the judicial function. However, when judges engage in conduct which is unrelated to any identifiable case or legal proceeding, or in a merely personal capacity, they are often judged by the test of whether their behavior may reflect badly on the reputation of the judiciary. The question that is thus raised reflects a concern for maintaining the trust and confidence of the public in all judges. In other words, the behavior is being evaluated for its impact on the external legitimacy of the judicial establishment. We will question this mixing of an external perspective on the law within the internal legal process of disciplining judges for improper relations with the public.

2.2 *Responsiveness*

It is a longstanding theme in socio-legal research to investigate the impact of law on society and of society on law. If a legal system and its actors are to be responsive to the society in which they are embedded then some such reciprocal influence must be present. According to the systems theory elaborated by Luhmann (2004) and Teubner (1993), society can be thought of as a system of subsystems such as the political system, the economic system, the education and health systems, and the legal system amongst others. Each subsystem should be considered "semi-autonomous" because they operate with concepts, norms and processes which are unique to them and are sometimes described as a "culture". A question then arises as to how a subsystem such as law can both maintain elements of autonomy while remaining in touch with and responsive to the wider society which forms its environment.

Teubner (2014) suggests that the mechanism of reciprocal influence between law and other systems forming a society is a communicative one. In other words, information and messages pass from one system to another but must undergo a type of "translation" before they become meaningful and relevant within the system that receives

[7]The Supreme Court of Canada has spoken about legitimacy of political and judicial institutions being supported by the Constitution in the case Reference re Remuneration of Judges of the Provincial Court of Prince Edward Island; Reference re Independence and Impartiality of Judges of the Provincial Court of Prince Edward Island (1997). Fallon (2005) provides a discussion of the legal, sociological, and moral concepts of legitimacy in the United States constitutional context. Bassok (2011) examines the sociological legitimacy of courts using the concepts of "institutional capital or institutional loyalty".

[8]Friedman (2003) discusses public opinion and the concept of "diffuse support" for courts while Strawn (2008) has conducted an empirical study of relations between judicial codes of ethics and public perceptions of judges' impartiality. See also Howarth and Stark (2014).

and evaluates them.[9] For us, this concept of communicating semi-autonomous systems is another application of I/E. Leading legal actors can be considered as a key part of the communicative mechanism by acting at times internally and at other times externally to a legal system. Thus, judges may function as influential messengers as well as “translators” in the interaction between law and society.

If judges are not attuned to the messages circulating in society their decisions are more prone to error and misjudgment. This may take the form of decision making which relies on “common sense” which is far from being common in the community or which ignores commonly accepted facts or propositions.[10]

2.3 *Comparativism*

The I/E distinction leads to a categorization of descriptions of judges’ actions based on searches for regularities in behavior (an external point of view) and for the meanings of those actions as understood by judges themselves (the internal point of view). The logical result is a table of possibilities as follows:

	Behavior (B) (external)	
Meaning (M) (internal)	Same B/different M	Different B/different M
	Same B/same M	Different B/same M

Admittedly this is an ideal scheme and there will always be gradations between the poles of “same” and “different”.

An example may help to understand this analytical tool. Let us say that three legal systems are studied to determine the frequency of judges meeting separately with one of the parties to litigation in the absence of the other. In System 1 this almost always happens; in System 2 almost never; and in System 3 about half of the time. One might conclude that System 1 and 2 are distinctly different while System 3 has some resemblance to both the other two. Looking further at the meanings ascribed to these practices by the judges engaged in them might reveal that in System 1 there is a strong norm that adjudication should be the last resort and judges have a duty to encourage parties to resolve their differences. In System 2 there is a strong norm of impartiality of judges which dissuades them from ever meeting privately with parties, although it is acceptable to encourage settlement in joint meetings. System 3 has a rule of court permitting judges to mediate cases before them, and some judges believe a private “caucus” with each party is appropriate as part of that process, while others do not. If a researcher from System 2 applied the norms of that jurisdiction (internal point of view) to the observed practices of the other two she might find

[9]Reichman (2007) describes the legal system in similar terms as “cognitively open” through the mediation of its judges who may act as learning agents.

[10]For studies of this problem see Burns (2016), Burns et al. (2016), and Blackham (2016).

them flawed and contrary to the "rule of law". However, an observer who adopted an external point of view and tried to make sense of the observations might conclude that all three systems encourage settlement, but adopt different approaches to achieve that goal. In terms of the categories shown above this would be a case of different behavior/same meaning.

3 Canadian Judges

3.1 *The Canadian Judiciary*

The judges of the higher courts in Canada, comprising the Provincial superior courts, the Federal Court, and the Supreme Court of Canada (Canada's highest court) are all appointed by the Federal executive branch and hold office in the words of the Canadian Constitution "during good behavior".[11] They may only be removed by a vote of both branches (House of Commons and Senate) of the federal Parliament. The *Judges Act* creates the Canadian Judicial Council (CJC) comprising the chief justices of all the higher courts and elaborates the grounds upon which it may decide to recommend that a judge be removed from office by Parliament.

The federal Minister of Justice selects appointees to the superior courts and the Federal Court after consultation with judges and lawyers and the Prime Minister chooses the judges of the Supreme Court of Canada after similar consultation. Following English practice most judges are selected from the ranks of senior lawyers, although some law professors have also been appointed. It is commonly believed that an individual's chances of appointment to a court are enhanced, though not guaranteed, if they have been associated with, or supported, the political party then in power as the Government in the federal Parliament. In a rather unique constitutional arrangement the courthouses and court staff of the superior courts are supplied and paid for by the Province in which the court sits while the judges' salaries of all the courts mentioned are paid by the federal government.

3.2 *Professional Ethics*

The CJC has adopted a document titled *Ethical Principles for Judges* (Canadian Judicial Council 2004) but have emphasized that it is not a code of rules of conduct but rather more in the nature of guidelines subject to flexible application.[12] Like similar documents in many other jurisdictions it highlights the need for judges to

---

[11]The same standard is found in the United States Constitution (Article III). See the commentary by a former American Supreme Court judge: O'Connor (2003).

[12]This publication follows on from several earlier ones: Wilson (1980), Canadian Judicial Council (1990, 1991a, b), and Friedland (1995).

be independent, to exhibit integrity and diligence, to respect the equality of persons before the court, and to demonstrate impartiality in judgment according to law.[13] The *Principles* deal with conduct both in court and out and considers situations in which a judge interacts with the public.

The commentary concerning integrity states in part:

> **4.** Judges, of course, have private lives and should enjoy, as much as possible, the rights and freedoms of citizens generally. Moreover, an out of touch judge is less likely to be effective. Neither the judge's personal development nor the public interest is well served if judges are unduly isolated from the communities they serve. Legal standards frequently call for the application of the reasonable person test. Judicial fact-finding, an important part of a judge's work, calls for the evaluation of evidence in light of common sense and experience. Therefore, judges should, to the extent consistent with their special role, remain closely in touch with the public....
>
> **5.** A judge's conduct, both in and out of court, is bound to be the subject of public scrutiny and comment. Judges must therefore accept some restrictions on their activities — even activities that would not elicit adverse notice if carried out by other members of the community. Judges need to strike a delicate balance between the requirements of judicial office and the legitimate demands of the judge's personal life, development and family. (Canadian Judicial Council 2004)

In its commentary on the principles the document quotes from a case in the Supreme Court of Canada:

> Both independence and impartiality are fundamental, not only to the capacity to do justice in a particular case but also to individual and public confidence in the administration of justice. Without that confidence the system cannot command the respect and acceptance that are essential to its effective operation. It is, therefore, important that a tribunal should be perceived as independent, as well as impartial... (Canadian Judicial Council 2004)

However, the document also acknowledges that a prudent judge is not required to sever all ties to the community which she serves:

> C.2 The judge administers the law on behalf of the community and therefore unnecessary isolation from the community does not promote wise or just judgments. The Right Honourable Gerald Fauteux put the matter succinctly and eloquently in *Le livre du magistrate* (translation):
>
>> [there is no intention] to place the judiciary in an ivory tower and to require it to cut off all relationship with organizations which serve society. Judges are not expected to live on the fringe of society of which they are an important part. To do so would be contrary to the effective exercise of judicial power which requires exactly the opposite approach. (Canadian Judicial Council 2004)

The Canadian judiciary is clearly aware of both the benefits and the dangers of judges engaging with the public outside their courtrooms. The next sections explore this tension as manifested in the lives of three Canadian judges.

---

[13]It has been noted that judicial independence functions primarily to support the appearance and actuality of judges' impartiality when deciding cases: Renke (1994).

3.3 *Law and Politics (Tom Berger)*

Most Canadian judges shy away from public attention outside their courtrooms. Justice Thomas Berger was an exception. In his career as a lawyer in the Province of British Columbia he often acted for aboriginal peoples (known in Canada as First Nations) in their claims for legal rights and recognition. Public attention to such struggles was welcomed. Further, as an active politician Berger was elected both to the Provincial legislature and the federal Parliament as a member of a left of center party. He was accustomed to, and comfortable with, public debate and this did not change when he was appointed to the superior court in 1972.[14]

Several years later Berger was appointed by the federal government to head a public inquiry (while remaining a judge) into a proposal to build a pipeline in Canada's north. The projected line was massive both physically and economically, but its route traversed lands subject to unresolved claims by the First Nations who lived there. After lengthy inquiries with much media attention a report was issued that recommended the land claims be settled before proceeding with construction. The pipeline was never built.

In the early 1980s Canada experienced widespread public political and legal debate over proposals to renew and revise its Constitution. Pierre Trudeau, the Prime Minister, (father of the current one) wished to add a bill of rights to the Constitution (the Canadian Charter of Rights and Freedoms) making it more like the American one, and less like the "unwritten" constitution of the United Kingdom. A very significant element of the proposed changes was to give the Canadian courts expanded authority to conduct judicial review of legislation and other government action at all levels from the federal, to the provincial and municipal. Prior to this the courts were limited to deciding which governmental level, the federal or the provincial, had jurisdiction to act according to the "division of powers" clauses of the constitution. Pursuant to the proposed Charter, however, Canadian judges would assume the obligation and authority to strike down and declare null and void laws passed at any level, and to interfere in any governmental activity, if they were found to contravene the rights set out in the Charter.

While this national debate was occurring Justice Berger authored a book, *Fragile Freedoms: Human Rights and Dissent in Canada*, (Berger 1981) in which he surveyed the rights (or lack thereof) of various minorities in Canadian history including the First Nations. One of the constitutional issues being debated was whether the rights of First Nations should be recognized and protected in the Charter. In 1981 the Prime Minister reached a negotiated agreement with the leaders of all the Provinces (except the Province of Quebec) on the wording of the Charter which omitted special

---

[14]Berger was not the first or the last Canadian judge to be politically outspoken. Before him the first judge of Canada's Northwest Territories (Jack Sissons) often criticized politicians and the civil service. See Sissons (1968). In 1995 Justice Angers of the New Brunswick Court of Appeal published an open letter to the Prime Minister criticizing the Government's proposed legislation on gun control. He was censured for his actions (Angers 1995).

mention of the First Nations. During a speaking tour promoting his book Justice Berger criticized this result in a public speech reported in part as follows:

> The constitutional agreement is a defeat for the native peoples but it is also a defeat for all Canadians. The agreement reveals the true limits of the Canadian conscience and the Canadian imagination. For the statesmen who signed the agreement of Nov. 5, 1981, represent us. They know us well, and they believed they could, with impunity, delete native rights from the Constitution. (Report 1983)

Recognition of First Nations was soon after reintroduced to the final Charter wording which eventually became part of the new Constitution. However, in the meantime the Prime Minister responded in a television interview to Justice Berger's comments in part as follows:

> He saw fit to get off the bench and enter into the political arena at a very inopportune time. I just regard this as the judiciary getting mixed into politics and I hope the judges will do something about it. (Report 1983)

Subsequently a judge of the Federal Court lodged a complaint with the CJC about Justice Berger's behavior and a committee of inquiry comprised mostly of chief justices was appointed to investigate and report to the CJC. That committee concluded Berger had engaged in misconduct which would justify asking Parliament to remove him from office, but recommended only censure because the rules and principles were not clear beforehand. The full CJC accepted that Berger had acted "indiscreetly", but that his conduct did not call for removal, and it only issued a warning that such action should not be repeated by any judge.[15] The Chief Justice of Canada (Chair of the CJC) however, continued to criticize Berger publicly, and the judge decided he had no choice but to resign his office.[16] Berger returned to the active practice of law, conducted more high profile cases on behalf of First Nations and continued his critical writing. (Berger 1985, 1991b, 2002).

In 1982, during what came to be called the "Berger affair", the *Ethical Principles for Judges* had not yet been adopted although there were influential Canadian books with similar messages. What interests us in this chapter is the use in this case of references to public opinion in order to justify judicial discipline. The inquiry committee reported as follows:

> It is important that public confidence in the judiciary and in its impartiality should not be impaired. Sir William Anson was of the view that Parliament could extend the term "good behaviour" to cover "any form of misconduct which would destroy public confidence in the holder of the office". (Anson, Law and Custom of the [… 115] Constitution, 3rd ed., p. 222). (Report 1983)

[15]The "chilling effect" on judicial speech of such warnings without punishment has been noted and criticized: Lubet (1989). See also McCormick (1998).

[16]Justice Berger had communicated his views forcefully in his own defence to Chief Justice Laskin in a letter later published as part of a symposium: Berger (1991a). Years earlier, Laskin, at the time only a member of the Supreme Court, had spoken of "the dilemma of the judge who must be very much of society and yet is compelled by the nature of his office to stand apart from it": Laskin (1972). As Chief Justice, Laskin clearly was of the opinion that Berger resolved this dilemma inappropriately.

They concluded as follows:

> The judicial office is one which confers important privileges, obligations and protections necessary to the carrying out of the duties of one of Her Majesty's judges. A judge must accept the duty to protect that office, his fellow judges and the public from political controversy as the best way of maintaining "the historic personal independence" of judges. (Report 1983)

No evidence was produced (other than the Prime Minister's statements) that the general public considered Berger's remarks out of line. Justice Berger argued in his defense that given his background, knowledge, and experience he felt a moral obligation to speak out in support of First Nations. It may well be that many members of the Canadian public accepted that stance and it would have been remarkable and more damaging to the reputation of the legal system in their eyes if he had stayed silent.[17] Our concern is with the ability of the legal system in an internal proceeding to integrate a concern for the perceived legitimacy of the judiciary which requires evaluation from an external perspective on the law.

3.4 *Local Involvement (Ted Matlow)*

Ted Matlow had a long and respectable career as a superior court judge in the Province of Ontario before becoming involved in a local building controversy involving the City of Toronto (Canada's largest). Matlow lived on a short "dead end" street with only one outlet to the local main road. At that intersection the City owned and operated a parking lot. The City, in cooperation with a land developer, proposed to rezone the land so that the developer could acquire it in order to build and sell some condominium residences. All was well until Matlow and his neighbors learned that the building plans had changed to become a multi-storey complex containing commercial spaces and more residential units than originally proposed. Many in the neighborhood, including Matlow, came to believe that the size and nature of the project had been illegally altered and they suspected improper behavior on the part of city officials (including its legal department) in collaboration with the developer.

A local group of residents, with Justice Matlow as its unofficial "Chair", took legal and political steps (lobbying) to try to stop the development. They were unsuccessful, but later Matlow was prompted to take his concerns to a national newspaper based in the city to gain exposure for what he continued to consider a failure of law and legal process. All the while these steps were being taken Justice Matlow continued to participate in judging cases involving the City of Toronto. Eventually, when the judge's latest media move became known the chief city lawyer (City Solicitor) complained of Matlows' actions to the CJC. An inquiry committee held a public hearing with witnesses and concluded that Parliament should be asked to remove the judge from his position. The full CJC disagreed, considering him to have engaged in misconduct, but not so serious as to warrant removal. The CJC imposed conditions

[17] Members of the legal profession were also critical of the handling of the affair by the CJC. See for example Webber (1984) and Felsky (1984).

on the judge, including apologizing to the City Solicitor, and the requirement to seek the advice and consent of the CJC before becoming engaged in any other public controversies. Justice Matlow later retired and criticized the process and outcome of the proceedings taken against him (Carville 2015).

In these proceedings Justice Matlow freely acknowledged that in retrospect some of the language he had used regarding the city lawyers was intemperate and ill-advised and that some of his actions displayed poor judgment. Nevertheless, he maintained that at all times he had acted out of an honest and sincere belief an injustice had been committed, that he had never been biased against the City in his judgments, and that his reputation remained intact, if not enhanced, as a result of his actions. In relation to the latter argument a commendatory statement from the local community and character references from colleagues and neighbors were placed before the inquiry committee. The committee at first doubted whether they should be admitted as evidence, and later chose to essentially ignore them in its decision making.

In reaching its decision the committee referred to the question of the confidence of the public in appearing before Justice Matlow or in the justice system as a whole. But rather than inquiring into any actual perceptions of members of the public the committee was content to reach a decision based on its own view of what a "reasonable, fair minded and informed person" would think of the judge's conduct. Although the "reasonable person" test is used in other branches of law we suggest it may be inappropriate when an external perspective is needed to test questionable behavior. The committee reached a conclusion of external fact (loss of public confidence) based solely on its own internal view of the law and judges.

The CJC did not question this approach to evaluating judicial conduct but qualified it to some extent, stating:

> [148] Justice Matlow submits that character evidence is relevant to the assessment of his integrity and credibility and also constitutes mitigating factors with respect to the appropriate penalty. Therefore, it should have been considered by the Inquiry Committee.
>
> [149] The reasons of the Inquiry Committee indicate that it viewed this evidence as partisan and, in any event, as representative of a small segment of the public only. We do not disagree with this assessment. But we also find the evidence to be relevant. Positing the opposite question, what if there were a deluge of letters from the local community, including Justice Matlow's peers and lawyers, to the effect that he was unfit to hold office? Would that be relevant as part of our deliberations? We think it may properly be. So too, are the support letters which have been accepted as evidence.
>
> [150] Character is certainly relevant to the assessment of a judge's attributes. The letters deal with various aspects of Justice Matlow's character, that is his integrity, honesty, conscientious work ethic, and commitment. While these letters are not relevant to whether the conduct complained of occurred, they may be relevant to why the acts occurred, the context of the acts, and whether the acts were committed without malice and without bad faith. Character is also highly relevant to the issue of what recommendations should flow from a finding of judicial misconduct. While the weight to be given to this evidence is admittedly for the inquiry committee, and while an inquiry committee may elect to give it little weight, still it is an error in principle to simply ignore this kind of evidence for all purposes. In particular, the evidence is relevant to the sanction phase of the proceedings and ought to have been considered in that context. It was not. (Canadian Judicial Council 2008)

If the only evidence of public opinion before the inquiry committee was that the "local community" supported the judge and approved of his conduct it is hard to understand how the element of "loss of public confidence" in the test for judicial misconduct was found to exist in Matlow's case. In the result, the CJC reviewed all the conduct complained of, finding that only some of it could be characterized as misconduct, and concluding that

> [184] After taking into account all relevant materials and factors, it is our opinion that while Justice Matlow made serious errors of judgement which constituted judicial misconduct and also placed him in a position incompatible with the due execution of his office, that a recommendation for removal from the Bench is not warranted in this case. In all the circumstances, we are of the opinion that Justice Matlow's conduct is not "so manifestly and profoundly destructive of the concept of impartiality, integrity and independence of the judicial role, that public confidence would be sufficiently undermined to render the judge incapable of executing the judicial office." Accordingly, we do not recommend that he be removed from office. (Canadian Judicial Council 2008)

The Council thus avoided the question of whether evidentiary proof of loss of public confidence might be needed.

3.5 *Judges' Public Role (Beverley McLachlin)*

Beverley McLachlin is the longest serving Chief Justice of Canada, having been appointed to that position in 2000 after serving as a member of that Court, and before that as Chief Justice of the Supreme Court of British Columbia. She has become known for her public expressions of concern for the state of the justice system in Canada including the pernicious influence of sexism, and the decline in the ability of ordinary citizens to access affordable legal services.

It is clear that Chief Justice McLachlin does not believe judges should be "monks" cloistered away from society, but rather that they should be engaged with their fellow citizens and responsive to the needs of the community in which they live and adjudicate.[18] As she put it in a speech given in 2001:

> The judges in modern society are not potentates: they are rather servants, servants of the people in the highest and most honourable sense of that term. The judge has a task, a more important task than ever before. It is precisely because of the importance of this task that the judge is expected to perform it well and efficiently, to be responsive and responsible. …
>
> The nature of the questions they decide, and the public expectation that they will decide them fairly and well, place new demands on judges. It no longer suffices to be a competent legal scholar and a fair arbiter. To perform their modern role well, judges must be sensitive to a broad range of social concerns. They must possess a keen appreciation of the importance of individual and group interests and rights. And they must be in touch with the society in which they work, understanding its values and its tensions. The ivory tower no longer suffices as

[18] Chief Justice McLachlin was not the first leading Canadian judge to advocate more active involvement of judges in society. In 1988 a member of that Court had spoken out in similar fashion; see L'Heureux-Dubé (1988).

> the residence of choice for judges. The new role of judges in social policy also demands new efforts of objectivity. Often the judge will have strong personal views on questions which a judge is asked to decide: questions like abortion, capital punishment or euthanasia. But the task of judging is not accomplished simply by plugging one's personal views into the legal equation. The judge must strive for objectivity. This requires an act of imagination. And it requires an attitude of "active humility", which enables the judge to set aside preconceptions and prejudices and look at the issue afresh in the light of the evidence and submissions. …
>
> The public that pays the judges and takes its cases before them increasingly takes the view that it is entitled to know who these people are. Judges are faced with the question of whether or how to respond to the new demands of the public - demands that are underlined by the new ubiquitousness of the media. …
>
> A recent report of the Canadian Judicial Council notes that "[t]here are many instances where judges themselves may be the best messengers, and the groups they should reach may prefer to hear directly from judges themselves."
>
> Needless to say, there is a spectrum of opinion on the issue. What seems clear, however, is that, over the last twenty or so years, the entire spectrum has shifted in favour of a greater willingness on the part of judges to speak out. This shift is a reflection of the changing role of the judiciary, and perhaps a reflection of the fact that our democracies are becoming more participatory, with citizens taking a more active interest in the way social policy is made. Judges must always remember, however, that this new openness must not be permitted to sully their perceived or actual impartiality. (McLachlin 2001)

In another address some years later McLachlin debunked the myth of judges as "living oracles":

> In short, judges are human beings. They are sons and daughters, husbands and wives, parents and friends. They coach the local soccer team, cook dinner when they come home at night, and line up in airports when they go on vacation. Insofar as their humanness may be a distraction, as Tolstoy suggests, judges must strive to overcome it. But the benefits of judges being human beings greatly outweigh the detriments. Judges deal with human problems. They must be able to relate to these problems, to understand them. We would not want a robot for a judge even if we could find one. We would worry that the robot would be unable to understand the human condition, the basic requirement for being a judge. …
>
> In sum, judges are not living Oracles. They are human beings, trained in the law, who struggle to understand the situations before them and to resolve them in accordance with the law and their consciences. [footnotes omitted] (McLachlin 2004)

Chief Justice McLachlin may thus be taken as a leading exponent of the view that law and society must interact in rich and mutually rewarding ways, and that judges have a significant role to play in that give and take, both by speaking as "messengers" and listening with "active humility". A recent public controversy involving the Chief Justice illustrates the complex nexus that such responsive judging entails.

The federal and provincial governments of Canada have been struggling for decades with the consequences of old and now abandoned policies towards the treatment of the First Nations peoples in Canada. Government action in the past has included the forced removal of children from Aboriginal families and placement of them in residential schools or in homes with non-Aboriginal foster parents. These and other discriminatory programs had a devastating impact on First Nations communities and the children themselves. Some of the responses to this sad history have been government apologies, and the creation of a government funded system to settle the many thousands of legal claims made by those who as children were mistreated in residential schools. Nevertheless, many injustices remain to be righted and further legal claims continue to be made.

One governmental response was the creation of a Truth and Reconciliation Commission which held hearings across the country to arrive at recommendations on ways to heal the relationship between the First Nations peoples in Canada and the non-aboriginal population. The Commission released its final report in July, 2015. In May of that year, before the report was published, Chief Justice McLachlin spoke in Toronto on the topic "Reconciling Unity and Diversity in the Modern Era: Tolerance and Intolerance" (McLachlin 2015). In her remarks she touched on the topic of the role of courts and judges in pluralistic societies such as Canada:

> Fear and hatred of the other in our midst is a disease that can destroy social peace. The best antidote to this fear is the assurance that everyone's basic right to hold their own beliefs and follow their own practices – provided they do not harm others – is the assurance of protection by the legal system. This requires that citizens must have access to the legal system, and that the legal system responds with integrity, even in the face of overweening pressure from the majority that sees the belief or practice as aberrant and wrong. It also requires commitment to a culture of legality – a culture that encourages debate about particular decisions, while maintaining respect for the principles and processes of the law and the Constitution.

These were not controversial ideas, but earlier in the speech she had described some of the past instances of intolerance in Canadian society, and highlighted the treatment of the First Nations:

> The most glaring blemish on the Canadian historic record relates to our treatment of the First Nations that lived here at the time of colonization. An initial period of cooperative inter-reliance grounded in norms of equality and mutual dependence ... was supplanted in the nineteenth century by the ethos of exclusion and cultural annihilation. Early laws forbad treaty Indians from leaving allocated reservations. Starvation and disease were rampant. Indians were denied the right to vote. Religious and social traditions, like the Potlach and the Sun Dance, were outlawed. Children were taken from their parents and sent away to residential schools, where they were forbidden to speak their native languages, forced to wear white-man's clothing, forced to observe Christian religious practices, and not infrequently subjected to sexual abuse. ... "Indianness" was not to be tolerated; rather it must be eliminated. **In the buzz-word of the day, assimilation; in the language of the 21st century, cultural genocide**. [emphasis added] (McLachlin 2015)

Coming from the Chief Justice of Canada these were strong and outspoken words indeed that were reported immediately in the media and generated vigorous debate.[19] Some commentators welcomed them as a statement of the obvious and First Nations were pleased to see that the tragedy they endured by government order was finally being understood for what it truly was. Other public voices were critical of the Chief Justice's statement, pointing out that the Supreme Court of Canada might still have to rule on claims arising out of the events she described. For these critics the speech represented prejudgment at its worst.

We believe Chief Justice McLachlin's public statements can be viewed as a worthy example of the working of reciprocal communication between law and society.

[19]See, for instance, Fine (2015), Coates (2015) and Gagnon (2015).

Although characterizing some government actions as "cultural genocide" may not have clear legal consequences in Canadian law, the fact that a leading jurist has done so at least symbolically shows that the legal system is listening to the society around it. McLachlin is one of those judges who can take both an insider's viewpoint on the law as well as that of the citizen on the outside with great hopes and expectations of justice through law. She is truly a responsive judge who bridges the internal/external legal divide and a role model for others.

4 Chinese Judges

4.1 The Chinese Judiciary

The Constitution of the People's Republic of China (PRC) provides that the people's courts are the judicial organs of the State. The State sets up the Supreme People's Court (SPC), local people's courts at different levels and special people's courts such as military courts. These people's courts adjudicate civil, criminal and administrative suits in accordance with laws, and carry out judicial activities including the execution of civil and administrative decisions and proceedings for state compensation.

The SPC, as the highest judicial organ of the PRC, is responsible for adjudicating cases that have material effects nationwide or are subject to its adjudication according to law, formulating judicial interpretations, supervising and guiding the judicial work of local people's courts at different levels and special people's courts, and managing certain judicial administration work of the courts nationwide within the scope of its functions and powers. Local people's courts at different levels include primary people's courts, intermediate people's courts and higher people's courts. Special people's courts include military courts, maritime courts and IP courts. A people's court at a higher level supervises the judicial work of the people's courts at the next lower level. In litigious activities, the people's courts adopt the systems of public trial, collegiate panel, challenge system for judicial bias, people's assessors, defense, and judgment of the second instance as final.

4.1.1 Chinese Judicial Reform

As early as in the 1990s, China's courts started reforms focusing on enhancing the function of court trials, expanding the openness of trials and improving judicial professionalization. Since the 15th National Congress of the Communist Party of China (CPC), the SPC has initiated a series of reforms in the areas of organization and system of courts; judge selection and appointment system, judge disciplinary system, and judges' compensation, among others which was mainly provided by The Judge Law; litigation procedure; method of trial; enforcement system; judicial management; and promulgated three "*Five-year Reform Program for People's Courts*" in

1999, 2005 and 2009. The three Programs served as the basis of China's court reform before 2013. To respond to the sentiments of the 3rd and 4th Plenary Session of the 18th CCCPC,[20] the SPC promulgated *the Opinions on Comprehensively Deepening the Reform of People's Courts* on February 4, 2015, putting forward 65 reform measures, which was served as *the Fourth Five-year Reform Program for People's Courts 2014–2018*. At of the end of 2016, 63 reform tasks had been basically accomplished or carried out in an all-round way.

The reform of the judicial system covers a wide range of issues and has high policy sensitivity. It mainly includes four aspects: improvement of classification and management of judicial personnel; improvement of judicial accountability; improvement of job security of judicial personnel; and promotion of centralized management of personnel, financial and material resources of local courts below the provincial level (Supreme People's Court 2017a).

4.2 *Professionalization of Judges*

4.2.1 Professionalization and Mass Line (Ma Xiwu)

The professionalization of Chinese judges can be viewed to some extent as a process of separating themselves from the society. But this is really a difficult and far from smooth process in China. In its long history, the Chinese judiciary has emphasized strongly the *mass line* which can be summarized as "*having faith in the masses and relying on the masses*". This principle distinguishes Chinese judges from their Western counterparts who are expected to be separate to some extent from society, thus maintaining judicial independence and impartiality. Since the establishment of PRC, China's courts and judges have been required to implement the *Ma Xiwu trial method*. The centerpiece of *Ma's Method* was "*trial at the edge of a field*", which entailed a bench trial at the corner of a farm or in the courtyard of a household. Driven by his belief that the judiciary must serve the people and that party policy was the most direct law, Ma Xiwu took the position that such a trial, out of a formal courtroom and with no legal jargon, was easiest for people to understand. He preferred to call his trials mediation rather than adjudication. It was also Ma's view that the satisfaction of the people was the major criterion for evaluating the outcome of the trial. *Ma's*

[20]The Decision of the Central Committee of the CPC ("CCCPC") on Some Major Issues Concerning Comprehensively Deepening the Reform adopted at the 3rd Plenary Session of the 18th CCCPC set an important task of advancing rule by law in China and deepening the reform of the judicial system. The Decision of the CCCPC on Some Major Issues Concerning Management of State Affairs under the Rule of Law in an All-round Way adopted at the 4th Plenary Session of the 18th CCCPC set the establishment of a socialist system of rule by law with Chinese characteristics and the building of a socialist country under the rule of law as the general objective of advancing management of state affairs under the rule of law in an all-round way, and put forward a series of major reform measures in scientific legislation, strict law enforcement, judicial impartiality, universal law abiding and other areas.

Method was hailed by many top leaders of China and Ma Xiwu himself was praised by Chairman Mao as a person closest to the people (Southern Weekend 2009).

The push for Chinese judges' professionalization began at the end of 20th century, led by then Chief Justice Xiao Yang. At that time, the SPC issued the *Basic Standards of the People's Republic of China on Professional Ethics of Judges* in 2001 and the Codes of Conduct for Judges in 2005. In line with the background of judicial reform focusing on enhancing the function of court trials and expanding the openness of trials, these two documents assisted China's judges starting on the road to professionalism.

However, in the era of Chief Justice Wang Shengjun, this road took a detour. From 2007 onwards, as Wang Shengjun replaced Xiao Yang as SPC President, populist trends—populist in that they emphasize judicial responsiveness to public opinion—swiftly grew in visibility. *Ma Xiwu trial method* was emphasized again by the SPC and spread quickly throughout the country (Wang 2009a, b; Bai 2009). Wang's reference to Ma Xiwu's example in his March 2009 Work Report to the National People's Congress was the first time an SPC report had done so since at least 1978. This prompted a senior American scholar to comment that "the populist, from-the-masses-to-the-masses, procedure-be-damned Ma Xiwu style is definitely making a rhetorical comeback" (Clarke 2009). There arose much discussion of this "populist turn" in Chinese legal reform.[21] Liebman (2011) provides a basic description of "legal populism":

> The Ma Xiwu method embodied core elements of the CCP's legal ideology. Law became inseparable from politics and was designed to advance Party policy. Law was practical and adaptable, not rigid or constraining. Legal institutions were neither independent nor specialized, and professionalism was explicitly rejected. Written law yielded to actual experiences; a correct decision was one that met the emotions of the masses. (Liebman 2011)

4.2.2 Stages of Achievement

Though the mass line remains in the era of Zhou Qiang, as Chief Justice nevertheless there has been great progress in judicial professionalization in recent years. To improve the regularization, specialization and professionalization of judicial personnel, the SPC has reformed the judge selection and appointment system, improved the system of classified management of judicial personnel, and promoted the establishment of a system of setting a separate rank of posts for judges and determining their remunerations. These measures were taken to enhance judges' sense of honor and dedication to their profession.

Carrying out the reform of the judge quota system in an all-round way.

Under the judge quota system before the reform all court personnel were named "judge", and after the reform only 39% or so of the court personnel will be named

[21]See Minzner (2011), Zang (2010), Peerenboom (2010), and Pils (2009) (discussing the SPC's embracement of populism under Wang Shengjun).

judge. Those designated as judges are in charge of trial work, while the rest engage in administrative and ancillary work. The higher people's courts in all provincial-level regions have scientifically set the judge quotas for the courts at three levels according to the number of cases handled, and the situations of economic and social development, population and other basic data of the places where the courts are located. Quotas also take into consideration the level of trial and functions of the courts, workloads of judges, staffing of auxiliary judicial personnel and other factors, and are dynamically adjusted according to changes in the number of cases and personnel structure. Some courts set the quotas lower than 30% and others higher than 50%, it depends on its specific situation in that court.

Reforming the judge selection and appointment system.

Pilot regions have established judge selection committees at the provincial level comprising judge representatives and relevant civilians, and formulated open, fair and just judge selection and appointment procedures, to ensure that only the outstanding legal practitioners who are upright in character and have rich experience and a high professional level will become judge candidates. In order to improve the system of selection of judges level by level, on May 13, 2016, the Organization Department of the CCCPC, the SPC and the Supreme People's Procuratorate jointly promulgated opinions on establishing the system of selection of judges and public procurators level by level, which have the result that the judges at lower level courts can be selected by the high level courts.

Promoting classified management of judicial personnel.

To further optimize the allocation of human resources of the courts, China's courts classify the judicial personnel into judges, auxiliary judicial personnel and judicial administrative personnel, and adopt different management systems for different categories of personnel, to ensure that each person is assigned to a definite post of duty and attends to his or her own duties. These changes have improved the management systems for judge assistants, clerks, enforcement personnel, judicial policemen and other auxiliary judicial personnel, and scientifically determined the proportion of judges to auxiliary judicial personnel, to effectively reduce the amount of routine and procedural work undertaken by judges.

Strictly regulating the after-hours acts of judicial personnel.

In conjunction with the related departments of the Central Government, the SPC has promulgated documents governing judicial conduct in the following areas:

- prohibiting judicial personnel from entering six kinds of contact or intercourse with litigants, lawyers, specially related parties or intermediaries
- requiring judicial personnel handling cases to receive litigants, lawyers, specially related parties or intermediaries at working places and during working hours
- prohibiting judicial personnel who have resigned from any judicial organs from acting as process attorneys or defenders in any cases handled by such judicial organs

- prohibiting judicial personnel who have been dismissed from public office due to violation of the law and discipline from practicing law for life. (Supreme People's Court 2017a)

Protecting Judicial Personnel to Lawfully Perform Statutory Duties.

Called on by the SPC, the General Office of the Central Committee of the CPC and the General Office of the State Council issued *the Provisions on Protecting Judicial Personnel to Lawfully Perform Statutory Duties* in July 2016. This document, which distinguishes the judge from a general civil servant, also differentiated judicial work from the Party's work and executive work, thereby pushing judicial professionalization forward. The Provisions state in part:

> Article 2 Where a judge or prosecutor handles a case in accordance with the law, he shall be free of intervention by any administrative departments, social organizations, and individuals, and entitled to refuse any organization or individual's requirements that violate the statutory duties or legal procedures or hinder judicial justice. Judicial personnel shall keep a complete and faithful record of the situation where any entity or individual intervenes in judicial activities, or the handling of specific cases. Relevant departments shall, in the light of the relevant provisions, circulate a notice on or hold liable the relevant responsible persons who intervene in judicial activities and handling of specific cases.
>
> Article 3 No entity or individual shall request a judge or prosecutor to engage in any affair beyond the scope of his statutory duties. A people's court or people's procuratorate shall be entitled to refuse the request of any entity or individual to make arrangement for judges or prosecutors to engage in any affair beyond the scope of their statutory duties.

The Supreme Court issued the document *Implement Methods of Provisions on Protecting Judicial Personnel to Lawfully Perform Statutory Duties* in February 2017, specifying in section 2 matters beyond the scope of judge's statutory duties:

> the people's court shall refuse and should not arrange any judge to do the following affairs demanded by any entity or individual: investment attraction, administrative law enforcement, police patrol, traffic dispersion, health campaign, democratic appraisal, etc. The personnel of court shall be prohibited from participating in local investment attraction, joint law enforcement, interfering in specific administrative activity including land expropriation, house demolition, etc., joining the various temporary organizations led by local government including leading groups for demolishment, project headquarters, and the like.

4.3 Law and Politics (Zhou Qiang)

Chinese judges, contrary to their Western counterparts, play an important political role in society, as stated in *The Code of Conduct for Judges.*

> *Article 1 Loyalty and steadfastness.* Insist on the supreme position of the Party's cause, the interests of the people, and the constitutional laws. Maintain consistency of thoughts and actions with those of the Party Central Committee. The words and behaviors shall not be in contravention with the basic policies of the Party and the State as well as the socialist legal system.

> *Article 2 Judicial justice.* Insist on taking the facts as the basis and using law as the criterion. Treat all parties fairly. Ensure justice in criteria and results, in procedures and in images. Strive to realize organic integration of legal effect and social effect of case handling. Do not abuse the power and abuse the law in making judgment.
>
> *Article 5 Serving the people wholeheartedly.* Implement the provisions and requirements of upholding justice for the people. Learn what the people say, what the people feel and what the people think. Adhere to active judicial enforcement. Establish service awareness. Make proper proceeding guidance, risk warning, legal interpretation and other services for the convenience of the people. Avoid undesirable work style such as being indifferent and tyrannizing.
>
> *Article 19* If a large-scale dispute is found or the conflict may be easily intensified, report to the leaders of the court promptly and contact the relevant department. Actively carry out the work on persuasion and prevent the conflict from being intensified.

Apart from these provisions on the books, the speeches of the Chief Justice are always regarded as guiding the whole judicial system. The incumbent Chief Justice, Zhou Qiang, also the Party Secretary of China's Supreme People's Court Party Group, gave an address to the National Conference of Courts' Presidents on January 14, 2017. In his address, Zhou Qiang pointed to the need to "raise the sword" against the ideologies of judicial independence, separation of powers, and constitutional democracy as follows:

> [China's courts] must firmly resist the western idea of "constitutional democracy", "separation of powers" and "judicial independence". These are erroneous western notions that threaten the leadership of the ruling Communist Party and defame the Chinese socialist path on the rule of law. We should raise our flag and show our sword to struggle against such thoughts. We must not fall into the trap of western thoughts and judicial independence. We must stay firm on the Chinese socialist path on the rule of law. (Hu 2017)

Zhou also stated that Party groups of courts at all levels must include ideological work on their agenda. This should be an important element of the administrative goals of leading groups and leading cadres, which must be deployed, implemented, inspected, and evaluated together with Party building and other work, guaranteeing the concrete nature and completeness of responsibility systems.

Zhou further stated that to strengthen the inspection of the implementation of the responsibility system in ideological work, ideological work must become a major item in the appraisal and reward of cadres, and it must be brought within the scope of Party discipline inspection, particularly the inspection of political discipline and political behavior. Accountability systems must be severe, and the responsibility for violations of the demands of ideological work, as well as for the weak resolution of problems, shall be severely investigated.

Zhou added that one must persist in combining rule by law and rule by virtue, and vigorously promote Socialist Core Values. The demands of socialist ethics must be applied to adjudication, emphasizing the resolution of outstanding issues in the field of morality through judicial means, and bring into play the judiciary's function of upholding virtue and condemning evil. In particular:

> "The use of the internet to endanger national security, spreading rumors, picking up quarrels and causing troubles, inciting mass incidents must be punished according to the law.

> Participation in the special action to severely strike at online political rumors and maintaining network security must be enthusiastic." Zhou Qiang stated that, we should draw on the adjudicative experience relevant to the ideological cases, enact a judicial interpretation on cases involving infringing the reputation and honor of heroes and historical figures, protect the image of leaders and heroes, and firmly safeguard the glorious history of the Party and the People's Army. (Supreme People's Court 2017b)

Zhou Qiang became the President of SPC in March 2013. Like other top Chinese leaders, Zhou formerly spoke often of promoting the "rule of law" and was thought aligned with CPC general secretary Xi Jinping's stated ambition to make the court system in China fairer. Indeed, in his first few years in office, Zhou overturned several unjust cases, including the wrongful execution of Nie Shubin in 1995; granted judges more independence; and restricted local officials' influence over court rulings, although ultimately courts at all levels still had to answer to the party leadership. His address above was interpreted by some media as self-protection amid a Communist Party power struggle ahead of the 19th National Congress of the Communist Party of China. One Western observer noted (Forsythe 2017): "People who know him find him a reasonable person who's had a good legal education and who had been open before he became Chief Justice to improvements in the legal system, ... This must be pretty bitter gruel for him to swallow in order to try to bring the courts into a kind of militant observance of the highest party leadership."

4.4 *Judicial Speech*

The citizen, including the judge, enjoys the freedom of speech. But there is some difference between the freedom of the general citizen and a judge, because a judge has a dual identity, one being that of a citizen, the other that of a judge. As a judge there are more limitations on speech than on the ordinary person when he or she expresses an idea or feeling. Following are two examples of problematic judicial speech, one which occurred before the final judgment was done, and the second an expression of feeling that had nothing to do with a particular case.

4.4.1 Pending Cases (Jiang Xingchang)

When Xu Ting used a debit card to withdraw RMB100, the defective ATM ejected RMB1000 while deducting only RMB1 from the card. Xu Ting decided to take advantage of this "God-given opportunity" (Guangdong High Court 2008), and withdrew over RMB 170,000 by using his debit card with a balance of RMB171 many times at the machine. Xu Ting was caught after a year's escape and was sentenced to life imprisonment at first instance in December 2007 by Guangzhou Municipal Intermediate Court for the offence of theft. Later the Guangdong High Court remanded the case to Guangzhou Municipal Intermediate Court for re-trial due to "insufficient evidence and unclear facts" (Guangdong High Court 2008). The finding of the case drew phenomenal attention from all kinds of media including the Internet, newspapers and television, and many people in legal circles commented on the conviction and punishment related to the case.

One commentator was Jiang Xingchang, the former vice president of SPC. When Jiang was interviewed during the National People's Congress (NPC) of 2008, he said, "the circumstance of Xu Ting's case is unusual, it is not suitable to convict Xu of a 'theft from financial institutions' rather than a 'crime of stealing', it is obviously too severe for the first instance court to sentence Xu to life imprisonment" (People.com.cn 2008). This was said twenty days before the judgment on retrial was to be given. Jiang's comment caused a hot debate among the media and the public. In fact, the development of the case was just as expected. The finding of the first instance of Xu Ting upon retrial was made on March 31, 2008. Guangzhou Intermediate Court still maintained that Xu Ting's act constituted "stealing from financial institutions in extremely huge amount of cash", but had activated the "special punishment reduction" procedure of clause 2 of article 63 of the Criminal Law according to the special circumstance of the case by sentencing Xu Ting to a fixed term of imprisonment of five years. The Guangdong High Court made the final ruling on May 22, 2008, "Rejecting Xu Ting's appeal according to the law and maintaining the original judgment" (of 5 years imprisonment). The SPC affirmed that decision on August 20, 2008 (China Supreme Court 2008).

The question here is whether Jiang's speech was appropriate before the final judgment was delivered. The answer is no. According to *The Basic Standards of the People's Republic of China on Professional Ethics of Judges*, article 14, "Respect the lawful exercise of judicial authority of other judges. Other than performance of work responsibilities or going through proper procedures, do not inquire into, interfere or comment on the cases currently under trial by other judges". Jiang's comment obviously violated this Basic Standard, because his interview was not related to "performance of work responsibilities or going through proper procedures".

4.4.2 Personal Attacks (Li Bingxiang)

The people's Internet network issued a blog describing and naming "one policeman of 57 years old being on duty in the snowstorm" with two photographs of a senior policeman who was on duty standing in the snowstorm and added the praising words, "the senior policeman of 57 years old, Zhang Hongcang, on duty during a snowstorm in Tongguan of Shanxi province on February 21, whose hair mixed with snow and his back moved the pedestrians. Please transmit it and pay our respects to him!" (South China Morning Post 2017) Li Bingxiang, a judge of Lijiang intermediate court, transmitted this blog and gave his own comment in his own online WeiChat on February 26, 2017, as follows: "there must be one story behind one story. Behind the story that the senior policeman was on duty in the snowstorm, there are three stories, one is being punished for his wrong-doing, another is putting on a show, the last one is still putting on a show!" (South China Morning Post 2017) Li's comment immediately generated discontent among netizens, and Lijiang intermediate court issued a circular in its official Micro Blog at 7:35 pm of that day, which said "Li's comment is wrong, and deeply hurt the policemen who strived in ice snow and the public", "the Party group of Lijiang intermediate court decided after discussion that Li should be suspended for the serious nature of his speech, and we will seriously handle this case after investigation" (Thepaper.cn 2017).

According to *The Codes of Conduct for Judges*, judges should respect social ethics and speak and behave properly, otherwise they could be punished accordingly.

Article 80 Basic requirements

(1) Abide by the social ethics. Observe discipline and abide by the law.

(2) Strengthen self-cultivation. Observe strict self-discipline.

(3) Constrain words and deeds outside work. Do not become addicted to undesirable hobbies and behaviors incompatible with the image of judge, and which may affect the impartial performance of duties. Conscientiously safeguard the image of judge.

Article 93 The People's Court at all levels and all the judges shall conscientiously comply and execute these Codes of Conduct. In respect of personnel in violation of these Codes of Conduct, where the circumstance is relatively mild and there is no harmful consequence, admonition and education through criticism shall be carried out. Where it constitutes violation of discipline, it shall be dealt with according to the relevant provisions of disciplinary sanction of the People's Court. Where it constitutes violation of law, it shall be dealt with sternly according to the provisions of the law.

4.4.3 Legal Explanations

Some high profile cases strongly attract public attention, and even after final judgment members of the public may still debate the case dramatically, expressing doubts, dissatisfaction and even great anger. The question is whether judges have an obligation to explain the final judgment when the public refuses to accept the judgment easily.

4.4.4 Example 1

Wu Ying, a female, the former legal representative of Zhejiang Ecru Group, was arrested on March 16, 2007, for suspicion of illegally taking public deposits for herself. In December 2009, she was sentenced to the death penalty in the first instance by Jinhua Municipal Intermediate People's Court. She appealed against the decision. On January 18, 2012, the appeal was rejected and the original decision was maintained in the second instance by Zhejiang Provincial Higher People's Court, which was submitted to the Supreme People's Court for verification and approval. On February 7, 2012, before the SPC made its decision whether to approve of the death penalty against Wu Ying, Shen Xiao-ou, the presiding judge of second instance in Zhejiang Provincial Higher People's Court, answered the angry questions advanced by the public in a press conference. These questions included: (1) Why did the second instance maintain the original judgment of death penalty? (2) What are the real facts of this case? (3) Why did the court convict Wu Ying of fund-raising fraud rather than private lending? (4) Why did the court find that Wu Ying took "funding from the public" when 11 victims were all the relatives of Wu Ying? (5) Why didn't the behavior of Wu Ying in informing against other officials constitute "rendering meritorious service", which is one of the conditions for obtaining a reduced punishment (6) Was the judgment influenced by some administrative interference?

On April 20, 2012, the Supreme People's Court did not approve of the death penalty against Wu Ying and remanded the case to Zhejiang Provincial Higher People's Court for retrial. On May 21, 2012, Zhejiang Provincial Higher People's court made a final judgment that Wu Ying was sentenced to the death penalty with a two-year suspension, revocation of political rights and confiscation of all personal property. This case received extensive attention in society as it raised many questions about informal financing issues in China. On May 21, 2012, the spokesman of the Zhejiang Provincial Higher People's Court answered questions about the retrial judgment when meeting the press, questions which mainly focused on the procedural aspects, such as the change of counsel, the constitution of the panel of judges, the procedure of seizure, and the like.

4.4.5 Example 2

Peng Yu's case, which will be discussed further below, is another example of a case that attracted a lot of public attention resulting in the presiding judge together with the leader in charge of the court meeting the press after entering the judgment.

The protocol for answering questions from the public after final judgment was provided by the SPC at the National Register and Trial Seminar in November 2005. According to the explanation from the vice director of the Register Tribunal of SPC, answering such questions requires both the judge who gave the judgment and the judge in charge of the register to listen to the petitioner, his first petition, and the reasons for applying for a retrial. However, the job of answering doubts mainly belongs to the judge who gave the judgment. The purpose of this regime is to increase the rate of ending litigation, reduce repetitive petitions, and ease tensions caused by the judgment between the court and the public (People's Daily 2006).

The Code of Conduct for Judges permits judges to meet the press, which means a judge may accept interviews by the media after finishing the judgment if the interview is arranged or approved by the related organization.

> Article 84 Accepting interviews related to court work of the news media
>
> (1) Accepting interviews of news media must be arranged or approved by the organization.
>
> (2) During the interview, comments which are detrimental to the judicial justice shall not be made. Commentary on cases currently under trial and the parties concerned shall not be made. The State's secret, trade secret and personal privacy as well as other non-public information obtained in the course of work shall not be divulged.

The SPC distinguished suspended cases and finished cases in *The SPC's Several Provisions about Court Accepting Supervision of Media* in 2009. As to suspended cases, judges and other personnel cannot accept interviews arbitrarily. With regards to finalized cases, the court can arrange related personnel to meet the press through the propaganda department.

4.5 *Judges' Public Role*

In carrying out their duties Chinese judges are in the public eye, and sometimes the public is aroused by their work. Judges may influence society and vice versa in a reciprocal relation.

4.5.1 Example 1

Peng Yu, an alleged Good Samaritan, lifted an elderly woman who had fallen at a bus stop in Nanjing on November 20, 2006. Peng had just got off one bus, while the woman was catching another bus driving into the bus stop. The woman was seriously injured and sued Peng, arguing that it was Peng who knocked her down. There was no direct evidence, only one witness who saw Peng walking towards the woman and lifting her, but he did not see how the woman fell. After the woman's son arrived, Peng accompanied the woman and her son to the hospital and paid 200RMB for her medical fee. This fact also became a disputed matter afterwards.

One important document given in evidence was an electronic document provided by the police office which recorded that Peng had admitted there was physical contact with the woman. However, Peng said it was the woman knocking him rather than the opposite. However, the original paper document was lost, and this electronic document was a photograph of it taken by the woman's son who was a policeman serving in another police office. Peng questioned the authenticity of this electronic document, so the policeman who was on duty that day gave a description about what had happened before him and confirmed the authenticity of the electronic document. The court adopted this evidence and entered judgment against Peng who was required to pay the woman 45,876.36 RMB as compensation, accounting for 40% of the whole damages found.

Public controversy about the judgment mainly focused on the judge's reasoning with "common sense", although the use of the electronic document was also questioned by the media and the public. For example, in the judgment, the judge stated that a reasonable Good Samaritan would first catch the wrongdoer who caused the accident rather than help the victim; and that the reasonable person would wait until the victim's family arrived, and then leave, rather than accompany the victim to the hospital. Further, according to the judge's common sense, strangers would not lend money to each other, and if they did, it was common for a reasonable person to ask for a receipt as a proof. If they ask for nothing, it was probably compensation being paid rather than lending money. This case caused dramatic public disputes nationwide, and the judge who decided it was even harassed by people dissatisfied with the judgment.

4.5.2 Example 2

Yu Huan, from Liaocheng in Shandong Province, was convicted of intentional injury and given a life sentence on February 17, 2017 after he stabbed four debt collectors who confronted him and his mother on April 14, 2016. One of the injured later died. Yu claimed he attacked the debt collectors after one of them exposed himself to his mother. The case quickly went viral on social media, with many saying Yu's penalty was too harsh, as well as some criticizing how the police handled the incident. The Shandong High People's Court accepted an appeal from Yu, while some police officers involved in the matter were probed for alleged misconduct in the case.

The dissatisfaction of the public was mainly caused by expressions in the judgment used to explain why Yu's behavior could not constitute legitimate "self-defense". For example: "although Yu's personal freedom was limited and he was also insulted by the collectors, the police had been there, and Yu and his mother were in little risk of being infringed in their rights of life and health. Therefore, there is no any urgency of defense." The facts affirmed in the judgment indicated that the policemen had come but they had then gone after saying "collecting is ok, but assaulting is prohibited". The question then, is whether Yu may defend himself and his mother after the policemen left while they were still controlled by the collectors. Apart from the legal question, the public especially questioned the ethical rule reflected in this case: if such a tremendous insult happened to your family, how would you react?

These examples show the potential for judges and the public to come into conflict over judicial rulings. The subject was raised by Shen Deyong, Executive Vice-President of the SPC, who hosted a seminar on criminal trials on April 5, 2017 in Shandong province. During the seminar, Shen said:

> Courts should take initiative to echo public concerns when some rulings stir the public, … What we can do is to improve our ability and efficiency of tackling cases and avoid verdicts that are obviously contrary to common sense, … while clarifying the facts of a case, judges should learn to understand the background behind an incident and take the social effects that a judgment may cause into consideration, … But it doesn't mean making rulings contrary to laws or facts, …. (People's Court 2017)

The judgment of the second instance entered by Shandong High People's Court on June 23, 2017 reflected public opinion in the way advocated by Shen Deyong. The life sentence of Yu Huan was reduced to five years in prison (China Daily 2017). Beijing News commented as following:

> In the end, justice has been done. On the one hand, the much-reduced sentence suggests that previous weighing up of the facts and the judgment were not flawless. On the other hand, the rectifications were made in the wake of the public's demand for fairness, highlighting that China's courts are subject to public supervision. Admittedly, judicial judgments require untainted professionalism and legal knowledge. But public opinion, which although less professional in a legal sense, matters a great deal to judicial justice. That explains why juries

in countries such as the United States are composed of people chosen from all walks of life. (Beijing News 2017)

The provisions which are relevant to the examples above in *The Codes of Conduct for Judges* are article 51 and article 52, which instruct judges how to narrate the facts and justify the conclusion.

Article 51 Account of the part on finding of facts in the judgment document of cases with general procedures

(1) Objective representation, rigorous logics, precise wording, avoiding the use of vocabulary which are obviously commendatory or derogatory.

(2) Accurately analyze and explain the reasons for why the evidence submitted by the parties is accepted or refused, as well as the facts that the accepted evidence supports.

(3) Rational explanation shall be carried out on issues such as burden of proof, probative force of evidence as well as the criteria of proof.

Article 52 Determination and analysis and argumentation of the trial outcome of cases under general procedures

(1) Accurate, objective and concise reasoning shall be carried out. Elaborate on the reasons as to whether to adopt the opinion of response, opinion of defense, and the opinion of the attorney, etc.

(2) In the trial of a criminal case, the verdict of guilty or not guilty shall be made according to the relevant provisions of the law and judicial interpretation and by incorporating the specific facts of the case. Where it is confirmed to be guilty, analysis and ascertainment of the statutory and discretionary circumstances for heavier, lighter, reduced or remitted punishment shall be carried out.

(3) In the trial of a civil case, the legal relationship of the case shall be clarified, and the relationship of rights and obligation among the parties, the responsibility as well as the degree of the responsibilities to be borne by the parties shall be summarized and judged with details according to the relevant provisions of law, regulations and judicial interpretation and by incorporating specific circumstances of the case,

(4) In the trial of an administrative case, carry out analysis and argumentation on whether the specific administrative conduct carried out by the administrative organ and its personnel is legitimate, whether the legitimate rights and interest of the plaintiff have been infringed upon, and whether causality exists with the specific administration conduct of the respondent according to the relevant provisions of law, regulations and judicial interpretation and by incorporating the facts of the case.

5 Comparisons

In this section we will try to sort the data and observations we have collected according to the comparative schema of behavior and meaning set out previously.

5.1 *Same Behavior/Different Meaning*

The governments of Canada and China both assert the value of the "rule of law". As scholars have pointed out,[22] this phrase has become so prevalent in the contemporary legal and political discourse of virtually all countries that it has become, if not meaningless, then at least capable of a bewildering number of diverse interpretations and applications.

There is no question that both Chinese and Canadian judges are obligated to reach their judgments based on rational decisions regarding the proven facts and the application of existing law to them. Using a broad interpretation of the "rule of law" the behavior of both judiciaries would therefore seem to be parallel. Judges in both countries must not act capriciously, with bias towards any party, or without legal justification.

In Canada, however, judges have no additional obligation to contribute to the edification and moral improvement of the community through their judicial work. One manifestation of this is the elevation in Canada and other Western countries of the delivery of procedural justice as the only practicable goal of law. By contrast, in China judges are required to aim at both "substantive and procedural justice", to ensure "the integrity of legal effect and social effect" as prescribed by *The Code of Conduct for Judges*. This is an expanded conception of the work of law as allied with moral norms in society and the expectations of the public. In China, the rule of virtue complements the rule of law, a conjunction that may be practicable there by reason of the country's relative cultural homogeneity in contrast to multiethnic, multicultural and pluralistic nations such as Canada. In cases like that of Peng Yu and Yu Huan Chinese judges who are insensitive to this expanded social role can precipitate moral crisis in the whole country. While adhering to the rule of law, as do Canadian judges, Chinese judges must acknowledge an additional responsibility and burden in the name of law.

Contrasting the treatment of the case of Judge Ted Matlow and the processes of professionalization of the Chinese judiciary presents another instance of similar action for different reasons. Recall that Judge Matlow was faulted in part for excessive and improper involvement in local property matters and that in its declaration of February 2017 (above), the Supreme Peoples' Court prohibited judicial involvement in many local matters including those involving property.

In relation to Matlow, one of the principal concerns was that he used the title "Judge" when interacting with city and provincial authorities and that this was an improper attempt to use the prestige and authority of his judicial office for personal purposes. The assumption that is being made is that a judge is in a position of power and influence over such officials. In the case of Chinese judges, however, it appears that the opposite assumption is at work and that the judiciary is being told to be wary of close involvement with local authorities who may be able to influence and even control the judges. Such ties may impair judges' actual or perceived impartiality and thus adversely affect their external legitimacy in the community. Therefore,

[22] See for instance, Krygier (2016).

although the prohibition against certain judicial behavior appears to be very much the same in Canada and China, the purpose underlying such action is quite different, reflecting different relationships of status and power between the judiciary and other government personnel in the two countries.

5.2 *Same Behavior/Same Meaning*

We see parallel actions for similar purposes by the judiciaries of China and Canada in relation to limiting judges' public speech. Judges everywhere today are neither expected to be saints, seers, or oracles, nor considered entitled to claim such a role for themselves. Rather, they are citizens like others, albeit with specialized legal training and experience, who have been entrusted by the state to administer law fairly and effectively. Modern judges thus have a dual identity in society, being both ordinary citizens with all the rights accorded by the state, and at the same time, always and everywhere they go, powerful officials with responsibility to the law and the legal system. A judge may not simply "turn on and off" at will their identity as judge. This dual status has been recognized in Canada and China as requiring some limits to be placed on judges' communication with the public outside of cases over which they preside.[23] These limits are balanced by the recognition that members of the judiciary must also have some freedom of personal speech because as has been said, "no man would be a judge, upon the condition of being obligated to be totally a judge."[24]

Thus, Canada's *Ethical Principles for Judges* cautions that "Judges must therefore accept some restrictions on their activities—even activities that would not elicit adverse notice if carried out by other members of the community" and goes on to note that in relation to public debate:

> [T]here are two fundamental considerations. The first is whether the judge's involvement could reasonably undermine confidence in his or her impartiality. The second is whether such involvement may unnecessarily expose the judge to political attack or be inconsistent with the dignity of judicial office. If either is the case the judge should avoid such involvement.

Similarly, China's *Code of Conduct for Judges* admonishes the judiciary to:

> Constrain words and deeds outside work. Do not become addicted to undesirable hobbies and behaviors incompatible with the image of judge, and which may affect the impartial performance of duties. Conscientiously safeguard the image of judge.

These similar restrictions on judicial activity including speech are, moreover, motivated by the same two concerns: preserving the appearance of impartiality and maintaining the dignity ("image") of judicial office holders. The first goal may be endangered by a judge who expresses opinions about pending court cases or other live legal issues and the second by a judge's comments that condemn the maker as ignorant or a fool for commenting on matters they are not particularly qualified to speak out

[23]In the United States a similar principle has been described as "judicial lockjaw": Westin (1962).
[24]The remark is from Boswell's *Life of Johnson* as quoted in Ross (1989a). See also Ross (1989b).

about. Both purposes in limiting judicial speech are based on the underlying goal to maintain the external legitimacy of the judiciary in society.

The Matlow case in Canada furnishes one example of this principle at work. Judge Matlow firmly believed that local officials had engaged in misbehavior in dealing with a neighboring property, and he expressed this belief in strong terms to others including sarcastic remarks. He was censured for such speech and required to apologize although he sincerely thought it was the right thing to do. The Canadian Judicial Council considered that such personal attacks were not in keeping with the dignity of the judicial office. Similarly, in the Chinese case of Li Bingxiang a judge who spoke out in a derogative way about another government official was suspended from his duties.

In relation to pending cases and decisions of other judges, *The Basic Standards of the People's Republic of China on Professional Ethics of Judges* provides in part in Article 14, "Other than performance of work responsibilities or going through proper procedures, do not inquire into, interfere or comment on the cases currently under trial by other judges." This standard was probably breached by the judge Jiang Xingchang discussed above. Canada's *Ethical Principles for Judges* comments that "Judges should, therefore, avoid deliberate use of words or conduct, in and out of court, that could reasonably give rise to a perception of an absence of impartiality." This and other principles have been interpreted to prohibit commentary on other judges or cases which shows that a judge has formed a different fixed opinion which would determine their judgment in a similar case. In other words, their mind has been made up in advance of any trial, and this is the very opposite of impartiality. The Chief Justice of Canada herself faced criticism for expressing a strong opinion concerning the attempted assimilation of First Nations peoples when cases based on those events might still reach the Supreme Court for decision. The restrictions on judicial freedom of speech in both countries appear to be motivated by the desire to maintain the internal and external legitimacy of the judicial branch. Concerning the internal aspect, the rules attempt to avoid disagreement and confusion among judges concerning the law to be applied, and in relation to the external, they support the appearance of judges' impartiality and avert public suspicion of a closed judicial mind.

There are thus similar limits on judges' freedom of expression in Canada and China designed to reach the same goal: legitimacy, which is dependent upon the trust and confidence of the public in the judiciary. Both countries recognize that the judicial institution requires the support of the public as well as the government to carry out effectively its function of delivering justice according to law.

5.3 *Different Behavior/Different Meaning*

We observe that the greatest differences between the judiciaries of Canada and China in both action and purpose are found in the complex nexus of law and politics. Canada's *Ethical Principles for Judges* makes it clear that judges should divorce themselves from politics: "All partisan political activity must cease upon appointment. Judges should refrain from conduct that, in the mind of a reasonable, fair minded and informed person, could give rise to the appearance that the judge is engaged in political activity." The key word here is "partisan" which reflects Canadian political traditions of contests for power among multiple political parties. Indeed, the Parliamentary system which Canada inherited from England is structured around the existence of one party which forms the Government, and another party playing the role of the Loyal Opposition. Further, the requirement for judges to refrain from engagement in politics follows from the "separation of powers" doctrine recognized in Canada according to which the judiciary is a distinct and independent authority alongside the Parliament (legislative authority) and the Executive (the Government acting in the name of the sovereign). Just as Parliament and the Executive must refrain from acting as judges, so are judges prohibited from acting as politicians.

In China the situation is quite different where judges are required to be loyal to the CPC and defer to its leadership in administering the law. As explained by Chief Justice Zhou, ideology as interpreted by the CPC must be embraced by judges and they should be assessed in part on their devotion to and application of socialist values in their work. The *Code of Conduct for Judges* makes this very explicit: "Insist on the supreme position of the Party's cause, the interests of the people, and the constitutional laws. Maintain consistency of thoughts and actions with those of the Party Central Committee."

These very different relations of judges to politics and political parties reflect divergent understandings of the role of politics in society that arise out of the historical trajectories of the state and the judiciary in Canada and China. The principle of separation of powers within the British state was adopted during the centuries' old process of political emancipation of society from governance by an absolute monarch. Since the *Magna Carta* (1215) Parliament assumed authority to pass laws which the monarch must accept, and since the *Act of Settlement* in 1701 it became acknowledged that the judicial branch exercises authority independent of Parliament, the Executive and the sovereign. Politics in this tradition was thus understood to include at its foundation the struggle for emancipation of British citizens as individual bearers of rights which could be maintained by the courts even against state action. The modern result is a system of government in which the power of the state is distributed among three basic institutions, one of which is the judiciary. Canada inherited this legal structure and political tradition.

The historical roots of the judiciary in modern China are quite different. Judicial techniques such as the Ma Xiwu method of trial were born in a revolutionary environment that prioritized the social and economic emancipation of society under the leadership of the CPC. First and foremost was the need to ameliorate inequality, poverty, and traditional hierarchies of power. The CPC cemented its position as the only legitimate political expression of these goals through its success in making good on many of these social promises. In parallel fashion, the Chinese judiciary gained legitimacy by complementing and supporting politics understood as being the struggle of the CPC for socio-economic transformation.[25]

We might, therefore, say that politics in the British (and Canadian) tradition was often concerned with limiting or least diffusing the power of the state, while in modern China a strong state unified under the guidance of the CPC presented itself as the best political arrangement to achieve social progress. These different conceptions of politics have in turn affected the role of judges in the two countries. Following British tradition, judges are expected to oppose the will of the state if required by law as interpreted by the judiciary. A dramatic example of just such an event has recently occurred: the "Brexit" decision by Supreme Court of the United Kingdom. In the case *R v Secretary of State* (2017) that Court declared that the Government could not unilaterally withdraw the country from the European Union by exercising the authority of the sovereign ("prerogative power") in whose name it governs. Rather, the Court said, the Government must secure the consent of Parliament because such withdrawal would change the laws applicable to British citizens, a legislative act which may only be taken by Parliament. This decision draws on ancient legal authority to delimit the powers of organs of the state, in this case the Government as the executive institution. It would be inconceivable for Chinese judges to attempt to exercise similar authority over the actions of the government and the CPC.

We might, therefore, conclude simply by saying that Canada's judiciary is the product of a political emancipation of society from domination by unitary state authority, while the modern Chinese judiciary originated as part of a socio-economic emancipation of society accomplished under the authority of a state unified through single party politics. The consequence is that Canadian judges are expected to be free from politics because they are relied on to protect individuals against unlawful political action while Chinese judges are expected to embrace and assist politics in achieving social goals.

However, despite these marked differences in judicial practice and purpose in the two countries, there are glimpses of some trends toward a convergence of judicial practices we should also note.

First, recall that Justice Berger was censured for intervening in a public debate over the amendment of the Canadian Constitution, an instance of judicial speech which was held to be inappropriate "political" activity. However, some of the very amendments which he commented on, particularly the *Charter of Rights and Freedoms*, introduced politics into judicial work in Canada in a way that had not been seen before. Under the *Charter*, Canadian judges are given the authority to declare null and void laws and other governmental activity which infringe legal and other rights the *Charter* establishes and protects. Governments at all levels in the federation are entitled to defend their actions which limit Charter rights provided such limits are "reasonable limits prescribed by law as can be demonstrably justified in a free and democratic society" (Section 1). The authority of courts to question and overturn legislation and government actions is known as judicial review. It is quite

---

[25]For another comparative perspective on the history of Western and Chinese judging see Jacob (2014).

evident that considering whether government action is reasonable and justified, keeping in mind the requirements of a free and democratic society, implicates Canadian judges in deciding what most people would call "political" questions. Indeed, the Supreme Court of Canada has been asked to give its opinion on several matters involving essentially political issues: for instance, the extent of agreement among the Provinces of Canada required to amend the Constitution (Reference re: Amendment 1982); whether the Province of Quebec had a legal right to secede from the federation (Reference re: Secession 1998); and whether the Senate of Canada could be abolished or restructured by the Federal Government without the consent of the Provinces (Reference re: Senate Reform 2014). Canadian judges are apparently not totally divorced from politics.

Next, consider a recent development in Chinese jurisprudence. Although Chief Justice Zhou rejects the separation of powers approach to judicial authority, perhaps at some point the CPC might see some advantage in bolstering the independence of China's judiciary. A Chinese legal scholar has, for instance, suggested giving a judicial body such as the SPC authority to review, and, if necessary, strike down laws and administrative actions of subordinate political institutions that contravene or are inconsistent with the Constitution or national laws. Judges given such power may assist the central government in ensuring that laws are applied consistently and uniformly across China (Ji 2014). In a large country like China with many regional and subordinate governmental institutions and actors, a limited form of judicial review may be accepted as compatible with the aims of the CPC. Chinese judges may have a future that includes some independence from politics.

An external perspective allows us to observe that Canadian judges do indeed confront and resolve some political issues while Chinese politics might conceivably lead to giving China's judges some authority to limit politics itself at some levels.[26]

5.4 *Different Behavior/Same Meaning*

Canadian and Chinese judges share the same goal of maintaining both the internal and external legitimacy of the judicial institution. In relation to the internal aspect of legitimacy the behavior of both judiciaries is also similar, but different actions are observed when it comes to concern for their external legitimacy.

We see parallel behavior arising out of concern for the internal legitimacy of the judiciary in Canada and China as follows: standards of fact finding and legal justification designed to ensure the fair and consistent application of the law throughout the country; respect for the decisions of other judges to maintain stability and certainty of the law; and practices that promote efficient and effective judicial work. These actions tend to support the fair and effective administration of the law in a way that is logical, coherent and consistent, thus contributing to its internal legitimacy.

[26]For a comparative study of the role of judges in promoting and supporting judicial review in different political settings see Roux (2017). See also Valois (2013).

Judges in Canada and China, however, pursue different strategies when it comes to maintaining and enhancing the external (sociological) legitimacy of the judicial branch. As the following analysis shows, Canadian judges tend to distance themselves from society while Chinese judges involve themselves more readily.

Chief Justice McLachlin has pointed out that Canadian judges were traditionally thought of as secluded oracles, appearing in public only in courtrooms. This practice of judicial non-involvement in society was criticized by one Judge of the Supreme Court of Canada who questioned "Should judges be monks?".[27] Chief Justice McLachlin further noted that times have changed and that Canadian judges are now expected to be in touch with the communities they work in, including awareness of people's current lives and attitudes which may be gained through some social contact. As the *Ethical Principles for Judges* states: "The judge administers the law on behalf of the community and therefore unnecessary isolation from the community does not promote wise or just judgments." Nevertheless, there is an enduring belief in Canada that judges should maintain some distance from the public to demonstrate their independence and avoid compromising their impartiality. As the *Ethical Principles* note: "Judges need to strike a delicate balance between the requirements of judicial office and the legitimate demands of the judge's personal life, development and family." In other words, "carry on with life but bear in mind that you occupy a special status in the community that should not be jeopardized." Most Canadian judges even today take this advice to heart by limiting their social involvement and visibility outside of court appearances.

In summary, we observe from an external perspective that Canadian judges try to maintain external legitimacy largely by distancing themselves from the public in line with legal traditions of independence and impartiality. Such action is endorsed by the ethical principles governing judges and supported by Canadian judges' sense of professional responsibility.

In China, judges demonstrate more concern for their external legitimacy and accordingly take different steps than their Canadian counterparts. A principal difference is adoption of the Ma Xiwu trial mode which is characterized by the mass line, and offering legal explanation after the final judgment to gain the comprehension and approval of the public. These steps are intended to demonstrate the harmony of the judges and the law with the needs and aspirations of the people. Further, since the rule of virtue still plays a big role in Chinese society, as constantly emphasized by the top leader (People's Daily 2016), its judges must demonstrate that they act accordingly in a moral way expected by the masses. There is currently not the same level of public trust and confidence in Chinese judges as exists in relation to Canadian judges, thus judges in China must make an extra effort to actively associate themselves with the people and respond to public doubts or anger concerning judges' work.

Chinese judges have traditionally been taught to be engaged with the communities they work in according to the expectations of society and the CPC. Such connections

[27] See Canadian Judicial Centre (1989), Sopinka (1991, 1996). Justice Sopinka appears to have agreed with Oliver Wendell Holmes's remark that a judge should take part in "the passions of his time": Sopinka (1991, at 142).

are supported by the principles of judicial conduct and the guidance of senior officials. However, the current trend of professionalization of Chinese judges may have the result of decreasing this close connection between judges and the public in the future. Recent directives have encouraged China's judges to separate themselves from local connections more than in the past, thus achieving greater independence which is viewed as being more professional in their roles. Chinese judges will thus have to negotiate a path between traditional public expectations of access to, and connection with judges, and competing professional standards of independence and impartiality which are being emphasized more today.

The judiciaries of both Canada and China face continuing challenges in remaining both relevant to, and respected by, the societies they serve, challenges that test their external legitimacy.

6 Conclusion

State-appointed judges everywhere pledge to support the *status quo*, understood as the fundamental legal and political institutions and arrangements under which they are to function, and this is no less the case in Canada and China. Accordingly, the first act which judges perform aiming at external legitimation of the legal system is accepting judicial appointment to start with. Judges then continue to perform their duties with legitimacy in the eyes of the public as one of their goals along with the goal of ensuring internal legitimation of legal actions and decisions. The judicial function is therefore not primarily directed towards social change, however, the demand for sociological legitimation of a legal system nevertheless requires a certain degree of responsiveness towards the public which it governs.[28] Judges must therefore respond to public needs and concerns while at the same time maintaining a certain degree of independence from society to demonstrate their impartiality and lack of bias when faced with conflicting claims and interests. Balancing independence with engagement is becoming increasingly challenging as judges and their decisions are made more visible through both mass and social media. As one judge has put it, there is now the possibility of judges being "publicized" out of office (Edwards 1989).[29]

In this chapter we have tried to describe how judges in Canada and China have met the challenge of fulfilling their duties from a position of what might be called "engaged independence" within society. Because Canadian and Chinese judges have no independent coercive power, unlike the science fictional Judge Dredd, they rely

[28] Siegel describes this task of judges as requiring "judicial statesmanship" in expressing social values and sustaining social solidarity: Siegel (2008). Canadian judges have been described as "socially embedded moral agents": Devlin et al. (2013).

[29] For further discussions of judicial conduct and communication in the modern media era see: Rupert (1990), Reinhardt (1995), Kelso (1995), MacKay (1996), Fortunato (1999), Ratushny (2000), Mellon (2002), Webb (2003), Sparling (2010), Dodek and Sossin (2010), MacKenzie (2012), Schmidt (2013), Sossin and Bacal (2013), Goodman (2014), Moran (2015), National Center for State Courts (2016), and Henderson (2016).

on the cooperation and support of other government actors, and the willingness of a great majority of the public to accept their decisions and the justifications given for them. For a society to believe in the wisdom and justness of its judges, the judiciary must balance an "objective", impartial view of the matters that come before it for judgment together with a "subjective" understanding of the human desires and aspirations which require resolution.

References

Angers J-C (1995) Gun controls and democracy. Univ New Brunswick Law J 45:183–189
Bai L (白龙) (2009) Wang Shengjun Yaoqiu Ganjing Xuexi Ma Xiwu Zuo Yi Xin Weimin de "Pingmin Faguan" (王胜俊要求干警学习马锡五做一心为民的"平民法官") [Wang shengjun Demands that Policemen Learn from Ma Xiwu and Become "Commoner Judges" that Only Serve the People], Renmin Ribao (人民日报) [People's Daily], Aug. 8. http://www.npc.gov.cn/npc/xinwen/fztd/sfgz/2009-08/08/content_1512847.htm. Accessed 9 Aug 2017
Barzun CL (2015) Inside-out: beyond the internal/external distinction in legal scholarship. Va Law Rev 101(5):1203–1288
Bassok O (2011) The sociological-legitimacy difficulty. J Law Politics 26:239–272
Beijing News (2017) Much reduced sentence reflects verdict of 'jury' of public opinion. China Daily. http://www.chinadaily.com.cn/opinion/2017-06/26/content_29881425.htm. Accessed 9 Aug 2017
Berger TR (1981) Fragile freedoms: human rights and dissent in Canada. Clarke, Irwin & Company Limited, Toronto
Berger TR (1985) The charter and the Canadian identity. Univ W Ontario Law Rev 23:1–8
Berger TR (1991a) Letter to Bora Laskin. Univ New Brunswick Law J 40:234–240
Berger TR (1991b) A long and terrible shadow: White values, native rights in the Americas since 1492, 2nd edn. Douglas & McIntyre, Vancouver
Berger TR (2002) One man's justice: a life in the law. Douglas & McIntyre, Vancouver
Blackham A (2016) Legitimacy and empirical evidence in UK courts. Griffith Law Rev 25(3):414–440
Burns K (2016) Judges, "common sense" and judicial cognition. Griffith Law Rev 25(3):319–351
Burns K, Dioso-Villa R, Rathus Zoe (2016) Judicial decision-making and "outside" extra-legal knowledge: breaking down silos. Griffith Law Rev 25(3):283–290
Canadian Judicial Centre (1989) A quantum leap in judicial ethics. Can Judicial Centre Bull 2(2):1–3
Canadian Judicial Council (1990) Principles governing relations between the judiciary and the news media. Can Judicial Centre Bull 3(2):1–2
Canadian Judicial Council (1991a) Commentaries on judicial conduct. Les Éditions Yvon Blais Inc, Cowansville (Que)
Canadian Judicial Council (1991b) The Canadian Judicial Council. Canadian Judicial Council, Ottawa
Canadian Judicial Council (2004) Ethical principles for judges. Canadian Judicial Council, Ottawa
Canadian Judicial Council (2008) Matlow inquiry: public documents. Canadian Judicial Council. https://www.cjc-ccm.gc.ca/english/conduct_en.asp?selMenu=conduct_inq_matlow_en.asp. Accessed 8 Aug 2017
Carville O (2015) Canadian Judicial Council under fire by federal judge. The Star, 12 February. https://www.thestar.com/news/gta/2015/02/12/canadian-judicial-council-under-fire-by-federal-judge.html. Accessed 8 Aug 2017
China Daily (2017) Much reduced sentence reflects verdict of 'jury' of public opinion. http://www.chinadaily.com.cn/opinion/2017-06/26/content_29881425.htm. Accessed 21 Dec 2017

China Supreme Court (2008) Xu theft case (2008) Criminal Code Zi No. 18 [(2008)刑核字第18号]. http://www.pkulaw.cn/case/PFnl_a25051f3312b07f3adff0d1266f0a2c59cf516734f81bfef.html. Accessed 21 Dec 2017

Clarke DC (2009) Supreme people's court work report: comments, Chinese law professors blog (9 Apr 2009). http://lawprofessors.typepad.com/china_law_prof_blog/2009/04/supreme-peoples-court-work-report.html. Accessed 9 Aug 2017

Coates K (2015) McLachlin said what many have long known. The Globe and Mail. https://www.theglobeandmail.com/opinion/mclachlin-said-what-many-have-long-known/article24704812/. Accessed 8 Aug 2017

Delgado R (1990) Judicial influences and the inside-outside dichotomy: a comment on Professor Nagel. Univ Colorado Law Rev 61:711–714

Devlin R, Adèle Kent C, Lightstone S (2013) The past, present … and future (?) of judicial ethics education in Canada. Leg Ethics 16(1):1–35

Dodek A, Sossin L (eds) (2010) Judicial independence in context. Irwin Law Inc., Toronto

Edwards HT (1989) Regulating judicial misconduct and divining "good behavior" for federal judges. Mich Law Rev 87:765–796

Fallon Richard H Jr (2005) Legitimacy and the constitution. Harvard Law Rev 118:1787–1853

Felsky M (1984) The Berger affair and the independence of the judiciary. Univ Toronto Fac Law Rev 42:118–125

Fine S (2015) Chief Justice says Canada attempted "cultural genocide" on Aboriginals. The Globe and Mail. https://www.theglobeandmail.com/news/national/chief-justice-says-canada-attempted-cultural-genocide-on-aboriginals/article24688854/. Accessed 8 Aug 2017

Forsythe M (2017) China's Chief Justice rejects an independent judiciary, and reformers wince. New York Times, 18 January. https://www.nytimes.com/2017/01/18/world/asia/china-chief-justice-courts-zhou-qiang.html. Accessed 9 Aug 2017

Fortunato SJ Jr (1999) On a judge's duty to speak extrajudicially: Rethinking the strategy of silence. Georgetown J Leg Ethics 12:679–716

Friedland ML (1995) A place apart: judicial independence and accountability in Canada. Canadian Judicial Council, Ottawa

Friedman B (2003) Mediated popular constitutionalism. Mich Law Rev 101:2596–2636

Gagnon L (2015) McLachlin's comments a disservice to her court, and to Aboriginals. The Globe and Mail. https://www.theglobeandmail.com/opinion/mclachlins-comments-a-disservice-to-her-court-and-to-aboriginals/article24879482/. Accessed 8 Aug 2017

Goodman MD (2014) Shame, angry judges, and the social media effect. Catholic Univ Law Rev 63:589–623

Guangdong High Court (2008) Criminal ruling (theft) (粤高法刑一终字第5号). http://www.pkulaw.cn/case/PFnl_a25051f3312b07f3f8a3baa3372d4a782417e79ce65fe20e.html. Accessed 21 Dec 2017

Henderson A (2016) The high court and the cocktail party from hell: can social media improve community engagement with the courts? J Judicial Adm 25:175–192

Howarth DR, Stark SW (2014) The reality of the British constitution: H.L.A. Hart and what "officials" really think. University of Cambridge Faculty of Law. https://papers.ssrn.com/sol3/papers.cfm?abstract_id=2466001. Accessed 8 Aug 2017

Hu J (2017) China's top judge warns against the 'threat' of judicial independence, Global voices, 20 Jan 2017. https://globalvoices.org/2017/01/20/chinas-top-judge-warns-against-the-threat-of-judicial-independence/#. Accessed 9 Aug 2017

Jacob R (2014) The judge and the sacred: notes for a comparative history of western and Chinese judicial cultures. Asian J Law Soc 1:17–30

Ji W (2014) The rule of law in a Chinese way: social diversification and reconstructing the system of authority. Asian J Law Soc 1:305–338

Kelso JC (1995) Time, place, and manner restrictions on extrajudicial speech by judges. Loyola Los Angeles Law Rev 28:851–868

Krygier M (2016) The rule of law: pasts, presents, and two possible futures. Ann Rev Law Soc Sci 12:199–229. https://doi.org/10.1146/annurev-lawsocsci-102612-134103
Laskin B (1972) The institutional character of the judge. Magnes Press, Hebrew University, Jerusalem
L'Heureux-Dubé C (1988) Notes from an address on judges' day. Can Judicial Centre Bull 1(1):6–7
Liebman BL (2011) A return to populist legality? Historical legacies and legal reform. In: Heilmann S, Perry EJ (eds) Mao's invisible hand: the political foundations of adaptive governance in China, pp 165–200. Harvard University Press, Cambridge
Lubet S (1989) Professor Polonius advises Judge Laertes: rules, good taste and the scope of public comment. Georgetown J Leg Ethics 2:665–689
Luhmann N (2004) Law as a social system. Ziegert KA (Trans). Oxford University Press, Oxford
MacKay AW (1996) Framing the issues for cameras in the courtrooms: redefining judicial dignity and decorum. Dalhousie Law J 19:139–168
MacKenzie B (2012) Extrajudicial speech: judicial ethics in the new media age. Reynolds Courts Media Law J 2:185–209
Mavis Baker v. Minister of Citizenship and Immigration (1999) Supreme Court of Canada. [1999] 2 S.C.R. 817. https://scc-csc.lexum.com/scc-csc/scc-csc/en/item/1717/index.do. Accessed 8 Aug 2017
McCormick P (1998) Twelve paradoxes of judicial discipline. Const Forum 9(4):105–113
McLachlin B (2001) The role of judges in modern society. Supreme Court of Canada. http://www.scc-csc.ca/judges-juges/spe-dis/bm-2001-05-05-eng.aspx. Accessed 8 Aug 2017
McLachlin B (2004) Judging in a democratic state. Supreme Court of Canada. http://www.scc-csc.ca/judges-juges/spe-dis/bm-2004-06-03-eng.aspx. Accessed 8 Aug 2017
McLachlin B (2015) Reconciling unity and diversity in the modern era: tolerance and intolerance. The Globe and Mail. https://www.theglobeandmail.com/news/national/unity-diversity-and-cultural-genocide-chief-justice-mclachlins-complete-text/article24698710/. Accessed 8 Aug 2017
Mellon H (2002) Meeting the public: the charter, public debate, and the judiciary. Windsor Yearb Access Justice 21:33–45
Minow ML (1990) Judging inside out. Univ Colorado Law Rev 61:795–801
Minzner CF (2011) China's turn against law. Am J Comp Law 59:935–984. https://doi.org/10.5131/AJCL.2011.0006
Moran J (2015) Courting controversy: the problems caused by extrajudicial speech and writing. Victoria Univ Wellington Law Rev 46:453–494
Nagel RF (1990) Political pressure and judging in constitutional cases. Univ Colorado Law Rev 61:685–702
National Center for State Courts (2016) Trends in state courts: special focus on family law and court communications. National Center for State Courts. http://www.ncsc.org/~/media/microsites/files/trends%202016/trends-2016-low.ashx. Accessed 8 Aug 2017
O'Connor SD (2003) Vindicating the rule of law: the role of the judiciary. Chin J Int Law 2:1–10
Peerenboom R (2010) Between global norms and domestic realities: judicial reforms in China. LAWASIA J 2010:1–16
People's Court (2017) Shen Deyong: Accurately grasp the method, use preciseness; strive at full speed to ensure that the task of judicial system reform is performed. http://mp.weixin.qq.com/s/pDBM57IDioU-atpY8PFCvw. Accessed 21 Dec 2017
People's Daily Overseas Edition (2006) (人民日报海外版), 18 Aug 2006, p 004
People's Daily (2016) Xi Jinping: Insisting the combination of rule by law and rule by virtue, improving the modernization of state governance system and ability (习近平:坚持依法治国和以德治国相结合, 推进国家治理体系和治理能力现代化), 12 Nov 2016, p 1
People.com.cn (2008) Jiang Xingchang, vice president of the Supreme People's Court: "Xu Ting case," the first sentence was significantly overweight. http://npc.people.com.cn/GB/28320/116286/116599/6983219.html. Accessed 21 Dec 2017

Pils E (2009) Yang Jia and China's unpopular criminal justice system. Human Rights in China. http://www.hrichina.org/en/content/3702. Accessed 9 Aug 2017
Posner EA, Vermeule A (2013) Inside or outside the system? Univ Chicago Law Rev 80:1743–1797
R (on the application of Miller and another) (Respondents) *v* Secretary of State for Exiting the European Union (Appellant) REFERENCE by the Attorney General for Northern Ireland - In the matter of an application by Agnew and others for Judicial Review REFERENCE by the Court of Appeal (Northern Ireland) – In the matter of an application by Raymond McCord for Judicial Review [2017] UKSC 5. https://www.supremecourt.uk/cases/docs/uksc-2016-0196-judgment.pdf. Accessed 9 Aug 2017
Rodriguez-Blanco V (2007) Peter Winch and H.LA. Hart: two concepts of the internal point of view. Can J Law Jurisprud 20(2):453–473
Ratushny E (2000) Speaking as judges: how far can they go? Natl J Const Law 11:293–409
Reference re: Amendment to the Canadian Constitution, [1982] 2 S.C.R. 791. https://scc-csc.lexum.com/scc-csc/scc-csc/en/item/5529/index.do. Accessed 9 Aug 2017
Reference re: Remuneration of Judges of the Provincial Court of Prince Edward Island; Reference re Independence and Impartiality of Judges of the Provincial Court of Prince Edward Island. 1997. Supreme Court of Canada. [1997] 3 S.C.R. 3. https://scc-csc.lexum.com/scc-csc/scc-csc/en/item/1541/index.do. Accessed 8 Aug 2017
Reference re: Secession of Quebec. 1998. Supreme Court of Canada. [1998] 2 S.C.R. 217. https://scc-csc.lexum.com/scc-csc/scc-csc/en/item/1643/index.do. Accessed 8 Aug 2017
Reference re: Senate Reform (2014) Supreme Court of Canada. 2014 SCC 32. https://scc-csc.lexum.com/scc-csc/scc-csc/en/item/13614/index.do. Accessed 9 Aug 2017
Reichman A (2007) The dimensions of law: judicial craft, its public perception, and the role of the scholar. Calif Law Rev 95:1619–1675
Reinhardt S (1995) Judicial speech and the open judiciary. Loyola Los Angeles Law Rev 28:805–813
Renke W (1994) Invoking independence: judicial independence as a no-cut wage guarantee. Points of View/Points de vue No. 5. Centre for Constitutional Studies, Edmonton
Report and record of the committee of investigation into the conduct of the Hon. Mr. Justice Berger and resolution of the Canadian Judicial Council (1983) McGill Law J 28:378–436
Ross WG (1989a) Extrajudicial speech: charting the boundaries of propriety. Georgetown J Leg Ethics 2:589–642
Ross WG (1989b) Rules for extrajudicial speech: too broad and too narrow. Georgetown J Leg Ethics 2:691–693
Roux T (2017) How, when and why does faith in law's autonomy from politics decline? A comparative constitutional-cultural analysis. In: Delaney E, Dixon R (eds) Comparative judicial review, forthcoming. Edward Elgar, Cheltenham. University of New South Wales. https://papers.ssrn.com/sol3/papers.cfm?abstract_id=2921602. Accessed 8 Aug 2017
Rupert B (1990) Judicial media relations. Can Judicial Centre Bull 3(2):2–4
Schmidt CW (2013) Beyond the opinion: Supreme Court justices and extrajudicial speech. Chicago-Kent Law Rev 88:487–526
Siegel NS (2008) The virtue of judicial statesmanship. Tex Law Rev 86:959–1032
Sissons J (1968) Judge of the far north: the memoirs of Jack Sissons. McClelland and Stewart, Toronto
Sopinka J (1991) Confirmation hearings and the proper role for judges in the public sphere. Windsor Rev Leg Soc Issues 3:139–146
Sopinka John (1996) Must a judge be a monk—revisited. Univ New Brunswick Law J 45:167–174
Sossin L, Bacal M (2013) Judicial ethics in a digital age. Univ Br Columbia Law Rev 46(3):629–664
South China Morning Post (2017) Chinese judge suspended over social media swipe at traffic policeman. http://www.scmp.com/news/china/policies-politics/article/2074417/chinese-judge-suspended-over-social-media-swipe-traffic. Accessed 21 Dec 2017
Southern Weekend (2009) The biggest controversy over judicial reform—the revival of Ma Xiwu. Southern Weekend, June 11 at A8

Sparling TA (2010) Through different lenses: using psychology to assess popular criticism of the judiciary from the public's perspective. Kansas J Law Public Policy 19:471–504

Strawn BB (2008) Do judicial ethics canons affect perceptions of judicial impartiality? Boston Univ Law Rev 88:781–813

Supreme People's Court of the People's Republic of China (2017a) Court reform in China. Supreme People's Court. http://english.court.gov.cn/2017-03/14/content_28552928.htm. Accessed 9 Aug 2017

Supreme People's Court of the People's Republic of China (2017b) Address by Zhou Qiang. http://www.court.gov.cn (最高人民法院网), 2017-01-12 09:19:00

Tamanaha BZ (1996) The internal/external distinction and the notion of a "practice" in legal theory and sociolegal studies. Law Soc Rev 30:163–204

Tamanaha BZ (2006) A socio-legal methodology for the internal/external distinction: jurisprudential implications. Fordham Law Rev 75:1255–1274

Teubner G (1993) Law as an autopoietic system. Blackwell, Oxford

Teubner G (2014) Law and social theory: three problems. Asian J Law Soc 1:235–254

Thepaper.cn (2017)Lijiang, a judge microblogging 57-year-old traffic police on duty is "show" was suspended. http://www.thepaper.cn/newsDetail_forward_1627575. Accessed 21 Dec 2017

Valois M (2013) Judicial independence: keeping law at a distance from politics. LexisNexis Canada Inc, Markham (Ont)

Wang S (王胜俊) (2009a) Zuigao Renmin Fayuan Gongzuo Baogao (2009) (最高人民法院工作报告[2009]) [Supreme People's Court Work Report (2009)], Standing Comm. Nat'l. People's Cong. Gazette, 1 Apr 2009

Wang Y (王烨) (2009b) Ma Xiwu Shenpan Fangshi Zhanting zai Gansu Luocheng (马锡五审判方式展厅在甘肃落成) [The exhibit hall of the Ma Xiwu adjudication method opens in Gansu], Zhongguo Fayuan Wang (中国法院网). Chinacourt.org. http://old.chinacourt.org/public/detail.php?id=341462. Accessed 9 Aug 2017

Webb D (2003) Judicial conduct in a very small place: some contextual questions. Leg Ethics 6(1):106–117

Webber J (1984) The limits to judges' free speech: a comment on the report of the committee of investigation into the conduct of the Hon. Mr. Justice Berger. McGill Law J 29(3):369–406

Westin AF (1962) Out-of-court commentary by United State Supreme Court Justices, 1790–1962: Of free speech and judicial lockjaw. Columbia Law Rev 62:633–669

Wilson JO (1980) A book for judges. Minister of Supply and Services Canada, Ottawa

Zang D (2010) Rise of political populism and the trouble with the legal profession in China. Harvard China Rev 6(1):79–99. https://papers.ssrn.com/sol3/papers.cfm?abstract_id=1585442. Accessed 10 Aug 2017

Archie Zariski is Professor of Legal Studies at Athabasca University, Canada, a lawyer and an experienced mediator. He has created and taught courses in ADR, negotiation and mediation at Athabasca and at Murdoch Law School, Australia. His research includes exploring the roles of lawyers and judges in dispute resolution processes. Archie is co-editor of the book *The Multi-Tasking Judge: Judicial Dispute Resolution in Comparative Perspective* and the author of *Legal Literacy: An Introduction to Legal Studies*. He is a member of the ADR Institute of Canada, and the Resolution Institute (Australia).

Changqing Shi is a Professor of Law at Shanghai University in the People's Republic of China. She is also a part-time lawyer and a former prosecutor in Yantai People's Procuratorate. She visited the University of Pennsylvania in 2017 and the Institute for European Tort Law in 2012 as a visiting scholar. Her research is mainly in the fields of civil procedure and alternative dispute resolution. Her many articles relate to mediation and the judiciary.

Judicial Practice in Action: Court Reform and Responsive Judges in Canada

Toby S. Goldbach

Abstract This chapter presents two examples of responsive judging *outside* of the courtroom. The chapter takes a socio-legal approach to the study of responsive judging, outlining the activities and practices of judges and the work that judges do on a day-to-day basis, from the mundane rule-making activities to the both visible and hidden work on architectural design and courthouse construction. The two examples feature judges in Ontario, Canada responding to critiques of formal legal institutions by working on court reform outside of, or in addition to, their regular case-work. First, judges in Ontario responded to calls for "faster, cheaper, and better" alternatives to trial by incorporating non-adversarial processes and procedures within the life of a case. Second, Ontario judges responded to the over incarceration of Aboriginal offenders by bringing culturally appropriate procedures into the criminal trial and building a physical space for Aboriginal justice within the courthouse. For better or worse, judges have responded to a variety of challenges by innovating, adapting, and reforming the practices and operation of activities at court, and specifically by incorporating "alternative dispute resolution" ("ADR") mechanisms into conventional court procedures. In presenting these examples of judicial responsiveness, this chapter provokes legal scholars to reflect on the various sites of judicial law-making, and, concurrently the various sites of the intermingling of law and politics.

1 Introduction

This chapter examines public or state-centered institutions by focusing on judges as ethnographic objects—considering judges as real people who work and practice at the nexus of law. It describes judges' work on court reform by featuring two examples of judicial responsiveness *outside* of the courtroom. In so doing, the chapter intends to provoke legal scholars to reflect on the role of the decision as the sole site of judicial law-making, as well as the various sites of the intermingling of law and politics.

T. S. Goldbach (✉)
University of British Columbia Allard School of Law, Vancouver, Canada
e-mail: goldbach@allard.ubc.ca

© Springer Nature Singapore Pte Ltd. 2018

T. Sourdin and A. Zariski (eds.), *The Responsive Judge*, Ius Gentium: Comparative Perspectives on Law and Justice 67, https://doi.org/10.1007/978-981-13-1023-2_8

Contemporary judges find themselves in a precarious position, cast as both heroes and villains in a narrative about whether law can effectively resolve disputes and deliver justice. Internationally, development practitioners, economists, and government officials appeal to judges for their practical and institutional support. Judges are seen as fulfilling a crucial role in supporting the rule of law in countries transitioning to democracy (Ginsburg 2012; Trubek and Santos 2006), or in guaranteeing a stable mechanism for resolving disputes in countries seeking foreign direct investment (Trebilcock and Daniels 2008; Trebilcock and Mota Prado 2011; Haggard et al. 2008). Human rights scholars look to judges to protect socio-economic rights (Gross Stein 2010; Rittich 2004). And particular courts—for example the South African Constitutional Court, the Israeli High Court of Justice, the Inter-American Court on Human Rights or the European Court of Justice—stand as emblems of humanitarian law and our collective aspirations for law and justice.

In contrast, legal scholars condemn judges for a myriad of wrongdoings. Judges are accused of overstepping their role and "judicializing" politics (Chemerinsky 2006; Mandel 1989). Judges are deemed to be ill equipped to decide complex cases (Zumbansen 2012; particularly medical malpractice or complex commercial cases), or are thought to be inflexible, too slow, and encouraging of calculating and unscrupulous behaviour in court (Galanter 2002, 291).

Legal scholars also forecast apocalyptic futures for the formal legal institutions where judges reside. The decline in the number of civil trials led one scholar to posit that the trial is vanishing (Galanter 2004), while another laments on the "empty halls of justice" (Resnik and Curtis 2011). These claims are supported by data. In Ontario, fewer than four percent of civil cases go through a full trial for final disposition (Winkler 2008b, 11).

Why, then, write about "responsive judging"? How can judges possibly respond to these challenges?

This chapter adopts a socio-legal empirical approach to the study of judges, examining and describing judges "in action" (Seron and Sibley 2004). In particular, the chapter describes the activities and practices of judges and the work that judges do on a day-to-day basis, from the mundane rule-making activities to the both visible and hidden work on architectural design and courthouse construction. For better or worse, judges have responded to a variety of challenges by innovating, adapting, and reforming the practices and operation of activities at court, and specifically by incorporating "alternative dispute resolution" ("ADR") mechanisms into conventional court procedures.[1] For example, judges responded to calls for "faster, cheaper, better" alternatives by incorporating non-adversarial processes and procedures within the life of a case. Judges responded to over-incarceration of Aboriginal offenders in Canada by bringing culturally appropriate procedures into the criminal trial and building a space for Aboriginal justice within the Canadian courthouse.

---

[1]It is with some reluctance that I refer to out-of-court dispute resolution as "alternative". There is an argument to be made that with only a small percentage of cases being disposed of at trial, negotiation, mediation and arbitration are no longer alternative. However, for this paper, especially with respect to the historical discussion, I will be following the convention of using the terminology "ADR".

Responsive judging has been broadly defined as "a range of behaviours and approaches used by judges to more effectively attend to issues and problems that emerge in the justice system" (Sourdin 2016). Several scholars describe responsive judging within the context of the engagement and connection of judges in the courtroom to litigants, witnesses, victims, or the accused (see e.g. de Hoon and Verberk 2014; Law Commission 2001). For example, de Hoon and Verberk (2014) in their research on judicial dispute resolution in the Netherlands, seek out "the new judge" who "looks further than the purely legal coordinates of the conflict" and who involves herself "in diagnosing the needs of the litigants" (de Hoon and Verberk 2014). This judge is responsive to the needs of those who come before her by recognizing that the "legal definition of a conflict as it is presented in court is often only a part of a more encompassing problem" (de Hoon and Verberk 2014, 40).

In contrast, a socio-legal or law-and-society study of responsive judging would examine legal activities "in all their guises," using "situated and contextualized analys[is]" to uncover the varied instances of social action that produce, shape, and encourage law and legality (Seron and Sibley 2004, 30). The socio-legal review may, therefore, entail moving beyond the courtroom, even in an examination of judges. The emphasis is on situated and contextualized analysis and the ways that law is created, constructed, and reformed through social action (whether or not through formal or informal means). This chapter is thus situated in a turn of phrase, moving from describing or promoting responsive judging to a description and analysis of the *responsive judge*. Considering that on a conservative estimate, upwards of ninety percent of filed actions do not go through a full trial, it hardly needs stating that a great deal of judicial activity happens outside of the courtroom. What are judges doing? What are the ways that judges are being responsive outside the space of the courtroom and beyond the confines of a trial?

Once we shift our view in that way, we find a myriad of activities that judges do to create, adapt, and reform law and legal procedure, through rules committees, in behind-the-scenes meetings, through reports and commissions, structuring the way cases are heard, configuring the processing of disputes and often situating judges in highly political debates even while remaining significantly understudied. Examples of these types of activities include judicial innovations in court procedures to design "problem-solving courts" (Berman et al. 2005) and "therapeutic judging" in specialized courts such as domestic violence courts, drug courts, and conciliation family courts (Winick and Wexler 2003; Bentley 2005).[2] Judges have developed case-management systems (Winkler 2008b) and procedures for multi-jurisdictional cases (Winkler 2016). Judges conduct civil justice reform reviews (Osborne 2007), participate in working groups and jury amendment committees to improve trial procedures for remote and indigenous communities, and oversee judicial research centers (e.g. the Israeli Courts Research Division). Judges also work with judges from other

[2]The National Judicial Institute established a Therapeutic Jurisprudence Planning Committee, to consult and provide editorial assistance on the publication of a bench-book on Problem Solving Courts. The committee included judges from Ontario, Quebec, and Alberta. The Toronto Drug Treatment Court was established in 1998 under the leadership of Justice Paul Bentley, then Chief Justice of the first level trial court in Ontario.

countries to design and implement case tracking systems, as well as to implement the transition from inquisitorial to adversarial criminal justice systems.

One effect of reforms to legal procedure over the last several decades is the co-mingling of dispute resolution processes as well as a shift from *alternative* procedures being on the margin of practice to their inclusion as one stage in the process of court adjudication (Hughes 2001). Thus Macfarlane (2012) describes the phenomenon of "hybrid models of dispute resolution in legal practice, judicial processes, and courthouse culture" (931). This is particularly true in the case of compositing adversarial and non-adversarial procedures. The "new environment of settlement processes" (Macfarlane 2012) means that, whether through formal or informal means, judges are also commonly practicing as judicial mediators in settlement conferencing and through case management facilitating settlements in addition to adjudicating disputes.

Legal scholars and scholars of courts and judges need to respond to these changing circumstances by adapting methodologies to reflect new forms of disputing and "extra-disputing judicial activity."[3] Work undertaken by contemporary judges which moves beyond the specific case still affects courts and the operation of trials (Goldbach 2016). This work has a facilitative impact on case-work and decision-making, changing the nature of disputing by changing the form and procedures for processing disputes. Moreover, the issues that concern scholars of courts and judges—bias, judicial independence, jurisdiction, etc.—do not abate because judges have moved part of their work out of the courtroom. Judges' response to critique of trials and state-centered dispute resolution are often channeled into behind-the-scene meetings and through reports or commissions—outside of the normal places where we expect judges to do their work. Thus, not all instantiations of judicial efforts at law reform and legal change are brought into view by a review of legal decisions alone. Scholars need to be responsive in their research about judges and find new ways to research judicial politics and judicial behaviour.

The chapter proceeds as follows. After a brief description of the new responsive judge, I present two examples of judicial responsiveness in Ontario:[4] (1) judges'

[3]I have coined this term as a kind of inverse of Legal Pluralism's exploration of the everyday life of the law. Where legal pluralism examines "extra-judicial dispute resolution," (Engel 1980; Merry 1988), e.g. law and dispute resolution that takes place outside of state-centered institutions, this research explores "extra-disputing judicial activity," work that judges do that is legal, judicial, and in particular related to state-centered institutions, but does not involve resolving disputes.

[4]While this chapter focuses on civil rule making in Ontario, judges in the U.S. similarly undertake a considerable amount of thinking and development of court procedure *outside* of the courtroom. Under the Rules Enabling Act in 1934, ch. 651, 48 Stat. 1064 (subsequently 28 United States Code, § 2072), Congress authorized the Supreme Court to prescribe general rules of civil procedure for the district courts. U.S. federal judges thus have the power to make "prospective, legislation-like rules" for procedures controlling civil litigation in lower federal courts. Much of this work takes place under the auspices of the Advisory Committee on Civil Rules (28 U.S.C. § 2073(a)(2), which now has a majority of judge members (10 of 17 in 2016). According to Burbank and Farhang (2014, 1583), judicial capture of rule-making authority for federal trials was itself the outcome of a protracted "decades-long campaign" to secure rule-making power similar to that of the court of equity.

response to the legal profession's interest in expanding the role of settlement in civil litigation; and, (2) judges' response to the over-incarceration of Aboriginal offenders and multiple calls from government commissions for culturally appropriate procedures in the criminal justice system. The chapter concludes with a discussion of the potential for scholarship to respond to the changing circumstances of judicial work.

2 Responsive Judges

The standard objects of the study for courts or judges are judicial decisions, the conceptual product (Pickering and Stephanides 1992) of judicial case-work. For example, scholars analyze the impact of judicial decisions on the political realm (Kapiszewski et al. 2013), or investigate behavioral and theoretical "determinants of decisions"—how judges decide and the factors that go into judicial decision-making (Epstein et al. 2013).

There are two problems with these standard approaches to researching judges. First, scholarship barely touches on the products of judicial work that are not related to a specific case. Judges and court staff are well aware of the work that judges do on court reform, court administration, public relations, maintaining and improving the reputation of the court in addition to case work. Judges sit as administrative heads of court, assigning cases, deciding on judicial rotations, or even structuring the way cases are heard. Judges are "not simply decision makers" but are also researchers, report writers, educators, "*thinking subjects* engaged in dialogue with a variety of broader intellectual debates and projects" (Miyazaki 2013, 6, italics in the original). Judges perform important "acts of making" (Pickering and Stephanides 1992, 3, ft1) which often come before or contribute to the progress of case-work and decision writing (Wolff 2013; Cover 1975). Judges engage in activities that do not necessarily relate to a particular dispute but which structure courts' practices and thus affect legal change.

The Commercial List in Toronto stands as an example of structural legal reform initiated by judges. The Commercial List, which provides "expert decision making on a 'real time' basis" for matters raising issues of commercial law, was established "in large part [due] to the efforts of a number of innovative and accomplished judges[5]… who created and led the Commercial List… [for] the timely and effective adjudication of commercial disputes" (Winkler 2008a, 4). "Extra-disputing judicial activity"—not all of what judges do is resolve disputes—shapes the structure of dispute processing and situates judges in highly political debates even while remaining significantly understudied.

---

[5]Former Chief Justice Winkler names the following judges as those who helped establish the Commercial List: Justices Marvin Catzman, Lloyd Houlden, Edward Saunders, Katherine Feldman, Robert Blair, James Farley and Sarah Pepall.

Second, scholars do not have an account of procedural and structural changes at court. Legal scholars are aware that legal knowledge is produced socially, but as it relates to judges and courts, they limit their view to one set of practices. Scholars explore the practices of knowledge formation during or about particular cases (Valverde 2003) but do not go further. In both instances, these are depictions of judges as they appear publicly. They are the "official portraits" (Lasser 1995) of judges, (also) the most visible and accessible sketches of a judge's work and judicial involvement in politics and legal change. However, to the extent that legal scholarship seeks an account of judicial practice—the study of what judges actually do—it must look beyond the written decision.

This chapter presents two short case studies of judges in Ontario engaging in extra-disputing judicial activity, responding to critiques of courts and the legal system by incorporating *alternative* and non-adversarial procedures into the civil and criminal trial.[6]

3 Civil Rules Response

3.1 ADR Pilot Project and Early Case Management

Amid concerns about the cost of civil justice, trial delays, and the rise in self-represented litigants, judges in Ontario have responded by introducing non-adversarial methods into the work at court. This includes, for example, the introduction of an ADR pilot program in Toronto in 1994, case management in Ottawa, Toronto, and Windsor, simplified procedures, mandatory mediation, and pre-trial conferencing. These reforms are part of a much larger and longer movement against formalism in law. While this anti-formalist sentiment can be said to have its roots—at least in the United States—in the Legal Realist Movement of the 1930s, the effort to de-formalize rules of civil procedure to make them more responsive and instrumental gained particular momentum with the modern "ADR movement" of the 1970s and 1980s (Menkel-Meadow 2000, 2).

Dispute resolution methods that would substitute for a trial have always existed (Pirie 1994, 170). Labour mediation and arbitration procedures began in the United States in the early twentieth century, including the U.S. Conciliation Service founded in 1918, the National Mediation Board in 1926, and the Federal Mediation and Conciliation Services in 1947 (Meyer 2004). However, beginning in the 1970s, community activists and consumers demanding greater participation began attacking the court system (Menkel-Meadow 1991, 8; Galanter 2002). Increasingly, the opinion was that the courts were overloaded, inefficient and unable to meet the growing demand for litigation.

[6]More detail on the changes to the Rules of Civil Procedure and sentencing reforms can be found in Farrow (2014) and Goldbach (2015) respectively.

The most striking example of a changing legal paradigm (Menkel-Meadow 2000, 1) was the 1976 Pound Conference, hosted by Chief Justice Burger to mark the seventieth anniversary of Roscoe Pound's celebrated address on "the Causes of Popular Dissatisfaction with the Administration of Justice." It was at the Pound Conference where Frank Sander gave the now famous speech on Varieties of Dispute Processing, calling for a "multi-door courthouse"[7] that would offer a variety of options for resolving disputes. In addition to being concerned about "contentious procedure" and gaming litigation, Pound's original piece lamented on the "individualist spirit" of the legal system, "which agree[d] ill with a collectivist age" (Pound 1906). Pound was clearly concerned with judges mechanically applying law without attention to social consequences (Pound 1908). On the other hand, the anniversary of Pound's original address to the American Bar Association was occasion for conversations about overburdened courts, the "ever-expanding demands for court intervention to address social problems" and "a general consensus that the courts should scale back their excursions into problem solving… by promoting the use of alternative dispute resolution" (Galanter 2002, 295).[8]

Throughout the 1980s, lawyers and the court system continued to be vilified. Writing in 1985, Sarat spoke of the phenomenon "[v]ariously described as 'hyperlexis,' 'the law explosion,' or 'the adversary society,'" where "an unprecedented number of cases" were straining courts' institutional capacity and repressing "the emergence of many cognizable legal claims" (Sarat 1985). The following year, Judith Resnik (1986) captured the sentiment of the turn against courts as a movement away from civil procedure. Whereas at an earlier time in U.S. legal history, dissatisfaction with litigation process at court drove procedural reform, at the time Resnik was writing, legal practitioners had:

> moved from arguments … about how to simplify procedure to foster judicial decisions 'on the merits' to conversations about the desirability of limiting the use of courts… Today's continuing legal education programs feature 'alternative dispute resolution,' advertised as preferable to trials, judges, and litigation. (Resnik 1986, 3)

At the same time, well respected scholars turned their mind to the science and psychology of negotiation. In 1981, Robert Axelrod produced research on the benefits of "being nice" using the Prisoner's Dilemma game to explore strategies for cooperation (Menkel-Meadow 2006). Harvard Law School established the Program on Negotiation in 1983 as a special research project that included faculty, students, and staff from Harvard University, Massachusetts Institute of Technology and Tufts University (Mnookin and Hackley 2008).

---

[7] An attendee of the 1976 conference, Earl Johnson, formerly of the California Court of Appeal, notes that Frank Sander's speech never actually referred to the 'multi-door courthouse'. He recalls that "a magazine editor coined the phrase when he used it in the headline for an article about Sander's speech. Yet 'multi-door courthouse' proved a perfect title for what Sander had envisioned and was forever attached to his influential recommendations for remaking America's dispute resolution system" (Johnson 2012).

[8] Johnson also recollects that while Sander's speech generated "a definite buzz", the committee tasked with following up on the conference recommended neighborhood justice centres located in the community, with the cooperation, but outside, of the courts.

ADR was the "faster, cheaper, better" alternative. The Canadian Bar Association urged lawyers to see their primary function as problem solving and embrace ADR as part of the profession's commitment to effective dispute resolution (Landerkin and Pirie 2005, 42). By 1996, the Canadian Bar Association Task Force on Systems of Civil Justice specifically called for ADR not to be considered an *alternative,* but instead as an integral component of the civil justice system (Canadian Bar Association 1996).

Within this context, judges of the highest level trial court in Ontario, now the Superior Court of Justice,[9] introduced case-management and court-annexed mediation. Superior Court judges practiced judicial mediation before any official rules were put into place. Their early practice was evaluative—giving parties a neutral evaluation of the case to encourage them to settle. For example, Justice Winkler, who served as Chief Justice of Ontario from 2007 until his retirement in 2013, had a background in labour law related mediation and moved the same skills over to his practice on the bench (telephone interview with Justice Winkler October 16, 2014).[10] Working between the long trial list and the Commercial list, Justice Winkler and a small number of other judges including Justice James Farley, started a "cottage industry" of "designated hitter" mediation (Winkler 2007a) where judges with expertise with the issues in dispute would act as mediators to help settle "the most intractable cases on the eve of trial, when costs are already out of control and the parties and their lawyers are dug into apparently irreconcilable positions" (Winkler 2008a, 4).

The 1990s saw a flurry of activity and reform in civil litigation in Ontario. In 1994, Attorney General Marion Boyd and Roy McMurtry, then Chief Justice of the higher level trial court, established a Civil Justice Review as a joint initiative to "develop an overall strategy… in an effort to provide a speedier, more streamlined and more efficient" civil justice system (Winkler 2008b, 3). Also in 1994, practitioners and judges introduced an ADR Pilot Project in Toronto. The ADR Centre of the Ontario Court General Division was the first court-connected ADR program in Canada, diverting four of every ten cases to mediation (Macfarlane 1995).

The Civil Justice Review, co-chaired by Justice Robert Blair, currently a judge of the Court of Appeal of Ontario, also evaluated the three case management pilot projects that were underway in Windsor, Sault Ste. Marie and Toronto. In a first report released in 1995, the Civil Justice Review recommended the "[i]ntegration of the various dispute resolution techniques and case management mechanisms into a

---

[9]In Ontario, two trial courts have jurisdiction over civil, criminal, and family matters. For the purposes of this chapter, it is sufficient to know that authority is divided over "higher" and "lower" level matters, such as murder, manslaughter, and drug trafficking (as higher level matters) in criminal offences. The lower level trial court is known as the Ontario Court of Justice. The higher level trial court has gone through several name and jurisdictional changes over the last thirty years: becoming the Ontario Court (General Division) in 1989 and then changing its name to the Superior Court of Justice in 1999. Each level trial court has a Chief Justice responsible for governance and administration. The Ontario Court of Appeal is governed by a President, who also sits as the Chief Justice of Ontario.

[10]Justice Winkler's role as a mediator includes the following disputes: Ontario Hydro and Power Workers 1996, TD Bank, Air Canada Restructuring 2003; (see also Law of Class Actions in Canada; also mentions Walkerton Tainted Water and Windsor-Michigan Tunnel).

co-ordinated whole" (Winkler 2008b, 4). Specifically, it recommended three types of meetings between judges and parties—case conferencing ("to deal with logistics and processing"), settlement conferences and trial management conferences—to move cases through to completion. Conferences between the judge and the parties would be required before a case could be listed for trial or given a trial date. The Civil Justice Review also reported that the Toronto team of twelve case management judges, led by Justice Douglas Coo, recommended universal case management to apply to all civil cases (Ontario Civil Justice Review 1995, s. 13.1).

In its Supplemental and Final report, released in 1996, the Civil Justice Review recommended ADR within two months of filing the first response (Winkler 2008b), a settlement conference "within three months of the close of pleadings for fast track cases and within eight months for standard track cases" and again the "integration of ADR and mandatory referral of all civil (non-family) cases to mediation after the close of pleadings" (Ontario Civil Justice Review 1996, s. 5.1).

The Civil Justice Review's recommendations triggered significant reforms including the introduction of simplified procedures for claims of $25,000 CDN or less (Rule 76), case management rules (Rule 77), and mandatory mediation (Rule 24.1).[11] Rule 24.1 of the Ontario Rules of Civil Procedure set out the definition of mediation and procedural rules for the conduct of the mediation, including attendance, authority to settle, signing of agreements and the writing of a mediator's report. The new rules also reflected the Civil Justice Review's recommendation to tie mandatory mediation to case managed actions in Toronto, Ottawa and Windsor.[12] Rule 77, which required mandatory mediation in all case-managed actions, was introduced in Ottawa in 1996, in stages in Toronto between 1997 and 2001, and in Windsor in 2003. The rules required mediation to take place within ninety days after the first defence was filed unless the parties obtained a court order abridging or extending the time. For standard track cases, parties could consent to a postponement of up to sixty days. Parties could opt out of mediation only by obtaining a court order, which was rarely

[11] In Ontario, a Civil Rules Committee has the authority to may make rules "in relation to the practice and procedure of those courts in all civil proceedings" even if "they alter … the substantive law". Rules are "subject to the approval of the Attorney General". See Ontario Courts of Justice Act, sections 65 and 66. As of June 2017, the Ontario Civil Rules Committee includes: the Chief Justice and Associate Chief Justice of the Court of Appeal and two additional judges (George R. Strathy, Alexandra Hoy, Kathryn Feldman, Justice Peter Lauwers); Chief Justice, Associate Chief Justice, the Regional Senior Justice and seven additional judges of the Superior Court of Justice (Heather Forster Smith, Frank N. Marrocco, G. Morawetz, Todd L. Archibald, Harrison Arrell, Peter A. Daley, James McNamara, Louise Gauthier, Thomas A. Heeney and Mark Edwards) and the Chief Justice of the Ontario Court of Justice represented by Justice Patrick Monahan as designate, Small Claims Court Judge P.A. Thomson, four representatives of the Ministry of the Attorney General, and nine lawyers from the private sector (Total membership: 29 Quorum requirement: 10).

[12] Similarly Judith Resnik depicts a judiciary in the U.S. that is "down in the trenches," playing "a key role in delineating the parameters of acceptable procedures, of what should be called ADR, of what kinds of resolutions are acceptable, of what kinds of negotiations the courts should sanction, enter into, or decline" (Resnik 1995, 1630).

given.[13] If the parties did not select a mediator within thirty days after the first defence, the court would appoint one.

3.2 *The Bar Strikes Back*

The Bar did not immediately embrace these judicial interventions. Writing at the time, prominent commercial litigator and mediator, Martin Teplitsky (2000) argued that mandatory mediation would not reduce costs or delay: "It is often said that about 95 percent of civil actions never get to trial. There is no evidence to suggest that this number can be improved upon" (Teplitsky 2000). Teplitsky argued that in smaller cases, mediation costs would make parties less likely to settle because of 'sunk costs'. Instead, Teplitsky described the pre-trial period as "a pro forma tactical or strategic event of little significance" (Teplitsky 2000). Echoing Teplitsky's concerns, a 2001 report noted that "only 40% of cases reached settlement at the mandatory mediation stage" (Winkler 2008b, 19).

The new rules, unintentionally of course, brought trial scheduling in Toronto to a gridlock. Prior to the rule changes, Toronto lawyers had the custom of not scheduling trial dates until both parties were ready to proceed. With case management, trial dates were set for every lawsuit filed in the process of being case managed by the judge. As a result, "waiting times for trial dates mushroomed" (Winkler 2007b, 105). When lawyers noticed this, they set trial dates for cases not yet ready to proceed on the assumption that their case would be ready to proceed by the time the trial date came. In many cases, however, lawyers were still not ready by the date of trial. Before long, "the trial lists were in shambles" (Winkler 2007b, 105). By mid-2004, routine motions had a six month wait time. Long trials were being scheduled three years in advance and short trials had wait times of over a year. And those delays had the additional effect of increasing the number of interlocutory motions. According to Justice Winkler (2007b) in 2004, the court had thirty-eight long trials that could not be heard because there were no judges available. With approximately 20,000 cases per year, Toronto could not handle all of the increased scheduling required for universal case management.

In response to the scheduling crisis, Justice Winkler, by this time the Regional Senior Justice of the Toronto Region (in charge of scheduling), took it upon himself to meet with those affected and design a solution. In the summer and early fall of 2004, Justice Winkler met with lawyers, judges, masters, mediators and court administrators. He established an ad hoc advisory committee to assist with consultations and reform proposals. The ad hoc committee then met with multiple stakeholders, including: "The Advocate's Society, Toronto Lawyers Association, Ontario Bar Association, The Law Society of Upper Canada, Canadian Defence Lawyers, vari-

---

[13]For example, in *Timron Investments Ltd. v. Baxter* (2002), Master Polika did not grant an order to exempt the parties from mandatory mediation even though both solicitors consented [*Timron Investments Ltd. v. Baxter*, [2002] O.J. No. 3551, 116 A.C.W.S. (3d) 493 (Ont. SCJ)].

ous mediation associations, judges and masters, and representatives from the Court Services Division of the Ministry of the Attorney General" (Winkler 2008b).

Based on input from the Bar and court staff, the court issued a Practice Direction[14] in December 2004 suspending automatic application of Rule 77 (case management) to claims filed in Toronto. In January 2005, the Civil Rules Committee enacted Rule 78 on an expedited basis, reverting case management back to pilot project status in Toronto. The new motto was: "case management where necessary, but not necessarily case management" (Winkler 2008b, ii). In other words, case management was no longer universal in the Toronto region. In addition, the time to schedule mediation was lengthened from sixty to ninety days.[15]

3.3 *Procedural Politics*

Rule 78 was in effect until December 2010, at which time the rules for civil case management in Toronto were incorporated back into Rule 77 applying to all case management in Ontario. Case management and mandatory mediation still apply to civil actions in Ottawa, Toronto, and Windsor. They are, however, no longer universal: "case management where necessary, but not necessarily case management" (Winkler 2008b, ii; Osborne 2007, 91) won the day. Under the current Rule 77, case management is only to be undertaken in "those proceedings for which a need for the court's intervention is demonstrated and only to the degree that is appropriate" (section 77.01 (1) O. Reg. 438/08, s. 64). The rules, however, only delineate vague criteria for this determination. Decisions regarding the nature and extent of case management are to be "informed" by the "relevant practices, traditions, customs or judicial resource issues that apply locally in the region" (section 77.01 (2) O. Reg. 438/08, s.64). The dates for mediation were modified to come later in the trial process, allowing time for discovery and for injuries to set in. Mandatory mediation was extended to cover actions that go through simplified procedure (claims for up to 50,000$ CDN). However, case management and mandatory mediation do not apply

[14] A practice direction is a "notice, guide or similar publication for the purpose of governing… the practice for proceedings" in the Superior Court; O. Reg. 132/04, s. 1. Superior Court of Justice. A practice direction allows the court to initiate procedural guidelines subject only to the approval and signature of the Chief Justice and the regional senior Judge. While the practice direction does not need the prior approval of the full Rules Committee, it does have to be filed with the secretary of the Committee. The practice direction comes into effect once notice of publication is made, by posting the direction on the Ontario Courts website and publishing it in the Ontario Reports.

[15] This was not the end of consultations with the Bar and review of the civil rules. In June 2006, the Attorney General asked former Associate Chief Justice of Ontario, Justice Coulter Osborne, to direct the Civil Justice Reform Project, with a mandate "to review potential areas of reform and deliver recommendations for action to make the civil justice system more accessible and affordable for Ontarians" (Osborne 2007, 137). In addition to receiving written submissions, Justice Osborne and counsel at the Superior Court of Justice and Project Director for the Civil Justice Reform Project, Mohan Sharma, met with regional bar associations, judges, litigant organizations, law firms, and officials at the Ministry of the Attorney General.

to Commercial List matters, estate proceedings, class actions as well as various other types of procedures.

During the course of this story of responsiveness and procedural reform in Ontario, the significant judicial players—justices McMurtry, Blair, and Winkler—were all promoted. Roy McMurtry became the Chief Justice of the Superior Court in 1994 and then Chief Justice of Ontario and President of the Court of Appeal in 1996, a position he held until 2007. Justice Blair—whose biography on the Ontario Courts website highlights his extra-disputing judicial activities: in "the development and implementation of alternative dispute resolution techniques"; as a "member of the Steering Committee which oversaw the implementation of a Court-connected ADR Center in Toronto"; and "with the Mandatory Mediation project in Toronto and the introduction of case management and mediation"—took on the role of Regional Senior Justice for the Toronto Region in 1999 and was appointed to the Court of Appeal in 2003. Justice Winkler served as the next Regional Senior Justice for the Toronto Region from 2004 to 2007, at which point he was appointed to the Ontario Court of Appeal directly as Chief Justice of Ontario and President of the Court of Appeal for Ontario.

I am by no means claiming that these judges participated in reforming regulations in anticipation of career promotion or that they were promoted because of this work. On the other hand, I want to recommend that legal scholars adopt a "defensible realism," which includes a realistic appreciation for "the judge as a human being" with several non-legal pecuniary and non-pecuniary goals (Epstein et al. 2013, 28). This would allow us to craft interesting projects inquiring into a variety of objectives and outcomes such as job satisfaction, the desire for a good reputation, promotion prospects as well as "the intrinsic interest of the work and the power or prestige and pride or self-esteem… that the job confers" (Epstein et al. 2013, 31).

In the U.S., for example, federal judges were also active users and early promoters of ADR techniques. Stephen Yeazell, in his compelling historical account of reforms to the Federal Rules of Civil Procedure, argues that a growing emphasis on pre-trial motions and negotiations helped shift the balance of power from appellate to trial level courts. According to Yeazell, contemporary federal district court judges devote the bulk of their time to pretrial motions and pretrial settlement conferences (Yeazell 1994). These tasks often effectively dispose of matters. In addition, pre-trial rulings in the U.S. are usually not appealable. Yeazell argues that the authority to control and manage the litigation process has thus shifted to trial level judges. Cases that settle "guarantee that appellate courts will play no role in the suit… Judicially encouraged settlement, to the extent that it succeeds, thus extends the reach of trial court power" (Yeazell 1994, 656).

Yeazell considers the institutional implications of centralized or decentralized judicial power as if similar to power in federal versus state legislatures and executives. Power and politics thus presents even in the mundane activity of procedural reform. The story of civil rule changes in Ontario similarly suggests that studying judicial behavior is relevant regardless of whether judicial law-making happens inside or outside of the courtroom.

4 Courthouse Construction and Sentencing Reforms

4.1 *The Aboriginal Conference Settlement Suite*

On April 23, 2014, the Attorney General of Ontario unveiled a new consolidated courthouse in Thunder Bay, northwestern Ontario. The courthouse houses fifteen courtrooms, including a larger courtroom for multiple offenders plus a conference area whose design was based on local native architecture. This conference area, called the Aboriginal Conference Settlement Suite ("ACSS"), consists of a centre circular room meant to emulate a traditional healing lodge, as well as several smaller meeting rooms. The Ministry of the Attorney General describes the space as "a culturally relevant Aboriginal space designed for case conferencing, pre-trials, Gladue Courts[16] and family and civil hearings" (Ministry of the Attorney General 2012–2013, 53). Judges in the Northwest region consulted on the new courthouse and were instrumental in getting, and keeping, the construction of a space for Aboriginal justice on the Ministry's agenda.

Recognizing the history and ongoing difficulties faced by indigenous populations in Canada, Aboriginal justice advocates pushed for comprehensive investigation into Aboriginal alienation and their effects. Throughout the 1970s-1990s, multiple government commissions and public inquiries examined the causes and effects of systemic discrimination against indigenous peoples in Canada (Culhane 1995, 151; Roberts and Melchers 2003). Many reports used incarceration rates as a way to draw attention to the extent to which indigenous populations were criminalized. Reports compared prison rates for Aboriginal peoples against incarceration rates of non-natives or against population rates of Aboriginal peoples, illustrating the disproportionately high incarceration of Aboriginal offenders.

The Royal Commission on Aboriginal Peoples, for example, noted that in 1976, a sixteen year-old treaty Indian boy in the province of Saskatchewan had a seventy percent chance of a stay in prison by the age of twenty-five, while a non-Native Saskatchewan boy only had an eight percent chance of imprisonment (Canada 1996a, 30). In 1992, in the Canadian Prairie Provinces of Manitoba, Saskatchewan, and Alberta, Aboriginal people represented approximately fifteen percent of the population, however, their percentage of total prison population could be as high as sixty percent (Canada 1996a). In 2000, the Department of Justice continued to report that Aboriginal people were overrepresented among admissions to adult correctional facilities, at fifteen percent of provincial/territorial admissions, while constituting less than three percent of the general Canadian population (Canada 2000).

Multiple reports and commissions came to the conclusion that in order to address feelings of alienation and the disproportionate incarceration of Aboriginal offenders,

---

[16]Gladue Courts are provisional or part-time courts that conduct bail and sentencing hearings for Aboriginal offenders. Following the instructions of the Supreme Court of Canada in *R. v. Gladue*, [1999] 1 S.C.R. 688, these courts will rely on a Gladue Report, a detailed pre-sentencing report outlining the particular circumstances that brought the Aboriginal offender before the court. See discussion *infra* at part 4B.

governments should work toward incorporating Aboriginal justice principles into the existing criminal justice system (see e.g. Canada 1996a, b; Law Reform Commission of Canada 1991; Manitoba et al. 1991). In 1996, Parliament amended the sentencing provisions of the Criminal Code and included a section directing judges to consider the circumstances of Aboriginal offenders (Roberts and Melchers 2003). The federal government also funded community justice programs, and ministries and court services supported diversion programs to Aboriginal councils (Goldbach 2015).

A number of judges across Canada responded to these reports and commissions by bringing Aboriginal justice methods into the criminal trial. In 1992, a judge of the Yukon Territorial Court adapted an approach based on local First Nations' methods for dealing with crime in *R. v. Moses*, [1992] B.C.W.L.D. 1294 (Can. Y.K.T.C.), additional reasons provided in *R. v. Moses*, [1992] 71 C.C.C. (3d) 347 (Can. Y.K.T.C.). Following this first use of a healing circle at a criminal trial, several judges participated in sentencing circles and incorporated Aboriginal justice methods into trials (Goldbach 2015) or as part of diversion programs. The Supreme Court of Canada endorsed these efforts in its reading of the 1996 amendments in *R. v. Gladue*, [1999] 1 S.C.R. 688 and then again in *R. v. Wells*, [2000] 1 S.C.R. 207, writing that "[t]he background considerations regarding the distinct situation of aboriginal peoples in Canada" included "[t]he types of sentencing procedures… which may be appropriate in the circumstances for the offender because of his or her particular aboriginal heritage or connection" (*R. v. Gladue* [1999] ¶ 66).

In Thunder Bay, once the government announced its intention to build a new courthouse, judges met with Ministry architects and architectural firms to consult on workload and courtroom size (Judge of the Ontario Court of Justice, personal interview, April 23, 2014). In this context of regular meetings and consultation on the construction of the new courthouse, judges of the Ontario Court of Justice, the lower level trial court which sees the bulk of criminal matters, responded to concerns about Aboriginal confrontation with the criminal justice system by spearheading a proposal to include infrastructure for Aboriginal justice programs.

Ontario is the site not only of the largest and busiest court system in Canada (Ministry of the Attorney General 2012–2013, i), it also hosts the largest number of people with Aboriginal ancestry—approximately twenty percent of the one million people with Aboriginal ancestry who live in Canada (Statistics Canada 2011). In addition, five of the twenty largest bands (the unit of government pursuant to the Indian Act) are located in Ontario. Almost half of the Registered Indian population in Ontario lives on reserves and settlements, but a large proportion of the population also lives in major urban centers in Thunder Bay, Sudbury, Sault Ste. Marie, Ottawa, and Toronto.

The percentage of Aboriginal offenders in jail in relation to the province's total population of incarcerated offenders has been less dire in Ontario compared to Canada's Prairie and Western Provinces (eight percent in Ontario compared to forty-nine percent in Manitoba) (LaPrairie 1992, 5). However, because Ontario has the largest off-reserve Aboriginal population, the real numbers of incarcerated indigenous offenders becomes problematic. In a paper commissioned by the Ipperwash Inquiry, Jonathan Rudin of the Aboriginal Legal Services of Toronto Legal Clinic notes that Ontario has the third-highest rate of over-incarceration of Aboriginal people in Canada (Rudin n.d.). That is, if one compares the percent of Aboriginal people in the general population against the percent of Aboriginal offenders within the corrections population, Ontario is behind only Alberta and Saskatchewan in the extent to which Aboriginal offenders are over-represented in prison populations (Rudin n.d.).

Thunder Bay is the largest community and the main urban centre for the Northwest judicial region. In 2009, eighty percent of the lower level trial court cases in Thunder Bay originated within the Aboriginal population (Facilities Management Branch 2009, 5). While the Ministry projects a decline in the overall population in the next twenty-five years, the Aboriginal population is expected to increase as a result of urban migration, in part as a result of a newly built high school in Thunder Bay, as well as better health care facilities and employment opportunities (Geraldine Phillet, Facility Program Thunder Bay Consolidated Courthouse, Ontario Ministry of the Attorney General, May 1, 2007) (on file with author).

Judges of the Northwest region sought to involve themselves in the construction of the new courthouse following a conversation at a meeting of the Chief Justice's Executive—the administrative group for the Ontario Court of Justice, composed of the Chief Justice, Associate Chief Justice, and the Regional Senior Judges. Judges in other regions had been through the construction process with the Ministry and recommended that judges get involved at the earlier stages of design (Judge of the Ontario Court of Justice (retired), personal interview, May 2, 2014). Regional judges met with Ministry staff for about a year before the design work-up phase, and with the design teams who were competing for the project.

One judge in particular promoted the idea of a space that could accommodate Aboriginal justice methods. The judge invited the court's Ojibway Interpreter and Aboriginal Liaison to a meeting with the lead architect. There they discussed how court in northern communities is often held in a circle. The judge and Aboriginal Liaison recommended that at least one room in the new courthouse be built in a way that would allow judges to conduct proceedings in a circle, and that could reflect traditional Aboriginal spirituality (Judge of the Ontario Court of Justice (retired), personal interview, May 2, 2014). After that meeting, the architect set out to learn about different Aboriginal building designs and the court interpreter helped the Ministry arrange an Elders advisory council for the construction project.

The design of the centre room of the Aboriginal Conference Settlement Suites emulates a traditional healing lodge. Entrances align with the solar directions and the color scheme replicates an Aboriginal medicine wheel (Ministry of the Attorney General, Facilities Management Branch, Aboriginal Conference Settlement Suite Final Report, March 2009) (on file with author). The ventilation system was designed to accommodate smudging and other traditional ceremonies to be part of legal proceedings. The suite of rooms is on the ground floor close to the courthouse's main entrance. This was a deliberate choice in order to facilitate public access outside of court hours. In the planning stage, the idea was that the room would be used for other kinds of ceremonies, such as weddings and funerals. It was designed so that it could be accessed on the weekend without the public having to access the entire building. The ACSS can also accommodate various court proceedings such as: case conferencing, pre-trials, Gladue Courts, as well as family law and civil proceedings. One of the judges that I spoke with described the goals of the new courtroom this way:

> We're hoping that room will give us the opportunity to consult more broadly with the Aboriginal community about issues that impact on them that are justice system issues, like how do we safely keep people out of jail, how do we protect community interest, protect individual interests and at the same time have… some kind of reconciliation. We view the room as a place, one place, for that discussion to take place. And because it's clearly designed to facilitate discussion about those issues, we hope it'll encourage that to happen more (Judge of the Ontario Court of Justice, personal interview, April 23, 2014)

The most recent use of the ACSS has been to provide a home for a community court program. On March 6, 2017, the ACSS welcomed the first case of the Indigenous People's Court, a diversion court program for criminal matters. A judge can refer a matter to the Indigenous People's Court which sits two times per month. Cases are heard by two local elders utilizing restorative justice principles for sentencing (Venetis 2017).

4.2 *Judges Other Work*

Ontario Court of Justice judges have participated in various other extra-disputing judicial work in attempts to ameliorate the circumstances of Aboriginal offenders, including committee work and procedural reform. In response to the Supreme Court of Canada's decision in *R. v. Gladue*, judges of the Ontario Court of Justice collaborated with Legal Aid lawyers to establish a "Gladue Court" in downtown Toronto. Following a presentation by the Aboriginal Legal Services of Toronto at a conference of the Canadian Association of Provincial Court Judges, University of Toronto Professor Kent Roach, Jonathon Rudin of the Aboriginal Legal Services, an Aboriginal court-worker, Justice Patrick Sheppard, and three other Ontario Court of Justice judges worked to establish a court that would implement the directives laid out in *R. v. Gladue*.

The Gladue Court opened in October 2001, and was the first Aboriginal court in an urban setting in Canada (Whonnock 2008). At the Gladue Court, "staff is trained to apply the Gladue decision and present the appropriate evidence" (Knazan 2003). A Gladue Caseworker writes a Gladue report, which focuses on the circumstances of the Aboriginal offender, and where appropriate "links that life story to broader issues facing Aboriginal people such as the intergenerational trauma of residential schools…" (Rudin 2006). The Gladue report might also suggest recommendations for sentencing.

Judges currently sit on a committee that is charged with overseeing the implementation of recommendations to address the low participation of First Nations peoples on Ontario juries. Based on the Iaccabuci Report on First Nation's representation on juries, the Attorney General established a First Nation Jury Review Implementation

Committee.[17] Justice Marc Bode of the Northwest Region in Ontario was on the Juries Review Implementation Committee. He was replaced by Justice Stach.[18]

Finally, judges in the Northwest region participated in a review and reform of the "Fly-In Court" procedure, which sets out the procedure for judges, prosecution and defense counsel who travel to northern remote communities for criminal matters. In Ontario, one in four First Nations communities live in locations accessible only by air or by ice road during the winter. As a result, in the 1970s, the Attorney General began flying court staff into remote communities. This would include all staff normally present at a trial—a judge, Crown prosecutor, defense lawyers, police, victim services and other essential court staff. This would also allow for the accused, as well as residents who were required to appear as witnesses, to attend court locally instead of travelling to the larger base courts further south. Currently, the Ontario Court of Justice conducts criminal and family court hearings in twenty-nine First Nations communities.

A Working Group on Fly-In Courts was formed in April 2012 as a joint initiative between the Ontario Court of Justice and the Ministry to assess problems and make recommendations to improve the Fly-In Court's operations. Then Regional Senior Justice for the Northwest region, Justice Bode, co-chaired the Working Group with JoDee Kamm, Director of Court Operations for the Northwest region (a ministry position through Court Services Division). The Working Group consisted of over twenty members, including judges, staff from Court Services Division, ministry officials, the Deputy Grand Chief of the Nishnawbe Aski Nation responsible for justice issues, members of the defense and family bars, and police services. Under the auspices of the working group, Regional Senior Justice Bode also met with the band council from the Matawa First Nations to discuss moving the base court locations for the Summer Beaver and Webequie communities from Kenora to Thunder Bay. The council advised Justice Bode that moving those communities base court to Thunder Bay would make it easier to organize bail sureties. They also advised that accused from the Summer Beaver and Webequie communities sometimes enter guilty pleas simply because it is too difficult to arrange for witnesses to attend court in Kenora (NAN Conference Report).[19]

[17]The Ontario government initially established a separate advisory group and implementation committees, which have now merged into a single committee. First Nations people are often excluded from the jury rolls due to criminal records for minor offenses (NAN Conference Report).

[18]The full list of the Juries Review Implementation Committee is available at the Ministry of the Attorney General's website, http://www.attorneygeneral.jus.gov.on.ca/english/juries_implementation_committee.asp (accessed October 12, 2017).

[19]The Working Group's report, submitted in August 2013, recommended using video conferencing for routine court appearances in criminal matters such as set dates and adjournments (remands) to save the court's time when it is in the community. The Working Group recommended providing dedicated child protection case conference times on a pilot basis because these matters were getting dropped when criminal matters ran overtime. The group recommended providing designated youth court days and using video conferencing for pre-trial motions in child protection cases so that residents of remote communities can participate.

4.3 Politics in Practice

The remote communities served by Fly-In Courts face a particular set of problems stemming from colonialism, climate change, globalization and increased regulation. One community, the Pikangikum reserve, is infamous for having the highest suicide rate in the world (Patriquin 2012). Over a twenty year period ending in 2011, ninety-six people—mostly youth—committed suicide. With a population of approximately twenty-four hundred people, the suicide rate in Pikangikum is close to twenty times higher than the average rate in Canada "and far and away the highest in the world" (Patriquin 2012). Residents of Pikangikum face desperate sociological conditions: housing with no sewage pipes or running water; close to five thousand calls to police in one year; desperately low high school graduation rates and high rates of referral to the First Nations child protection agency (Patriquin 2012).

Judges can travel to communities such as Pikangikum many times over a period of several years. One of the judges I interviewed had been traveling to remote northern communities for thirty-two years, twelve as a defense lawyer and twenty-five years as judge. This judge spoke to me about the high suicide rate in Pikangikum and the disproportionate number of charges being laid in relation to the size of the population. He expressed concerns for the youth in the communities, who had no job prospects and no connection to traditional income sources, especially since the ban on trade of seal products in the EU.[20]

Judges' extra-disputing work in Ontario's Northwest region highlights the problematic, almost abstruse, nature of the separation between law and politics. In particular, it illustrates the extent to which judges are immersed in the political. Standard debates about judicial politics focus on the ways that judges bring their political preferences to bear in cases brought before them. The concern is that judges will affect outcomes and legal rights by deciding according to their politics and ideology, or that judges engage in a kind of judicial capture by expanding what they consider to be justiciable. Overall, this area of scholarship seems to insinuate that just as judges choose their ideological affiliations, they also choose which part of politics they wish to engage. Judges may be acting within the confines of "the preferences of other actors, the choices they expect others to make, and the institutional context in which they act", but they are still "strategic actors" seeking to "achieve their goals" (Epstein and Knight 2013).

Yet judges are often thrown into politics in the sense of being constituted as political actors because of the particular roles they play (Wendt 1999; Barnett and Duvall 2005). Judges are empowered through social processes that constitute them as judges and are by right of that social identity thrust into a position of power most simply

[20]Similarly, the Fly-In Courts Working Group took notice of the daunting socio-economic circumstances of these communities: As the mandate of the Working Group suggests, its work focused on the operation of the OCJ court system in fly-in remote communities. At the same time, the Working Group was very aware of the serious systemic problems that affect these First Nations communities. These systemic problems present broader policy issues for the justice system to grapple with as it tries to provide relevant and appropriate justice services for these communities.

defined as "the ability … to control the circumstances of … existence" (Barnett and Duvall 2005). Even in rote cases such as public intoxication, theft or misdemeanor assaults, judges who fly into remote northern communities are implicated in the way power and politics plays out in the Canadian legal system. Through the Fly-In Courts, judges are physically immersed in a history of confrontation and subordination. Political matters as they relate to Aboriginal peoples do not just arise in land claims, disputes over treaty rights or fishing rights—the well-publicized cases of the Supreme Court of Canada (see, e.g. *Haida Nation v. British Columbia* (Minister of Forests), [2004] 3 S.C.R. 511; *R. v. Van der Peet*, [1996] 2 SCR 507). They also arise in the "small" or "unimportant" cases which ultimately contribute to an overall experience of alienation and over-incarceration.

This assertion is not new. But it is significant in this context to recall that judges do not always "seek to etch their political values into law" or "use the law to achieve their ideological or partisan ends" (Epstein and Knight 2013). Moreover, judicial politics does not always manifest as the left-right politics that so dominates U.S. scholarship in this area. Judges in the Northwest region continuously re-enact the politics of culture (Weiner 1999; Demian 2003) and a history of confrontation between Canadian governments and First Nations peoples. Whether by physically attending at remote northern communities or reserves through the Fly-In Court program, or conceptually considering the circumstances of Aboriginal offenders and orienting themselves to the particular history of confrontation between Euro-Canadian settlers and the First Nations people as mandated in section 718.2 (e), judges interact with a politics that is historical *and* ongoing.

On the other hand, at the end of the case, judges fly out. Whatever connection judges have are (and must be) partial. Judges must remove themselves in an ongoing process of affecting separation and distance. As described above, however, many moments in a judge's work-life strain the notion of separation. Judicial independence and impartiality are not things-in-the-world, but ideals, which judges strive to enact in practice. Judges navigate their distance to the personal and political in a series of partial connections (Strathern 1991), which in many ways resemble most legal actors' engagement with the personal and the political.

5 Responsive Research

If judges' conceptual products—their decisions—ignite passionate debate, the work they do to get there remains hidden, behind the scenes, unknown and not discussed. Work such as developing and implementing new case-management systems, simplified procedures, systems for populating the jury roll or video-conferencing appear to be on the sidelines. Legal procedures and other work which are constitutive of decisions and declarations on rights and entitlements are the "quotidian, humdrum" (Riles 2011) legal devices that are utilized to achieve (other) goals. But, if as Kapiszewski et al. (2013) point out, "judges taking on more expansive roles in politics and governance… often engage in various kinds of legal creativity and innovation relating to procedure, remedies, case selection, and standing" (at 31–32), ignoring procedural and administrative interventions means that a particular kind of judicial foray into legal change escapes review.

In addition to responding to the needs of victims, defendants, or witnesses, judges are also responsive in the sense of being aware of and attempting to respond to the legal community outside of the courtroom. Ontario trial court judges responded to the crisis in litigation and over-incarceration of Aboriginal offenders by working on regulations, reforming legal procedure, and consulting on courthouse construction and design. Judges do more than sit on cases, and, even when judicial work is limited to case-work, outcomes may not be reported if the matter does not result in a decision.

Legal scholars need to respond to the changing circumstances of legal practice by moving beyond reported decisions as the source of data on judicial work. This does not mean that the issues or questions change. Scholars will still be concerned with judicial independence and impartiality. But scholars also need to be concerned about the ways judges are situated in political debates outside of their case-work. Judges are implicated in politics beyond the written decision. Moreover, framing all concerns about judicial politics as part of a liberal-conservative divide ignores the ways that power and politics are central to the practice of law.

Inquiries into judges and politics are often expressed in terms of judicial independence—either the judiciary's institutional independence from the other branches of government (Monahan and Shaw 2011; Dodek 2010) or a judge's personal independence that enables her to decide in an impartial manner. For example, judges are thought to bring "an aura of credibility, authority and impartiality due to their institutional independence from the executive and legislative branches of government" (Monahan and Shaw 2011, 438). But what does judicial independence look like *in action*? Adam Dodek (2010) quotes Justice Dickson noting that while impartiality "refers to a state of mind or attitude", independence "refers to the 'status or relationship to others'" (quoted in Dodek 2010, 302). How do judges navigate these "relationships"? How do we make sense of independence constituted through relationships?

Judges participate in court reform in a variety of contexts that are more and less removed from the personal and political. Judges from Toronto, Vancouver, Phoenix and New York are reforming civil litigation through the International Insolvency Institute by developing guidelines for cross border communication in insolvency cases. Judges report on recommendations for meeting the needs of unrepresented litigants and compile guidelines for complex litigation. In the criminal context, judges sit as chairs and commissioners of the U.S. Sentencing Commission, develop methods to bring information about the circumstances of Aboriginal offenders to sentencing, and use alternative methods for constructing sentences. Judges participate in law reform projects and produce legal change. They take part in a multitude of activities that affect dispute processing, but whose remnants are not necessarily found in the artifact of a decision. Legal scholars can respond to this opportunity by crafting socio-legal empirical projects that inquire into the variety of judicial responsiveness and extra-disputing work.

References

Barnett M, Duvall R (2005) Power in international politics. Int Org 59(1):39–75
Bentley P (2005) Forward. In: Goldberg S (ed) Judging for the 21st century: a problem-solving approach. National Judicial Institute, Ottawa, Canada
Berman G, Feinblatt J, Glazer S (2005) Good courts: the case for problem-solving justice. New Press, New York
Burbank S, Frahang S (2014). Litigation Reform: an institutional approach. U Pa L Rev 162:1543–1618
Canada. Royal Commission on Aboriginal Peoples (1996a) Bridging the cultural divide: a report on Aboriginal people and criminal justice in Canada. Royal Commission on Aboriginal Peoples, Ottawa
Canada (1996b) Report of the royal commission on Aboriginal peoples, vol. 1: looking forward, looking back. The Commission. 1996, Ottawa
Canada (2000) Final evaluation aboriginal justice strategy. Department of Justice. http://publications.gc.ca/collections/collection_2007/jus/J3-6-2000-1E.pdf. Accessed 7 Jan 2018
Canadian Bar Association. Task Force on Systems of Civil Justice (1996) Report of the task force on systems of civil justice. Canadian Bar Association, Ottawa
Chemerinsky E (2006) Seeing the emperor's clothes: recognizing the reality of constitutional decision making. Boston Univ Law Rev 86(5):1069–1081
Cover RM (1975) For James Wm. Moore: some reflections on a reading of the rules. Yale Law J 84(4):718–740
Culhane D (1995) Justice and healing: Aboriginal peoples in Canada. J Hum Justice 6(2):140–160
de Hoon MW, Verberk S (2014) Towards a more responsive judge: challenges and opportunities. Utrecht Law Rev 10(4):27–40
Demian M (2003) Custom in the courtroom, law in the village: legal transformations in Papua New Guinea. R J Anthropol Inst 9(1):97–115
Dodek A (2010) Judicial independence as a public policy instrument. In: Dodek A, Sossin L (eds) Judicial independence in context. Irwin Law, Toronto
Engel D (1980) Legal pluralism in an American community: perspectives on a civil trial court. Am Bar Found Res J 5(3):425–454
Epstein L, Knight J (2013) Reconsidering judicial preferences. Annu Rev Polit Sci 16(1):11–31
Epstein L, Landes WM, Posner RA (2013) The behavior of federal judges: a theoretical and empirical study of rational choice. Harvard University Press, Cambridge
Farrow TCW (2014) Civil justice, privatization, and democracy. University of Toronto Press, Toronto
Galanter M (2002) The turn against law: the recoil against expanding accountability. Tex Law Rev 81(1):285–304
Galanter M (2004) The vanishing trial: an examination of trials and related matters in federal and state courts. J Empirical Legal Stud 1(3):459–570
Ginsburg T (2012) Courts and new democracies: recent works. Law Soc Inq 37(3):720–742
Goldbach TS (2015) Instrumentalizing the expressive: transplanting sentencing circles into the Canadian criminal trial. Transnational Law Contemp Probl 25(1):61–107
Goldbach TS (2016) From the court to the classroom: judges' work in international judicial education. Cornell Int Law J 49(3):617–682
Gross Stein J (2010) Going too far too fast: judicial independence and political judgment. In: Dodek A, Sossin L (eds) Judicial independence in context. Irwin Law, Toronto
Haggard S, MacIntyre A, Tiede L (2008) The rule of law and economic development. Annu Rev Polit Sci 11(1):205–234
Hughes P (2001) Mandatory mediation: opportunity or subversion? Windsor Yearb Access Justice 19:161–202
Johnson E (2012) The pound conference remembered. Dispute Resolut Mag 19(1):6+

Kapiszewski D, Silverstein G, Kagan RA (2013) Consequential courts: judicial roles in global perspective. Cambridge University Press, Cambridge

Knazan B (2003) Sentencing Aboriginal offenders in a large city—the Toronto Gladue (Aboriginal persons) Court. National Judicial Institute Aboriginal Law Seminar. http://www.aboriginallegal.ca/assets/gladuesentencingpaper.pdf. Accessed 7 Jan 2018

Landerkin HF, Pirie AJ (2005) What's the issue?: Judicial dispute resolution in Canada. Law Context 22(1):25–63

LaPrairie C (1992) Aboriginal crime and justice: explaining the present, exploring the future. Can J Criminol Crim Justice 34:281–298

Lasser MS-O-l'E (1995) Judicial (self-)portraits: judicial discourse in the French legal system. Yale Law J 104(6):1325–1410

Law Commission of Canada (2001) Safeguarding the future and healing the past: the government of Canada's response to the law commission of Canada's report restoring dignity: responding to child abuse in Canadian institutions. The Dept, Ottawa

Law Reform Commission of Canada (1991) Report on Aboriginal peoples and criminal justice: equity, respect and the search for justice. Law Reform Commission of Canada, Ottawa

Macfarlane J (2012) ADR and the courts: renewing our commitment to innovation. Marquette Law Rev 95(3):927–940

Macfarlane J (1995) Court-based mediation for civil cases: an evaluation of the Ontario court (general division) ADR centre. Queen's Printer for Ontario, Toronto

Mandel M (1989) The charter of rights and the legalization of politics in Canada. Wall & Thompson, Toronto

Manitoba, Hamilton AC, Sinclair CM (1991) Report of the Aboriginal justice inquiry of Manitoba. Public Inquiry into the Administration of Justice and Aboriginal People, Winnipeg

Mayer BS (2004) Beyond neutrality: confronting the crisis in conflict resolution. Jossey-Bass, San Francisco

Menkel-Meadow C (1991) Pursuing settlement in an adversary culture: a tale of innovation co-opted or "The Law of ADR". Fla State Univ Law Rev 19:1–46

Menkel-Meadow C (2006) Why hasn't the world gotten to yes? An appreciation and some reflections. Negot J 22(4):485–503

Menkel-Meadow CJ (2000) Mothers and fathers of invention: the intellectual founders of ADR. Ohio State J Dispute Resolut 16(1):1–37

Merry S (1988) Legal pluralism. Law Soc Rev 22(5):869–896

Ministry of the Attorney General, Facilities Management Branch, Aboriginal Conference Settlement Suite Final Report (March 2009) (on file with author) [Facilities Management Branch]

Ministry of the Attorney General (2012–2013) Court services division annual report 2012–2013. Queen's Printer for Ontario

Miyazaki H (2013) Arbitraging Japan dreams of capitalism at the end of finance. University of California Press, Berkeley

Mnookin R, Hackley S (2008) Welcome to the program on negotiation (PON). Harvard Law School. http://www.pon.harvard.edu/about/. Accessed 7 Jan 2018

Monahan P, Shaw B (2011) The impact of extra-judicial service on the Canadian judiciary: the need for reform. In: Lee HP (ed) Judiciaries in comparative perspective. Cambridge University Press, Cambridge

Ontario Civil Justice Review (1995) Civil justice review first report. Toronto. https://www.attorneygeneral.jus.gov.on.ca/english/about/pubs/cjr/. Accessed 13 Oct 2017

Ontario Civil Justice Review (1996) Civil justice review: supplemental and final report. Toronto. https://www.attorneygeneral.jus.gov.on.ca/english/about/pubs/cjr/ Accessed 13 Oct 2017

Osborne CA (2007) Civil justice reform project: summary of findings and recommendations. Ontario Ministry of the Attorney General, Nov 2007. https://www.attorneygeneral.jus.gov.on.ca/english/about/pubs/cjrp/. Accessed 13 Oct 2017

Patriquin M (2012) Canada, home to the suicide capital of the world: in Pikangikum, gas sniffing is rampant and young people are taking their own lives at a shocking rate. Martin Patriquin explores a community shattered, Rogers Publishing Ltd.

Pickering A, Stephanides A (1992) Constructing quaternions: on the analysis of conceptual practice. In: Pickering A (ed) Science as practice and culture, University of Chicago Press

Pirie AJ (1994) Manufacturing mediation: the professionalization of informalism. In: Morris C, Pirie AJ (eds) Qualifications for dispute resolution: perspectives on the debate. UVic Institute for Conflict Resolution, Victoria

Pound R (1906) The causes of popular dissatisfaction with the administration of justice, address before the annual convention of the American Bar Association. Am Law Rev 40:729–749

Pound R (1908) Mechanical jurisprudence. Columbia Law Rev 8(8):605–623

Resnik J (1986) The declining faith in the adversary system. Litigation 13(1):3–6

Resnik J (1995) Procedural innovations, sloshing over: a comment on Deborah Hensler, "a glass half full, a glass half empty: the use of alternative dispute resolution in mass personal injury litigation. Tex Law Rev 73(7):1627–1645

Resnik J, Curtis DE (2011) Representing justice: invention, controversy, and rights in city-states and democratic courtrooms. Yale University Press, New Haven

Riles A (2011) Collateral knowledge: legal reasoning in the global financial markets. University of Chicago Press, Chicago

Rittich K (2004) The future of law and development: second generation reforms and the incorporation of the social. Mich J Int Law 261:199–243

Roberts J, Melchers R (2003) The incarceration of Aboriginal offenders: trends from 1978 to 2001. Can J Criminol 45(2):211–242

Rudin J (2006) A court of our own: more on the Gladue courts. Nishnawbe-Aski Legal Services. http://www.nanlegal.on.ca/upload/documents/legal-articles/a-court-of-our-own—more-on-gladue-courts.pdf. Accessed 7 Jan 2018

Rudin J (nd) Aboriginal peoples and the criminal justice system. [Toronto, ON]. [Ipperwash Inquiry]. http://www.deslibris.ca/ID/251083. Accessed 7 Jan 2018

Sarat A (1985) The litigation explosion, access to justice, and court reform: examining the critical assumptions. Rutgers Law Rev 37(2):319–336

Scron C, Sibley S (2004) Profession, science, and culture. An emergent canon of law and society research. In: Sarat A (ed) Blackwell companion to law and society, Blackwell Publishing, Oxford, pp 30–60

Sourdin T (2016) Responsive judging. Roundtable presentation, law and society association conference, New Orleans (3 June 2016). Definition available at http://www.lawanddsociety.org/NewOrleans2016/docs/2016_Program.pdf

Statistics Canada (2011) Provincial/territorial distribution of Aboriginal identity population, Canada. Available at Population and geographic distribution—Aboriginal statistics at a glance, 2nd edn, http://www.statcan.gc.ca/pub/89-645-x/2015001/pop-concept-eng.htm#a4. Accessed 7 Jan 2018

Strathern M (1991) Partial connections. Rowman & Littlefield Publishers, Sabage

Teplitsky M (2000) Excessive cost and delay: is there a solution? Advocates Soc J 19(2):5

Trebilcock MJ, Daniels RJ (2008) Rule of law reform and development: charting the fragile path of progress. Edward Elgar, Cheltenham

Trebilcock MJ, Mota Prado M (2011) What makes poor countries poor? Institutional determinants of development. Edward Elgar, Cheltenham

Trubek D, Santos A (2006) The third moment in law and development theory and the emergence of a new critical practice. In: Trubek DM, Santos A (eds) The new law and economic development: a critical appraisal. Cambridge University Press, Cambridge, pp 1–18

Valverde M (2003) Pragmatist and non-pragmatist knowledge practices in American Law. Polit Legal Anthropol Rev 26(2):86–108

Venetis T (2017) First of its kind indigenous people's court in Northwestern Ontario. The Lawyer's Daily, Monday, 27 Feb 2017

Weiner J (1999) Culture in a sealed envelope: the concealment of Australian aboriginal heritage and tradition in the Hindmarsh Island Bridge affair. J R Anthropol Inst 5:193–210
Wendt A (1999) Social theory of international politics. Cambridge University Press, Cambridge
Whonnock K (2008) Aboriginal courts in Canada. The Scow Institute. http://scow-archive.libraries.coop/library/documents/Aboriginal_Courts.pdf. Accessed 7 Jan 2018
Winick BJ, Wexler DB (2003) Judging in a therapeutic key: therapeutic jurisdiction and the courts. Carolina Academic Press, Durham
Winkler WK (2007a) Access to justice, mediation: Panacea or pariah? Can Arbitr Mediat J 16(1):5–9
Winkler WK (2007b) Civil justice reform—the Toronto experience: The Warren Winkler lectures on civil justice reform. Ottawa Law Rev 39(1):99
Winkler WK (2008a) The vanishing trial. Advocates' Soc J 27:3–5
Winkler, The Honourable Chief Justice Warren (2008b) Evaluation of Civil case management in the Toronto region: a report of the implementation of the Toronto practice direction and rule 78. (Submitted to the Attorney General of Ontario and the Superior Court of Justice, Feb 2008)
Winkler WK (2016) Access to justice: personal reflections, University of Saskatchewan College of Law Silas E. Halyk, Q.C. Lecture
Wolff TB (2013) Managerial judging and substantive law. Wash Univ Law Rev 90(3):1027–1069
Yeazell SC (1994) The misunderstood consequences of modern civil process. Wis Law Rev 631–678
Zumbansen P (2012) Transnational private regulatory governance: ambiguities of public authority and private power. Osgoode CLPE Research Paper No. 45/2012 (4 Dec 2012)

Toby S. Goldbach is an Assistant Professor of Law at the University of British Columbia, Allard School of Law. She holds an LL.M. and J.S.D. from Cornell University Law School, and a J.D. and LL.M. specializing in ADR from Osgoode Hall Law School. Dr. Goldbach's research stands at the intersection of comparative law, international relations, and anthropology of law, with a particular focus on the transnational movement of norms related to court procedure and dispute resolution.

Judging in a Therapeutic Way: TJ Audit of Juvenile, Probation and Criminal Procedure Law in Pakistan with Reference to Therapeutic Design and Therapeutic Application of Law

Muhammad Amir Munir

Abstract In Professor Wexler's "bottle-liquid" metaphor, the legal landscapes or legal structures are "bottles," and the roles, behaviors, practices and techniques used by legal actors (judges, lawyers, therapists) are "liquid". Within this framework responsive judging requires judges to use Therapeutic Jurisprudence (TJ) practices to promote procedural fairness and better outcomes. However, enabling judicial responsiveness may also require legislative changes consistent with therapeutic design. This Chapter describes changes made in Pakistan, where the *Juvenile Justice System Ordinance 2000*, the *Control of Narcotics Substance Act 1997* the *Criminal Procedure Code 1898* and probation law contain therapeutic provisions. These laws, thus, are therapeutic in design—*the bottles*. However, the practice in trial courts and the decisions of constitutional courts suggest that there exists no mechanism and training regime for judges, prosecutors and lawyers to provide them with guidance into the humane side of law, i.e., TJ application—*the liquid*. This paper will provide a TJ "audit" of these Pakistani laws in accordance with the Therapeutic Design of Law (TDL) and Therapeutic Application of Law (TAL). It gives examples of judicial education concerning TJ in the form of joint lectures of the author and Professor Dr. David B. Wexler (who was available through Skype) at the Punjab Judicial Academy. The paper also discusses TJ literature produced in Pakistan, including reference to some court opinions, in relation to mainstreaming therapeutic jurisprudence practice.

Paper presented at the Law and Society Association (LSA) Meeting, Isabel Maria Sheraton Hotel, Mexico City, Mexico, 22 June 2017.

M. A. Munir (✉)
Punjab Judicial Academy, Lahore, Pakistan
e-mail: bionic4@hotmail.com

© Springer Nature Singapore Pte Ltd. 2018

T. Sourdin and A. Zariski (eds.), *The Responsive Judge*, Ius Gentium: Comparative Perspectives on Law and Justice 67, https://doi.org/10.1007/978-981-13-1023-2_9

1 Introduction

Therapeutic Jurisprudence (TJ) (Wexler 2000) aims to find the healing capacity of the law (Flies-Away and Garrow 2013). In juvenile law, "healing capacity of law" is generated through a special way of applying the law where the well-being and rehabilitation of the juvenile is the required outcome (Munir Muhammad Amir 2007). It is indeed interdisciplinary (Chesser 2016). This is to ensure that juveniles do not become victims of concurrence and recidivism (King and Auty 2005)—a phenomenon of great concern for a state, social scientists, judges, lawyers and law enforcement agencies. Professor James Gillian,[1] highlighted that in the United States, "[t]wo-thirds of prisoners reoffend within three years of leaving prison, often with a more serious and violent offense" (Gillian 2012). This shows the failure of the system of punishment and imprisonment, at least in one of its dynamics—deterrence.[2] The situation in Pakistan is the same where "life conditions in prisons is (sic) closely related with recidivism rate and criminal behaviour" (Akbar and Bhutta 2017). The Federal Shariat Court (FSC), a constitutional court of Pakistan, has also observed that the "prevailing prison system, does not envision rectification, reform, reformation, or rehabilitation of the convict and advised the managers of prison systems to adopt an objective attitude and bring a change in the prison discipline as well as in the outlook" (Muhammad Aslam Khaki v State 2009). However, prison becomes the abode of a convict only when no alternative sentence is deemed appropriate for his or her well-being or rehabilitation, or alternatively, when legal actors (judges, lawyers, police, probation officers, guardian etc.) are either unaware of a structure to facilitate rehabilitation, or they are indifferent in their roles, behaviour or practices to considering a therapeutic way of doing things. The latter may either be due to bias, prejudice,[3] or merely because of a lack of training in the use of the TJ tools. Hence, we can say that sometimes law is therapeutic in design but is not applied in a therapeutic way and vice versa (Syed Walayat Shah v Qaisar Mahmood 2015).

The role of the judge as going beyond simply providing justice according to law is emphasised in this chapter. Judging in context, essentially responsive judging, is finding its roots in recent cases of constitutional import. The Supreme Court of Pakistan has very recently held that if the confession of a child must be recorded, "it was appropriate and desirable that the accused should have been provided counselling/consultation facility of natural guardian or any close blood relative of mature age, having no clash of interest with him". These observations were made with respect to the non-therapeutic role of the magistrate in terms that "…the recording

[1]Professor Gillian is a clinical Professor of psychiatry and an Adjunct Professor of law at New York University. He is the author of, among other books, "Preventing Violence" and "Why Some Politicians Are More Dangerous Than Others".

[2]At this moment, we are not entering into the debate with respect to the death penalty and its impact on crime reduction. Our focus mainly will remain on other less harmful crimes.

[3]When legal actors presume that the law may be abused by the accused. It is general opinion in Pakistan that the softness in juvenile laws provides an opportunity for using children to commit crimes (Author's informal discussions with a number of judges, lawyers, probation officers, and police).

Magistrate did not provide him [the child defendant] sufficient time for reflection to recompose himself" (*Hashim Qasim v State,* 2017 SCMR 986). With respect to social context judging in rape cases, the Supreme Court has guided all legal actors in the following terms (*Salman Akram Raja v Government of the Punjab*, 2013 SCMR 203):

- every police station that receives rape complaints should involve reputable civil society organizations for the purpose of legal aid and counselling;
- a list of such organizations might be provided by bodies such as the National Commission on the Status of Women;
- on the receipt of information regarding the commission of rape, the Investigating Officer/Station House Officer (S.H.O.) should inform such organizations at the earliest possible time;
- the administration of DNA tests and preservation of DNA evidence should be made mandatory in rape cases;
- as soon as the victim was composed, her statement should be recorded under S. 164 of the Code of Criminal Procedure (Cr.P.C.), preferably by a female Magistrate;
- trials for rape should be conducted in camera and after regular court hours;
- during a rape trial, screens or other arrangements should be made so that the victims and vulnerable witnesses did not have to face the accused persons; and
- evidence of rape victims should be recorded, in appropriate cases, through video conferencing so that the victims, particularly juvenile victims, did not have to be present in court.

In the same vein, an earlier decision shows that exemption from the death penalty for children convicted of offences carrying capital punishment prior to the enforcement of the *Juvenile Justice System Ordinance* was only granted by the Supreme Court in the course of interpreting a Presidential Order based on the constitutional principle of equal treatment (*Nazir v State,* PLD 2007 SC 202). According to the Presidential Order the death sentence of some children was converted to that of life imprisonment. Likewise, giving importance to peace and harmony in the community, the Lahore High Court has observed that the "[c]ompromise between parties was relevant as it would imprint beneficial effects in relations between the parties and promote peace, tranquillity and harmony" (*Faiz Rasool v Province of Punjab*, 2017 YLR 134). Accordingly, the death penalty was converted into that of life imprisonment.

The court has also expanded the meaning of compensation which has to be awarded to a person who has suffered mental anguish or psychological damage due to a crime. In this way, a "minor baby girl born in result of crime [of rape] committed by the appellant" is declared as "'a person' suffering mental anguish and psychological damage for her whole life, thus, she is entitled for the compensation provided under the law." (*Nadeem Masood v State,* 2015 PCrLJ 1633). In the ways described above, Pakistan's judges and courts are now more relevant to society by practicing responsive judging in context.

2 Therapeutic Design and Application of Law (TDL and TAL)

The liquid/bottle metaphor identified by Professor Wexler is useful in understanding the interconnection between the therapeutic design of a law and its therapeutic or responsive application by legal actors. He writes:

> To examine the law and its administration, we are using a metaphor of "[liquid] and bottles", looking at the law itself—the legal landscape or legal structure—as "bottles," and at the roles, behaviors, practices and techniques used by legal actors (judges, lawyers, therapists) as "liquid" …." (Wexler 2015).

Thus, there may be a law that may be classified as therapeutic in its design, e.g., a law dealing with juveniles (bottle) has provisions for rehabilitation and restoring the well-being of juveniles. Although the law seeks rehabilitation of a juvenile as a first option for the courts, the trend of court decisions may reflect the attitude of legal actors who are indifferent towards the concept of rehabilitation (liquid). TJ techniques suggest that instead of the court imposing a rehab plan (Wexler 1993), it is advisable to ask the juvenile to propose his or her own conditions of future behaviour so that compliance is optimal, and relapse is minimal (Wexler 2015). By training and discussion, legal actors may be sensitized to TJ by interdisciplinary studies establishing that a juvenile, if treated differently and humanely, may become a responsible citizen again. In this way, the old bottle (law, rules) will carry new liquid (roles, practices and techniques of legal actors).

To determine if a penal law is therapeutic in design (TDL), the criteria to be applied is whether it takes into account the rehabilitation and well-being of the accused. It should also be determined if the punishment is immutable, and what objective circumstances/factors may be taken into consideration when imposing a sentence especially where the court must use its discretion in reaching a decision.

To determine if a law is being administered in a therapeutic way (TAL), the criteria focusses on the roles and attitudes of legal actors in relation to their support to enable the accused to enter into a process for his or her own rehab and well-being planned in an integrated way. A team decision making approach by legal actors will be a plus point as well. The supervisory role of the judge and other legal actors should also be considered at the execution stage of a convicted person's behavioural contract. Another factor to be considered is whether the convict was provided an opportunity to give his or her input if a sentence is necessarily passed after conviction.[4]

[4]In Pakistan, it is generally presumed that the criminal courts are bound to pass sentence immediately after recording conviction of an accused at trial. There is no concept of post-conviction sentence hearings.

3 TDL and TAL Analysis of the *Pakistan Penal Code*

This study examines three laws, viz., the *Juvenile Justice System Ordinance 2000*; the *Code of Criminal Procedure 1898* and the *Probation of Offenders Ordinance 1960* with respect to TDL and TAL. The first is a special criminal procedure law for the trial of juveniles/children in conflict with the law; the second is a general criminal procedural law, and the last is the probation law that empowers courts to consider imposing alternative sentences of probation in appropriate cases. However, it would be best to start with the *Pakistan Penal Code 1860* (hereinafter PPC), a general penal law,[5] that prescribes acts and/or omissions (sections 33 and 36) as offences punishable in the form of prescribed or discretionary sentences.

The PPC provides punishments for the offences it defines (section 2 and Chapter III). The preamble to PPC is indifferent towards any rehabilitation theory of punishment in simply stating: "Whereas it is expedient to provide a general Penal Code for Pakistan". The sentences which a court can impose on an accused on conviction range from simple imprisonment to the death penalty,[6] according to the nature of the offence.[7] There are certain Islamic punishments prescribed as well for qisas[8] and diyat[9] offences. Chapter III of PPC provides an interesting structure of punishments in which the role of the courts is to consider, subjectively, why a specific sentence must be imposed. Section 60 of PPC provides discretion to a trial court to impose a sentence of imprisonment either rigorous (with labour) or simple (mere confinement):

> 60. *Sentence may be (in certain cases of imprisonment) wholly or partly rigorous or simple*: In every case in which an offender is punishable with imprisonment which may be of either description, it shall be competent to the Court which sentences such offender to direct in the sentence that such imprisonment shall be wholly rigorous, or that such imprisonment shall be wholly simple, or that any part of such imprisonment shall be rigorous and the rest simple.

Through TJ lenses (Munir Muhammad Amir 2008), there is much of therapeutic jurisprudence in such a provision leaving aside the question that the sentence still focuses on incarceration or is custodial in nature.[10] For example, in a sodomy case where the offender himself was a child/juvenile, the appellate court converted his sentence of rigorous imprisonment to that of simple imprisonment (*Qayyum Ullah v*

---

[5] There are many special criminal laws with specific offences defined therein along with their punishments. However, we will not go into detail of those laws for brevity and time constraints.

[6] There are very few offences having capital punishment.

[7] Other punishments include rigorous imprisonment, fine, life imprisonment, arsh, daman, ta'zir, and forfeiture of property: See section 53 PPC.

[8] "qisas" means punishment by causing similar hurt at the same part of the body of the convict as he has caused to the victim, or by causing his death if he has committed qatl-i-amd, in exercise of the right of the victim or a wali: See section 299(k) of PPC.

[9] Compensation payable to legal heirs of victim: See section 323 PPC.

[10] We have to note that the TJ literature does not support custodial rehab programs for different reasons and its anti-therapeutic impact on the psychology of a convict.

State 2016, YLR 178). Likewise, in another case where a former legislator was tried for contesting an election using fake educational certificates, the High Court in appeal reduced his sentence to simple imprisonment (*Abdul Qayyum v State* 2013, MLD 1750). Further, there is no ground to impose rigorous imprisonment if the offender commits the offence for the first time and has no other criminal record. In a murder case, the appellate court converted the sentence of a child offender to that of simple imprisonment for 14 years by reason of his being a minor, i.e., less than 18 years of age. It should also be mentioned that the punishments prescribed for offences in PPC are mostly variable, i.e., either rigorous or simple. Very few offences have only rigorous imprisonment as the only option for sentencing by the court. However, the research at Pakistanlawsite (2018)[11] shows that there are very few cases where the appellate courts have converted the sentences of rigorous imprisonment to that of simple imprisonment. The author could not locate a case where this provision is applied to impose the lesser of the two options.

In the same vein, most offences have an alternative punishment of a fine only, i.e., a non-custodial sentence. However, it is rare to find a conviction recorded where a mere fine is imposed as a sentence. Courts are rigorously applying imprisonment as a first option of their sentencing behaviour. In this connection it should be mentioned that the Lahore High Court, in *Ali Muhammad v State* (PLD 2009 Lahore 317) elaborated on the sentencing policy for harms punishable under Qisas and Diyat law. It was held that the first option for the courts is to pass a non-custodial sentence. Imprisonment can only be inflicted if certain pre-conditions are met.[12]

It thus appears that the courts are still without good guidance on whether to impose rigorous imprisonment only at first instance. These dynamics of the sentencing regime should be considered in relation to the therapeutic or detrimental impact on those convicts for whom rigorous imprisonment may be physically and mentally harmful.[13] Thus, law in this perspective is seen to be 'unfriendly' to TJ but on a deeper analysis, some therapeutic impact can be created for the convicts. This law may be therapeutic in design, but the above analysis shows that it is not being applied in a therapeutic way. Here the role, behaviour and practices of legal actors are causes of the non-application of TJ.

Two other important provisions of PPC should also be considered. Section 82 provides that nothing is an offence which is committed by a child under 10 years of age. Section 83 deals specifically with children between 10–14 years of age. It says:

> 83. *Act of a child above ten and under fourteen of immature understanding:* Nothing is an offence which is done by a child above ten years of age and under fourteen, who has not attained sufficient maturity of understanding to judge of the nature and consequences of his conduct on that occasion.

---

[11]This is commercial website of Pakistani case law reported in Pakistan Legal Decisions and other journals issued by M/S PLD Publishers.

[12]This judgment is under challenge before the Hon'ble Supreme Court of Pakistan which has yet to expound the law on this point.

[13]For example, women, children, the infirm and the elderly. So far, there are no sentencing guidelines provided by the legislature in this respect.

For children under 10 years of age, there is no criminal responsibility. However, to make this provision operational, it is imperative that either age is not at dispute, or if disputed, the question needs to be resolved at the earliest stage (Munir Muhammad Amir 2007). This issue is taken up again below when section 7 of the *Juvenile Justice System Ordinance 2000* is discussed.

TJ literature suggests that it has its origins in mental health cases—where medical jurisprudence entered legal jurisprudence. Section 84 of PPC says that a person of unsound mind cannot be held criminally liable. The Balochistan High Court, in *Abdul Ghaffar v State* (PLD 2017 Balochistan 46) held that the burden of proof of insanity lay on the accused, and under section 84 of PPC, the crucial point of time at which unsoundness of mind should be established is at the time when the act, constituting the offence, was committed. In this case, the medical report submitted by the Standing Board had revealed that the accused was suffering from "Bipolar disorder" and the court held that with this illness the petitioner could not be considered a person of unsound mind (*Abdul Ghaffar v State* 2017). Likewise, in the case of *Safia Bano v Home Department* (PLD 2017 SC 18), the Supreme Court of Pakistan rejected the plea of a wife of a convict that his paranoid schizophrenia entitled him to a halt of his execution. These opinions reinforce the assertion that knowledge of mental health science is of crucial importance in applying penal law. However, the international literature on mental health is critical of judicial systems with the allegation that "the judicial system does not give as much weight to a diagnosis of mental illness as it should when determining the proper sentence upon conviction" (Padowitz 2015).

Thus, the design of these provisions may be somewhat therapeutic (old bottle); however, their application is non-therapeutic at the moment (no new liquid).

Another provision of the PPC concerns the right of self-defence against persons being a child or under mental disability or unsoundness of mind. Section 98 PPC provides that if any of these persons do an act or omission which would otherwise be an offence, although they are a child or insane, they may be harmed at the hands of a prospective victim within their right of self-defence. The juvenile or person of unsound mind may even be killed. This area is of great concern for the development of law, judicial precedent and TJ.

Another important provision is section 306 PPC which states that the punishment of qisas cannot be inflicted on a minor or insane person. Thus, for these, the law is therapeutically designed. However, the question of determination of age at the relevant time may become a crucial point of controversy if this issue is not taken seriously by legal actors and guardians of the minor or the insane. In recent cases, the Supreme Court of Pakistan has held that the defence of juvenility, if not taken at the earliest possible opportunity, cannot be of any help to the convict to escape the death penalty in a murder case. In *Muhammad Aslam v State* (PLD 2009 SC 777), the Court observed that where an accused claims minority, such a plea must be taken by him at the earliest available opportunity and he should not be allowed to throw surprises at the prosecution at the end of the trial or at the appellate or revisional stages, thereby depriving the prosecution of opportunities to rebut such claims in a proper manner. The same was recently reaffirmed when the Court held: Any belated attempt made by the accused [alleged juvenile] in such regard before the Supreme

Court may not be met with approval or acceptance (*Muhammad Raheel v State*, PLD 2017 SC 145). Thus, if the legal actors are not friendly to TJ practices as reflected in section 306 there is a chance that a child may suffer the death penalty through no fault of their own.

4 TDL and TAL Analysis of the *Juvenile Justice System Ordinance* 2000 and the *Probation of Offenders Ordinance* 1960

Pakistan enacted its formal *Juvenile Justice System Ordinance* (hereinafter JJSO) in the year 2000. Its preamble reads:

> Whereas it is expedient to prove for protection of children involved in criminal litigation, their rehabilitation in society, re-organization of Juvenile Courts and matters connected therewith and incidental thereto.

This law focuses on the rehabilitation of children who come in contact with the criminal law and courts. It has brought a fundamental shift to the juvenile justice system of Pakistan. Thus, it has been held by the Sindh High Court in *Ghulam Rasool v State (*PLD 2010 Sindh 384) that:

- *Juvenile Justice System Ordinance 2000* was a special law and would take precedence over the general law;
- The Ordinance did not give any discretion to a Trial Court to ignore its mandatory provisions;
- The purpose of the Ordinance is to provide protection to children in criminal litigation and their rehabilitation in society.

Likewise, in an earlier case, *Zia Ahmad Awan v Govt of Sindh* (2002 PCrLJ 659), the Sindh High Court emphasised that responsibility lay with the Provincial Government to ensure that the provisions of the law were complied with by agencies and officials, as the issue involved in the petition was not only legal, but also had social and moral dimensions. The Court also emphasised that the government and legislature should bring about a unified juvenile law as there were other laws that also deal with the matter of juveniles.

The Courts are cognizant of the seriousness of the issue as when the Sindh High Court in *Afsar Zamin v State* (PLD 2002 Sindh 18) held that the JJSO needs to be interpreted liberally. It was observed:

- *Juvenile Justice System Ordinance 2000* is aimed at extending protection to children involved in criminal litigation and their rehabilitation in society;
- The Ordinance in a way safeguards the human rights of a section of society who deserve reasonable concession because of their tender age and, therefore, it is to be construed liberally to achieve the said object.

In a paper for the 3rd International Conference on Therapeutic Jurisprudence, Muhammad Ahmad Munir (2007) has remarked:

> This law introduces therapeutic jurisprudence in Pakistan. It is interesting and surprising to note that that the terms "well-being", "bond for good behavior" and "Court controlled probation" used in this law are key words for the TJ community and courts around the world wherever TJ is practiced.

The first element in the TJ design of this law is its preamble. Later, remarkably, except for its title which contains the word 'juvenile', nowhere in the text of the Ordinance has the word 'juvenile' been used. Instead, the law focuses on the word 'child'[14] whenever it refers to a person in conflict with the law who is under 18 years of age. In the definition clause the word 'child' is defined. This, in the author's view, has a healing impact in that a child is not referred to as a "juvenile" which can have the association of "juvenile delinquent" and so stigmatize the child. Literature on labelling theory also supports this assertion (Hora 2016). The law is thus consistent with TDL in this aspect. However, it remains to consider this Ordinance in relation to TAL on which there is little research.

Twenty judgments of the Supreme Court of Pakistan have been surveyed, spanning over a period between 2003 to 2017 (15 years).[15] Three terms are used by the apex court for children who come in conflict with the law. These are:

- "Accused"
- "Juvenile offender"
- "Juvenile"

The behaviour noted will not be much different for the other courts of the country with few exceptions. It is apparent from this record of litigation that the use of words that may stigmatize the child needs to be avoided not only in literature but also in other writing like news items, judgments, and publicly available records. The JJSO has used the phrase 'child accused of' in some places. Perhaps the legislature should consider the approach used in India which favours the term 'child in conflict with law' to avoid any stigma to the child. The TAL in relation to the Ordinance in this respect is a little foggy and the fog can be easily removed by producing more literature and awareness of the importance of terminology.

The JJSO, in its section 3, casts a duty upon the state to provide free legal assistance, if requested, to every child in conflict with law. There is little ambiguity in the legislative words which are "shall have the right of legal assistance at the expense of the State". However, the state may argue that the child had a right of free legal assistance, but he or she never used his or her right to it. Though hypothetical, that argument may have force in terms that it is not the 'duty' of the state, but only an obligation to act if the same is requested by the child. The Child Rights Convention

---

[14] See section 2(b) of JJSO where the term 'child' has been defined as "a person who at the time of commission of an offence has not attained the age of eighteen years".

[15] I used the Pakistanlawsite search engine and searched for the term 'juvenile justice' with the limitation that only cases of the Hon Supreme Court of Pakistan be searched. It brought 20 titles as such.

(CRC) in Article 40 places a duty on states to ensure that every child has legal assistance. However, Article 35 of the CRC only provides a right to the child, as is the case in our legislation. Thus, reading Articles 35 and 40 of the CRC, the national laws may cast a duty upon the state through prosecutors and/or courts to immediately provide free legal assistance to a child irrespective of the fact that he or she asserts his or her right in this regard.

Joint trial of children with adults is prohibited in JJSO. This provision is therapeutically oriented to prevent children from meeting and interacting with adults accused of offences. However, practically speaking, the environment in courts is not conducive to implementing this provision in letter and spirit. Courts are overburdened with case backlogs and thus violations of this provision are noted by appellate courts. In *Adnan Zafar v State* (2005 YLR 1281), the Lahore High Court observed:

- The Record had shown that the trial Court, instead of conducting a separate trial, had tried both the accused as well as his co-accused jointly and used carbon copies of the record;
- Such procedure adopted by the trial Court on the face of it, militated against mandatory provisions of *Juvenile Justice System Ordinance, 2000*.

In an earlier case, *Liaquat v State* (2001 YLR 3278), the Sindh High Court also declared joint trial of a child with an adult to be an illegal procedure and direction was made for re-trial.

This stream of case law suggests that the legislative intent is not followed in practice. The law, which is consistent with TDL, is actually having anti-therapeutic impacts on children because legal actors seem indifferent to the physical and psychological impact on children who come in contact with accused adults during trial and imprisonment. Training and sensitization of legal actors is necessary to ensure the therapeutic application of this law.

A well written law cannot be as beneficial for a child if a key question is not resolved at the earliest possible point: the question of age of a person for the purposes of JJSO (Munir Muhammad Amir 2007). This is a matter of great debate in judicial decisions in Pakistan because of the availability of fake birth certificates. In *Faisal Aleem v State*, PLD 2010 SC 1080, the apex Court did not accept a birth certificate on the grounds that the date of birth of the accused was just few months different to his brother and this does not seem possible. There is also malpractice by birth registration officers. In *Muhammad Nasir v State*, 2007 MLD 148, the Lahore High Court observed: the intention of the Legislature was very clear that determination of the age of an accused person based on a School Leaving certificate or birth certificate was not safe, hence, a report from the Medical Board was to be obtained for determination of age. Another weak area is the issuance of school certificates with manipulated dates of birth in school records. The JJSO in its section 7 has thus focused on two elements: documentary and medical evidence. In *Muhammad Aslam v State*, the Supreme Court has provided detailed guidelines for trial courts on how to resolve the controversy of age of the accused. In this case it was observed by the Court that medical evidence must also be considered along with documentary evidence, but keeping in view the principles of the *Qanun-i-Shahadat Order 1984*.[16]

The Lahore High Court in *Mohammad Ilyas v State* (2017 YLR 71) observed carefully that "the issue about the age of an accused at trial, which can result in punishment of death, is of vital significance." Thus, the whole therapeutic design of the law may be of no use for a child if his or her age could not be determined at the earliest stage if age is in controversy. "This is only possible if we apply the JJSO with an 'ethic of care'" (Munir Muhammad Amir 2007).

The Supreme Court of Pakistan has settled the controversy as to who may initiate the query about the age of the person alleged to be a child. In *Sultan Ahmad's case* (PLD 2004 SC 758), it was held:

- The Court is not to wait until someone raises the question of age;
- It is the obligation of the court to suspend all proceedings until the question is resolved;
- The Court must hold an inquiry to determine the child's age.

Recently, the Supreme Court, in *Muhammad Aslam v State* (PLD 2009 SC 777) has provided a distinct procedure to be followed by the courts to determine the age of the person alleged to be a child to make the process simple and clearer. If legal actors take the proper steps well within time the therapeutic application of laws may be ensured.

With respect to arrest and bail, the JJSO seems to be consistent with TDL. This is because it focuses on two important therapeutic values:

- Avoiding incarceration where appropriate (non-custodial process) (Murrell 2017);
- Ensuring the presence of a guardian (Hora et al. 1999).

In a case of unnatural lust, the plea of the child was accepted for a grant of bail because of his age below 18 years (*Zaher v State*, 2007 SCMR 1178). There are some heinous cases where bail was granted to children who have committed crimes, but after the lapse of some reasonable time in custody, e.g., after five months of arrest in 2012 MLD 1965, after 18 months of arrest in 2017 MLD 399, and after 3 and a half years of arrest in 2014 YLR 422. It is a prime duty of courts to apply the exceptions in the law of bail for juveniles when the offences committed by them are serious, heinous, gruesome or brutal.[17] For non-serious offences, the law provides that bail must be granted as a first option even in non-bailable offences if a child is below 15 years of age. Case law referred to above dictates that the trial courts are still reluctant to grant bail at the earliest stage and thus these matters have to go to the High Courts or Supreme Court of Pakistan. There is a lack of empirical analysis of the culture of decisions on bail by trial courts to provide an informed view of the behaviour of courts in this area. The National Judicial (Policy Making) Committee, however, when considering the aspect of non-grant of bail by trial courts to deserving accused

[16]This is a present law of evidence in Pakistan.

[17]Section 10 of JJSO has special exceptions to refuse bail to children on these grounds.

persons, has issued policy guidelines for the courts to grant bail in appropriate cases. It has further emphasised that cases of juveniles must be disposed of within given timelines (Law and Justice Commission of Pakistan 2009). There is no consistent therapeutic application of the JJSO in this aspect as well.

In relation to the presence of the guardian or parent of a child after his or her arrest and appearance before courts the law is therapeutic in providing an opportunity for a team decision making process. However, the practice in courts and by the police is not good enough and this provision of law is mostly neglected. In a case where the confessional statement of the child was recorded by the magistrate in the absence of any guardian or other protector the Supreme Court of Pakistan observed:

> Being a juvenile (minor), it was appropriate and desirable that the accused should have been provided counselling/consultation facility of natural guardian or any close blood relative of mature age, having no clash of interest with him (*Hashim Qasim v State,* 2017 SCMR 986).

This provision of the JJSO has embedded the concept of 'team decision making' (Munir Muhammad Amir 2006) about a child. At different procedural steps, the team may consist of different persons. For example, as per section 10(1)(a) & (b), at the time of first appearance before a magistrate the presence of guardian and probation officer is made mandatory by the law itself. However, the magistrate is not constrained by law from involving other specialists like psychologists, psychiatrists, medical officers, school teachers, employers or any other suitable persons. The probation officer, being a member of the statutory team, is also empowered to consult any relevant person for writing his special report about the child to be submitted in court under section 9 of JJSO.[18]

A report by the probation officer is a mandatory requirement of law according to section 9(1) of JJSO:

> The Probation Officer shall assist the Juvenile Court by making a report on the child's character, educational, social and moral background.

The impact this report may have remains unclear. Courts must be sensitized to the importance of the report produced by the probation officer so that the law is administered in a better and informed way. A law with TDL features is not being applied (TAL) by legal actors to bring about its full potential.

---

[18]It is interesting to note that no law has yet developed about the report of a probation officer which he or she is bound to prepare and submit before a juvenile court (I have made this assertion on the basis of searching case law on section 9 of JJSO by using Pakistanlawsite. No case is reported there).

4.1 *Probation*

Section 11 of the JJSO is an impressive legislative intervention to provide a therapeutic track for dealing with a child before the Court. Although the probation law[19] was present since 1960, JJSO has now provided that a juvenile court, as a first option, must use its discretion, after convicting a child before it, to send him or her on probation (non-custodial sentence) for his or her well-being and good behaviour. This is also mandated in the United Nations Standard Minimum Rules for Non-Custodial Measures (The Tokyo Rules) (UNGA 1990). This is indeed an instance of TDL, as a brief study of the scheme of this law will show.

In section 11 of JJSO, the word 'may' has been used to provide juvenile courts a discretion to consider two options after convicting a child before it: either to send the child on probation or to order custodial care in a borstal institution. The first option is to send the child on probation, therefore if the court decides to use second option it is imperative for the court to justify its skipping of the probation option. The Supreme Court of Pakistan has observed: "The word 'may' involves a choice and the word 'shall' involves an order…. Such would be the customary usage of the terms when they appear in a statute…. Even an enabling word like 'may' would become mandatory, when the object was to effectuate a legal right." (*Muhammad Sadiq v University of Sindh* 1996). How the discretion is to be used by an authority is further explained by the Court in another case:

- Discretion must not be exercised to curtail the purpose of law and offend the statute, rather the discretion must be exercised to advance the cause of justice in a just, fair and reasonable manner;
- Failure to exercise discretionary power under the statute without any legal justification amounts to refusal to use such power in an arbitrary and capricious manner (*Abu Bakar Siddique v Collector of Customs*, Lahore, 2006).

Thus, in a narcotics substance case, the Lahore High Court has remarked that the "[c]ourt in narcotic case, if deemed it proper, could send accused on probation" (*Anti Narcotics Force v State* 2016). Giving preference to non-custodial sentences brings a therapeutic impact and meets the objectives of the law as well. Here, there is both TDL and TAL in action.

4.2 *Court Controlled Probation*

An interesting departure from the ordinary course of legal action was also made by the JJSO which introduced the concept of a court-controlled probation system. This approach is clearly in line with the literature on therapeutic jurisprudence. Professor Arie Freiberg (2017) from the University of Melbourne, has aptly remarked:

[19]The Probation of Offenders Ordinance, 1960.

> Problem-solving courts rely upon the active use of judicial authority to solve problems and to change the behaviour of litigants. Instead of passing off cases – to other judges, to probation departments, to community-based treatment programs – judges at problem-solving courts stay involved with each case throughout the post-adjudication process….

This is now the regime under JJSO in relation to probation. The judges of juvenile courts need to use this authority in a manner such that the purpose of the law is served the most. The court has even been granted a discretion to reduce the period of sentence if it is satisfied that further probation is not necessary (Munir Muhammad Amir 2005).

As a corollary to this discussion, it is also important to note that the *Code of Criminal Procedure 1898* has also given a role to trial court judges when the government must consider the release of a convict on the basis of good conduct in prison. Section 401(2) of CrPC provides:

> …may require the presiding Judge of the Court before or by which the conviction was had or confirmed to state his opinion as to whether the application should be granted or refused, together with his reasons for such opinion and also to forward with the statement of such opinion a certified copy of the record of the trial or of such record thereof as exists.

Thus, as early as 1898, a role for judges concerning the question of release of prisoners for good conduct was part of the law. When and how many times it has been used is not traceable due to a lack of empirical studies on this provision of law.

4.3 Death Penalty and Handcuffs

The JJSO bars trial courts from imposing the death penalty on children convicted of an offence having capital punishment. This provision is still a matter of controversy due to the concern that that this immunity may lead to a rise in the number of serious offences committed by persons below 18 years of age. However, so far, no empirical study is available to prove or disprove this assertion and more research is required to bring to bear empirical evidence and analysis.

With respect to the prohibition of handcuffs for children, magistrates are now much more conscious to keep an eye on police investigating officers for any such violation. Thus, some judicial officers have described their experience during training sessions at the Punjab Judicial Academy such that whenever they have found a child produced in court in handcuffs, they have made an order to remove them for the psychological benefit of the child. The author himself has made such orders in the past while a magistrate. That experience has shown that if a judge is aware of even a small therapeutic opportunity, its exploitation can have a positive impact not only on the accused, but also on other legal actors such as police so that they do not repeat the anti-therapeutic acts.

5 Legal and Judicial Education on TJ[20]

Professor Wexler from the University of Puerto Rico and the University of Arizona is a key exponent of therapeutic jurisprudence and its application. In 2005–06 the author started communicating with Professor Wexler through emails (Munir Muhammad Amir 2017) so as better to understand TJ concepts and their application to local laws in Pakistan, particularly to the JJSO. In wake of this connection, the author has written several articles and essays on TJ[21] and in this way, TJ literature in Pakistan began its journey. Thereafter, the author's father[22] and brother[23] have also developed a great interest in TJ and have written articles on this topic. The author's father has translated the baseline TJ article (TJ: An Overview) by Professor Wexler into the Urdu language (Mughal 2006).

It was an honour for the author when in 2015 Professor Wexler accepted a request to deliver presentations through Skype from Puerto Rico to Lahore at the Punjab Judicial Academy (PJA). These were joint presentations by Professor Wexler and the author (who was a senior instructor in the PJA at that time) on TJ and juvenile law. Almost 350 civil judges and judicial magistrates were trained on TJ in a series of lectures. The records of feedback at the PJA establish that the judicial officers found these lectures very informative and practical. Late last year, the Lahore High Court established child and gender-based violence courts in Lahore District. These courts must look at the humane side of law and should employ therapeutic jurisprudence principles while dealing with the cases where children and women are the victims or the defendants (accused).

6 Practicing TJ in Court

Over the last ten years or more, the author has been a TJ practitioner and has tried to apply TJ principles while on the bench as a magistrate. It has shown good results in several cases involving juveniles. In one of these cases, the child was charged with the offence of theft. Through a TJ dialogue and team decision making process, he was sent on probation for good conduct on his own behavioural terms agreed to by his father as guardian as well. The child completed his probation successfully and was released from probation even earlier than the initial period.

[20] See Munir Muhammad Amir (2008).

[21] To read TJ literature in Pakistan, visit my SSRN page at http://ssrn.com/author=670902.

[22] Justice Dr. Munir Ahmad Mughal, a former judge of the Lahore High Court and a Member of the Council of Islamic Ideology. His research can be accessed online at http://ssrn.com/author=1697634. He can be contacted at justicemunir@gmail.com.

[23] Muhammad Ahmad Munir, a Ph.D. fellow at the McGill University, Canada. Under the guidance of Prof David Wexler, he has written and presented a paper in 3rd International Conference on Therapeutic Jurisprudence held in Perth Australia. He can be contacted at ahmad.munir@mail.mcgill.ca.

Likewise, the author has also written in judicial orders about the use of language and its impact on litigants. Most important among these was a case relating to an intellectually challenged person. The pleadings and litigation used the word "lunatic" to describe said person. Taking guidance from the Lahore High Court Rules and Orders and TJ literature, the author held that the word 'lunatic' should not be used in a derogatory manner and against the fundamental right of human dignity (*Syed Walayat Shah v Qaisar Mahmood* 2015). A copy of the judgment was also sent to the Law and Justice Commission of Pakistan to consider legislative improvements where the word 'lunatic' occurs in different pieces of legislation.

7 Conclusion

This study has shown that the law relating to child offenders in Pakistan is fundamentally therapeutically designed. Many of its provisions are also being applied therapeutically but more legal and judicial education is required. Legal actors must be sensitized to TJ principles for administering the law in a responsive manner where welfare and well-being and rehabilitation in society are the prime objectives. There is much research, however, still required on the empirical side to analyse the TJ potential of JJSO and TAL with respect to the desired outcomes.

Acknowledgements The author wants to acknowledge guidance of Prof. Dr. David B Wexler and critical review by his Father Justice Dr. Munir Ahmad Mughal in writing this paper. For all the errors, omissions and assertions, the author is, however, solely responsible. The views reflected by the author do not reflect the official view of any of the institutions to which he represents. Thanks are also due to Professors Tania Sourdin (University of Newcastle, Australia) and Archie Zariski (University of Athabasca, Canada) for providing ample support in preparing and presenting at the LSA 2017 Conference through a generous financial grant by the National Science Foundation, USA.

References

Abu Bakar Siddique v Collector of Customs (2006) Lahore, SCMR 705 (Supreme Court 2006)

Akbar MS, Bhutta MH (2017) Prison reforms and situation of prisons in Pakistan. A Sociological Association of Pakistan. http://sapandssrp.com/attachments/File/Prison_reforms.pdf. Accessed 17 June 2017

Anti Narcotics Force v State (2016) PCrLJ 953 (Lahore High Court 2016)

Chesser B (2016) Therapeutic jurisprudence. Oxford Bibliographies. http://www.oxfordbibliographies.com/view/document/obo-9780195396607/obo-9780195396607-0203.xml. Accessed 17 June 2017

Flies-Away TJ, Garrow CE (2013) Healing to wellness courts: therapeutic jurisprudence. Mich St L Rev 2013(2):403–450

Freiberg A (2017) Specialized courts and sentencing. http://www.aic.gov.au/media_library/conferences/probation/freiberg.pdf. Accessed 17 June 2017

Gilligan J (2012) Prison could be productive. New York Times, 18 Dec. https://www.nytimes.com/roomfordebate/2012/12/18/prison-could. Accessed 17 June 2017

Hora PF (2016) Therapeutic jurisprudence, procedural justice and labelling theory—a continuum of fairness. Justice Speakers Institute, 18 Oct. http://justicespeakersinstitute.com/therapeutic-jurisprudence-procedural-justice-and-labeling-theory-a-continuum-of-fairness/. Accessed 17 June 2017

Hora PF, Schma WG, Rosenthal JTA (1999) Therapeutic jurisprudence and the drug treatment court movement. Notre Dame L Rev 74(2):439–538

King MS, Auty K (2005) Therapeutic jurisprudence: an emerging trend in courts of summary jurisdiction. Altern Law J 30(2):69–74

Law and Justice Commission of Pakistan (2009) National judicial policy. Law and Justice Commission of Pakistan, Islamabad. http://ljcp.gov.pk/nljcp/assets/dist/NJP/njp.pdf. Accessed 17 June 2017

Mughal JD (2006) Mualjati Usul Qanun: Aik Jaiza. Pak Law J 37. http://www.pljlawsite.com. Accessed 17 June 2017

Muhammad Aslam Khaki v State (2009) Shariat Petition No. 68/I (Federal Shariat Court 28 Aug 2009)

Muhammad Sadiq v University of Sindh (1996) PLD, SC 182 (Supreme Court 1996)

Munir Muhammad Amir (2005) The TJ elements in juvenile justice system of Pakistan: problems for a juvenile court to act therapeutically. University of Arizona Law School (1 July 2005)

Munir Muhammad Amir (2006) Family courts in Pakistan in search of 'better remedies' for women and children. Lawasia J 2006:191–226

Munir Muhammad Amir (2007) Juvenile justice system ordinance 2000: theory. Pak Law J 2007:52–56

Munir Muhammad Ahmad (2007) Therapeutic jurisprudence in Pakistan: juvenile delinquency & the role of the defense lawyer. In: Reinhardt G, Cannon A (eds) Transforming legal processes in court and beyond, Australasian Institute of Judicial Administration, Perth, pp 85–106

Munir Muhammad Amir (2008) Therapeutic jurisprudence and legal education in Pakistan: a quest for innovation in study of law to mend attitudes of law professionals towards litigants. Pak Law J 2008. SSRN. https://papers.ssrn.com/sol3/papers.cfm?abstract_id=1917748. Accessed 17 June 2017

Munir Muhammad Amir (2017) Mainstreaming therapeutic jurisprudence in Pakistan: a historical discourse (18 Aug 2017). SSRN. https://papers.ssrn.com/sol3/papers.cfm?abstract_id=3021643. Accessed 17 June 2017

Murrell H (2017) Therapeutic jurisprudence. Learned friends. http://learnedfriends.com.au/getmedia/601fdf90-4dfd-48e8-9425-616cbea333af/Therapeutic-Jurisprudence-H-Murrell.aspx. Accessed 17 June 2017

Padowitz K (2015) Psychology of law and criminal behaviour. http://www.psychology-criminalbehavior-law.com/2015/01/bipolar-disorder/. Accessed 17 June 2017

Pakistanlawsite (2018) Pakistanlawsite. http://www.pakistanlawsite.com/Login/MainPage. Accessed 28 Feb 2018

Syed Walayat Shah v Qaisar Mahmood (2015) Application No. 8/2012 (Muhammad Amir Munir, Additional District and Sessions Judge, Jhelum. 26 June 2015)

UNGA (1990) United Nations Standard Minimum Rules for Non-custodial Measures. 14 December. Tokyo, Japan. http://www.ohchr.org/Documents/ProfessionalInterest/tokyorules.pdf. Accessed 17 June 2017

Wexler DB (1993) Therapeutic jurisprudence and the criminal courts. William Mary Law Rev 35(1):279–299

Wexler DB (2000) Therapeutic jurisprudence: an overview. Thomas Cooley Law Rev 17:125–134

Wexler DB (2015) Moving forward on mainstreaming therapeutic jurisprudence: an ongoing process to facilitate the therapeutic design and application of the law. Arizona Legal Studies Discussion Paper No. 15–10. SSRN. https://papers.ssrn.com/sol3/papers.cfm?abstract_id=2564613. Accessed 17 June 2017

Muhammad Amir Munir holds an LLB and LLM from the University of the Punjab, Lahore. Presently, he is a Ph.D. law candidate at the International Islamic University, Islamabad. He is also a Fellow of the Commonwealth Judicial Education Institute, Canada. He is a trial judge both for civil and criminal cases of a serious nature (murder, rape, abduction, narcotics etc.) and also hears civil, criminal, family and rent appeals from the orders/judgments of courts of first instance. He has written on TJ and its application in Pakistan. He has also delivered lectures on juvenile law and its TJ potential both at the Federal and Punjab Judicial academies. In recent past, he has delivered joint presentations on TJ for almost 325 trainee judges/magistrates at the Punjab Judicial Academy with Prof David B Wexler (who joined from Puerto Rico through Skype). He is also a TJ practitioner and has written Guest Columns for the International Network on Therapeutic Jurisprudence (INTJ).

The #BlueWhale Challenge to the Indian Judiciary: A Critical Analysis of the Response of the Indian Higher Judiciary to Risky Online Contents with Special Reference to the BlueWhale Suicide Game

Debarati Halder

Abstract Since July 2017, shocking reports of suicides of teenagers and young adults started surfacing in Indian news media. These were unique because of their possible links with the notorious BlueWhale challenge, an online game, offering a 50 step challenge including suicide. The Madras High Court was the first High Court in India to take cognizance of the matter suo motu. Immediately after it, other High Courts in India were also approached by social cause lawyers through public interest litigations with similar prayers to direct the government and public stakeholders, including the intermediaries and website companies, to take preventive steps against the BlueWhale game. The multiplicity of the public interest litigations motivated the Supreme Court of India to take up the matter as one single matter, and it directed other High Courts not to deal with it to avoid a multiplicity of judicial responses. The case covered a tussle between the emotional intelligence of young people and the artificial intelligence used by the administrators and group members of the game to reach the teenagers and young adults and "trap" them in this dangerous game. This chapter analyses how the judges have responded to the issue and concludes with suggestions for sensitising the higher judiciary regarding the legal-technological issues involved in online games which may prove extremely dangerous for women and children. Finally, the chapter outlines the need for stricter judicial decision-making attitudes towards the liability of foreign hosted Internet service providers.

D. Halder (✉)
Unitedworld School of Law, Gandhinagar, India
e-mail: advocateresearcher@gmail.com

© Springer Nature Singapore Pte Ltd. 2018

T. Sourdin and A. Zariski (eds.), *The Responsive Judge*, Ius Gentium: Comparative Perspectives on Law and Justice 67, https://doi.org/10.1007/978-981-13-1023-2_10

1 Introduction

Post July 2017 the High Courts of Madras,[1] Calcutta,[2] Delhi (LiveLaw Network 2017a) and Bombay (PTI, Mumbai 2017) were one by one approached by social cause lawyers through public interest litigation praying for the same cause, i.e., directing the government to take steps to stop the BlueWhale suicide game and to direct the internet service providers to prevent circulation/creation/facilitating/uploading/downloading of the BlueWhale suicide game. While the Madras High Court, which took cognizance of the issue first, provided its detailed order for the public interest litigation ('the order'), other High Courts were directed by the Supreme Court of India not to deal with the matter as it had taken up the matter preferred by social cause lawyers with a prayer for directing the government specifically to improve "the filtering services at Indian shores like having firewalls in each cable landing station or having DNS blocking wall with brain scanner (at underground submarine optical fibre cable connecting the operators abroad) to be installed at Indian shores to prevent and filter the virtual online games which are harmful and life-threatening and morally degrading" (PTI 2017). This is probably the first time in Indian legal history that five High Courts of India, including three High Courts which were entrusted with the original jurisdiction since the inception of modern law and judiciary concept in India during the colonial rules, i.e., High Courts of Calcutta, Bombay and Madras were approached simultaneously for regulating the internet, which is largely regulated by the US laws and internet borne behaviour of children and youth. On 27th October 2017, the Supreme Court of India took up the matter for hearing and passed orders containing a set of directions to the government for taking steps to prevent the children and youth from playing dangerous online games and directing the intermediaries to take down any such gaming contents which will be detrimental to the children and youth (Express Web Desk 2017). This chapter considers judicial responses towards dealing with the public interest litigations related to online contents, especially BlueWhale games, the judicial understanding and sentencing policies in such cases and the positive and negative aspects of such sentencing policies (if any).

It is important to note that earlier social activists and cause lawyers had preferred public interest litigations on several issues related to public health and morality which had adversely affected children and women in general; consider the case of Kamalesh Vaswani versus Union of India and others (2013)[3] where the Supreme Court was approached for passing order to ban porn sites. It maintained a very mature judicial stand not to interfere with the personal choice of an adult to view porn contents within the four walls of his own room. Chief Justice H. L. Dattu in his order dated 8th July, 2015 observed that:

---

[1]The Registrar (Judicial), Madurai Bench of Madras High Court, Madurai versus The Secretary to Government, Union Ministry of Communications, Government of India, New India & others, Suo Motu W.P. (MD). No.16668 of 2017.

[2]In Re: Ayushman Foundation versus State Of West Bengal & Ors, W.P. No. 23537(W) of 2017.

[3]Writ Petition (Civil) No. 177/2013 in the Supreme Court of India.

> Such interim orders cannot be passed by this court. Somebody can come to the court and say 'Look, I am an adult and how can you stop me from watching it within the four walls of my room? It is a violation of Article 21 [right to life and personal liberty] of the Constitution.' Yes, the issue is serious and some steps need to be taken… the Centre has to take a stand… let us see what stand the Centre will take (Nanisetti 2015).

But at the same time, the court also did not neglect its duties to direct the government to take steps to ban the porn sites, especially those which contained child pornographic materials or which could have been easily accessible to children below 18 years of age because of the absence of a proper age filtering mechanism. As a result the Indian Ministry of Communication and Information Technology Department of Telecommunication, Government of India through its order dated 31 July 2015, blocked 857 websites which were stated to contain pornographic materials.[4] But the BlueWhale game phenomena is not something where the judges could distinguish between the danger of exposing children to sexually explicit contents online and allowing adult people's personal choice to view contents which will be sexually erotic (without knowingly harming anyone). It needed technical understanding of the online phenomena. Also, the issue called for judicial review of the government monitored system for counselling and preventing young inquisitive minds from falling into the dangerous trap of violent online games.

2 The BlueWhale Game Phenomena in India

Around the last week of July to the first week of August in 2017, Indian media was flooded with reports on suicides of children and youth due to the online game named "BlueWhale challenge". The suicide of a 14-year-old boy in Mumbai, India is presently the first known case of "taking the BlueWhale Challenge" (Vaktania 2017) of completing the final task of "jump off a high building. Take your life" (Sarkhel 2017). After this case, several suicides of teenagers and young adults were reported by the Indian media, which were also mentioned in the public interest litigation filed by one Gurmit Singh in the Delhi High Court (LiveLaw Network 2017a). The suicide cases in the above mentioned court cases show a similar trend, i.e., ending life by jumping off high rise buildings. In all cases, the media reports stated that the police investigations found a linkage with motivation to suicide which was communicated via websites including Facebook or digital messaging services like WhatsApp. The Madras High court in its order (in the nature of Mandamus) to the government stakeholders on creating a mechanism to block the online BlueWhale game and to spread awareness regarding the negative effects of such self-destructing online games, analysed the basis and structure of the BlueWhale challenge game on the basis of the information provided by the police and other stakeholders, which is worth mentioning here. According to paragraph 6 of the order, "The Blue Whale challenge is of fairly recent origin. It is believed to have been started in Russia in

[4]See Centre for Internet & Society (2015) for a copy of the order.

2013 and gained its notoriety among teenagers and more particularly, students. We are informed that this game was invented by a Russian Psychopath, who stated that he wanted "to clean the Society of those who are not fit to live". The judges further observed in the order as below:

> On account of the steps taken by the Central and State Governments, Blue Whale challenge is no longer downloadable. But then it continues to be played online. There is information that the game is even now available under other names such as 'A Silent House', 'Wake me up at 4.20 a.m' etc. It is played by using smartphones or similar devices. Cases of suicidal deaths because of this game are being reported throughout the world including India. On account of the intervention of the Police, there has been a case of rescue of a woman at Puduchery. It came to be known that she was using a Russian based social media platform known as "Vkontakte". This networking application is similar to Facebook and is available over Android, iOS and Windows platforms. But no direction can be issued by the Indian Authorities to "Vkontakte" as it is not governed by the laws of India … Even though Blue Whale game is no longer downloadable, it is still available. The administrator is able to reach out to the potential victims through what is known as "Over the top services" like Whatsapp, Telegram, Wickr, Silent Circle, osTel, ChatSecure, Signal, ShareIt etc. They can create closed communication/chatting fora which ensure anonymity of the users.[5]

The petitioner in the Delhi High Court public interest litigation case further provided that there are 50 tasks that are assigned to the gamers or challengers; these include taking dare devil steps and documenting them through selfies as "proof", such as waking up at early hours, locking themselves up in a dark room for several hours, watching a horror movie and listening to music sent by the curator/administrator to the player, climbing cranes, standing on the top of a high rise building, piercing a needle through one's own arms or legs, and jumping from a high rise building (LiveLaw News Network, 2017a). The list of these tasks is also available in the media reports on the BlueWhale suicide challenge.

However, it needs to be understood that the BlueWhale challenge game which was initially known as "Blue whale app" is not a software application like general "apps" which may be downloaded and run in computer devices. The term "app" was probably related by the media to associate it with online games which are generally available in the "play stores".[6] This is also supported by the response given to the Madras High Court's query to Google Play. As the Delhi High Court public interest litigation petition suggested (which is supported by the observation of the Madras High Court in its order), interested players may use hash-tags to attract the attention of administrators/curators, who would provide them links which may be clicked open for registering with email ID and/or phone numbers. This observation is supported by the reports of some journalists who did investigative journalism in this regard. One such journalist from Economic Times, India mentioned that he created multiple fake profiles of 17-year-old boys and girls and had used hashtags like #BlueWhalechallenge, #moderatorfindme, #F57, #IAmAWhale on social networking sites

[5]See paras. 12 & 13 of the order.

[6]According to Android Central (2016), "Google Play, which was originally born and referred to by Google as the Android Market, is Google's official store and portal for Android apps, games and other content for your Android-powered phone, tablet or Android TV device".

like VK, Twitter, Instagram, and Facebook to attract the attention of the administrators/curators. But he had remained unsuccessful as he was blocked by VK every time he created the profiles with such hashtags.[7] Some reports have suggested that once registered, the senders of the link may get unauthorised access to the digital data of the player (Ranjani 2017). The Madras High Court, however, observed in its order that once registered, the player would be instructed to provide personal details, photographs, email ID and a phone number. This means that the player's personal digital data would not be automatically accessed, but the players would be asked to provide this information as per the rules of the game. Further, as per the rules of the game, once registered, they would not be permitted to withdraw from the game. They have to complete the game.[8] The Madras High Court has also observed that it is more out of fear of future misuse of personal digital data that the players compulsorily take up the last challenge, i.e., ending life in the way suggested by the administrator/curator. The Madras High Court has also observed that there is a possibility of "customised" instructions from the curator/administrator in the player's country, depending upon the accessibility of high rise buildings by the players; this was proved in the suicide case of a youth from Madurai, who was reportedly asked to "hang" himself because apparently there were no high rise buildings near his place.[9] It may be observed that the main concern of the social cause lawyers and the courts in the BlueWhale game phenomena was the growing rate of suicides and self-harming among teenagers and young adults.

Whilst almost all reports, petitions, and the Madras High Court order, stated that the BlueWhale challenge phenomena may be new to India in 2017, this was not a new phenomena in other countries; for example, there has been reports from Russia, the UK and other European countries of teenagers reportedly getting involved in playing the BlueWhale challenge (Mann 2017). Several reports also suggested that the police had arrested two masterminds of the BlueWhale challenge game in Russia, and further investigations were going on (Mann 2017). The media reports suggest that one of the masterminds behind BlueWhale game was found to be a curator of the group and not the creator of the BlueWhale game.[10] However, several investigative journalistic reports have also refuted the connection between playing the BlueWhale challenge game and committing suicide due to a lack of proper police reports showing corroborative evidence of cause and results in this regard (Angiolino 2017).

---

[7] See para. 6 of the order.

[8] See para. 7 of the order.

[9] See para. 6 of the order.

[10] See Angiolino (2017) for more information.

2.1 *Deciding upon the Cause of Concern for Online Issues: A Challenge to the Judiciary*

Analysing the prayers in the public interest litigation petitions that were filed to several High Courts, including the Supreme Court and the concern of the Madras High Court in its suo motu public interest litigation, it may be seen that the main concern was the psychological vulnerability of the teenagers and young adults that was being affected through such mind challenging games. However, the social cause lawyers and the courts were also concerned about creating preventive mechanisms to stop the accessibility of such online games by young people. Clearly, there are two issues wrapped up in one that threw challenge to the Indian judiciary: one is related to framing policy guidelines to control the adolescent and young adults from becoming victims of "challenges" to win and one is related to controlling the Information Technology networks as per the Indian laws for preventing circulation of contents which may divert young minds towards dangerous ends. While the first may be an easier task for the Indian judiciary, the second is not so easy because of involvement of numerous issues including lack of technical understanding, presence of services providers who claim to be ruled by foreign laws, and lack of cross border treaties for cyber issues especially in this regard. The higher judiciary in India had earlier provided certain landmark judgements regarding regulating people's behaviour online. In certain cases, the Supreme Court had been lenient towards the behaviour of people online and refused to abide by the strict laws enacted by the legislature.

One such example could be the case of *Shreya Singhal Versus Union of India*, 2012,[11] where the Supreme Court showed its concern for people's right to speech, especially the right to criticise the government over S.66A of the *Information Technology Act*, 2000 (amended in 2008) which prescribed punishment for annoying, insulting, intimidating etc. speech. A brief overview of the facts of the case may be worth mentioning here: after the death of Bal Thackeray, the political supremo of Shiv Sena, a regional political party having its ideological base on Hindu nationalism, the Shiv Sena party members called for a "Mumbai bandh" or shutdown of the city of Mumbai in memory of Thackeray. One young woman from Mumbai in her Facebook timeline commented on such decision on shutdown of Mumbai city on the occasion of the death of Thackeray. Her friend showed thumbs up for the comment. Within a few hours of posting the comment and the thumbs up, the police arrested both of the women on the charge of posting annoying, insulting comments against Thackeray and sedition. Noticeably, the charge was made mainly on S.66A of the *Information Technology Act* which, due to its poor framing, gave a long hand to everyone and anyone to lodge a police complaint for speech which the complainant feels is offensive within the meaning of the section. This author in her earlier article on the analysis of the Supreme court judgement on S.66A of the Information Technology Act has shown that such complaints based on S.66A of the Information Technology Act were made largely by political party leaders and workers who

[11] WP. (criminal) no.167 of 2012.

wanted to curb speech against their political ideologies (Halder 2015). While the lawyers for the petitioner were successful in drawing the judges' attention to the misuse of the provision as a whole, judges were more concerned about the abuse of law by the government machinery in the name of restrictions of freedom of speech which has been given the status of a fundamental right under Art 19(1)(A) of the Indian Constitution. The judges' response to the "promises" made by the defence lawyers representing the government to execute the said provision with caution is noteworthy here. They observed "Governments may come and Governments may go but Section 66A goes on forever. An assurance from the present Government even if carried out faithfully would not bind any successor Government. It must, therefore, be held that Section 66A must be judged on its own merits without any reference to how well it may be administered."[12]As such, the judges were clearly anticipating another clamp down on freedom of speech which had occurred during the emergency period in the 1970's in the regime of the then Prime Minister Indira Gandhi (Rajagopal 2011). The court in Singhal's case definitely did not want to neglect the judgement in *Bennett Coleman & Co. & Ors. v. Union of India & Ors.* 1973,[13] which secured people's right to criticise the government and press freedom in India against the arbitrary legislations created at the whims of the Prime Minister to restrict publication of any information and freedom to criticise the government. But this author in her earlier publication criticised this point of view of the court, which according to her was extremely narrow. Her observation in this regard was as follows:

> … the trends of the cybercrimes that are presently recognised by the Indian criminal justice system, can also be found in various other legislations like the Indian Penal Code or the Protection of children from sexual offences Act, 2012, or Protection of Women from Sexual Harassment at Workplace Act, 2013 or in the Indecent representation of women (Prohibition) Act, 1986. The decision of rejection of the constitutionality of Section 66A by the Supreme Court in the case of Shreya Singhal also relied on these facts. 47 But the author argues that the provisions dealing with offences under Chapter XI of the Information Technology Act or any other laws currently in force for that matter are not fully equipped to deal with online crimes, especially when 'bad talk' is involved. The court did not consider examining the scope of such laws elaborately while deciding the fate of Section 66A. The court however put much emphasis on the issue of right to information, especially information regarding public officials, political decisions affecting public welfare etc., which may fall well within the scope of Art. 19(1) of the Constitution, as well as within the exceptions mentioned in Section 499 IPC. This is evident from the myriad of judgments; including foreign judgments cited in the Singhal's case. But a brief over view of the judgement may show that there are several issues which the Court did not address or left unattended while judging the necessity of the existence of Section 66A. One such issue is the decision or the lack of on the type of "information" that may not be considered as open to be viewed by cyber bystanders. In the cyber space communication, certain information may essentially involve questions of privacy. Chilling of speech becomes essential when such privacy is infringed. Internet speech can become viral in nature if the harasser wishes to gather more viewers to witness humiliation of the victim. If such information consists of speech which may turn its character from a 'free speech' to a dangerous information due to the viral nature of the internet, 48

[12]See p. 96 of the order of the court in *Shreya Singhal Versus Union of India* (2012).

[13]Bennett Coleman & Co. & Ors. v. Union of India & Ors., [1973] 2 S.C.R. 757 at 829.

> the person who makes such speech must be made liable for punishment, depending upon his prior knowledge about the consequence of such use of internet. Further, the Information Technology Act has vested responsibility of investigation of 'any' case under this Act to 'any officer not below the rank of an inspector'. Also, cases punishable with three years imprisonment or more have been made cognizable offences. It is a hard truth that majority of the police officers in the rank of inspectors in India lack proper training to handle cases related to cybercrime. The author argues that both these provisions cushioned the misuse of Section 66A by stake holders who may have used the ignorance of the criminal justice machinery. The court should have paid more consideration to the effect of these provisions while deciding the fate of 66A (Halder 2015, 120–121).

But unlike Singhal's case, in *Kamalesh Vaswani versus Union of India & others*,[14] the court was concerned with two different issues: one was regarding the personal right of adult individuals to view erotica contents privately and the other was related to legislative and executive efforts to curb circulation of obscene, sexually explicit contents. It needs to be understood that right to view sexual erotica contents has not been recognised as a fundamental right, neither has it been recognised as a separate statutory right in India. It is rather a much suppressed and typically "private" right under Art 21 of the constitution guaranteeing right to life and liberty. This is considered as a right flowing from the right to marry and found a family under Art 16 of the Universal Declaration of Human Rights, which states that "(1) Men and women of full age, without any limitation due to race, nationality or religion, have the right to marry and to found a family. They are entitled to equal rights as to marriage, during marriage and at its dissolution. (2) Marriage shall be entered into only with the free and full consent of the intending spouses. (3) The family is the natural and fundamental group unit of society and is entitled to protection by society and the State." The right to watch sexual erotica content by adults privately and without harming others may be considered as an obvious component to the reproductive rights. However, in India watching sexual erotica has been considered a moral wrong even though world-wise India is the first producer of sexual erotica for the purpose of personal enjoyment as well as for reproduction in the form of the ancient text Kama Sutra, as well as ancient sculptures especially in Khajuraho Temple (Bastia 2006). But the cyber era legislations, however, made an attempt to distinguish between creation/publication/distribution of sexual erotica content which may be sexually explicit or obscene and watching the same for scientific and other purposes (which very well fits in the essential element of the right to reproduction) and for offensive purposes. This is apparent from the exceptions to the offences mentioned in Ss. 67[15] and 67A[16] of the *Information Technology Act*, 2000 (amended in 2008) which states as follows:

[14]Writ Petition (Civil) No. 177/2013 in the Supreme Court of India.

[15]See S.67 of the Information Technology Act, 2000 (amended in 2008) which speaks about punishment for publishing or transmitting obscene material in electronic form.

[16]See S.67A of the Information Technology Act, 2000 (amended in 2008) which speaks about punishment for publishing or transmitting material containing sexually explicit acts, etc. in electronic form.

> This section and section 67 does not extend to any book, pamphlet, paper, writing, drawing, painting, representation or figure in electronic form-(i) the publication of which is proved to be justified as being for the public good on the ground that such book, pamphlet, paper, writing, drawing, painting, representation or figure is in the interest of science, literature, art, or learning or other objects of general concern; or (ii) which is kept or used bona fide for religious purposes.

The court in Vaswani's case relied upon the personal rights to watch sexual erotica from this aspect as well. But at the same time, the court wanted to shift the responsibility of detecting and blocking websites containing child pornography and child sexual abuse to the executive through its technical committees. Unfortunately the executive failed to execute this duty with expertise and blocked more than 850 websites some of which were not offensive and were meant for adult entertaining. The government faced huge criticism for such a ban without properly detecting the contents and the websites' policies to take down offensive and child pornographic contents (Khomami 2015).

However, in the Re Prajwala case,[17] the court showed its concern not for the personal right to view sexual erotica, but for developing a preventive mechanism to prevent wide circulation of sexual abuse videos. Before delving into the facts of the case, it would be necessary to know about certain procedural issues for public interest litigations for the cause of women and children. India has an orthodox social setup which does not necessarily allow women to report crimes including sexual victimisation, domestic violence and harassment, and inhuman condition of living. During the 1970s–80s, two judges of the Supreme Court, namely Justices P. N. Bhagwati and Krishna Iyer, created a silent revolution in the field of public interest litigation in India by way of judicial activism for the cause of groups of people who fall in the socially and economically weaker sections by broadening the concept of locus standi. This group of special beneficiaries also included women and children because it was understood by the judges that they may not be able to access justice easily even though their families (excluding them) may be able to access the same through private interest litigations. Especially Justice P. N. Bhagawati, therefore, delivered a landmark judgment in allowing letter petitions as a mechanism to access justice, especially in matters concerning women and children (Baxi 1985). This tradition of accessing the courts for women and children's interests through letter petition has gone through reforms from the docket management perspective: these letters, addressed to the senior judges of the Supreme Court or the High Courts generally go through the court's administrative sections where the contents of the litigations as stated in the letters are screened by senior court officers. This not only saves time for the court, but may also distinguish genuine cases from frivolous cases.[18]

Suo motu cases by the courts originating from journalistic reports, have specifically been considered in sexual offence cases and cases involving gross violations of

[17]SMW (Crl.) No(S).3/2015 In Re: Prajwala Letter Dated 18.2.2015 Videos Of Sexual Violence And Recommendations.

[18]It is an unfortunate fact that the concept of public interest litigations has been subjected to wide range misuse for gaining publicity by the petitioner. A recent report suggested that the Chief Justice of India has taken strong note of the same. See LiveLaw (2017b) for more information.

women's and children's rights. This is evident from the research of Galanter (2014) who analysed the Indian Supreme Court's initiative to take up suo motu cases to ensure justice in regard to inter caste love marriages, intervention by the Khap panchayats and rapes. Prajwala's case involves one such letter petition which complained about widely spreading gang rape videos, rape videos and child pornographic contents through various content hosting platforms, social media platforms and search engines. This case is mentionable for two specific reasons: the judicial understanding related to the acceptance of letter petition for the cause of women and children regarding cyber victimisation and cyber aided victimisation, and the judicial understanding for the solution of the issue through the public-private partnership. The letter petition mentioned specifically about WhatsApp as a mechanism to spread the rape and gang rape videos and child porn contents. Interestingly WhatsApp, an instant digital messaging service available for android phones, is extremely popular among the Indian users and at the same time has a notorious review because of its nil reporting mechanism for offensive contents. As such, while in other content hosting platforms and social media platforms like Facebook, a cyber victim as well as a bystander can not only block the offender, but also report offensive content to the website, WhatsApp does not allow reporting the content and the content sender to the company. It allows only privately blocking the sender of content. As a result, the, the content may float through different users if the content has been forwarded to multiple users (Halder and Jaishankar 2016).

The judges in their latest order showed their concern towards the effectiveness of the proposals and recommendations offered by the government and the website companies for developing a mechanism to prevent circulation of offensive videos. In the order dated 23rd October 2017, the court acknowledged the creation of the committee under the chairmanship of the executive secretary of the Ministry of Electronics and Information Technology, as was directed by the court in its earlier order, and the consensus that had been reached by the government and private stakeholders in the form of proposals and recommendations.[19] These proposals and recommendations included expanding the list of the key words on the websites concerned, so that the detection of the offensive contents would be easier; the proposals also included creation of the key words in the Indian languages, creating administrative mechanism to facilitate reporting, conferring more responsibilities on the websites for acting on the reports of rape videos that may be given by civil society members, taking down the contents, and the creation of the photo-DNA data bank to act on the complaints of the victims faster and more effectively. It may be seen in the order that the judges could recognise the need for assistance of the expert committee to address this issue and the necessity for the united efforts of the legislative, administrative and judiciary in this issue. However, the judges did not put major emphasis upon awareness creation by the government and private stakeholders, including the NGOs, to not share such offensive videos as a mechanism for public shaming. Rather, the recent order showed that the judges were more concerned about the technical understanding of

[19]The proposals and recommendations can be seen in the order copy: SMW (Crl.) No(s).3/2015 In Re: Prajwala Letter Dated 18.2.2015 Videos Of Sexual Violence And Recommendations.

the issue by the expert committee and the possibilities of curbing the issue by developing effective digital technology. But at the same time, the judges did not put much emphasis on the enactment of cross border treaties to facilitate the investigation and arrest of perpetrators staying in different jurisdictions. It is presumed that the judges may have been more concerned about speedy development of a technical mechanism with the available resources for addressing the burning issue, rather than involving diplomatic involvement for the enactment of treaties which may take more time and cordial political relationships between stakeholder countries and organisations.

In the BlueWhale case, the judges of the Supreme court, however, neither put much emphasis on the enactment of treaties, nor on stricter enactment of new laws related to intermediary liability or enforcement of existing laws in this regard.

3 The BlueWhale Challenge to the Judiciary

Unlike the other cases, the BlueWhale issue was dealt with by the Madras High Court first. Thereafter the Supreme Court also took up the matter, not as an appeal against the judgment of the Madras High court, but as an independent matter. This author therefore feels that the responses of both courts must be analysed to understand the judicial response in this regard.

The Madras High Court was the first judicial authority to provide a comprehensive judgment on the BlueWhale challenge. A brief reading of the order of the court dated 12th September 2017, would show that the judges took suo-motu cognizance of the BlueWhale challenge following a newspaper report of the suicide of a 19-year-old boy. The reason behind such suo motu action was the unique reason behind the boy's suicide and the inability of the police to proceed further in arresting the abettor because of no possible way to approach the latter. The judges, while going through the facts of the suicide case and analysing the possible connection between the suicide and the BlueWhale challenge, also arrived at a disturbing understanding that teenagers and young adults are getting connected with curators/administrators of the group who would provide customised directions regarding the process to take up the final challenge and end their lives to suit the Indian conditions.[20] The court felt it was pertinent to add 14 respondents, including the central government department of the computer emergency response team of the ministry of communication, the police department, especially the cyber crime cell, the department of social welfare, and school education and other stake holders including educational and research institutes who had been working on cyber security and the mental health of the young people, because the judges understood that this not only involved questions of data privacy, but also general behaviour of new age youngsters who may use cyber space to beat depression and frustration. It may be pertinent that both the Indian penal code and the Indian Information Technology Act, 2000 (amended in 2008) provide provisions for arresting the abettor for crimes: the former for any offence, including

[20]See p. 12 of the order.

for committing suicide,[21] and the latter, for abetting to commit any offence.[22] But the Madras High Court did not show reliance on these provisions. Rather, the judges were more concerned with the responsibility of the service providers to block the circulation of the content related to the BlueWhale Suicide challenge. It may also be pertinent to note that the Information Technology Act provides extra territorial jurisdiction for addressing offences. The Act also holds the intermediary responsible for failing in its due diligence under S.79(3) of the Information Technology Act.[23]

The Madras High Court, while analysing the responsibility of Google India as a service provider under the above mentioned provision, observed that Google India denied all responsibility in this matter.[24] However, as discussed above, it is necessary to note that later investigations revealed that Google as a web company may not be liable for the creation of any BlueWhale Suicide app because the challenge game was not an application within the meaning of apps. The court, however, openly acknowledged the fact that neither of the judges was well versed in the digital technology and hence they largely relied on the expert comments of police officers who had knowledge of cyber security. But still then, they also acknowledged the fact that even the police are clueless due to the apparent non-cooperation of the service providers. The judges, however, were also concerned about loose policies of data protection, as are provided by the service providers, and observed that if curators/administrators can reach out to possible challengers on the basis of well framed keywords (which were probably created and circulated by the BlueWhale challenge creator/s), and could influence the players to take extreme steps like ending their lives in a way which can be availed by the players easily, then terror outfits may find such loose policy guidelines appropriate to target Indian young people to radicalise and create large scale destructive operations.

One of the interesting points to be noted in this specific order was the understanding of the judges regarding the web companies constant ignorance of the duty to abide by the laws of the victim's country in regards to the service provider's liability to exercise due diligence regarding offensive contents. It may be pertinent to note that website companies and search engines like Facebook, Twitter, WhatsApp, and Google are hosted in the US and are governed mainly by US laws. The immunity provisions regarding third party liability for any content is therefore also regulated by US laws. This author in her Ph.D. thesis had made extensive observation regarding such immunity cloak of the web service providers and the related effects of the same in the countries of the victims: her observation is as follows:

> Edwards (2011), pointed out that as per the US laws, the internet service providers and hosts can get two distinct types of immunities (i) immunity covering all types of liability materials except liability regarding the copyright infringements; and (ii) immunity covering materials

[21]See S.306 of the Indian Penal Code which defines abetment of suicide.

[22]See S.84B of the Information Technology Act which prescribes punishment for abetting an offence.

[23]See S.79 of the Information Technology Act, which speaks about nil liability of the intermediaries and the exceptions to this rule.

[24]See p. 7 of the order.

> that infringe copyrights. While the first type of immunity is covered by section 230© of the Communication Decency Act, codified at 47USC,150 the second type of liability is covered by Digital Millennium Copyright Act (DMCA) Title 512. Section 230 of the CDA under clause © with the heading "Protection for 'Good Samaritan' Blocking and Screening of Offensive Material" in sub clause (1) exempts the service providers and hosts as publishers or speakers of any information provided by any user and declares that "no provider or user of an interactive computer service shall be treated as the publisher or speaker of any information provided by another information content provider". Saying this, the law further strengthens the stand of the provider of the Interactive computer service regarding civil liability through sub clause (2) it states "no provider or user of an interactive computer service shall be held liable on account of (A) any action voluntarily taken in good faith to restrict access to or availability of material that the provider or user considers to be obscene, lewd, lascivious, filthy, excessively violent, harassing, or otherwise objectionable, whether or not such material is constitutionally protected; or (B) any action taken to enable or make available to information content providers or others the technical means to restrict access to material described in paragraph (1)". Thus as it can be seen, section 230(c) of the CDA in one hand gives the immunity to the provider and host of the interactive computer services from being considered as the publisher or speaker of any information that is published through the services by any other content provider; on the other hand it restricts any civil and also criminal liability on the provider for the "good Samaritan" action for either restricting any access to or availability of any material that the provider considers unwanted, or enabling or providing information to the 'content providers' about the technical means to restrict access to the materials discussed above, which are often seen as safety measures and buttons to block, report etc. available in the social networking sites. It needs to be pointed out that section 230(c) of the CDA is exercised by the ISPs and hosts to resist defamation based cases from the users as well as victims who may be non users. The greatest example of this could be Doe v. MySpace, where the court held that the case fell under typical characteristics of the section 230, CDA and it attracted the provisions on the said provision as the dispute was actually based over the content published in the site MySpace and negligence on the part of the site for content filtering or screening. Apart from this, section 230 CDA immunes the actions of the providers and host in regards to "editorial functions" (Donato v. Moldow, 865 A.2d 711 (N.J. Super. Ct. 2005), such as editing the content, removing the content for want to accuracy etc.; encouraging users to submit content on particular aspect (Best Western International, Inc. v. Furber, No. CV-06-1537 (D. Ariz. Sept. 5, 2008);158 paying third party for creating or submitting any content when the third party is not the employee of the site (Blumenthal v. Drudge, 992 F. Supp. 44 (D.D.C. 1998);159 providing "neutral forms" for submission of content by the user/s (Prickett v. info USA, Inc., 2006 WL 887431 (E.D. Tex. Mar. 30, 2006);160 not removing the content even after the provider has received private "defamatory notice" from any individual (Zeran v. America Online, Inc., 129 F.3d 327 (4th Cir. 1997)161 etc. However, in the last case, if the provider of the services promises in the site's terms and conditions to remove the content after receiving such defamatory notice, and he fails to remove the same after receipt of the said notice, he may not avail the benefits of the immunity clause of section 230 CDA for failure on the rounds of promissory estoppels (Barnes v. Yahoo!, Inc., 570 F.3d 1096 (9th Cir. 2009).162 (Halder 2013, 116-118).

The author further observed as follows:

> … immunity clause provided by section 230CDA has been the basis for preparations of the user's activities regarding uploading the content and SNWSs limits of liabilities towards judging the righteousness of such contents. Title 512 of the DMCA on the other hand looks after the issues involving copyright infringements in the interactive computer services and the service providers can be said to have exercised "due diligence" to avail the immunity in case of infringement of materials hosted in their website, as has been set out in the said provision, when they have fulfilled the following basic conditions:

- The provider must not have the requisite level of knowledge of the infringing activity.
- If the provider has the right and ability to control the infringing activity, it must not receive a financial benefit directly attributable to the infringing activity.
- Upon receiving proper notification of claimed infringement, the provider must expeditiously take down or block access to the material (Halder 2013, 118–119).

The author further observed that:

> … All of these websites specifically provide in their "report abuse section" that if the victims claim for victimisation due to any violation of policies by other users, and the same claim is not seen as violation of the policies as per the laws of California and also in the light of free speech guarantee, the victims must bring court order, seeking account information. This may include search warrant, court orders to remove content or subpoenas. Only in this clause the websites indicate about abiding by the laws of the land of the victim (Halder 2013, 119–120).

The understanding of the judges of the Madras High Court relating to the liability of the service providers regarding the content consisting of violent online game is at par with the above mentioned observation of this author. Assuming that the websites concerned will continue to ignore the laws of the land by promising only "monitoring" of the issue, the judges also observed that it is high time that service providers should be brought within the regulatory framework of the law of the land to restrict the floating of dangerous contents within the jurisdiction of India in the web platforms hosted in the US. In short, the court wanted to impose domestic laws on the US hosted web companies for their failure to restrict the floating of dangerous and offensive contents from other jurisdictions within Indian cyber space. This understanding was reached in the case of *Google Spain Versus Agencia Espanola* (2014) whereby the Court of Justice of the European Union ruled that "an Internet search engine operator is responsible for the processing that it carries out of personal data which appear on web pages published by third parties" (Court of Justice of the European Union 2014).

Simultaneously, the court also showed its concern towards growing emotional distance between teenagers and young adults and their families, especially parents. In an era when both parents are busy in their respective workplaces, such distance becomes obvious. Modern Indian social structure hardly includes joint families residing in the same house. The nuclear family set up makes both the parents and the children live in their own worlds with their own happiness and frustration and their own procedures to enjoy or beat such frustrations. The judges in this case took special note of these modern phenomena and instead of holding parents absolutely liable for the addiction of their children to take up such risky online challenges, directed the social welfare departments to spread awareness through schools and NGOs. This is indeed commendable because the court showed maturity to engage the government and private stakeholders along with the parents in educating children about the dangers of online predators in the name of online games.

It needs to be noted that the Madras High Court judgement was the last comprehensive response of the higher judiciary in regard to the BlueWhale challenge game before the issue would be taken up by the Supreme Court of India. But unlike Prajwala's case, the gravity of the issue was judged to be of prime importance because this involved the challenge between the welfare of children, their emotional intelligence and artificial intelligence, which proved extremely dangerous for young people. Hence in the Supreme Court of India, the coram of judges included senior most judges including the Chief Justice of India, and Justice D. Y Chandrachud who was an instrumental force in making the right to privacy a fundamental right under Art 21.[25] The judges in the BlueWhale suicide case did not want to disturb the observation of the Madras High Court regarding the necessity to grow cyber security measures to restrict the flowing of offensive contents within Indian cyber space and the liability of the services providers. A plain reading of their order dated 27th October 2017 on the issue of the BlueWhale suicide game may show that while the judges shifted the responsibility of creating a mechanism to detect the contents of the game and prevent the same from reaching the Indian users, including teenagers and young adults, to the government departments managing information and communication technology, they laid more emphasis on public awareness regarding the dangers of such violent games.[26]

The Supreme Court would further show that the judges preferred national television channels to create awareness materials in consultation with the ministry of women and child development. This is because the judges felt that children and their parents in different parts of India must be reached through audio visual media, especially television. They necessarily felt that in several families, adults may be completely unaware about the perils of information and digital communication technology due to lack of education and awareness. But simultaneously, children may be cyber smart and reach out to strangers to prove heroism or even to overcome low levels of confidence, without understanding the vicious effects of the dark web. It may be seen that the Supreme Court restricted its role in directing the government stakeholders to develop a proper preventive mechanism in this regard; the judges neither touched the issue of enacting mutual assisting treaties with other countries for eliminating the problem from the roots, or for creating strict precedence to make the web-service providers liable, like the Irish High Court which ordered Facebook to pay compensation to a 14-year-old girl who was victimised by way of revenge porn in Facebook. The news media report on this issue states that the victim sought damages from Facebook, as the service provider, for negligence, misuse of private information and breach of the Data Protection Act (IANS 2018). The response of the judges in India was more towards securing the welfare of the children and not going into technical post mortem of informational-technological reasons for a group of people from unknown destinations to access the information of youngsters and continue to coerce them to remain trapped in the dangerous challenges.

[25] See Writ Petition (Civil) No. 494/2012 in the Supreme Court of India.

[26] See Writ Petition (Civil) No. 872/2017 in the Supreme Court of India.

4 Conclusion

An unfortunate truth that haunts the efficiency of the higher judiciary in India is a lack of proper and basic understanding of the information and digital technology and its related effects on laws regulating corporate behaviour as well as human behaviour. In other countries, the judges have taken positive steps when it comes to regulating the elasticity of immunity clauses in the policies of US hosted web companies. This is evident from cases like the Google Spain case (Court of Justice of the European Union 2014). But India's higher judiciary has hardly taken similar steps on the liability of the web service providers, even though the Indian legislation under S.69(b)(4) of the Information Technology Act, 2000, amended in 2008, provides for punishment for the intermediary for intentionally failing to provide technical assistance and extend all facilities to government agencies to enable online access or to secure and provide online access to the computer resource generating, transmitting, receiving or storing traffic data or information.

This author argues that this attitude of the Indian higher judiciary towards the foreign web service providing companies has made them continue to ignore the domestic legal provisions by providing a monotonous fruitless promise to practice due diligence in monitoring the issue. While the thoughtful and therapeutic response of the judges by way of directing the public and private stakeholders to spread awareness about the perils of the BlueWhale suicide challenge game is commendable, it is suggested that the judges should also throw light on developing judicial mechanisms to regulate the negligent attitude of the web service providers. Further, it is essential that judges of the higher judiciary also encourage research, seminars and workshops of cyber related issues concerning the safety of women and children. But this author further opines that the purpose of such seminars or workshops would become meaningless if the judges of the higher judiciary do not join these seminars as participants. In India it has become a trend for the judicial academies, law schools and private seminar/conference organisers to invite the members of the higher judiciary as key-note speakers and chief guests. This makes the judges speak about their own experiences and ways of settling the matters. But they are hardly receptive of the researches and suggestions made by legal academia and independent researchers. This makes the judges rely more on submissions and opinions made by legal practitioners, police officers or private practitioners of cyber security which may lack scientific research. This further restricts the transfer of ideas from researchers, professors, lawyers and judges who are also restorative justice practitioners from within the country as well as from abroad.

It can be further observed that the training academies for judges, including the judicial academies, may arrange for conferences as part of their curriculum. For example, the National Judicial Academy of India, Bhopal, conducts several national workshops and seminars where trainee judges and acting judges are sensitised about court procedures, new laws and social phenomena (Himachal Pradesh Judicial Academy 2011). Nevertheless, some judges may not participate in the academic conferences as receivers of knowledge while in service. This may be due to several reasons including a self-built ego of being a judge in the courts of law, or codes of conduct that prevent the judge from participating in any conference as a 'learner/participant' without the order of the superior judges. However, this attitude of judiciary may be contrasted with the situation in the United States, if, for example, reference is made to the explanatory comments under Rule 3.14 of the Code of Judicial Conduct of Connecticut (2011). The Code provides: "Judges are encouraged to attend educational programs, as both teachers and participants, in law related and academic disciplines, in furtherance of their duty to remain competent in the law. Participation in a variety of other extrajudicial activity is also permitted and encouraged by this Code." Such codes of conducts may make it mandatory for judges to participate in academic (and not necessarily judicial) seminars and conference as learner/participants to broaden their knowledge. It is therefore suggested that members of the higher judiciary may consider participating more in therapeutic justice or restorative justice seminars or workshops on cyber crimes and effective legal ways to deal with the same.

References

Android Central (2016) Google Play Store. https://www.androidcentral.com/google-play-store/home. Accessed 23 Feb 2018

Angiolino A (2017) The man who stopped the Blue Whale hoax in Bulgaria: an interview with Georgi Apostolov. http://www.gioconomicon.net/modules.php?name=News&file=article&sid=9088&title=ecco-chi-ha-fermato-la-bufala-del-blue-whale-in-bulgaria#EnglishArticle. Accessed 15 Sept 2017

Bastia BK (2006) Socio-cultural aspect of sexual practices and sexual offences—an Indian scenario. J Clin Forensic Med 13(4):208–210

Baxi U (1985) Taking suffering seriously: social action litigation in the Supreme Court of India. Third World Leg Stud 4(6):107–132

Centre for Internet & Society (2015) DOT order blocking 857 websites on grounds of decency and morality. Centre for Internet & Society, 31 July. http://cis-india.org/internet-governance/resources/dot-morality-block-order-2015-07-31/view. Accessed 1 Jan 2018

Court of Justice of the European Union (2014) Judgment in Case C-131/12 Google Spain SL, Google Inc. v Agencia Española de Protección de Datos, Mario Costeja González (Press Release, No. 70/14, Luxembourg, 13 May). https://curia.europa.eu/jcms/upload/docs/application/pdf/2014-05/cp140070en.pdf. Accessed 12 Sept 2017

Express Web Desk (2017) Blue Whale challenge: Supreme Court wants DD to air programme; this is what other courts have ordered. The Indian Express, 27 Oct. http://indianexpress.com/article/india/blue-whale-challenge-supreme-court-wants-dd-to-air-programme-this-is-what-other-courts-have-ordered-4908861/. Accessed 27 Oct 2017

Galanter Marc (2014) Snakes and ladders: Suo Moto, intervention and the Indian judiciary. FIU Law Rev 10(1):69–83

Halder D (2013) Cyber socialising and victimisation of women: a comparative analysis of laws in India, UK and Canada (Unpublished PhD thesis submitted to National Law School of India University, Bangalore)

Halder D (2015) A retrospective analysis of S.66a: could S.66a of the information technology act be reconsidered for regulating 'bad talk' in the internet? Indian Student Law Rev (ISLR) 3:91–118

Halder D, Jaishankar K (2016) Cyber crime against women in India. Sage Publications, New Delhi

Himachal Pradesh Judicial Academy (2011) Judicial ethics and conduct of judicial officers. http://hpsja.nic.in/ethics.pdf. Accessed 12 Jan 2018

IANS (2018) Irish teenager wins Facebook payout over revenge porn. Business Standard, 2 Jan. http://www.business-standard.com/article/news-ians/irish-teenager-wins-facebook-payout-over-revenge-porn-118011200349_1.html. Accessed 18 Jan 2018
Khomami N (2015) India lifts ban on internet pornography after criticism. The Guardian, 5 Aug. https://www.theguardian.com/culture/2015/aug/05/india-lifts-ban-on-internet-pornography-after-criticisms on 5 Aug 2017. Accessed 10 Sept 2017
LiveLaw News Network (2017a) PIL filed in Delhi HC against 'Blue Whale Challenge'. Live Law News Network, 16 Aug. http://www.livelaw.in/pil-filed-delhi-hc-blue-whale-challenge-read-petition/. Accessed 16 Sept 2017
LiveLaw News Network (2017b) CJI fumes at Rampant misuse of PILs. Live Law News Network, 28 Oct. http://www.livelaw.in/cji-fumes-rampant-misuse-pils/. Accessed 28 Oct 2017
Mann T (2017) Girl, 17, exposed as being mastermind behind Blue Whale suicide game. Metro, 30 Aug. http://metro.co.uk/2017/08/30/girl-17-exposed-as-being-mastermind-behind-blue-whale-suicide-game-6889363/. Accessed 16 Sept 2017
Nanisetti S (2015) Is watching porn a fundamental right? The New Indian Express, July 10. http://www.newindianexpress.com/cities/hyderabad/Is-Watching-Porn-a-Fundamental-Right/2015/07/10/article2911541.ece. Accessed 1 Jan 2018
PTI Mumbai (2017) HC refuses to hear PIL on Blue Whale as matter is before SC. Business Standard, 21 Sept. http://www.business-standard.com/article/pti-stories/hc-refuses-to-hear-pil-on-blue-whale-as-matter-is-before-sc-117092100882_1.html. Accessed 21 Sept 2017
PTI (2017) SC seeks government's reply on plea to firewall Blue Whale game. The Hindu, 13 Oct. http://www.thehindu.com/news/national/sc-seeks-governments-reply-on-plea-to-firewall-blue-whale-game/article19852049.ece. Accessed 13 Oct 2017
Rajagopal A (2011) The emergency as prehistory of the new Indian middle class. Mod Asian Stud 45(5):1003–1049
Ranjani L (2017) Blue Whale Challenge: at least 75 whalers in Tamil Nadu's Madurai. Indian Express, 1 Sept. http://www.newindianexpress.com/states/tamil-nadu/2017/sep/01/blue-whale-challenge-at-least-75-whalers-in-tamil-nadus-madurai-1651006–1.html. Accessed 23 Sept 2017
Sarkhel A (2017) Another teen dies but is it really because of Blue Whale Challenge. India Times, 12 Sept. https://tech.economictimes.indiatimes.com/news/internet/another-teen-dies-but-is-it-really-because-of-blue-whale-challenge/60049646. Accessed 15 Sept 2017
Secretary of the State of Connecticut (2011) Code of judicial conduct. https://www.jud.ct.gov/Publications/PracticeBook/Judicial_Conduct.pdf. Accessed 12 Jan 2018
Vaktania S (2017) Blue Whale suicide: 'Only thing you'd be left with is a picture of me', wrote Mumbai teen who jumped to death. India Today, 31 July. http://indiatoday.intoday.in/story/mumbai-suicide-boy-kills-self-teenager-suicide-andheri-blue-whale-online-game-online-challenge-bluewhale/1/1015159.html. Accessed 15 Sept 2017

Debarati Halder (LL.B., LL.M., Ph.D. (Law) (NLSIU, Bangalore)) is presently working as a Professor at Unitedworld School of Law, GandhiNagar, Gujarat. Dr. Halder is the Honorary Managing Director, Centre for Cyber Victim Counselling, and also the founding Secretary of the South Asian Society of Criminology and Victimology.

The Responsive Judge: Comparative Perspectives of Korea and Japan

Young Hoa Jung

Abstract This chapter begins by outlining the legal culture of citizens, judges, and courts in two countries' modern history—that of Korea and Japan. It first examines the Constitutional Court of Korea as compared to the Supreme Court of Japan, focusing on the role and function of constitutional adjudication and examining the judicial responsiveness of each through judicial review of legislation. The chapter then examines the judiciaries of each country in their role as adjudicators of litigants' rights through civil litigation. The core of this chapter is an evaluation of the most significant features of the Korean and Japanese judiciaries in these legal areas—the activism of the former in constitutional matters compared to the passivism of the latter in similar situations, and differences in approach to alternative dispute resolution in civil litigation. Korea's Constitutional Court exemplifies the autonomy of justice from external control or influence through a process of active constitutional adjudication, while Japan's Supreme Court has played a more passive constitutional role. By contrast, Japan's judiciary and its judges are more responsive in their embrace of settlement and mediation in civil litigation than their counterparts in Korea. Some explanations for these differences amongst the judiciaries of these two countries are advanced.

1 Introduction

In the Confucian tradition of Korea and China, judges traditionally applied a combination of mediation and adjudication in the resolution of disputes because of a deep gap in legal culture between legal professionals and laymen (Jung 2013a). The modernization of Korea's legal system occurred in 1894 when the court system was established by the European system. Korea's present legal system may well be evolved by a civil law institution which Japanese colonialism transplanted between 1910 and 1945. Owing to this legacy of Japan's ruling, the present legal system of Korea remains formally European Civil Law with some influence of American Com-

Y. H. Jung (✉)
Chonbuk National University, Jeonju, South Korea
e-mail: hoajung@gmail.com

© Springer Nature Singapore Pte Ltd. 2018

T. Sourdin and A. Zariski (eds.), *The Responsive Judge*, Ius Gentium: Comparative Perspectives on Law and Justice 67, https://doi.org/10.1007/978-981-13-1023-2_11

mon Law. Consequently, Korea and Japan's legal systems share the same roots and many features in their modern legal histories (Hahm 1986). Due to differences in Confucian legal culture, Korea's legal system and laws were repressive. Korea now has a tool to ensure the enforceability of the laws and norms of the dominant group in the vertical social structure.

Before the Meiji restoration in 1868, Japan had developed a legal system based on custom. Until the Meiji era, there were no lawyers in Japan on the terms of modern society (Hahn 1983). The Tokugawa government adopted Confucianism, and its doctrines of social hierarchy and 'wa' (harmony,和), as a state orthodoxy in an effort to prevent commercial disputes from reaching any formal stage. They used these tenets as societal pressures to force potential litigants to settle their problems by themselves, refrain from litigation, and preserve the harmony of society (Henderson 1965). To have one's own rights emphasized in court meant telling another that he or she had erred. The Tokugawa system abhorred such judgments. By viewing the pursuit of individual rights in court as a disruption of societal harmony, the system strongly discouraged litigation. Thus, conciliation dominated civil procedure in the Tokugawa period (Henderson 1965). In fact, the concept of individual rights mattered little against the state in the era of Tokugawa (Tanaka 1976; Hahn 1983). The Meiji Government took steps to import the Western law system (Lockwood 1968). The German civil law system most heavily influenced Japan's modern legal system.

My aim in this chapter is first to describe the features and changing trends in legal culture, constitutional review, and civil litigations in Korea and Japan's judiciaries. I begin by outlining the legal culture of citizens, judges, and courts in the two countries' modern history. The chapter first examines the Constitutional Court of Korea as compared to the Supreme Court of Japan, focusing on the role and function of constitutional adjudication and examining the judicial responsiveness of each through judicial review of legislation. The chapter then examines the judiciaries of each country in their role as adjudicators of litigants' rights through civil litigation. The core of this chapter, however, is an evaluation of the most significant features of the Korean and Japanese judiciaries in these legal areas—the activism of the former in constitutional matters compared to the passivism of the latter in similar situations, and differences in approach to alternative dispute resolution in civil litigation. Korea's Constitutional Court exemplifies the autonomy of justice from external control or influence through a process of active constitutional adjudication, while Japan's Supreme Court has played a more passive constitutional role (Yang 1993; Ginsburg 2003; Higuchi 2004; Jung 2011). By contrast, Japan's judiciary and its judges are more responsive in their embrace of settlement and mediation in civil litigation than their counterparts in Korea. Further, many Japanese judges are mentored and monitored by seniors and peers.

2 Legal Culture of Korea and Japan

Korea and Japan have relatively enjoyed a Confucian tradition, with an attitude of distrust toward litigation and a preference for internalized norms as a means of social ordering. The civil law tradition is thus the starting point for any analysis of Korean law, but not the only source of influence. Since independence in 1945, Korea has had six republics and nine constitutional amendments until 1987. While the regime types have varied, there have been certain constants in postwar Korean politics (Yoon 1995; Choi 1995; Ahn 1998). Gregory Henderson claims Korean politics can be understood as a vortex, with all power at the center (Henderson 1968). The political rulers have continuously depended upon the law to make use of political authority and legality. After the assassination of Park Chung-hee by his subordinate, the chief of Korea's CIA, a military group subsequently took power in a coup in December 1979.

In 1987, the civilian democratic movement finally overcame its military suppression. Consequently, the Congress of the three main political parties agreed upon the amendment of the Constitution. The ruling parties made the decision to reestablish the Constitutional Court that had the power of constitutional review at that time. Why did the political parties agree to a designated Constitutional Court? There were some important causes for the creation of the Constitutional Court (hereafter 'the Court') in the amendment of the Constitution in 1987. On the one hand, the Supreme Court itself may have been reluctant to take on the power of constitutional review (West and Yoon 1992). The Supreme Court does fundamentally prefer to avoid "the politicization of judiciary" due to its involvement in constitutional controversies (Yoon 1995). On the other hand, the Constitutional Court draws its considerable strength from the reaction to the authoritative and military regimes of the pre-democratic period. These regimes abused people's rights and many people disliked and distrusted the Supreme Court. It was necessary to create a strong Court to guard human rights in the future. While legislators did consider the Constitutional Court and its role, they mainly took into consideration the traditional questions of how to separate law and politics, what kind of judicial or political institutions would exercise constitutional review, and how this new institution should be constituted.

The Constitutional Court is the highest court in the judicial system. The Court is the cornerstone of constitutional democracy just as Parliament is the hallmark of representative government. The idea of constitutional justice lies in the legal force that it has acquired in the eyes of the citizens. The Court has a monopoly of binding constitutional interpretation (Dressel 2012). It has jurisdiction to hear and decide certain kinds of constitutional cases. The Court makes decisions within a legal framework. Legal institutions are responsive to social change. Many basic questions about the relationship of law to social change and to cultural development are completely neglected (Friedman 1969). Today, the concept of culture—and perhaps legal culture—remains useful as a way of referring to clusters of social phenomena (patterns of thought, and belief patterns of action or interaction, characteristic institutions) coexisting in certain social environments, where the exact relationships existing among elements in the cluster are clear or are not of concern. In this sense, legal culture may have the same degree of significance for the sociology of law that the idea of legal families has for the comparative law (Cotterrell 2006).

2.1 *Korea's Legal Culture*

In 1961, the military government took a revolutionary revocation of a former colonial legislature in accordance with the "Act on Special Measures for Consolidation of the old laws" (15 July 1961) until the end of 1961. Further, the government took action to automatically abolish all colonial acts without exception until January 20th, 1962. Although this transformative legislative revolution seemingly revoked Japanese colonial legal institutions during three decades all at once, what Japan's colonial professors cultivated through legal education has overtly remained in current legal terminologies and legal professional practices within courts and prosecution proceedings (Jung 2010). The hallmark of the law becomes its association with, and subordination to, the requirements of government.

The first Constitution of 1948 was not only influenced by the Weimar Constitution in the sense of modern constitutionalism, but the judicial system was also substantially influenced by legal formalism in the USA. Korea's constitutional democracy was not realized until the ninth amendment of its Constitution. Before this transformative Constitutional amendment in 1987, the mere existence of law did not guarantee fairness, much less substantive justice. Just as the "monopoly of legitimate violence" is celebrated as a major achievement of the modern state, the main implications of the long authoritative regime (1961–1992) were the repressive laws, vortex political culture, and a rigid formalism of judicial process (Jung 2013b, 2014a). However, the democratic movement resulted in the separation and independence of law and politics and led to the transformative current Constitution and Constitutional Court, which, since 1987, has imported the style of the German Constitutional Court.

In other words, legal culture may not only relate to economic development, democracy, and political certainty, but these are also the important factors for the enhancement of human rights. In particular, existing political elites could hardly overcome the political culture of the centralized vortex in real life The question of how Korea's democracy has developed therefore relies upon the change of legal culture that may have determined Korea's advanced democracy and rule of law.

According to Henderson's (1968) analysis of Korean history and political culture, the pattern of "the vortex"[1] constitutes the single magnet of political culture in the past and present. Moreover, it appears that the current presidential system has been "the greatest vortex summoning men/woman rapidly into it, placing them briefly near the summit of ambition, and then sweeping them out both political decision and economic

[1] "Vortex" means the powerful, centripetal, and vertiginous updraft that sucks "all components" of a "mass society" toward the power apex (Henderson 1968).

interest" (Jung 2016). Since Korea's economic development in 1962, all governments have consistently interfered in the market through resources central and selective investment of resources as economic coordinator and regulator so far (Jung 2014b). Korean legal culture has led to a surge in court litigation since the establishment of the Constitutional Court in 1988. In this chapter, I propose to consider the ways in which judges give expression to political and moral values through civil litigations and constitutional adjudications under the rule of law.

2.2 *Japan's Legal Culture*

Japan was strongly influenced by the United States' legal system after World War II. Japan's current Constitution, which took effect in 1947, reflects the American influence. The Japanese corporate, civil rights, securities regulation, income tax, and labor laws have also carried a strong overtone of American law, as did Japan's antitrust laws initially after 1947. Thus, Japan's commercial legal system is a unique hybrid of German civil law and Common law systems grafted onto the legal system based on traditional customs and values which have held paramount importance in Japan for centuries and remain vibrant today (Hahn 1983). Japan has been incredibly successful in absorbing features of foreign legal systems without sacrificing its own indigenous values.

Japanese legal history is particularly interesting because it contains a significant discontinuity. In the course of the Meiji Restoration, in the middle of the nineteenth century, Japan adopted western codes of law. This move turned Japan into a civil law country. It aligned Japan with a legal tradition that, in some regards, harked back to the days of the Roman Empire. Obviously, Julius Caesar and the Roman emperors never quite got to Japan. Nonetheless, Japan opted to join the civil law family. The government was in the process of modernizing Japanese society, and it was plausible to include the legal system in their plans. The ruling circles looked, not unnaturally, to advanced European countries as models. Of course, after more than a century and a half, Japanese lawyers do not see their legal system as some sort of 'alien intrusion', any more than they would consider tempura an alien intrusion, despite the fact that they owe this marvelous food to Portuguese Jesuits.

Almost all countries have constitutions with bills of rights, and most of them have some sort of judicial review. To be sure, judicial review may be an American invention; it has been part of the American constitutional system for the last two hundred years. But as the world modernizes and globalizes, these institutions have spread all over the world. To a large extent, judicial review does not work the same in each country. The Japanese Supreme Court does not have the same record of activism as both the Korean and German Constitutional Courts. The United Kingdom and the Netherlands still lack judicial review, but both of these countries adhere to international human rights treaties and to the European Court of Human Rights (Friedman 2002).

A focus on the court system, the predictability of court decisions, and the costs of litigation, is much more profitable than discussing the problems in general terms of legal cultural dichotomy. Japan's legal culture has the following features: First, Japan's law is characterized by uniformity in the source of law: a centralized legal system under a unitary national government. This uniformity can be contrasted with the pluralism built into the structure of the federal system in the USA. It also fosters conformity among individual and group/community values. Second, a traditional system of social relations favors resolving disputes informally over an extended period of time. Defining issues is avoided in order to leave room for mutual compromise and litigation is viewed as a last resort which leads to a complete termination of the relationship. Third, law furnishes a formal framework to maintain social order and processes such as conciliation, mediation, and arbitration are actively employed. Finally, a law is not regarded as a major source of normative decision-making, affecting public as well as private conduct (Fujikura 1996).

3 The Comparison of Constitutional Review in Korea and Japan

We can see constitutional democracy through the lens of constitutional justice. The structural differences between constitutional review in the USA and the European model of constitutional justice are well known. The characteristics of the latter originate from the first constitutional court of Czechoslovakia and Austria, established in 1920. These courts are inseparable from democratic changes. The three generations of the European model emerged from a "system change".[2] Many constitutions have created constitutional courts following this model, not only in Europe, but also in Asia, Latin America and Africa (Lopez 1994). The Korean Constitutional Court fundamentally adopted the jurisdiction and structure of the Federal Constitutional Court in Germany. This model of constitutional justice provides for a court which is distinct and separate from the ordinary court system and has the power to examine the constitutionality of laws passed by parliament and, if necessary, to annul any laws found to be in conflict with the constitutional text.

[2]The first generation, the German and Italian constitutional courts, was set up after the fall of the Fascist regimes, in the early 1950s. The second generation, the Spanish and Portuguese courts, followed the collapse of the authoritarian regimes of Franco and Salazar in the 1970s. The third generation, the constitutional courts in the new post-Soviet democracies, were founded in the 1990s, this time expressly as symbols of the new democratic system and as the latest link in the chain of an established tradition (Sólyom 2010).

3.1 *Korea—Judge's Responsive Activism*

Korean Constitutions have provided an overview of various judicial review systems in the constitutional history. The Constitution of the First Republic (1948–1960) established the Constitutional Committee that was a mixed American model and European Model. The Committee had the power of judicial review of legislation, and made decisions over seven cases, including two cases which struck down laws restricting the right of appeal to the Supreme Court. The Constitution of the Second Republic (1960–1961) introduced the judicial control system of the German Federal Constitutional Court, but regretfully, could not operate the Court due to the coup in 1961. The Constitution of Third Republic (1961–1972) adopted the judicial system of the U.S. Supreme Court. During its operation over ten years, the Supreme Court held a clause of "State Damage Redress Act" unconstitutional in only one case, which challenged restrictions on compensation for military armies and policemen seeking to claim damage redress against the state.[3] Moreover, the purport of this decision was overturned by a subsequent amendment of the Constitution. Constitutions of both the Fourth Republic (1972–1980) and the Fifth Republic (1981–1987) maintained a judicial control system of the Constitutional Committee that remained strictly a nominal constitutional institution which never referred to any case under the repressive laws of authoritative regimes. From this overview of Korean judicial control in our constitutional history, we can learn an important lesson: the autonomous law cannot operate the constitutional control system without a real political democracy.

The Justices of the Constitutional Court may be appointed by the President with the consent of Congress. Candidates are nominated by Congress, the President, and the Chief Justice of the Supreme Court. All candidates should be qualified as judges, be more than 40 years of age, and have more than 15 years of career experience as a judge, prosecutor, or attorney. The terms of office and the retirement age of Justices are the same as those of Justices of the Supreme Court. Justices are subject to constitutional obligations not to join a political party or participate in politics. Justices of the Constitutional Court shall not be expelled from office except by impeachment or a sentence of imprisonment without prison labor or heavier punishment (Article 112(3) of the Constitution). The Constitutional Court may review the legislation by the Congress and equivalent statutes by other entities. However, according to Article 107(2) of the Constitution, the constitutionality of subordinate legislation, such as administrative orders, regulations, rules, and measures, is subject to the judgment of the Supreme Court. Consequently, a dualism causes a serious conflict of law between the Constitutional Court and the Supreme Court. If a different interpretation of the Constitution arises between both Courts, the Constitution does not expressly prescribe whose opinion shall be final. This incomplete dualism undermines the

[3]The Government was concerned about the decision in the context of claims of redress for Vietnamese war veterans. Most justices of the Supreme Court concerned with the decision of unconstitutionality of that law resigned from the bench and the law was subsequently amended.

uniformity and consistency of constitutional order. The Constitutional Court's jurisdiction has fundamentally been important in relation to judicial review of statutes and determination of constitutional complaints.

3.1.1 Judge's Purposive Interpretation

The Court was established on the basis of the Constitutional Court Act (hereafter 'CCA') of 1988. Under Chapter VI of the Constitution, the Court has the following jurisdiction: adjudicating the constitutionality of a law upon the request of a court; Impeachment; deciding on the dissolution of a political party; resolving jurisdictional disputes among state agencies and local governments; and hearing constitutional complaints (public petitions relating to the Constitution) as prescribed by the Act.[4] As the jurisdiction of the Constitutional Court excludes both an abstract judicial review and the constitutional complaints against a court trial, some scholars and lawyers have argued that the scope of its jurisdiction was insufficient to readily take a constitutional adjudication. In the course of legislation of the National Assembly, the CCA has reflected three limitations of the Court's power on request of the Supreme Court. First, only ordinary courts can request the Court to review the constitutionality of statutes.[5] However, litigants can file a challenge to the constitutionality of a law through a constitutional complaint, meaning the above restriction is void.[6] Second, under Article 107(2) of the Constitution the Supreme Court has strongly campaigned for the intrinsic power to review the constitutionality of administrative legislation such as administrative orders, rules, and regulations excluding the Court. Third, Article 68(1) of the CCA excludes the judgment of an ordinary court from the object of an adjudication complaint by the Court (Yang et al. 1999).

Although the Court has encountered institutional inertia in constitutional adjudication,[7] nonetheless, the Court has actively worked towards enforcing a constitutional order. In general, a concrete control of law may be distinguished from an abstract control on the constitutionality of the law, with a reference to a concrete conflict

[4]Article 111(1) provides that the Constitutional Court shall have jurisdiction over the following matters: 1. The constitutionality of a law upon the request of the courts; 2. Impeachment; 3. Dissolution of a political party; 4. Competence disputes between State agencies, between State agencies and local governments, and between local governments; and 5. Constitutional complaint as prescribed by Act (Article 3(1) of Constitutional Court Act is contained same provisions).

[5]When the constitutionality of a law is at issue in a trial, the court shall request a decision of the Constitutional Court and shall judge according to the decision thereof (Article 107(1) of the Constitution).

[6]If a request made for adjudication on the constitutionality of a law under Article 41(1) is dismissed, the party who has made the request may request adjudication on a constitutional complaint to the Constitutional Court. In this case, the party shall not request again adjudication on the constitutionality of a law, for the same reason in the litigation procedure of the case concerned (Article 68(2) of CCA) [This Article Wholly Amended by Act No. 10546, Apr. 5, 2011].

[7]The Court's institutional inertia mainly resulted from the interest conflicts of both political parties and the judiciary itself (West and Yoon 1992, 15–18).

arising from the application of the law in a particular case after a law has been put into effect.

As the Court has the competence to annul unconstitutional laws in their adjudications, the principle that all powers are subject to the law while guaranteeing that the law will conform to the Constitution can be maintained. Even though the Court has some role in resolving jurisdictional disputes between organs of governments, this differs from an abstract review. In particular, Article 61(2) of the CCA restricts this form of review to those cases where the act or omission of the responding agency "infringes on or is in obvious danger of infringing on" the abstract review, and requires the presence of at least a threat to a concrete interest. The creation of constitutional jurisdiction is linked with a guarantee of constitutional democracy in the light of past dangers and the need to keep constitutional mandates from being suppressed by an authoritarian regime threatening the Constitution.

In fact, Article 45 of the CCA provided for a dichotomous decision as to constitutionality. The Court adopted from the German Constitution various other categories of decision that the Court can render. First, the Court can hold an act unconstitutional, voiding the act immediately. The Court can find the act to be non-conforming with the constitution, in which case the Congress may be required to amend the act in the near future. The Court can find that the act is conditionally constitutional as long as it is interpreted in the instant case. Finally, the Court may uphold the act as constitutional. These various types of declarations of constitutionality and unconstitutionality may place the Court in dialogue with the legislators and executive agencies. In other words, the Court can also provide guidance for enforcement agencies as to how to apply the law to avoid constitutional defect (Ginsburg 2003).

The Constitutional Court provides the other powers of the State with conceptual tools and criteria for their conduct through the interpretation of the Constitution. Thus, the Court plays the dual roles that defend and create the legal order. The judicial character of the Courts means that they cannot act on their own accord, but rather, only in legal procedures initiated by others or in specific cases provided for in the Constitution. They must follow criteria determined by the Constitution, and not by political opportunity or convenience (Lopez 1994).

When a person's constitutional rights have been infringed by executive or administrative action or nonfeasance, she or he may directly make a complaint to the Court for relief on the basis of Article 68(1) of the CCA. There are two separate grounds for such complaints. Article 68(1) of the CCA may allow complaints after all available legal remedies have been exhausted by plaintiffs whose rights have been infringed by unconstitutional state action.[8] Moreover, Article 68(2) of the CCA relates to cases in which the plaintiff has unsuccessfully sought referral by the ordinary courts under Article 41 of the CCA, and leads to a stay in ongoing adjudication pending the Constitutional Court judgment. This system is designed to partially remedy the lack of

[8]Most of these cases have involved allegations of abuse of prosecutorial discretion when prosecutors did not indict, however, before the related article of the Criminal Procedure Act was amended in 2010, Article 68(1) cases predominated because decisions of ordinary courts were excluded from the jurisdiction of the Constitutional Court.

jurisdiction over the decisions of ordinary courts. If the right of the petition did not exist, ordinary courts' processes would be unreviewable by the Court.

However, they are heard, the original concept that the Court has been designed as an instrument only to defend the Constitution is no longer valid. This is because there is explicit evidence of so many cases of specific procedures before the Court which seek to guarantee the protection of the constitutional fundamental rights of individuals. In Korea and Germany, constitutional complaint is of the utmost significance and is designed as a means by which the Court can remedy individual violations of any fundamental rights defined in the Constitution. The relevant characteristic of this procedure is that it does not seek a ruling of the Court on general legislative or administrative statutes, but rather on the individual acts of specific executive powers and of individuals (by means of the application of the doctrine of public function). In Germany and Spain, a constitutional complaint may be raised against all public powers in the event of the violation of a fundamental right, in a procedure which has often been described as a "universal appeal" (Lopez 1994). By means of the constitutional complaint, the Court may guide the action of the judicial, executive and legislative powers in all matters concerning constitutional rights. But in the case of Korea, the constitutional complaint has been the instrument for orienting the actions of executive and legislative powers, excluding the judgment of ordinary courts in Article 68(1) of the CCA.[9] Actually, the vast number of constitutional complaints in annual constitutes a strain on the efficacy of the Court and this result in the necessity of establishing a type of filter, both outside and within the realm of constitutional jurisdiction. In constitutional theory, as the Court should itself be prevented from reviewing the judgments of ordinary courts involving violations of constitutional rights, some serious tensions have arisen between the Court and the ordinary courts, and particularly the Supreme Court, in cases in which they believe the Constitutional Court to have acted ultra vires, reviewing judicial decisions not directly related to the protection of constitutional rights.

3.1.2 Constitutional Court's Responsive Autonomy

Just as the "monopoly of legitimate violence" is celebrated as a major achievement of the modern state, the essential implications of a long authoritative regime (1961–1987) have been the repressive laws, vortex political culture, and a rigid judicial formalism. In short, since the achievement of political democracy and the amendment of the Constitution in 1987, the Court of September 1988 has been work-

---

[9]CCA 68(1): Any person whose basic rights guaranteed by the Constitution are infringed due to exercise or non-exercise of the governmental power, *excluding judgment of the ordinary courts*, may file a constitutional complaint with the Constitutional Court: Provided, that if any remedy is provided by other laws, no one may file a constitutional complaint without having exhausted all such processes.

ing under an autonomous law. The Constitutional Court has been quite active in its five terms of operations.[10]

The 1st Court's term operated from September 1988 to August 1994.[11] Relying on the accumulation of the Court's precedents, laymen have also directly resorted to the Court as a tool for the remedy of their rights and controlling the executive powers. In short, the said Court was established in the wake of rapid social changes, and its major efforts went into remedying many statutes which had accumulated over many years under the authoritarian regimes, the constitutionality of which was relatively easy to adjudicate.

The 2nd Court's term (1994–2000) faced ever harder and more sophisticated adjudications and a constitutional complaint was filed challenging the prosecutor's decision not to indict the former presidents, who Mr. Chun and Mr. Roh involved in the military coup d'etat in 1979.[12] The Court decided to include the prosecutor's decision not to indict as a proper subject matter for constitutional complaints on the ground that there were no other effective control mechanisms checking the prosecutor's power to prosecute because appeals on such decisions could be made only under exceptional circumstances. This is because the control over the prosecution's arbitrary exercise of its powers is a matter of legislative discretion.[13]

The 3rd Court's term (2000–2006) made a contribution to criminal human rights and was proactive in fields where violations of rights had been condoned due to Confucian social custom or the traditional convention that the system of family registry (patriarchy, 'hojuje') is discrimination based on outdated notions of gender roles, and is incompatible with the Constitution because the individual is being treated merely as an instrument in the service of the maintenance and preservation of the family. Hot political controversies such as the construction of administrative capital and impeachment of the president were decided by the Court.

The 4th Court's term (2007–2013) had important goals such as a social integration through constitutional adjudication. The Court consistently expanded the scope of constitutional protection over freedom of speech. Such unconstitutional decisions were "a rating system of video materials case",[14] "a prior review of broadcasting

[10]The 1st term Court (September 1988–September 1994); the Second Term Court (September 1994–2000); the third term Court (September 2000–2006); the Fourth Term Court (September 2007–2013); the Fifth Term Court (September 2013–2017).

[11]By the first term in 1988–1994, the Court was composed of six permanent judges and three non-permanent judges. It has been widely acknowledged that the Court was established as the final resort which the people trusted and turned to for the protection of their fundamental human rights under the Constitution. The Constitutional Scholars' Society and Attorney's Community evaluated favorably the Justices' efforts to firmly establish the constitutional adjudication. In a survey of lawyers and law professors conducted by a citizen group in September 1994, the overwhelming majority of respondents gave high marks for the Court's activities during its first six years.

[12]The Campaign to "rectify the past" continued in a series of similar challenges against the non-institution of prosecution of those involved in the May Incident of 1980. Over this complaint adjudication, the Court upheld the Special Act on the May Democratization Movement, which suspended the statute of limitations for prosecuting those involved in the coup.

[13]94 Hun-Ba 2, August 21, 1997.

[14]2004 Hun-Ba 36, Oct. 4, 2007.

advertisements case",[15] a "restricted screening rating case",[16] "a withholding of video product classification case",[17] a "nighttime outdoor assembly ban case",[18] a "ban on internet distribution of obscene materials case",[19] a "real name verification of internet news site case",[20] and an "identity verification system on the internet".[21] The above decisions made a substantial contribution to enhancing the freedom of speech and liberal democracy in Korea (Constitutional Court 2010).

The 5th Court's term (2013–2017) decided the hot case of the dissolution of 'the Unified Progressive Party' after its major members' actions violated the liberal democratic order of the Constitution in 2014.[22] Moreover, the Court made the rigid decision that the respondent, President Park Gun-hye, was to be removed from office in the adjudication on the impeachment of the President on 10 March 2017.[23]

In recent years, the Court decisions of unconstitutionality have explicitly decreased compared with former Courts.

Table 1 describes the Court's caseload through thirty years of operations (1988.9–2017.10). Of the 32,844 filed cases, the Court has decided on merits 12,181 cases, with 879 merits of unconstitutional review over legislation, 2 impeachment merits, and 1 party dissolution merit (including a petition of retrial). There are 8687 petitions of Article 68(1) constitutional complaints over state action, 2523 petitions

---

[15]2005 Hun-Ma 506, June 26, 2008.

[16]2007 Hun-Ka 4, July 31, 2008.

[17]2004 Hun-Ka 18, Oct. 30, 2008.

[18]2008 Hun-Ka 25, Sept. 24, 2009.

[19]2006 Hun-Ba 109, 2007 Hun-Ba 49, 57, 83, 129 consolidated, May 28, 2009.

[20]2008 Hun-Ma 324, 2009 Hun-Ba 31 (consolidated), Feb. 25, 2010.

[21]2010 Hun-Ma 47, 252 (consolidated) Aug. 23, 2012.

[22]2013 Hun-Da1, Dec. 19, 2014.

[23]It was in the outline of petition for adjudication on impeachment of reasons that the respondent publicly announced her intention to resign from the presidency in accordance with the National Assembly's decision. The National Assembly formed a special committee and conducted an investigation of state administration into suspicions that a civilian had intervened in state affairs, and on December 1, 2016, appointed a special prosecutor. On December 8, the National Assembly presented to the plenary session a 'motion for the impeachment of the President (Park Geun-hye),' proposed on December 3, 2016, by 171 National Assembly members including Woo-Ho, Park-Won and Roh-Chan. The motion to impeach the respondent passed with 234 members in the 300-seat National Assembly voting in favor, at the 18th plenary of the 346th session (regular session) on December 9, 2016. The impeachment prosecutor requested impeachment adjudication against the respondent by submitting the original copy of the impeachment resolution to the Constitutional Court pursuant to Article 49 section 2 of the Constitutional Court Act (2016 Hun-Na1, March 10, 2017). By contrast, the Court rejected the case concerning the impeachment of former President Roh Moo-hyun on May 14, 2004 (2004 Hun-Na1). The question of whether to remove the President from office when he or she has violated the law should be determined by whether this violation is of such gravity in terms of protecting the Constitution, that it is required to preserve the Constitution and restore the impaired constitutional order through a decision in favor of removal; or whether the President, through a violation of law, has betrayed the trust of the people to such an extent that said public trust vested in the President should be forfeited before the presidential term ends (*see also* 2004 Hun-Na1, May 14, 2004).

of Article 68(2) constitutional complaints, and 37 cases of competence disputes between public entities.

The Court has found 1502 of 12,181 cases, or 12.3% of cases, unconstitutional in whole, or in part, in their application. The percentage of laws struck down has been the highest at 40.7%. Petitions under Article 68(1) of the CCA have been occupied in 60% of cases in which the Court dismissed a prosecutor arraignment not to prosecute. Some prosecutors interpret the findings as an instruction to reinvestigate the case; others, including scholars and activists, see it as an order to prosecute. As a result, findings of unconstitutionality do not always lead to prosecution. However, after the scope of application for adjudication of the Criminal Procedure Act was amended in 2008, Constitutional complaints apparently decreased. If a person who has filed a criminal complaint, with a right to file such criminal complaint, receives a notice of non-prosecution from a prosecutor, she/he may file an application for adjudication to find out whether such disposition is properly made, with the High Court having jurisdiction over the venue where the District Prosecutors' office to which the prosecutor belongs is situated (hereinafter referred to as the "Competent High Court"). With respect to a crime referred to in Article 126 of the Criminal Act, an application for adjudication shall not be filed against the clearly expressed intent of the publicized [Criminal Procedure Act, Article 260(1)].

The Court found 326 of 2523 cases, or 12.9% of cases, unconstitutional in whole, or in part, in their application. Constitutional complaints under Article 68(2) of the CCA have been heard less on the merits than as a result of an Article 68(1) petition, but the chances of success are higher for those that reach the merits stage. After a law upon the request of the courts is rejected by the ordinary courts, the ongoing litigation can be referred to the Court by litigants as a constitutional complaint under Article 68(2) of the CCA. Indeed, one factor in the relatively high "strike rate" of this petition of Article 68(2) of CCA shows the capacity of judges' constitutional interpretation in ordinary courts. While a speedy trial shall be applicable to the constitutional adjudication within 180 days in the course of proceeding, an excessively delayed trial, such as more than four or five years, results in a high rate of 7.3% of unsettled pending cases, as shown in Table 1.

On the one hand, it is important to emphasize that the rule of law (Rechtsstaat Principle) requires executive power to be enforced according to statutes and any wrongful administrative action should be redressed in the judicial process. As the notion of democratic constitutionalism evolved, the importance of the rule of law moved from the formal conception to the substantive one. The current Constitution adopts constitutional litigation, including constitutional review as well as constitutional complaints. It seems clear that the Constitutional Court has firmly applied a legal formalism on the basis of Justice's value neutrality, derived from the work of the United States Supreme Court. In other words, it is assumed that the Constitutional Court is independent of political powers, in accordance with a strict separation of law and politics. The Constitutional Court has contributed to the establishment of the rule of law by presenting the clear limits and precise standards regarding the exercise of executive power. As the source of constitutional jurisprudence in legal practice and education, the Constitutional Court may scrutinize orders that offend

Table 1 The caseload of the constitutional court (1988.9–2017.10)

Classification	Total	Constitutionality of laws	68(1) Complaint	68(2) Complaint	Competence dispute	Dissolution of party	Impeachment
Filed	32,844	935	25,443	6360	102	2	1
Settled	31,953	879	24,936	6046	88	2	2
Dismissed by panel	19,772		16,246 (14,737)	3523 (3192)			
Unconstitutional	580	274	104	202			
Unconformable	206	59	59	71	17		
Conditional Unconstitutional	70	18	20	32			
Conditional Constitutional	28	7		21			
Constitutional	2410	329	4	2077			
Upholding	618		616			1	1
Rejected	7254		7233		20		1
Dismissed	1929	69	1512	312	35	1	
Withdrawn	900	123	643(8)	118(2)	16		
Total decisions on merit	12,181	879	8687	2523	37	2	1
Number struck out	1502	358	799	326	17	1	1
Percentage struck out (%)	12.3	40.7	9.2	12.9	46	50	100
Pending cases	891	56	507	314	14	–	–
Pending percentage (%)	7.3	6.3	5.8	12.4	38		

Source Extracted from Constitutional Court Statistics. In the legal practice of Korea, merits cases include rejections but not dismissals by litigants. Partially/fully struck out includes all decisions but "constitutional" and "rejected."

1. "Unconstitutional": Used in the constitutionality of laws cases
2. "Unconformable": This conclusion means the Court acknowledges a law's unconstitutionality but merely requests the National Assembly to revise it by a certain period while having the law remain effective until that time
3. "Conditionally Unconstitutional": In cases challenging the constitutionality of a law, the Court prohibits a particular way of interpretation of a law as unconstitutional, while having other interpretations remain constitutional
4. "Conditionally Constitutional" means that a law is constitutional if it is interpreted according to the designated way. This is the converse of "Unconstitutional, in a certain context". Both are regarded as decisions of "partially unconstitutional"
5. "Upholding": This conclusion is used when the Court accepts a Constitutional Complaint which does not include a constitutionality of law issue

the protection afforded by fundamental rights and freedoms. Another issue involves determining what kind of constitutional issue is raised when fundamental rights and freedoms are restricted. Here, it is useful to examine whether the order's restriction of those rights and freedoms can be justified (Jung 2011, 2016).

As noted above, if a matter does not fit within the scope of protection of those rights and freedoms (i.e. it is outside the restriction's ranges), it would constitute a failure to qualify for constitutional protection (for example, violence incitement). Second, it needs a legal basis or rationale for restricting those rights and freedoms (statutory requirement). A restriction of those rights and freedoms must meet substantial standards such as 'compelling public interest' and 'legitimacy', as well as the scrutiny standard of the principle of proportionality.

Accordingly, the Constitution is vested with due process of law [Art. 12(1), (3)], and the requirement of protection against restriction of fundamental rights and freedoms, and the prohibition of laws infringing an essential element of fundamental rights and freedoms in accordance with Article 37 section 2. If the four requirements for restricting fundamental rights are not all met as above, fundamental rights protection will supersede the doctrine of general statutory reservation by which fundamental rights and freedom may be restricted.

On the other hand, the Constitutional Court is faithful to the purposive constitutional interpretation. Justices may interpret the Constitution in the context of the current situation so that the legal source of the written Constitution is applied to bring about the expected constitutional order and its associated legal culture. The Justices shall not be unconditionally bound to the intent of the Drafters, but must precisely interpret the objective purpose of the Constitution. Therefore, the Constitutional Court has consistently adopted a purposive interpretation which is able to explore the purpose of constitutional provisions.[24] Ultimately, the Constitutional Court should be established to faithfully apply the doctrine of purposive constitutional interpretation of the United States Federal Supreme Court and general Constitutional Court. Based on this premise, if the democratic constitutionalism may rationally improve the method of selecting judges, who can participate in the expert of the Constitutional court, it is expected to improve the efficiency of the Constitution culture.

3.2 *Japan's Less Responsive Supreme Court*

The constitution of Japan took effect on May 3, 1947, and was enacted as the mainstay of the democratizing reforms after Japan's defeat in World War II. Its preamble declares: "resolved that never again shall we be visited with the horrors of war through the action of government, [we] do proclaim that sovereign power resides with the people." The Constitution is also founded on the principle of separation of powers as following: "the whole judicial power is vested in a Supreme Court and such inferior

[24] Japan's Supreme Court has also the same way of purposive interpretation as Korea's Constitutional Court (Ito 1995; Jung 2011).

Courts as are established by law" [Art. 76(1)] and "all judges shall be independent in the exercise of their conscience and shall be bound only by this Constitution and the laws" [Art. 76(3)]. The Constitution solemnly pledges the guarantee of fundamental human rights (Art. 11), coupled with the power of the Supreme Court, as the court of last resort, to "determine the constitutionality of any law, order, regulation or official act" (Art. 81). This power of judicial review represents the most salient feature of the Constitution inspired by America law and is interpreted to reside in all the inferior courts as well.

The Japanese court system is made up of a hierarchy of three levels of ordinary courts, in accordance with the "three instances principle" that had been adopted in the Meiji era: the Supreme Court, 8 High Courts, and 50 District Courts. In addition, to constitute the fourth level of court hierarchy, there are about 440 Summary Courts with limited jurisdiction over the lightest civil and criminal cases, excluding family matters, placed under the District Courts. The Summary Court's civil jurisdiction presently covers claims valued at 1.4 million yen or lower. There are three kinds of ordinary courts: the District Court, Family Court, and Summary Court. Japanese courts are unique in other respects as well. Judicial corruption is virtually unknown. Judges do not take bribes. A combination of factors helps to explain this extraordinary integrity (Haley 2007).

3.2.1 The Features of Constitution Interpretation

The Japanese Constitution made clear that it is the supreme law of the land and any legislation or acts of the government which would violate the Constitution are invalid. Chapter X—Supreme law, of the Constitution thus provides that "[t]his Constitution shall be the supreme law of the nation and no law, ordinance, imperial rescript or other act of government, or part thereof, contrary to the provisions hereof, shall have legal force or validity" [Article 98(1)]. The supremacy of the Constitution is derived from the foundation law for freedom, and the Bill of Rights is the core of the Constitution which may protect positive natural rights deriving from human dignity (Ashibe 1994). Stated positively, the important issue is whether all statutes and orders enacted under the Meiji constitution have an effect. Article 98(1) of the Constitution allows those statutes and orders under the Meiji Constitution to be valid so long as they do not violate the Constitution.

Since 1947, the United States Constitution has contributed to the Japanese Constitution on the concepts and foundations in both political democracy and judicial review. It cannot be denied that the Meiji Constitution represented pseudo-constitutionalism in the light of democratic constitutional history. To be sure, the pre-war political regime was absolute monarchy sovereignty in pursuit of a continental civil law system and military imperialism. Similarly, the Constitution relied on the concepts of both legal positivism and reactive rights derived from the German Rechsstaat Principles in the 19th Century (Jung 2011). In contrast, the post-war current Constitution has declared the national sovereignty of the people who shall govern and a preference for a bicameral system in the British parliamentary cabinet style. But the so-called MacArthur Draft had to introduce unicameralism on the ground that bicameralism is not wholly democratic (Okudaira 1990). While the Japanese founders were sticking to the ideas of bicameralism, the House of Councilors, as well as a House of Representatives, adopted a house of vocational representation, similar to the two Councils of both Labor and Management in the Weimar Constitution of 1919.[25] Judicial review was enacted and implanted in line with the judicial review to which the United States Supreme Court was entitled pursuant to the Supremacy Clause of US Constitution and the judgment in *Marbury v. Madison* (5 U.S. 137, 1803) (Corwin 1929). While the judicial review was established in some cases, the more general abstract judicial review, however, under which the judiciary can exercise a broader discretion for protection of the Constitution in constitutional adjudication, is not vested in due to the principles of separation of power and national sovereignty (Ito 1995; Jung 2011). Subsequently, as concrete judicial review has the main purpose of settling an individual litigation, the Supreme Court can impose the self-restriction of judicial review, if it is possible to solve the case without making the decision a constitutional issue. Japanese Justices may obey the doctrine of "Constitutional avoidance." In *Ash wander v. Tennessee Valley Authority* [297 U.S. 288 (1936)], Brandeis set out a broad formulation of the avoidance doctrine. This reluctance to use the power of judicial review was, according to Brandeis, predicated on the principle of separation of powers that one branch must not "encroach upon the domain of another." Brandeis identified two prominent limitations on the federal judicial power based on the separation principle: the "case or controversy" requirement and the rule that federal courts have no power to render advisory opinions.[26] Brandeis linked a host of justiciability doctrines, including a political question and standing inquiries, to these limitations. In particular, Japan's Supreme Court has ruled only nine statutes to be unconstitutional in 70 years of constitutional litigations (1947–2017).

---

[25]Der Arbeiterrat und der Wirtschaftsrat, art. 165 von der Weimar Verfassungsrecht, August 11, 1919.

[26]Brandeis described how the Court had developed "prudential" rules—meaning non-constitutional, self-imposed restraints—by which to avoid "passing upon a large part of all the constitutional questions" presented to it, despite having jurisdiction to hear them. He described the avoidance doctrine as consisting of a "series" of seven rules: (1) "The Court will not pass upon the constitutionality of legislation in a friendly, non-adversary, proceeding"; (2) "The Court will not 'anticipate a question of constitutional law in advance of the necessity of deciding it"; (3) "The Court will not 'formulate a rule of constitutional law broader than is required by the precise facts to which it is to be applied"; (4) "The Court will not pass upon a constitutional question, although properly presented by the record if there is also present some other ground upon which the case may be disposed"; (5) "The Court will not pass upon the constitutionality of a statute unless the plaintiff was injured by the operation of the statute"; (6) "The Court will not pass upon the constitutionality of a statute at the instance of one who has availed himself of its benefits"; (7) Even if "serious doubt[s]" concerning the validity of an act of Congress is raised, the Court will first ascertain "'whether a construction of the statute is fairly possible by which the question may be avoided". Brandeis concludes his discussion of the avoidance doctrine with this warning: "One branch of the government cannot encroach upon the domain of another, without danger. The safety of our institutions depends in no small degree on a strict observance of this salutary rule": Ash Wander, 297 U.S. [quoting Sinking-Fund Cases v. U.S. Central Pacific Railroad Co., 99 U.S. 700, 718 (1871)] (Katzmann 1988; Frohnmayer 1973).

Human rights under Japan's Constitution have adopted the concept of the American notion of civil liberties derived from natural law as well as various unique American ideas and legal concepts such as individualism, fundamental human rights, freedom, and equality. Moreover, the Constitution enumerates some social economic rights in pursuit of the principle of the welfare state which stemmed from the Weimar Constitution and the United States' New Deal policies. The Constitution prescribes that all people shall have the right to maintain the minimum standards of wholesome and cultured living (art. 25), in addition to freedom of thought (art. 19), freedom of religion (art. 20), freedom of speech and of press (art. 21), and freedom of assembly and association (art. 23).

However, the Supreme Court has applied the double standard of scrutiny: the strict scrutiny and rational basis test, which originated in Justice Stone's footnote four in *United States v. Caroline Products Co.*[27] By contrast, the American Supreme Court has generally maintained the level of scrutiny and burden of proof that relies upon the three classifications of strict scrutiny, intermediate scrutiny, and rational basis test. Even though the Japanese Constitution entails more lists of human rights than the United States Constitution, the Japanese Supreme Court has never applied the scrutiny to social human rights (Ashibe 1994). In the Japanese Constitution, freedom of speech and political freedom may be entitled to protection as "it is politically free, but is socially not free." Still, everyone may enjoy the freedom of expression and keep a delicate balance between formal and informal social relationships due to the symbiotic feature of traditional hierarchical culture (Okudaira 1990). In sum, the Supreme Court receives and decides over 4000 civil, administrative, and criminal cases including constitutional cases per year. Except for constitutional cases, the Court rarely decides cases "en banc". Most cases are decided by one of the three petty benches, each with five justices, into which the court is divided and cases assigned in sequence (Beer and Itoh 1996).

3.2.2 Formalism and Constraint of Politics

Over seven decades, there have been nine cases in which the Supreme Court has ruled statutes to be invalid for violating the Constitution. There have been various comments or opinions regarding the function of judicial review. Many scholars and

[27] Footnote 4 introduced to the Supreme Court jurisprudence the idea of levels of judicial scrutiny. In keeping with the New Deal Revolution, Footnote 4 established the rational basis test for economic legislation, an extremely low standard of judicial review. The rational basis test mandates that legislation (whether enacted by Congress or state legislatures) which deals with economic regulation must be rationally related to a legitimate state interest. Therefore, Footnote 4 outlines a higher level of judicial scrutiny for legislation that meets certain conditions: (1) On its face violates a provision of the Constitution (facial challenge); (2) Attempts to distort or rig the political process; and (3) Discriminates against minorities, particularly those who lack sufficient numbers or power to seek redress through the political process. This higher level of scrutiny, now called "strict scrutiny", was first applied in Justice Black's opinion in *Korematsu v. U.S.* (1944). In fact, the cited work above (while quite useful on the origin and growth of the Footnote) does not claim that the law clerk was the author, and implies the opposite through letters between the justices: 304 U.S. 144 (1938).

lawyers have observed that the Supreme Court's attitude has been one of rigid passivism of judicial review, allowing for broader legislative discretion on Constitutional interpretation.[28] Generally, the Supreme Court relied upon the broad "public welfare" standard. However, the Court prefers to give weight to the wide discretion of the legislature (Okudaira 1990).

3.2.3 Why Has the Japanese Supreme Court Shown Very Passive Judicial Review?

First, Japan's legal culture has been more collective and collaborative, and less autonomous due to its strong symbiotic tradition. In fact, the legal culture is used to emphasize collectivism rather than individualism. The long experience of the rule of law for more than one hundred years inherently established the autonomous laws.

Second, the Supreme Court's constitutional interpretation inherited a more rigid approach based on formalism and textualism from the American Supreme Court and remained wedded to a 'Rechtsstaat' principle derived from the German Constitution since the 19th Century. With regard to the incidental system of judicial review, some members have questioned the adequacy of deciding the constitutionality of laws and other measures after the fact and in conjunction with litigation on specific cases.

Third, since the Meiji Constitution and Weimar Constitution that was run on the passive interpretation of constitutional provisions by the judiciary, Justices of the Supreme Court must rigidly obey the doctrine of Constitutional avoidance under the legal culture. Judicial review according to this approach included the following: guaranteeing human rights and protecting the Constitution. Maintaining an appropriate tension between the judicial and political branches through the medium of judicial review is very important to constitutional democracy. Judicial review also serves to stimulate constitutional debate.

Fourth, Supreme Court justices, with their large caseload of final appeals, are too busy to decide questions of constitutionality. The passive stance of the judiciary may be attributed in large part to: (1) the restraints on judicial review due to the fact that Japan's system is construed as being a U.S. style system of incidental review; (2) the influence of the idea that the executive branch takes precedence; and (3) the fact that, in the absence of free debate on constitutional revision, any Supreme Court decision on the constitutionality of a high-level matter of governance risked drawing intense scrutiny as a political issue. In particular, an environment in which the Constitution could be amended when a law was ruled unconstitutional was lacking, mainly due to the strict amendment procedure laid down by Article 96. The problem lies in the political coloration of appointments of Supreme Court justices and other judges,

[28]The Public Officials Election Act absolutely prohibits door-to-door election canvassing. Since 1950 the Supreme Court has continuously held that such regulation is constitutional: 4 Keishu 1799 (Sup. Ct., G.B. Sept. 27, 1950); 21 Keishu 1245 (Sup. Ct. 3rd. P.B., Nov. 21, 1967); 38 Keishu 387 (Sup. Ct., 3rd, P.B., July 21, 1981).

and in the judicial bureaucracy, which does not adequately ensure their freedom and independence.

Lastly, citing evidence such as the rarity of Supreme Court rulings that find statutes unconstitutional, some scholars have expressed the view that the judiciary is reluctant to decide questions of constitutionality ("judicial passivism") and is not adequately fulfilling the role entrusted to it in guaranteeing the Constitution (Matsui 2011). Other scholars have also criticized the courts' tendency to avoid rendering a decision by invoking the "act of state" doctrine on the grounds that the case is highly political in nature. Some scholars have expressed the view that the judiciary should have a limited involvement in acts of the state, leaving decisions in that area to the political branch,[29] while others have commented that whether the courts rule on constitutionality is a question that affects the autonomy of the judicial branch, and the legislative branch should not intervene (Haley 2007).

Under the unitary social structure and implied unilateral political governance, the Supreme Court hears very diverse cases in addition to ordinary litigations related to the bylaws of local government, and most Justices are inclined to follow the typical thought and conduct of a career judge. This is because the Cabinet will appoint the Justice, whom the ruling party may substantially select as a candidate from among career judges, prosecutors, practicing attorneys, and law professors, according to the recommendations of some sections of the legal community. A significant element of judicial passivism is attributed to a highly bureaucratic machinery, a rigid formalism, and a conservatism concerned to avoid "depoliticization" of controversies which should remain within the realm of politics (Matsudaira 2011).

4 Civil Litigation and Conciliation in Korea

4.1 Less Responsive to Civil Litigation

What factor(s) brought about Korea's economic miracle? Korea achieved one of the most rapid economic growths among developing countries during the 1960s–1980s. But until 1997, politics gradually changed from a rigid military authoritarian regime toward a post-democratic government. Advanced judicial states such as the Common Law and EU legal system have focused on a new area of therapeutic jurisprudence for lawyer's competence to resolve legal disputes. The adjudication has generally evolved in accordance with the legal culture and characteristics of social structures. In Asian countries, the judicial role is more likely to be limited to the adjudication rather than the settlement of legal disputes. Economic development requires various kinds of investment such as time and effort. Without the diligence of economic agents, it is impossible for a country to develop its economy. The economic development of a country is an essential investment in human capital, and a highly educated

[29]In fact, the Japanese Supreme Court employs both conservatism and activism in order to avoid judicial depoliticization (Matsudaira 2011).

and skilled workforce is a prerequisite for the production of all goods and services (Becker 1993).

First, a judicial system fully enforces a formal contract by way of a court trial, judgment, and judicial enforcement proceedings if required. By negotiation between the parties, the full execution of the contract, if necessary by means of judgment given at trial is at the Pareto optimality[30] (Johnson et al. 2002). Thus, informal contract enforcement (compromise through reconciliation, mediation, etc.) appears to be a solution to the lack of a court trial and less than Pareto optimal (Djankov et al. 2002).

Second, in most developed countries, courts which are guaranteed by a rule of law and independent jurisdiction have a lower risk of private property rights infringement (North 1990). In other words, the property rights system proved to be an important element of economic development (La Porta et al. 2003).

Third, the rule of law and private property rights in any country are the essential elements of economic development. The effectiveness of the judicial system has a significant impact on economic and social development (Hall and Jones 1999; Acemoglu et al. 2001).

4.2 *Statistic Trends of Civil Litigation*

Table 2 shows the trends related to the amount of civil litigation filed in all courts between 1960 and 2015. Litigation refers to civil litigation merits, including small claims cases. As shown in Table 2, the total amount of civil litigation sharply increased during the late 1980s. However, small claims cases were introduced not exceeding the monetary value of 20,000 USD (20 million KRW) in 1973 in the ordinary courts as well as the municipal courts. The common procedure in small claims cases has been to resolve matters at the pretrial stage in contrast to ordinary civil litigation.

During the fifty-five years from 1960 to 2015, the statistics show some characteristics which rely not only on the legal culture of Korean citizens but also on various societal economic factors. The population in 2015 was twice that of 1960, and the rate of civil litigation cases was 44 times that of 1960. The GDP in 2015 was 54 times that of 1960 and the figure of practicing attorneys was 44 times that of 1960. The number of litigation cases per 1000 citizens increased from 1.2 cases (1960) to 25.8 cases (2015). In particular, small claims cases have constituted the main source of civil litigations during 1975–2010. The rate of small claims has exceeded 70% of the total civil litigations per year. However, the curve of small claims has gradually decreased in contrast to the trend of civil merits cases since 2005 (Kim and Han 2007). In short, it has been shown that the increase in civil litigation was directly correlated with the increase in GDP and population.

[30] Pareto optimality is a state of allocation of resources from which it is impossible to reallocate so as to make any one individual or preference criterion better off without making at least one individual or preference criterion worse off.

Table 2 Statistic trend of civil litigation, population and real GDP (1960–2015)

Year	Civil litigation[a]	Small claims (B)[b]	Practicing attorney[c]	Population (thousand)[d]	GDP(Billion KRW)[e]
1960	29,863	–	456	25,012	27,305
1965	73,400	–	662	28,704	38,821
1970	68,847	–	719	32,882	67,650
1975	102,138	88,610 (86.7%)	809	35,280	108,549
1980	134,204	84,560 (63%)	940	38,123	163,065
1985	316,177	165,316 (52.3%)	1320	40,805	254,991
1990	302,156	136,075 (45%)	1983	42,869	419,518
1995	524,065	308,269 (58.8%)	3078	45,092	628,442
2000	771,551	495,814 (64.3%)	4228	47,008	820,843
2005	1,121,889	868,370 (77.4%)	6997	49,267	1,034,337
2010	1,133,188	687,449 (60.6%)	10,263	49,554	1,265,308
2015	1,318,640	686,407 (52%)	20,200	51,075	1,466,788

Source [a,b](Supreme Court, Judicature Yearbooks)
[c](Korea Bar Association Yearbooks)
[d](Statistics Korea)
[e](Bank of Korea's Economic Statistics System)

If it is difficult for litigants to access small claims cases, Fig. 1 shows that the judicial system may not work due to the costs of litigation. Civil litigations have increased to more than twice that of the 1980s since the crisis of currency in 1997, due to a harsh increase in small claims cases which were equivalent to an average rate of 70% in total civil merits until 2010 (Jung 2015a). This is plain evidence that Korea was under the explosion of civil litigation during two decades (1990–2010). The ratio of civil litigation in proportion to the population has rapidly increased because of small claims by banking creditors against debtors, from 45% at the end of 1990 to 77% in 2005. For example, 66 banking and financial companies sued 560,000 debtors through small claims actions under 20,000 USD among a total of 1,121,889 merits civil cases in 2005 (Jung 2015a). If we can easily control lots of small claims litigation, apart from merits of civil cases, this study may examine the essential relationship between judicial disputes and court trials, as well as the underlying reasons why Alternative Dispute Resolution ('ADR') in various forms has not flourished in social disputes resolution for a long time (Jung 2014b).

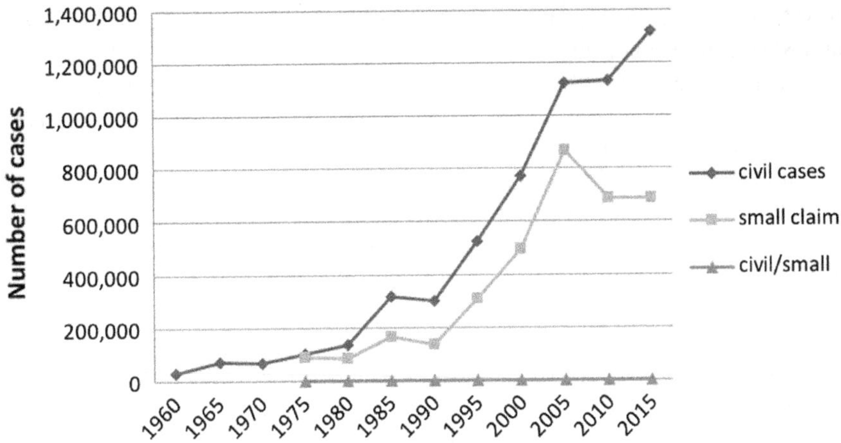

Fig. 1 The curve of Civil litigation and small claims in Korea (1960–2015)

As a rule, Korean people have traditionally avoided court trials as a form of dispute settlement due to a legal culture and tradition of avoiding a lawsuit in accordance with the maxim "litigant makes himself ruin by the lawsuit." In the Ly Dynasty, all of the public agencies had to carry out both administrative and judicial power, but they did not have the professional responsibility of a judge. Most litigants had to spend significant time and money to settle a legal dispute. For this reason, they have generally emphasized the importance of the professional responsibility of judges in the resolution of a legal dispute. When a plaintiff sues a defendant for a breach of contract, there is a de facto bias regarding the litigation as a zero-sum game in which the plaintiff will be a winner against the defendant. Two parties will not take into consideration alternative dispute resolution options such as a conciliation or mediation process by a non-judge. Although there is clear positive evidence of cost and time savings, and numerous other benefits of some judicial resolution programs, it is evident that ordinary parties to civil litigations depend on the results of civil adjudication and the winner's feeling of gratification against the loser in that lawsuit (Jung 2010).

4.3 *Relative Responsive Type of Court Mediation*

4.3.1 The Introduction and Management of Early Mediation

The original function of law focuses on maintaining social order and resolving disputes, but the function of modern law is creating and promoting social change. The function of laws promoting social change has recently emerged as a legislative trend (Jung 2014b). In 1990, the Court enacted the Civil Conciliation Act (hereafter

'CMA') in order to facilitate the small claims in civil litigation. The civil conciliation procedure can economically resolve civil disputes, with a judge or conciliation committee of the court able to hear an allegation from parties to the lawsuit, and suggest mediation plan by taking into consideration various circumstances. Compromise is reached through mutual concession. The civil conciliation has some advantages for the parties, courts, and judges. First, it is a fundamental, final, and early resolution of legal disputes for both the court and the parties. Second, civil conciliation minimizes judicial expense, constituting one-tenth of the cost of ordinary civil litigation. Third, parties can easily use civil conciliation procedures and can be freed from the strict formalism of legal procedure. Fourth, since it may not apply to the zero-sum game, even the worst resolution is better than the judgment (Schlichten ist besser als Richten). Fifth, civil conciliation respects the decision of the parties and makes it possible to voluntarily carry out the dispute, which makes it less vulnerable to neighbors. Sixth, the burden of the court or judge can be alleviated, and a fair and speedy trial can be achieved (Jung 2014b). In the CMA, the conciliating agencies are a subordinate judge, annexed court, and the conciliation committee (judge or annexed court). During the period of 2002–2009, conciliation cases by litigants in civil cases were below 1%, but in the case of court decisions, most mediation cases by an annexed court have exceeded 90% in civil litigation cases (2014a).[31] In particular, "the early mediation" was introduced because the rate of applications for mediation was very low at 1% during the 1990s, and civil conciliation procedure has been conducted at the discretion of the civil court or mediating judge (Jung 2014a). Before the Court-Annexed Mediator Committee and Trial-Day Mediation System were introduced in civil disputes resolution in the District Courts in 2009 and 2010, most of the civil conciliation cases were dependent upon the litigants' will or the judge's discretion due to the inclination of the zero-sum game from traditional legal culture (Jung 2014b).

According to the CMA, "early mediation" is a tribunal attempting to wait for the trial period before the trial on the merits of the case. In other words, it intends to resolve the dispute early after the investigation of the previous evidence or before/after the closing of the pleading of litigation. Before the trial court appoints the first date of the trial, or before the commencement of the trial, the case is referred to the mediation procedure by the trial court and the mediation committee exercises early mediation at its discretion not involving the court. If the trial court submits the case to the mediating judge, the judge assigns the early mediation to the court mediator [CMA 7(2)], or the non-standing mediation committee, or an external mediating agency who shall hear the opinions of the parties and carry out the necessary investigations [CMA 7(3)]. The standing mediator shall himself process it, and the non-standing mediator and the external mediator shall report the results to the judge in charge within two months. If the parties reach an agreement on their dispute, the judge shall make a decision or amendment to the mediation procedures. If an agreement is not reached, it will be referred to the trial court proceedings.

---

[31] Judge Lee Young-jin carried out Mediation Procedure in the Seoul District Court from 2010 to 2014, and he presented at the performance of the Court Conciliation System in 2014.

Table 3 Statistic trend of mediation cases in 2002–2012 (Korea)

Year	Civil cases	Small claims (A)	Party's mediation (B)	Judge's mediation (C)	Court-annexed mediation		Total mediation
					Committee mediation (D)	Court's mediation (E)	B + C + D + E sub total
2002	1,015,894	795,371	6918	4564	5362	47,971	64,815 (8.15%)
2003	1,151,072	906,205	7283	3260	4127	44,905	59,575 (6.6%)
2004	1,190,231	934,378	7041	2749	3319	49,650	62,759 (6.7%)
2005	1,121,889	868,370	6660	2594	2983	49,706	61,943 (7.1%)
2006	1,288,987	967,588	5800	2838	2838	43,015	54,581 (5.6%)
2007	1,213,805	901,488	6848	49,346	2780	46,566	105,540 (11.7%)
2008	1,259,031	944,712	9216	57,824	1546	56,278	124,864 (13.2%)
2009	1,074,236	780,220	11,382	58,459	2226	56,446	128,513 (16.5%)
2010	981,188	687,449	10,166	64,93	6206	58,729	140,036 (20.3%)
2011	985,533	690,239	7722	67,090	9616	57,474	141,901 (20.6%)
2012	1,044,928	739,842	8112	75,033	15,378	59,655	158,175 (21.4%)

Early Mediation has the following characteristics in Table 3: (1) At the beginning of a civil trial, the early mediation may heal up litigants' torments by prompt resolution of his/her legal dispute to the courts; (2) The expertise and experience of the mediation committee can facilitate communication and reconciliation between litigants; and (3) The mediating committee may hear the opinions of parties regarding the time and place, and shall establish conditions for the coordination of the meeting time and place where possible. While dispute settlement has been increased by early mediation, the success rate of mediation is not high. The mediating effort of judges and mediators in courts is affecting the settlement of disputes by mediation. For example, it is difficult for a mediating judge or court mediator to transfer the civil litigation case of a lawyer into the early mediation procedure in practice. In fact, most litigants or judges have been inactive and passive for the civil mediation cases, but improvements to the mediation institution have rapidly enhanced the early mediation of small claims cases through annexed-court judicial resolution since 2009. Consequently, in recent years, most judges in district courts have gradually been responsive by encouraging early mediation for uni-litigants in 90 percent of total small claims litigation cases.[32]

[32] According to the statistics of Supreme Court's Judicature Yearbook, the rate of uni-litigants consistently appeared at about 90 percent among total small claims litigation until the 2000s (Jung 2014a).

5 Pro-responsive Type of Court Mediation in Japan

5.1 Responsive Civil Mediation

The first comprehensive overhaul of Japan's Civil Procedure Code, since it was enacted in 1890 drawing primarily on German law (Taniguchi 1997), took effect in 1998 and added discretionary restrictions on the final right of appeal to the Supreme Court. Under Japan's current judicial system, whilst litigants of civil dispute may file a lawsuit to a court, there are also other litigation procedures as follows: (1) ordinary civil lawsuits, bankruptcy procedures, and civil preservation procedures can be brought to a district court or summary court; (2) small claims procedures and dunning procedures (request for payment of a fixed sum of monetary claim on debt) can be brought to a summary court; and (3) conciliation litigation prior to a lawsuit can be brought to a summary court.

During the first industrialization of Japan, the rate of civil litigation cases hardly increased from 146,855 cases (1960) to 148,920 cases (1975), but the rate of civil Summary cases did gradually increase by 22% from 155,981 (1960) to 190,782 cases (1975). This shows the impact of a stable social structure and the politics of Japan at that time. As almost Japanese remained true to traditional values including avoiding lawsuits in this period (1960–1975), Kawashima saw a gap between Japanese citizen's legal consciousness and principles of modern law (Kawashima 1967).

By contrast, the trend of civil litigation and conciliation cases sharply increased by 267% from 1975 (148,920 cases) to 1995 (397,765 cases). There was also a large fluctuation from −42 to 110% between 1985 (360,965 cases), 1990 (208,949 cases), and 1995 (397,765 cases) due to civil litigation cases in Courts. As shown in Fig. 2, the small claims of summary courts have consistently increased about 300% in civil litigation from 1970 (190,782 cases) to 2000 (573,366 cases). Most of the small claim cases have not exceeded 900 thousand yen (9000 USD) and 93% of the increase in litigation from 1974 to 2003 (367,759 cases) can be accounted for by small pecuniary claims (342,717), 83% of which were summary court cases (287,230 cases).[33] Those kinds of small pecuniary claims have been filed and won by credit loan companies via default judgments or instant adjustments (Tanase 2001; Hamano 1999–2000). Most litigants in small pecuniary claims have hardly made use of attorneys (Hamano 1999–2000).[34] These phenomena indicate two factors. First, in the 1970s, consumer credit loans and sales rapidly came into wide use among individuals in a period of a low growth economy. Second, repeat litigants of credit firms have made use of the instrumental litigation and judicial system.

[33]In 1982, the value of the subject matter of jurisdiction for Summary Courts was raised from 300 thousand yen to 900 thousand yen. In 2004, it was raised again to 1400 thousand yen.

[34]The rate of attorney-less cases in all of the Summary Courts was about 68.9% in 1973. This rate continued to rise to about 90% in 1995 and later (Ozaki 2007).

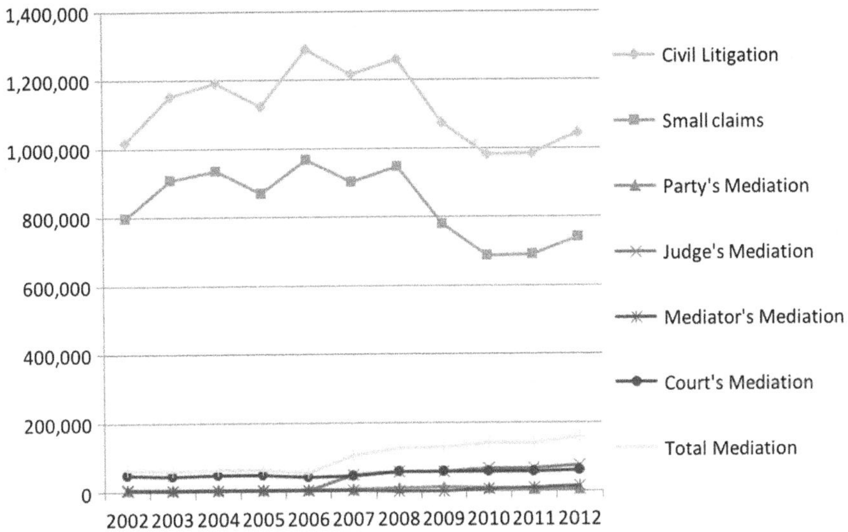

Fig. 2 Mediation curve of civil litigation and small claims in Korea (2002–2012)

The trend of civil litigation has shown large-scale fluctuations between 1980 and 1995, with a 'bubble economy' emerging between 1985 and 1990.[35] Although the ratio of summary procedures, including civil mediations, slightly increased between 1985 and 1990, this kind of civil procedure was not a complete substitute for civil litigation. During the bubble economy in the 1990s, small claims cases rapidly increased 23.7% from 1990 (435,967 cases) to 1995 (539,541 cases). However, the increasing rate (10%) of civil litigation in this period (from 360,965 to 397,765 cases) remained the same level (17.6%) as it was from 1970 (174,013 cases) to 1980 (204,801 cases) (Fig. 3 and Table 4).

5.2 *Conciliation of Summary Court*

Conciliation may be disposed of by the court based on the mutual consent of parties to settle a dispute on certain conditions. A Judge in a lawsuit can make a settlement pending the lawsuit. The Judge may intervene after having heard the evidence or part of the evidence. It is normal practice that the Judge sets a date for a conciliation conference instead of a trial (Rokumoto 1986). The Judge may form her/his legal evaluation of the trial case on the basis of evidence already taken or submitted before she/he suggests to the parties to seek a mutually agreeable solution or to consider a proposed solution. If a settlement is reached in this way, which the judge approves, then the terms of a settlement are registered in the court's protocol and they acquire

[35] The Plaza Agreement depreciated the dollar value between America and Japan in 1985.

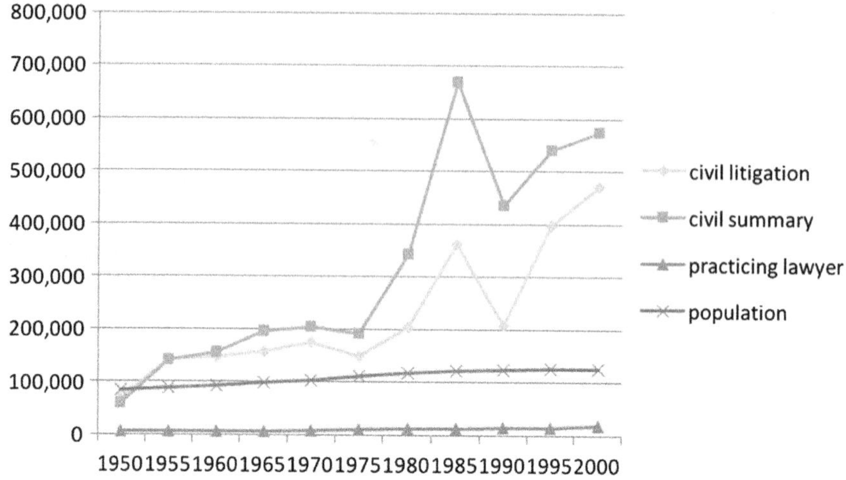

Fig. 3 The curve of civil litigation, lawyer and GDP in Japan (1950–2000)

Table 4 Statistic trend of civil cases, population and GDP in Japan (1950–2000)

Year	Civil litigation[a]	Civil summary[b]	Practicing lawyer[c]	Population (thousand)	GDP (Billion Yen)
1950	66,746	58,761	5804	83,200	–
1955	142,975	141,217	5967	89,276	–
1960	146,855	155,981	6439	93,419	71,683
1965	158,355	195,981	7343	98,275	111,294
1970	174,013	204,556	8797	103,720	188,323
1975	148,920	190,782	10,421	111,940	234,459
1980	204,801	342,209	11,624	117,060	310,720
1985	360,965	669,439	12,830	121,830	365,304,
1990	208,949	435,967	14,080	123,611	463,059
1995	397,765	539,541	15,456	125,570	498,697
2000	471,770	573,366	18,243	126,926	534,411

Source [a,b]Supreme Court of Japan, Annual Report of Judicial Statistics (Shibo Tokei Nenpo) [c]Hayashiya & Sugawara 2001 and Japan Federation of Bar Associations, Liberty & Justice (Jiyu to Seigi), No. 627, 639, 664

the same final effect as a formal judgment of the court. Litigants can appeal following the conciliation. The aim of conciliation and mediation is to reach a legally binding settlement of the dispute. However, the difference between conciliation and private mediation is that the former includes discovery of evidence and statement of claim and allegation in open court.

Furthermore, mediation refers to another way of bringing a civil case to court. It may take place informally out-of-court, with a third party assisting the parties to reach a settlement.[36] Mediation takes into consideration not only the legal merits of the case, but also any other aspects of the case relevant to its resolution between both parties. As the judge is normally too busy to take part in the hearing sessions of mediation, a layman may also attend to assist the litigants in the mediation procedure. After the fluctuation of litigation in the 1990s, civil litigation cases constantly increased. Civil mediation cases also accounted for the increase in Summary Cases which composed more than 95% of the mediation litigation during the 1990s.[37]

6 Conclusion

Korea and Japan have some common characteristics in their legal culture and legal system which have rooted from their Confucian heritages and colonial Civil Law as well as a political culture of the vortex and symbiotic societal environment. In Korea and Japan, most judges are politically independent and professionally competent in the world today. Organized as an autonomous bureaucracy, the judiciary comprises a small, largely self-regulating cadre of elite legal professionals who enjoy with reason an extraordinarily high level of public trust. The vast majority of judges begin their careers in their mid-to-late 20s upon graduation from the court-administered Legal Training and Research Institute (LTRI) and Law School. Most spend a professional life of 20–30 years within the nation-wide structure of courts that they themselves administer. Assignments and promotions are determined by a central personnel office staffed by peers.

In Korea's politics, however, authoritarian governments emphasized political efficiency through economic modernization rather than political legitimacy based on democracy until the late 1990s. Moreover, the military elite had an affinity for the instrumental value of economic development rather than the democratic value in Korean modernization and post-democracy (Jung 2015b). Furthermore, the judicial culture has shown the characteristics of the pursuit of jurists' rent-seeking that limit the opportunities for legal services of citizens in a legal market. Authoritarian political power guaranteed monopoly rents to minority lawyers based on repressive law. In fact, the term "preferential treatment" refers to the endowment of making an income several times higher than their former job as a judge or prosecutor, even after their retirement. This legal culture may violate the fairness and efficiency of the judiciary and is contrary to the legal ethics of judges and lawyers. Moreover, the culture may threaten the justice of the judiciary and result in a rigid formalism in the judicial procedure.

---

[36]Japan's civil mediations are composed of civil mediation procedures and family matter mediation procedures. Civil mediation is a procedure involving the litigant's choice to bring his/her complaint before the Summary Court or a District Court. Family matter mediation is a proceeding instituted in the Family court for matrimonial disputes, including those involving divorce.

[37]This expulsion of civil litigation cases strikes a sharp contrast to the mediation system in Korea, which failed before the introduction of early mediation in 2009.

There is a slight difference in the concept of "civil litigation" which Korean courts deal with in civil trials, including "small claims" that are conducted on the legal merits of the dispute. However, Japan's civil litigation excludes the cases of "dunning procedures" which is only preliminary to a lawsuit proper, as well as the cases of "civil motion" and "civil execution", which are both only auxiliary to a lawsuit (Choi and Rokumoto 2007). Korea's civil litigation does not cover the family litigations or administrative litigations, but family mediation procedure is compulsory for family disputes under the Family Litigation Act. In fact, in Korea and Japan it is mandatory for family matter litigants to resort to family mediation procedure first, and only when attempts at mediation procedure have failed are litigants then allowed to file a lawsuit to the ordinary court. In particular, although the constitutional review is contrasted with the activism of the Constitutional Court and conservatism of the Supreme Court, both judiciaries of Korea and Japan are equally remarkable in terms of their statistical similarity of mediation cases.

But Japan's Supreme Court has hardly had this kind of judicial responsiveness and autonomy from political influence and control. It seems that Japanese judicial conservatism stems from the pre-war reception of German statutory positivism. However, the German legacy establishes itself as an invisible constitution, rather than judicial philosophy. In sum, the Japanese Supreme Court can be active or conservative, depending on how it assesses the risk of judicialization (Matsudaira 2011). However, Japan's judiciary and its judges are more responsive and autonomous for mediation cases in civil litigations than Korea's judiciary, because the Japanese judiciary has a relatively long comparative legal history which commenced from the civil law of 1868 and common law of 1947. Furthermore, most judges have been mentored and monitored by seniors and peers.

In addition, a major disincentive to litigation has always been the longstanding delay of most constitutional adjudication and civil litigation in both Korea and Japan. Japan's reforms implemented in 1998 have helped keep this issue on the agenda, and an aim of the reforms seems to be to make the courtroom less daunting by involving more laypersons. This parallels the reintroduction of a jury or lay assessor (saiban-in) scheme for serious criminal cases, which was enacted in 2004 and took effect from 2006 in Japan (Nottage 2005; Ambler 2007; Corey and Hans 2010).

References

Acemoglu D, Johnson S, Robinson JA (2001) The colonial origins of comparative development: an empirical investigation. Am Econ Rev 91(5):1369–1401

Ahn K (1998) The influence of American constitutionalism on South Korea, Southern Ill. ULJ 22:71–115

Ambler L (2007) The people decide: the effect of the introduction of the quasi-jury system (Saiban-In Seido) on the death penalty in Japan. Northwest J Int Hum Rights 6(1):1–23

Ashibe N (1994) Constitutional Law (Japanese version). Yuhikaku, Tokyo

Becker Gary (1993) Human capital: a theoretical and empirical analysis, with special reference to education, 3rd edn. University of Chicago Press, Illinois

Beer LW, Itoh H (1996) The constitutional case law of Japan. University of Washington Press, Seattle

Choi D (1995) Informal ways vs. the formal law in Korea (Paper presented at Research Committee on the Sociology of Law, Tokyo, July 2015)

Choi D, Rokumoto K (eds) (2007) Judicial system transformation in the global world. Seoul National University Press, Seoul

Constitutional Court of Korea (2010) The twenty years of the constitutional court of Korea. The Constitutional Court, Seoul

Corey Z, Hans VP (2010) Japan's new lay judge system: deliberative democracy in action? Asian-Pac Law Policy J 12:72–94

Corwin E (1929) The "higher law" background of American constitutional law. Harvard Law Rev 42:149–185

Cotterrell R (2006) Law, culture & society. Ashgate, London

Djankov S, La Porta R, Lopez-de-Silans F, Shleifer A (2002) Court: The Lex Mundi Project. Working paper 8890. National Bureau of Economic Research, Cambridge

Dressel B (2012) Courts and governance in Asia: exploring variations and effects, international political science association (Paper presented at the XIV World Congress of Political Science, Madrid, 8–12 July 2012)

Friedman LM (1969) Legal culture and social development. Law Soc Rev 4:29–44

Friedman LM (2002) American law in the twentieth century. Yale University Press, New Haven

Frohnmayer DB (1973) The separation of powers: an essay on the vitality of a constitutional idea. Or Law Rev 52:211–219

Fujikura K (ed) (1996) Japanese law and legal theory. New York University Press, New York

Ginsburg T (2003) Judicial review in new democracies. Cambridge University Press, Cambridge

Hahm P (1986) Korean jurisprudence, politics and culture. Yonsei University Press, Seoul

Hahn EE (1983) An overview of the Japanese legal system. Northwest J Int Law Bus 5:520–521

Haley JO (2007) The Japanese judiciary: maintaining integrity, autonomy and the public trust. In: Foote DH (ed) Law in Japan. University of Washington Press, Seattle, pp 99–135

Hall RE, Jones CI (1999) Why do some countries produce so much more output per worker than other? Quart J Econ 114(1):83–116

Hamano R (1999–2000) Shihokaikaku no Teii [Context of Judicial Reform] *Rikkyo Hogaku* 53:101–148 and 55:172–203

Henderson DF (1965) Conciliation and Japanese law: Tokugawa and modern. Association for Asian Studies, Washington University Press, Seattle

Henderson Gregory (1968) Korea: politic of the vortex. Massachusetts Harvard University Press, Cambridge

Higuchi Y (2004) Lösung politischer Streitfragen durch die Verfassungsgerichsbarkeit [Solving Political Controversies through Constitutional Adjudication]. In: Starck C (ed) Fortschritt der Verfassungsgerichtsbarkeit in der Welt [Progress of Constitutional Adjudication in the World], pp 35–45

Ito M (1995) Constitutional law (Japanese version). Koubundou, Tokyo

Johnson S, McMillan J, Woodruff C (2002) Property rights and finance. Am Econ Rev 92:1335–1356

Jung YH (2010) The limit of rule of law in economic development in South Korea (Paper presented at the Annual Meeting of the Law & Society Association, Chicago, May 2010)

Jung YH (2011) Constitutional law. East Group Co., Seoul

Jung YH (2013a) Dispute resolution and the role of law and lawyers in compensation system (Paper presented at the Annual Meeting of the Law & Society Association, Boston, 31 May 2013)

Jung YH (2013b) The crisis of Korea democracy and problems of legal reformation—the critics of constitutional sociology on the vortex-centralized political culture. Law Rev 27:2–45

Jung YH (2014a) The role of court and lawyers in changing of legal culture in Korea: Revitalization of court annexed-civil mediation. Law Rev 42

Jung YH (2014b) The economic development and governance of industrial policy in Korea (1961–2014). In: Kim K, Jung YH (eds) The institution and policy for industrial upgrading:

Korean experiences and implications for developing countries, Seoul, Korea Industrial Economic Institute (KIEA)
Jung YH (2015a) The international comparison of Korean judicial system and renovation of its efficiency: the adoption of compulsory mini-mediation on small claims. J Justice 146:142–186
Jung YH (2015b) Constitutional Sociology. Chonbuk National University Press, Jeonju
Jung YH (2016) The comparative study of constitutional interpretation between U.S. Supreme Court and East Asian Constitutional Court (Korea & Japan). Paper presented at the Annual Meeting of the Law & Society Association, New Orleans, June 2016
Katzmann RA (1988) The underlying concerns. In: Katzmann RA (ed) Judges and legislators: toward institutional comity, Brookings Institution, Washington, D.C., pp 14–15
Kawashima T (1967) Nihon-jin no Ho-ishiki [The Japanese Legal Consciousness]. Iwanami Shoten, Tokyo
Kim D, Han S (2007) Civil litigation in Korea: trend and analysis. In: Choi D, Rokumoto K (eds) Judicial system transformation in the globalizing world: Korea and Japan. Seoul National University Press, Seoul, pp 69–104
La Porta RF, Lopez-de-Silance CP-E, Shleifer A (2003) Judicial checks and balances. J Polit Econ 112(2):445–470
Lee Y (2014) The significance and performance of court conciliation system. Semin Court's Mediat Issue Perspect Oct. 21 2014:1–14
Lockwood W (1968) The economic development of Japan. Princeton University Press, Princeton
Lopez Guerra L (1994) The role and competencies of the constitutional court. European commission for democracy through law. Paper presented at the UniDem Seminar Bucharest, 8–10 June 1994
Matsudaira T (2011) Judicialization of politics and the Japanese Supreme Court. Wash Univ Law Rev 88:1559–1569
Matsui S (2011) Why is the Japanese Supreme Court so conservative? Wash Univ Law Rev 88(6):1375–1423
North DC (1990) Institutions, institutional change and economic performance. Cambridge University Press, Cambridge
Nottage L (2005) Civil procedure reforms in Japan: the latest round. Ritsumeikan Law Rev 22:81–86
Okudaira Y (1990) Forty years of the constitution and its various influences: Japanese, American, and European, law and contemporary problems. Law Contemp Probl 53:17–49
Ozaki I (2007) Civil litigation in postwar Japan. In: Choi D, Rokumoto K (eds) Judicial system transformation in the globalizing world: Korea and Japan. Seoul National University Press, Seoul, pp 105–136
Rokumoto K (1986) Hōshakaigaku. Yūhikaku, Tokyo
Sólyom L (2010) The role of constitutional courts in the transition to democracy. Int Sociol 18(1):133–161
Tanase T (2001) Soshoriyo to Kindaika Kasetsu [Litigation and the Modernization Hypothesis]. In: Aoyama Y et al (eds) Minjisoshoho Riron No Aratana Kochiku [New Constructions in civil Procedure Law Theory]. Yuhikaku, Tokyo, pp 287–322
Tanaka H (ed) (1976) The Japanese legal system: introductory cases and materials. University of Tokyo Press, Tokyo
Taniguchi Y (1997) The 1996 code of civil procedure of Japan—a procedure for the coming century? Am J Comp Law 45:767–791
West J, Yoon D (1992) The constitutional court of the Republic of Korea: transforming the jurisprudence of the vortex. Am J Comp Law 40(1):73–119
Yang K (1993) Judicial reviewing and social change in the Korean democratizing process. Am J Comp Law 41(1):1–8
Yang K, Kim M, Nam B (1999) Report on reform of the Korean constitutional court act (Korean version). Constitutional Adjudication No. 10, The Constitutional Court
Yoon D-K (1995) New developments in Korean constitutionalism: changes and prospects. Pac Rim Law Policy J 4:395–418

Young Hoa Jung is a Professor at the Chonbuk National University School of Law. He holds a Ph.D. in Law, LLM and LLB from Seoul National University, and LLM from Northwestern University Law School. Professor Jung was a visiting scholar at Northwestern University Law School in 2006–2007 and 2009, and Wisconsin University Madison Law School in 2015–2016. He has also been a member of the Law and Society Association (USA) since 2000.

Mansfield, Atkin, Weinstein: Three Responsive Judges at the Nexus of Law, Politics, and Economy

Archie Zariski

Abstract This chapter examines a judge's role and function in responding to those unique, but not uncommon, cases which attract public attention to civil litigation normally considered to be of a "private" nature. It suggests that in such situations judges have an additional responsibility and opportunity to be responsive. The chapter surveys leading cases of responsive judging to draw out commonalities and lessons for the future. Three remarkable judges and their responsive decisions are discussed: *Somerset's Case (Somerset v Stewart)* before Chief Justice Mansfield, *Donoghue v Stevenson* as considered by Lord Atkin, and the *Agent Orange* litigation dealt with by the American Judge Jack Weinstein. A theme is developed from these cases which may be stated as the judge's overriding concern for doing justice in a way which will resonate with the public while at the same time respecting law and the legal system. Judges who navigate the nexus between law and justice while in the public eye use their legal skills, social knowledge, and human responsiveness to do justice to those who appear before them. Judges in an era of increasing openness of courts and pervasive social media may find valuable guidance in these iconic cases. By way of conclusion some thoughts are offered concerning responsive judging focusing on a judge's responsibility to secure as substantively just a result as possible, within the limits of the law, which is not limited to providing the appearance of justice through procedural propriety.

1 Introduction

This chapter is about judging legal disputes which do not involve the State as a party or the consideration of laws of general application to everyone in a State. From the perspective of the common law the core cases in this category are disputes involving torts or contracts between individuals or corporations. What is unique about the cases to be discussed is that they drew great public attention either at the time they were

A. Zariski (✉)
Athabasca University, Edmonton, Canada
e-mail: archiez@athabascau.ca

© Springer Nature Singapore Pte Ltd. 2018

T. Sourdin and A. Zariski (eds.), *The Responsive Judge*, Ius Gentium: Comparative Perspectives on Law and Justice 67, https://doi.org/10.1007/978-981-13-1023-2_12

being decided or subsequently. Judges face significant challenges when the public or its putative representatives becomes directly involved in litigation such as cases with intervenors or *amicus curiae*, public interest litigation (see Friedlander 1995), and also when the public interest becomes an explicit factor for consideration in decision making, but that is not the focus here. Further, the public interest in the efficient administration of the legal system, while important, is not considered by this chapter. Thus we set aside considerations relating to the provision of courts and adjudication as a public service, and as a public good from the economic perspective. Rather, this study is about what wise judges do when the public is just watching intently and waiting for a just result. Judge Jack Weinstein, speaking about cases involving large numbers of litigants which naturally attract public attention, affirmed his position as follows:

> Mass tort cases unfortunately do not involve the application of legislative schemes representing careful analysis of the policy problems presented. By their very nature, these cases involve unanticipated problems with wide-ranging social and political ramifications.
>
> A judge does not "legislate from the bench" simply because he or she considers the broadest implications of his or her decisions in such a case. Judges not only may take such a view; they must. (Weinstein 1995, 541)

The concerns expressed by Judge Weinstein illustrate the broad and compassionate view that all responsive judges bring to their craft.[1]

Such a perspective on judging raises difficult questions including the values of litigant self-determination and autonomy in conducting litigation juxtaposed to public expectations, and the independence and objectivity of the judicial branch set beside public demands for justice. Today there may be increased actual interest of the public in litigation as channeled and expressed through mass and social media. In Canada, for instance, the national television provider, CBC, allows people with legal disputes to "Go Public" with their complaints and in doing so seek redress via the influence of the "court of public opinion". To what extent is this a sign of increasing competition for the role of dispensing justice and what is the appropriate response of judges? Public interest in just decision making in particular cases also brings into play the ongoing debate ignited by Fiss (1984) concerning the role of settlement in legal dispute resolution (Luban 1995; Menkel-Meadow 1995; Carrington and Apanovitch 1997).

The challenges and issues mentioned above will be applied in the context of several notable historical and contemporary cases within common law systems. These case studies help to illuminate the tension inherent in the judicial role between satisfying the interested public's desire for justice and the fair application of the law in the context of the private interests of litigants. The first case discussed below is that in which Lord Mansfield was faced with a decision whether to uphold rights of dominion over a slave: *Somerset v. Stewart*. What interests were at stake in that litigation and

[1]Responsive judges can partly be distinguished as those who perceive in some cases before them wider ramifications for society than the narrow legal and factual issues put in dispute by the parties. They thus approach some cases as if they were "public law litigation" although not actually involving public law. See Chayes (1976) and Fiss (1979).

how did he resolve them in the name of justice? The next case explored is the famous one of *Donoghue v. Stevenson*, in which a rather modest claim for personal injury made its way to the highest court in the land and there became a landmark of common law jurisprudence. How did this happen in the context of a society in which consumers were not yet recognized as the face of the public? The *Agent Orange* litigation is then examined as a modern leading example of managerial judging and court sanctioned settlement processes used in a search for justice. What private interests were at play and how were they considered and balanced by the judge in the intense glare of public scrutiny? Following exploration of these questions, limits to the practice of responsive judging are examined as well as some interesting conceptual and doctrinal links among the cases considered here.

2 Somerset's Case

2.1 Background

Somerset's Case (1772, properly cited as *Somerset v Stewart*), was a proceeding claiming *habeas corpus* which questioned the right of a master of a ship (Stewart) to detain on board a black man (Somerset) on the instructions of Somerset's purported owner, a man originally from the American colony of Virginia. The writ had been issued by Chief Justice Mansfield to activists for the abolition of slavery and was returned to him for trial of the issue as to whether the detention was lawful. It was not the first case in which the legality of slavery had been raised before the Chief Justice, and it was not the last. In a prior case for assault by a purported master against his slave Mansfield had seen to it that the jury recognized weakness in the proof of ownership of the black man in question, and therefore found against the master on that factual ground (*Rex ex rel. Lewis v Stapylton* 1771). Subsequently, the defendant was never brought back before him for assessment of damages. In a later case (Gregson 1783) Mansfield was able to avoid the issue of the legality of slavery, but Somerset's case, in contrast to these others, clearly and inescapably presented that burning legal question.

Somerset should be considered in the context of serious related legal, political, and economic issues as well as momentous events such as the American Revolution which would erupt four years later. The legal status of slaves in England had been debated by lawyers and considered in the English courts for over a century before *Somerset* arose. Some decisions pointed to its illegality (*Smith* 1701, 1705), while an influential legal opinion authored jointly by the Solicitor General and Attorney General supported the legal status of slavery and denied one popular proposition that slaves were automatically freed upon entry into the mother country (quoted in Knight 1778). Some arguments revolved around the supposed exemplary nature of the common law and its support for the freedoms of all persons, sometimes in opposition to the will of Parliament and the Crown. Complicating the legal picture were a number of English statutes encouraging, supporting, and regulating the slave trade abroad such as *An Act To Settle the Trade to Africa*, (1698) 9&10 Will. Ill, c. 26., and *An Act for the more easy Recovery of Debts in His Majesty's Plantations and Colonies in America*, (1731/2) 5 Geo. II, c. 7. Accordingly, it might be open to argument that Parliament had already spoken on the matter. Finally, questions were raised about the applicability of the English common law in the colonies and whether this raised issues of conflict of laws, or indeed of the invalidity of colonial legislation in some cases (Wiecek 1974).

Some of these legal questions had direct political parallels and echoes. The governability of the rising British Empire was at stake when choices had to be made between a universal common law, British Statutes and Crown decrees, and local colonial laws and regulations, many of which either explicitly established or recognized the legal status of slavery (see Van Cleve 2006a, b; Hulsebosch 2006). This was one crux of American dissatisfaction which spurred the independence movement. Slave owners in the colonies were wealthy and powerful and could influence public opinion on that question. Many of them also resided in England and maintained a strong lobby on the home government. Law and politics, as always, were inextricably mixed (see Paley 2006).

Finally, slavery was also related to pressing economic questions and controversies. Should trade (including that in slaves) be made freer or more restricted? What would be the effect on plantation economies in the colonies of freeing slaves? What impact would there be on the capital markets if slave owners were suddenly disposed of a substantial part of their assets in the form of slave workers? Such questions pointed to the key role of slavery in contributing to the advance of the Empire at this point in its history. Mansfield was well aware of all these competing influences which were connected to important political and economic interests of the day.

2.2 Chief Justice Mansfield

William Murray, later Earl Mansfield, was an outsider in the English establishment.[2] A Scot, he made his way up the legal ranks in London despite prejudice against his countrymen and suspicions of his personal loyalty to the British Crown. Nevertheless, through hard work, the application of his considerable intelligence, and advantageous noble connections he succeeded in becoming a leading barrister, then Solicitor General, Attorney General and finally Chief Justice of the Court of King's Bench, the leading common law court in the country. Along the way he was a Member of Parliament and for a time, a Cabinet Minister. As Chief Justice he was very seldom overruled by the Lords, and was respected widely throughout the judiciary. Consequently, his word on the common law most often became the law of the land. In time he became the most famous jurist of his day and a public figure to the extent

[2]The following portrait of Lord Mansfield is largely drawn from Oldham (1992) and Hutchinson (2012).

that at one point his London house was burned down by those protesting his decisions on religious freedom.

Although Mansfield was devoted to the common law and its improvement, notably in commercial areas, he was also a staunch monarchist, supported George III in opposition to the criticisms of the colonies, and welcomed the ultimate authority of Parliament. He was a friend of the merchant class, members of which he invited on special juries to advise the court on business practices, and a supporter of free trade which he considered the lifeblood of the Empire. It has been said that his primary aim and legacy to the development of law was to bring coherence and certainty to the common law. Many of the principles and doctrines he enunciated remain established law today. Oldham (1992, 197) proposes that Lord Mansfield's judicial work was guided by six overriding objectives including those above, but also that of "accomplishing individual justice through notions of fairness and equity".

One feature of Mansfield's private life is notable in the context of *Somerset*. He maintained in his household, on an equal footing with family members, a black woman named Dido Elizabeth Belle. It is supposed that she was the illegitimate daughter, born of a slave, of one of his nephews, a sea captain. In his last will and testament Mansfield "confirmed" her freedom and left her substantial property. Although one might assume that this personal experience would strongly incline the Chief Justice towards outlawing slavery, it is likely that such a decision was much more difficult for him. If such a judgment were to be made applicable to the colonies it would be a strong statement in favor of central rule by London (Van Cleve 2006a). To impeach slavery would also court the wrath of slave owners in the colonies who might thus find an additional reason to reject the Crown. Many established and wealthy merchants in England and abroad might be seriously affected in their trade and assets, not to mention the unpredictable impact of many thousands of freed slaves living in England on the economy and society of the motherland. For Mansfield, the question of slavery was likely anything but black and white so to speak!

2.3 Outcome

Mansfield allowed the case to drag on for many months with several adjournments in the hearing. Several eminent and upcoming counsel spoke on both sides. During this time a fierce public debate ensued about the case, with the actual arguments presented in court being published and commented on. All of the issues surrounding the case were in play including the fledgling concept of universal human rights and its relation to the common law, the potential economic consequences to merchants and the Empire of abolishing slavery, and the implications of a decision either way on the political and legal relations between London and the colonies.

Reports suggest that Mansfield strenuously tried to persuade the parties to settle by allowing the purported slave owner to grant "manumission" or freedom to Somerset (Fiddes 1934; Oldham 1988). It appears both sides rejected such a solution, the abolitionists because it would deny them a clear legal precedent, and slave owners, who supported and financed the other side, because it would signal weakness in their position and encourage others to escape (Fisher 1943).

Finally, Mansfield could do nothing other than give judgment. After reportedly describing the status of slavery as "odious" he found for Somerset and released him. His reasons were carefully crafted in the time honored common law practice of deciding only the case before him without speculating on other potential disputes or proclaiming broad generalizations concerning the law. He did not base his decision, as the abolitionists had hoped, on the essential repugnance of the English common law for the condition of slavery. Neither did he mention the English statutes concerning the colonial slave trade which the slave owners had relied on. Rather, emphasizing the onus on the respondent to demonstrate proper grounds for seizing and detaining Somerset, he found merely that no sufficient legal justification had been advanced. In his words (*Somerset* 1772, 510), this would require demonstration of "positive law" which allowed such extraordinary action in England and no such law had been produced to the court.

In so couching his judgment Mansfield could credibly assert that it decided nothing more than that there was no explicit law in England existing at the time which authorized the seizure and detention of a supposed slave. The abolitionists could rightfully claim a victory, but could not honestly announce that slavery had been abolished. On other side, slave owners could lobby and hope for passage in Parliament of a statute which would provide the required "positive law", but meanwhile could not avoid the precedent of *Somerset* in future similar *habeas corpus* cases. Despite its very limited holding, *Somerset* has nevertheless been considered in historical retrospect as a watershed in the abolitionist cause. It shifted the onus to the nation to make a moral-political choice through democratic means between the value of human dignity and the pursuit of slave-generated profit. The result in *Somerset* may have opened a better way forward for British society at the time than a judicial declaration of emancipation by force of law could have done.

2.4 *The Snail in the Bottle*

2.4.1 Background

In the early twentieth century English tort law, and in particular the law of negligence, was still relatively undeveloped. This may have been a consequence of the preoccupation in the preceding century with contracts as the foundation of most rights and obligations, and of the continuing influence of the old causes of action. In the field of negligence as applied between "strangers" who, legally speaking were those who had no contractual relationship, liability for injury was limited by a duty of care only on the part of those who purveyed goods which were dangerous in themselves, or dangerous if not used properly. Over the centuries judges had singled out certain goods and situations for imposition of liability as cases randomly came before the courts, but there was nothing that could be called a coherent theory or doctrine of negligence which tied them together.

The early 1900s were also a time when what we now identify as the modern consumer society and economy was first emerging. Everyday goods were beginning to be industrially produced in such volumes that an increasing proportion of the population could afford to purchase them. One consequence of this was the increasing commercial distance between manufacturer and consumer, making them both factually, and legally, complete strangers.

In Scotland, as in much of the rest of the world at this time, ginger beer was popular. One zealous Glasgow solicitor was apparently an early advocate of consumers' rights since he backed several cases for damages in negligence brought against ginger beer manufacturers for allowing mice to get into their bottles. These cases were unsuccessful in the Scottish courts. Then he came upon a new client, Mrs. Donoghue, who complained of finding a snail in ginger beer which had been purchased for her at a cafe by a friend.[3] Mrs. Donoghue's case gained more support from the trial judge who decided to allow it to proceed to proof of the facts, but the Scottish appeal court followed what they considered solid precedent and non-suited her. It was inconceivable that ginger beer could be considered dangerous as understood in any of the authorities. No duty of care had been recognized in such circumstances and therefore no liability attached, regardless of the existence or not of a snail in the bottle.

Fortunately for Mrs. Donoghue and her solicitor one of the judges on the appeal panel dissented. This gave them an opening to apply for leave to appeal to the House of Lords, which, according to its practice at the time, granted it in such circumstances. It is reported that upon hearing the application for leave the presiding law Lord suggested to the defendants that they might make it easier on themselves by simply settling with Mrs. Donoghue. This was rejected perhaps out of fear of a deluge of what they considered to be nuisance claims. Thus, Mrs. Donoghue's modest claim for damages arising from enteritis caused by contaminated ginger beer proceeded to the pre-eminent common law court for determination of the question whether the manufacturer owed a duty to the non-contracting consumer.

2.5 *Lord Atkin*

James Atkin, later Lord Atkin of Aberdovy, was born in Brisbane, Australia, of parents who had emigrated from Britain.[4] Atkin, however, returned to Wales with his mother as a young child while his father was ailing in Queensland. James thus grew up not far from Aberdovy and considered himself a Welshman, having never returned to

[3]The description of the litigation in *Donoghue v Stevenson* which follows is largely drawn from Chapman (2010).

[4]The following sketch of Lord Atkin is largely drawn from Lewis (1999) and Hutchinson (2012). See also Carney (2005), Applegarth (2015) and Luck (2015).

Australia. Shortly before his death, Atkin's father wrote a letter admonishing his son James to be ever modest and honorable—"a nice unaffected gentleman". It appears that Atkin fulfilled his father's dying wishes. As a trial judge in the King's Bench, then on the Court of Appeal, and finally in the Lords, it seems Atkin retained the humble touch. He continued taking London buses to and from the court into his final years, rode his bicycle around the countryside near his estate at Aberdovy, and regularly sat as a magistrate in the local court there during breaks from London. Through such everyday routines it appears that Atkin maintained in his thinking a strong dose of common sense that pervaded his perceptions of justice.[5]

Atkin enjoyed his work as a trial judge but apparently regretted his time on the Court of Appeal, partly because he was not in contact with the litigants themselves. He supported public legal education and commended the study of law to all educated people as conducing to better citizenship (Atkin 1932). It seems he consciously considered the role of law in society and its impact on the common person. As a devout member of the Welsh church he believed in the relevance of Christian principles to everyday life (see Castle 2003; Chamberlain 2010).

2.6 Outcome

Eminent counsel represented both Appellant and Respondent in *Donoghue v Stevenson* before the House of Lords panel hearing the matter which included Lord Atkin, but on which he was not the senior judge. The Appellant's arguments favored broadening the class of cases in which a duty of care could be found, focusing on the inability of anyone to examine the contents of the bottle after manufacture due to its opacity. This element could be considered to make the matter similar to a dangerous situation arising from the use of a product. For the Respondent it was argued that the authorities simply did not recognize a duty in such situations and there was no need to look any further. No precedent, no duty, no claim.

There was a substantial delay between hearing the appeal and delivery of the judgments and there is reason to think that some interaction took place between the members of the panel during this time. Another Law Lord not involved in the case had access to Atkin's and other draft speeches and commented on them. It is thus reasonable to suppose that Atkin had some part in persuading at least two other judges to follow his lead and allow the appeal, sending Mrs. Donoghue back to trial to prove her case.

A striking divergence emerged in the reasons for judgment of the majority and minority in *Donoghue v Stevenson*. Lord Buckmaster, in dissent, had scathing words for those who would extend the authorities beyond the categories of "inherently

[5]Harding (1964, 435) notes: "The primary impression that remains after reading a wide selection of his judgments is one of his profound and all-pervading common sense. It is not a spectacular quality, except when it is absent, but it would seem to be his most typical and valuable single virtue, a touchstone to warn him when legal jargon and analysis begin to impede a just determination."

dangerous" and "dangerous in use" that had been long established. Lord Tomlin agreed with him in that conclusion. For the majority, legal doctrine was much more malleable in order to meet the changing needs of society. Thus, Lord Thankerton enunciated the principle that the categories of negligence were never closed. However, it was Atkin who went further still and in so doing revolutionized tort law in the field of negligence. Atkin favored the "neighbor principle", drawn from Christian parable, which recognized the potential responsibility of any person to any other if harm to a "neighbor" legally speaking should have been foreseen and prevented from happening (see Kleefeld 2013).

Donoghue v Stevenson was reported on in the newspapers as a "test case" when it was decided in 1932, but there appears to have been little further local public attention paid to it at the time. In contrast, word quickly spread throughout legal communities in Commonwealth jurisdictions and the United States where judges and lawyers debated its implications. It took years, however, for its true impact to be recognized in the courts and beyond, and its legal significance continues to be explored (Chan 2011). Today *Donoghue v Stevenson* is considered to be one of the iconic common law cases and it is not a stretch to say that many, perhaps most, well educated people in English speaking countries around the world today recognize the story of the "snail in the bottle".[6]

Donoghue contributed to the transition of Britain's economy into a modern consumer based one in which the moral duty of care of manufactured goods was transformed into an active principle of law. Externalized costs to the public were henceforth to be internalized, spurring the development of the liability insurance industry.

3 Agent Orange

3.1 Background

Agent Orange was a compound used in creating herbicides which contained a chemical known to be toxic to human beings called dioxin. These products had been produced in the United States for many years before they were adopted by the United States military for use as a defoliant in the war in Vietnam. In the course of that war many military personnel were exposed to a greater or lesser extent to dioxin. After the war ended many veterans back in the United States began to complain of serious diseases and adverse health and reproductive effects which they linked to their exposure to *Agent Orange* overseas. Although some adverse effects of exposure to dioxin had been known for years by the manufacturers of these products these were considered to be relatively minor and the veterans' claims were not taken seriously. The government agencies responsible for veterans' health and wellbeing also did not recognize a causal connection and thus provided no special benefits or services.

[6]See, for instance, Paisley Snail (2017), Donoghue (2017) and Chapman (2010).

Veterans began to feel that the toll taken on them through service for their country was not being properly recognized. This dissatisfaction was compounded by their awareness of public distaste for the Vietnam war in general and a pervasive lack of sympathy or respect for veterans who had fought there.

Responding to veterans' anguish and desire for help and compensation, lawyers in several parts of America began individual and class action claims principally against the manufacturers of *Agent Orange* for injuries sustained through exposure to dioxin in Vietnam. A campaign to bring the plight of exposed veterans to the attention of the public accompanied this legal action. Some of the defendants were in the top tier of American corporations, and a material shock to their balance sheets or reputations would reverberate throughout the "military-industrial complex" and the economy as a whole.

Hundreds of these claims with many thousands of plaintiffs were eventually consolidated for adjudication in a Federal District Court in New York. After a period of management by another judge, Judge Jack Weinstein was assigned to try this mass litigation.

3.2 *Judge Jack Weinstein*

Jack Weinstein rose to become a noted legal scholar and judge from humble beginnings in Brooklyn New York.[7] A master of procedure and evidence law, he eventually gained a reputation for skill in conducting complex litigation often involving scientific issues and expert witnesses. Weinstein was also at the forefront of the developing law of class actions which sought to bring justice to individual claimants who ordinarily could not afford to litigate on their own (see Mullenix 2015). Thus, he seemed an ideal judicial choice for the *Agent Orange* cases.

But Weinstein was also a strong-willed judge who did not hesitate to reach decisions which he well knew might be challenged in a higher court. Sometimes he used his vast procedural knowledge to steer cases in the direction he thought they should go, even advising counsel of his suggested strategies (see Morris 2015). It seems that he always had a firm view of the justice of the matter before him and wasn't hesitant to tell anyone what he thought on that score. Many of these traits and qualities were on display in his handling of the *Agent Orange* litigation.

3.3 *Outcome*

Judge Weinstein had it seems a well-deserved reputation of being among the most hard working Federal judges. Through great effort and application of his high intel-

[7]Biographical details and description of the professional life of Judge Weinstein are drawn from Morris (2011).

lectual capacity he was soon completely familiar with the complexities of the *Agent Orange* cases to which he had been assigned.[8] Weinstein was thus at the time probably one of the most knowledgeable people in America concerning the production, use, and possible health effects of products containing dioxin. His conclusion, based on this vast knowledge and the evidence likely to be presented, was that the claims would fail. It was not that causation could be disproven, just that the weight of evidence available then was not sufficient to tip the balance in favor of the veterans.

Soon after being assigned to *Agent Orange* Weinstein called counsel together and told them the cases should be settled. He then proceeded to ensure that all parties progressed speedily towards a trial date within a few months which he made clear would not be changed on any account. Weinstein appointed two special Masters of the court to advise him and assist with ongoing settlement negotiations. However, as the date of trial approached no settlement had been reached.

On the Friday before the Monday on which the trial was to start Weinstein directed counsel for all parties to attend settlement discussions at the court which would last all weekend. By virtue of Weinstein and his Master's intense argument and persuasion a settlement agreement was reached on Sunday which involved the payment of almost 200 million dollars by the manufacturers into a fund to be administered for the benefit of affected veterans. Subsequently Judge Weinstein conducted hearings across the country to inquire into the fairness and reasonableness of the settlement which had been reached (*Agent Orange* 1984b). Not surprisingly he found it fair, and the core provisions of the settlement withstood challenge on appeal.

After this settlement there were other *Agent Orange* related matters which Weinstein dealt with. For one, he dismissed the claims of those who had withdrawn from the class action because they did not wish to settle. Much later he also dismissed the claims brought on behalf of Vietnamese who had been exposed to *Agent Orange*.

4 Common Factors

4.1 Philosophy of Law

A similar approach to the relationship of law and society can be seen to run through the work of these three extraordinary judges. For them, law and the legal system were not autonomous institutions with a self-absorbed focus. Rather, they were essential components of society which contributed to progress towards a better life for its members. Through their decisions these judges attempted in their own ways to do justice to their compatriots and were not content to simply administer the law as a comfortable and predictable routine.

Mansfield believed that the keys to the progress and prosperity of British society in the eighteenth century lay in the hands of merchants and men of commerce.

[8]The following description of Judge Weinstein's involvement in the case is largely drawn from Schuck (1987) and Sills (2014) which are the most detailed account of the litigation.

Thus, he regularly sought information and advice from them about their practices and expectations through the use of special juries in order to understand how the law could be improved. In return, he largely succeeded in bringing coherence and certainty to principles of law in fields such as bills of exchange, banking and insurance in decisions which have stood the test of time. Lord Mansfield also encouraged the engagement of all citizens in government and promoted this in decisions upholding the rights of members of the Roman Catholic Church to participate in public life. In the *Somerset* case it is clear that he appreciated the serious legal, political, and economic consequences that could flow from his decision, but nevertheless managed to achieve a result which respected the equal dignity of all humanity.

Lord Atkin believed that law played an important part in the advancement of society by helping to refine its moral and ethical order and to educate citizens concerning their rights and obligations. Accordingly, he supported public legal education and advocated the study of law by all. His decisions show an acute awareness of the impact they might have on the society in which he lived much as others did, and from which he did not feel elevated or estranged. Atkin's holding in *Donoghue v Stevenson* shows clear concern for the "common person" engaged in everyday pursuits which might be made dangerous through remote careless commercial and manufacturing activity. The result of that case was to impose a more progressive commercial morality on businesses which is still being developed today. In another notable later wartime case (Liversidge 1941) Atkin, dissenting, refused to allow government to treat law as a convenient tool for its own purposes without regard for the integrity of judicial oversight in the public interest. Lord Atkin was a judge of his own society, but not above it.

Judge Jack Weinstein understood the role of law to be clearly about doing justice in society. In particular, he considered it to be one of the primary goals of law to empower those who otherwise would be powerless and unable to assert their rights. In his involvement in class action cases such as *Agent Orange*, and civil rights matters, he tried to achieve just that. As a trial judge he welcomed the direct contact with litigants and went out of his way in the *Agent Orange* fairness hearings to give voice to veterans and their families throughout the country, meeting them where they lived. Weinstein was an uncommon judge who sought justice for the common man and woman.

4.2 Skill in Legal Technique

In addition to their common desire for justice Mansfield, Atkin and Weinstein were also distinguished by their exemplary knowledge of the law and skill in legal technique. As judges of undoubted integrity they accepted that the ends of justice were to be pursued through sometimes unaccommodating legal concepts, categories and processes.

Mansfield displayed his legal acumen in *Somerset* primarily through recourse to the principle and practice of judicial restraint. On the one hand he was invited to invoke the spirit and intent of the common law to emancipate slaves throughout England (and perhaps the Empire), while on the other to acknowledge that Parliament had sanctioned slavery through statutes regulating the slave trade among the colonies. He chose neither course, but instead restricted himself to the technicalities of the proceedings before him, resting his decision on onus of proof and lack of evidence of explicit authority to imprison Somerset. However, Mansfield was also judicially creative in using the phrase "positive law" without apparently clarifying exactly what he meant by this term. It seems likely that he considered it to be equivalent to statute law, but there is the possibility that he also had royal decrees in mind, a type of law that was hotly contested in the colonies at the time.

In *Donoghue v Stevenson* Lord Atkin was faced with a mass of longstanding cases on the duty of care which were either unhelpful or contradictory to the position of Mrs. Donoghue. Through a masterful display of legal research and reasoning he managed to distinguish all of the apparently contrary authorities and to highlight those few which were supportive. Although his senior colleague Lord Buckmaster came to exactly opposite conclusions, and ridiculed the reading which Atkin chose to give these cases, Atkin had provided a credible basis for his view that a new principle could be introduced to the law of negligence without doing damage to the fabric of the law as it then stood. Then he proceeded to enunciate the neighbor principle based on a paraphrase of the biblical parable of the Good Samaritan, a strikingly creative and unorthodox fusion of morality and law.

One of the techniques that Judge Weinstein used to great effect in the *Agent Orange* litigation was issuing "tentative" or "preliminary" findings on issues of law, evidence or procedure in order to help nudge the parties towards settlement. Predictably, these "rulings" sometimes seemed to favor one side, then the other. As a trial judge and procedural expert he was well aware that his interim decisions would almost always be immune from appeal, thus preventing the parties from delaying the matter in hopes of obtaining certainty from the appeal court on some issues prior to trial. But Weinstein also demonstrated legal creativity when faced with the conflict of laws problem of trying a case with plaintiffs from virtually all of the different States of America. He first advanced the proposition that there was a Federal common law which could be applied to all claims. When that position was rejected on appeal Weinstein then stated he would use a novel approach, applying "national consensus law" (*Agent Orange* 1984a, 696) based upon commonalities in the laws of the States to the case. It is quite clear that Judge Weinstein used whatever procedural and doctrinal avenues were available to him from his vast judicial repertoire to ensure that the case ended justly, which in his mind meant settlement.

4.3 *Perception of Public Interest as a Desire for Justice*

Lord Mansfield and Judge Weinstein were well aware that the eyes of the community were on them as they dealt with the *Somerset* and *Agent Orange* cases. The media of the time communicated details of the litigation to the public knowing the interest there was in the outcome. There was much at stake to the parties in both cases, as well as to distinct segments of the population. However, I suggest that both Mansfield and Weinstein perceived as well that these high profile cases were also a test of the court's ability to achieve justice. In such situations it is not sufficient for a judge to reach a legally justifiable result but it is also necessary to ensure that the public perceives that justice has been done. To achieve this requires the judge to act justly towards all the litigants in the case. Seemingly it is not enough to just declare one party successful, the other not.

Mansfield was likely aware of divided opinion on the matter of slavery in England at the time *Somerset* arose. Although the abolitionist movement was gaining steam that view was not yet in the majority and it would not be for almost a hundred more years before slavery was abolished completely. Through his Christian upbringing and familiarity with Dido Mansfield had reason to favor Somerset, but he had also dedicated himself as a judge to supporting trade and commerce which would be adversely affected by abolition. Mansfield's decision in *Somerset* was probably a disappointment to both sides of the matter. But it dealt with the question in a way which allowed both sides to continue their struggles and protected the court from being labeled partisan. *Somerset* therefore represents a victory for law as affording justice to all.

Judge Weinstein foresaw the terrible consequences that a trial might have for all parties involved in *Agent Orange*. An outright loss in front of a jury would confirm the veterans in their despair that the American people had rejected them. On the other hand, given the weaknesses in their case, if a sympathetic jury sided in their favor that would undoubtedly lead to one or more appeals with the real possibility that the verdict would be overturned. The anguish of hope dashed would perhaps be an even greater blow to the suffering plaintiffs. The defendant manufacturers, many of them among the largest and well known American companies, would also be dragged through the mud of evidence of knowledge of the toxicity of their products and lack of response. Needless to say both sides would be required to spend millions of dollars in legal and other fees and wait years before the litigation came to an end. All the while the American public would look on, some perhaps affected by the suffering of veterans, and others suspicious of dubious claims against wealthy corporations. With hindsight it is perhaps easier for us to understand why Judge Weinstein acted as he did in forging a settlement in such an emotionally, politically and economically charged situation. The veterans would get some assistance, but the amount of the fund provided was not astronomical, and the defendants were allowed to assert no wrongdoing. A settlement might encourage healing of wounds related to the Vietnam war in the community at large and draw more attention to the need for appropriate government assistance. One can conclude that settlement in this case did more to protect the reputation of the court than a trial ever would have.

Donoghue v Stevenson is somewhat different regarding public interest, because there was little at the time the decision was reached. But the judges clearly had the public in mind as they contemplated the case. For the two dissenting Lords a relaxation in the duty of care would unleash a torrent of litigation by everyone injured in accidents involving manufactured goods. They envisioned the consumer society and its litigious nature and did not like what they saw. Atkin, however, considered the case as the most important that had come before the court because it permitted an improvement in the protection of ordinary people from avoidable injury due to careless business practices. His view was that the public would see the result as common sense justice being done, in contrast to lawyers who were blinded by precedent. *Donoghue* set in motion a rebalancing of the rights of consumers and the duties of business people that has since been embraced as a just result not only by the public but by lawyers themselves. If the case had not gone the way it did we might well look back at the House of Lords as an obstruction rather than as a pathway to the achievement of justice.

4.4 Agony of Decision

It should be apparent from the discussion above that the judges in these cases had no easy time. Mansfield had to struggle with the possibly momentous consequences of his decision for the Crown, the Empire, and the economy, balanced against the pitiful condition of the imprisoned Somerset. In addition, for a judge with a passion for legal certainty the limited, inconclusive, decision in *Somerset* must have been difficult for Mansfield to deliver and support. For his part, Lord Atkin went out on a limb in advocating an entirely new principle of negligence law against the withering criticism of fellow judges, but foreseeing the benefit to the public which might result. In *Agent Orange* Judge Weinstein was faced with plaintiffs who desperately wanted their day in court, defendants who were willing and able to fight all the way, a public that was keen to put the past behind it, and his own well-formed conviction that trial would end in tears all round. For Weinstein the rock was compromise through settlement as against the hard place of the torturous prolonged litigation.

When the public is interested in private litigation much is at stake, and much is demanded of a judge. A decision must be made that is not dictated by precedent, questions are not just solved by evidence, and a just outcome is hazy and indeterminate. This is the agony of decision of a judge who takes seriously the responsibility of bringing forth justice in the glare of public attention. It is the ultimate test for a responsive judge.

5 Limits and Links

The greatest judges speak in their judgments not only to legal professionals, but also to the society in which they live where law forms a dynamic nexus with politics and the economy. This characterizes their responsibility to the law combined with their humane devotion to social responsiveness. However, it should not be assumed that responsive judges simply look to public sentiment or opinion as their guiding light and shape the law to suit those perceived concerns and interests. Three significant decisions, one from each of the exemplary judges described here, demonstrate that responsive judges try to balance deep respect for the dignity and integrity of law with service to society's needs in their judicial craft.

Lord Mansfield's judicial, intellectual, and moral independence is unquestioned. Far from being a mere reflection of popular sentiment, his judgments display fidelity to law and justice as he saw it. One example of this was his decisions in relation to Dissenters (also known as Nonconformists)—those who did not support the established Anglican Church and were generally persecuted as a result such as by the *Test Act* of 1673 which required public office holders to embrace Anglicanism or be penalized. Judgments by Mansfield upholding their civic rights led a mob to burn down his London home. However, an even more notable case conducted by Lord Mansfield demonstrates his devotion to law. It is the infamous matter of *The Zong*, a slave ship owned and insured out of Liverpool. The case is *Gregson v Gilbert* (Gregson 1783), pronounced 11 years after *Somerset*, in which the ship owners sued an insurance syndicate for loss of cargo thrown overboard, ostensibly to save the crew and the remaining cargo in a situation of dire necessity. Such a claim was recognized in law and supported by the insurance policy wording (Webster 2007; Lobban 2007). However, the "cargo" lost in this case was 132 slaves (men, women, and children) who were bound and jettisoned on several occasions before the ship reached its destination in Jamaica. The "necessity" alleged was insufficient supply of water to sustain all lives aboard.

Lord Mansfield presided at the trial and affirmed the jury's verdict in favor of the ship owners. Someone present provided an account of the case in a letter to a newspaper and it came to public notice (Rupprecht 2007a). Granville Sharp, the slavery abolitionist who assisted in *Somerset*, was notified and started a campaign to have the responsible parties charged with murder. Meanwhile, the insurers sought a new trial based on proposed new evidence and facts. Mansfield conducted the hearing of the application for retrial sitting with two other judges. In the course of those proceedings the Lord Chief Justice is reported to have declared that although it was "shocking" to say, in the case of marine insurance slaves as cargo were to be treated no differently than "horses" being transported (Oldham 2007; Krikler 2007). Mansfield was an acknowledged expert in insurance law, deciding many cases that clarified and systematized that important emerging area of finance (Oldham 2004; Lobban 2007). A contemporary textbook on the law of insurance was dedicated to him. In the matter of *The Zong* Lord Mansfield showed his fidelity to law despite undoubted moral reservations concerning the case. A new trial was, however, ordered based on the allegation that rain had fallen on the vessel, replenishing the water supply, despite which more slaves were subsequently sacrificed. Since the "necessity" may thus have abated continued jettison of slaves was arguably unwarranted, thereby possibly reducing the allowable insurance recovery. In the result, it appears no further trial occurred, the owners no doubt being concerned about the damage to their business and reputations which would be done by a full examination of the horrors of the event. One suspects that Mansfield foresaw this outcome. But no criminal charges were ever laid.

The second example of a responsive judge's dedication to law notwithstanding the public mood is the dissenting opinion of Lord Atkin in the infamous case of *Liversidge v. Anderson* (1941). In that case the House of Lords was asked to determine the extent of the statutory power of a government minister to detain indefinitely, without charge, individuals who he had "reasonable cause to believe" were a danger to the state. At the time of the decision in *Liversidge* Britain was at one of the lowest points of the war against Germany, suffering daily bombardment, and as yet without American aid. Liversidge (an alias for a man with a German name) contended that the government must provide detailed information to substantiate the reasonableness of the minister's decision to imprison him. The government objected, contending it was sufficient that the minister simply stated reasonable grounds existed, and the Law Lords found it necessary to decide which argument prevailed. All the Lords hearing the case agreed with the government except Atkin. In an impassioned opinion he showed that judicial review of the reasonableness of executive action was a foundational principle in British jurisprudence and its abandonment due to wartime circumstances would sacrifice the rule of law. Here are his memorable words:

> In this country, amid the clash of arms, the laws are not silent. They may he changed, but they speak the same language in war as in peace. It has always been one of the pillars of freedom… that the judges are no respecters of persons and stand between the subject and any attempted encroachments on his liberty by the executive, alert to see that any coercive action is justified in law. (As quoted in Bingham 2009, 38)

Reaction to Lord Atkin's view was very mixed, the newspapers being divided and much of the public undoubtedly critical of anything that might aid the enemy. The judgment of posterity, however, has upheld Lord Atkin's position as being in the finest tradition of judicial independence and integrity (Bingham 2009). Atkin showed in *Liversidge* that although the inclinations of society must be considered, nevertheless the law must be vindicated where it achieves justice through the application of fundamental principles which remain essential in the long term.

Judge Weinstein, in the case *United States v Concepcion* (1992) provides the final example of responsive, yet independent, judging with integrity. In this and related cases Weinstein presided over the trial, conviction for welfare fraud, and sentencing of 20 Latinas, many of whom were only permanent residents and not United States citizens. Judge Weinstein faced two strong popular views in connection with the sentencing of these women. Beginning in 1976, with the campaign of Ronald Reagan for President, the figure of the "welfare queen" was brought to public attention. This stereotype was based on a singular actual example but exaggerated and broadened to include all those (presumably black, but also potentially Latina) women who lived extravagant lifestyles by exploiting the public welfare systems (Levin 2013; Cammett 2014). Public sentiment against such "welfare cheats" continued for decades, resulting in statutory changes to American welfare programs in the mid-1990s that limited the scope of their assistance (Gear Rich 2016; Parker West 2016). The second popular sentiment surrounding Judge Weinstein's decisions in these cases was that associated with the contemporary "truth in sentencing" movement. Many politicians and others criticized judges for their uneven and supposedly lenient sentencing decisions. One result of this advocacy was the United States Federal Sentencing Guidelines which attempted to bring more standardization, and ultimately severity, to sentencing practices among Federal judges such as Weinstein. Many judges believed the Guidelines to be an improper encroachment on judicial discretion and Judge Weinstein was one of those who sought ways to circumvent their strict requirements regarding imprisonment among other punitive measures (Weinstein 2008). In *Concepcion*, therefore, Judge Weinstein confronted the problem of imposing punishment on women identified in the public mind as undeserving "welfare queens" under an increasingly punitive and retributory sentencing regime that apparently had public support.

The decision in *Concepcion* is remarkable in several ways. In Judge Weinstein's judgment on sentencing (which runs to 45 pages in length) he first notes the deficiencies in the welfare system administration which contributed to the ease of making fraudulent claims, and the complicity of several government employees who were also convicted. He then reviews and considers all the relevant legal provisions regarding sentencing, placing the Guidelines within a conceptual framework that allows him to consider other factors besides retribution. Finally, he highlights the irony involved in sentencing mostly single mothers of young children for fraud on welfare programs intended to benefit those very children in poor households. In the result, Weinstein sentenced only 5 of the 20 women to jail terms, the two longest periods of imprisonment being reserved for two former government employees. The most frequent punishments he imposed were home detention (allowing for absence during work at employment) and restitution. In this way Judge Weinstein found a way to reconcile the evident public desire for retribution with a result that promised to achieve humane justice, noting:

> Experience in this district has demonstrated that imprisonment of a parent tends to result in the child ending up in prison as well. Even incarceration within the community and forced work for the community without pay is bound to have some adverse effects on the child. Nevertheless, these consequences cannot be entirely avoided. While the sins of the mother should not be visited on the child, the child may learn from her experience that crime does not go unpunished. (Concepcion 1992, 1283)

There are also some notable echoes and coincidences among the three leading cases of *Somerset*, *Donoghue*, and *Agent Orange* that illustrate the ongoing influence of responsive judges. These links are briefly described here.

First, some years after the decision in *Somerset* the same issue came before a Scottish court. That court accepted the argument that slavery was incompatible with the *Scottish* common law and thus effectively abolished it in that jurisdiction. This was the same court that gave Mrs. Donoghue her initial victory, but in the course of *Donoghue v Stevenson* all parties and courts accepted the proposition that in relation to the law of negligence the common law of England and Scotland did not differ.

Next, as described above, *Somerset* effectively raised conflicts of laws issues in relation to the common law of England, whether it applied to the colonies, and what effect it might have on incompatible colonial laws, plus the effect of British statutes on the slave trade. Similar questions would bedevil American jurisprudence for a hundred years as it struggled to define the interaction between Federal and State law as it applied to slaves and other matters (see Webb 2014). For instance, *Somerset* was cited in the infamous *Dred Scott* (1856) decision in which the United States Supreme Court declared that black slaves could not be citizens of the United States and that Federal laws could not emancipate them. Both the majority and the dissenters cited Lord Mansfield's judgment in *Somerset* in an effort to reconcile international, Federal, and State law. When Weinstein came to the *Agent Orange* litigation similar questions arose. Would State law apply to the many claims, Federal common law, or something else?

On a practical, procedural level, parallels can be drawn between Lord Mansfield and Judge Weinstein. In a way similar to Mansfield, Weinstein was known to use "advisory juries" to assist him to fully understand cases before him which presented situations with which he had no personal experience or exposure (Lahav 2015). Both responsive judges found similar ways to bridge the gap between limited judicial experience and the lived reality of litigants who appear in court.

Next, *Donoghue v Stevenson*, while a foreign decision, was undoubtedly also influential in the United States and contributed to the development and expansion of tort law there, especially in the area of product liability. The dissenting judges in *Donoghue* foresaw the phenomenon of mass litigation as practiced in *Agent Orange* and used that as one of the reasons not to extend the duty of care. However, the wisdom of Atkin's approach in *Donoghue* has been vindicated in such notable cases of public harm as the dangerous Pinto vehicles produced by Ford (*Grimshaw* 1981).

There are remarkable similarities in Lord Mansfield's views expressed in *Somerset* and Lord Atkin's remarks in his opinion in *Liversidge*. Recall that Somerset sued for *habeas corpus*, a proceeding designed to test the lawfulness of his imprisonment and to set him free. Liversidge, on the other hand, sued the government for the tort of false imprisonment, and for damages. In both cases the liberty of the individual was in question. Mansfield's response was clear:

> So high an act of dominion must be recognized by the law of the country where it is used. The power of a master over his slave has been extremely different, in different countries. The state of slavery is of such a nature, that it is incapable of being introduced on any reasons, moral or political; but only positive law, which preserves its force long after the reasons, occasion, and time itself from whence it was created, is erased from memory: it's so odious, that nothing can be suffered to support it, but positive law. Whatever inconveniences, therefore, may follow from a decision, I cannot say this case is allowed or approved by the law of England; and therefore the black must be discharged. (Somerset 1772, 510)

Atkin is equally clear and echoes the same sentiments regarding the freedom of the subject:

> The appellant's right to particulars, however, is based on a much broader ground, a principle which again is one of the pillars of liberty in that in English law every imprisonment is prima facie unlawful and that it is for a person directing imprisonment to justify his act. The only exception is in respect of imprisonment ordered by a judge, who from the nature of his office can't be sued, and the validity of whose judicial decisions cannot in such proceedings as the present be questioned. (Liversidge 1941, 245–246)

Finally, there is a conjunction between *Somerset*, *The Zong*, and the rise of class actions and mass claims in the United States, an area of law and practice in which

Judge Weinstein is an acknowledged expert. For some time in America the question of reparations for the era of slavery in that country has been debated and sometimes litigated. One of the legal techniques used has been the commencement of class actions by slave descendants as representatives of their enslaved ancestors. Such actions face numerous legal issues such as the indeterminacy of the class of plaintiffs, as well as identification of defendants and proof of causation in relation to them (Fortson 2004). A leading case in this area which dismissed such claims is *In re African-American Slave Descendants Litigation* (2005, 2006) heard by a Federal judge in Illinois, with an appeal dismissed by the Circuit Court of Appeals. Among other defendants the action included Lloyd's of London as a marine insurer of slave ships. One wonders whether such litigation would have taken a different course in the hands of Judge Weinstein.

A postscript to the reparations question illustrates the haunting specter of slavery that still hangs over America (See Quéma 2016). Several of the American States have passed legislation requiring companies to disclose their historical involvement with slavery. In California one insurer reported that a predecessor company was the London Assurance, and a published history of that company recorded as follows:

> … There is a tradition in the Corporation, though no written evidence of it has come to light [footnote 1: many records of the period have unfortunately been destroyed], that in the middle of the eighteenth century a cargo of slaves (each of whom was branded on the thigh) was insured, and heavy weather being encountered on the voyage, some of the Negroes were jettisoned, and in the consequence a claim for General Average was presented by the owners. (As quoted in Rupprecht 2007b, 23)

6 Conclusion

Responsive judges who perceive the actual or potential interest of the public in an otherwise private legal dispute face unique challenges. Since the general public is not a participating party in the litigation onlookers cannot be expected to value procedural fairness and due process as highly as the litigants. As a consequence, providing procedural justice, while necessary, is not a sufficient judicial response. Further, such cases have the potential to generate doubts among members of society that its legal system is dedicated to the search for justice in a more absolute sense. The foundational trust of society in its legal institutions may thus be weakened. A judge in such cases is faced with the agonistic task of ensuring that substantive justice is done and not merely facilitating an appearance of justice through dutifully following the law and legal procedure. When justice appears through responsive judging it can astound the powerful, confound the obvious, and rock the foundations of routine.

To judge in the public eye is an unenviable and almost impossible burden for a judge to bear because it requires her to see that justice is done to all parties. It is not enough to rely on relatively mechanical procedures such as "weighing" evidence or summing up the number of precedents for and against a particular argument. As Jacques Derrida (1990) describes it, a judge in such cases must confront an indeterminate result for which she bears unlimited responsibility towards each and every party, all the while being intensely scrutinized by the public which hopes and expects to be reassured in its faith in the law.

These case studies of responsive judges contribute to two important debates relating to contemporary judging. The first concerns the place of settlement in private litigation. *Somerset* shows us that settlement could potentially be used to defuse pressing social issues raised in highly charged cases. It is to the credit of Lord Mansfield that he not only encouraged settlement, but, when unsuccessful, pressed on to judgment with the remark "*Fiat justitia ruat cælum*—let justice be done whatever be the consequence" (*Somerset* 1772, 509). In *Donoghue* the effect of a settlement might have been more mixed. Rather than stifling litigation, paying out Mrs. Donoghue, to the knowledge of others, might simply have stimulated more such litigation, some of it possibly with only nuisance value. It would also have deprived an exemplary judge like Lord Atkin of the opportunity to bring the law of negligence more in line with popular expectations of justice. Finally, the *Agent Orange* case tells us that ameliorative justice may appear through settlement in some cases just as it may through judgment in others. Through the efforts of an extraordinary judge like Jack Weinstein the injustice which would have been inflicted on all parties by years of protracted litigation was averted through settlement.

The second debate revolving around judges concerns the openness of courts and judicial processes. The case studies here point to the salutary effect on judges, and the legal system as a whole, of an interested public demanding justice. Not many civil cases will attract general public attention, but the potential for it to arise should be preserved. Recent cases such as *Bock v Hansen* (2014) in the United States in which the court acted despite a purported settlement between the parties may indicate growing awareness among judges of the need to speak to the public about issues of wide concern *whether or not* the parties welcome the attention.[9]

To paraphrase Judge Weinstein: "These are my conclusions. Tentatively."

References

Applegarth PDT (2015) Lord Atkin: principle and progress. Supreme Court of Queensland Library. http://media.sclqld.org.au/documents/lectures-and-exhibitions/2015/Justice-Applegarth-paper-final.pdf. Accessed 8 Sept 2017

Atkin J (1932) Law as an educational subject. J Soc Public Teachers Law 1932:27–31

Bingham TH (2009) The case of Liversidge v. Anderson: the rule of law amid the clash of arms. Int Lawyer 43:33–38

Bock v. Hansen (2014) 225 Cal. App. 4th 215 (Cal. App. 1st Dist. 2014). Justia. http://law.justia.com/cases/california/court-of-appeal/2014/a136567.html. Accessed 8 Sept 2017

Cammett A (2014) Deadbeat dads & welfare queens: How metaphor shapes poverty law. Boston Coll J Law Soc Justice 34:233–266

[9]But see the refusal of the United State Supreme Court to hear a case it deemed moot after offer of full settlement: *Genesis Healthcare Corp. v Symczyk* (2013).

Carney G (2005) Lord Atkin—his Queensland origins and legacy. Supreme Court of Queensland Library. http://media.sclqld.org.au/documents/lectures-and-exhibitions/2015/gerard-carney-lord-atkin.pdf. Accessed 8 Sept 2017

Carrington PD, Apanovitch DP (1997) The constitutional limits of judicial rulemaking: the illegitimacy of mass-tort settlements negotiated under Federal Rule 23. Ariz Law Rev 39:461–495. ResearchGate. http://www.researchgate.net/publication/37810295. Accessed 8 Sept 2017

Castle R (2003) Lord Atkin and the neighbour test: origins of the principles of negligence in Donoghue v Stevenson. Ecclesiastical Law J 7:210–214

Chamberlain E (2010) Lord Atkin's opinion in Donoghue v Stevenson: perspectives from biblical hermeneutics. Law Humanit 4(1):91–114

Chan AB (2011) Who then—in law—is my neighbour?: Lord Atkin's 'neighbour principle' as an aid for the principled delineation of the boundaries of negligent liability. Faculty of Law, University of Toronto. https://tspace.library.utoronto.ca/bitstream/1807/27336/6/Chan_Adrian_B_20113_LLM_thesis.pdf. Accessed 8 Sept 2017

Chapman M (2010) The snail and the ginger beer. Wildy, Simmonds & Hill, London

Chayes A (1976) The role of the judge in public law litigation. Harvard Law Rev 89:1281–1316

Derrida J (1990) Force of law: the 'mystical foundation of authority'. Cardozo Law Rev 11:920–1045

Donoghue v Stevenson (1932) [1932] All ER Rep 1; [1932] AC 562. Scottish Council of Law Reporting. http://www.scottishlawreports.org.uk/resources/dvs/donoghue-v-stevenson-report.html. Accessed 8 Sept 2017

Donoghue v Stevenson: Digital Resources (2017) Scottish Council of Law Reporting. http://www.scottishlawreports.org.uk/resources/dvs/donoghue-v-stevenson.html. Accessed 8 Sept 2017

Dred Scott v Sandford (1856) 60 U.S. 393. Justia. https://supreme.justia.com/cases/federal/us/60/393/. Accessed 8 Sept 2017

Fiddes E (1934) Lord Mansfield and the Sommersett case. Law Q Rev 50:499–511

Fisher RA (1943) Granville Sharp and Lord Mansfield. J Negro Hist 28(4):381–389

Fiss OM (1979) Foreword: the forms of justice. Harvard Law Rev 93:1–58

Fiss OM (1984) Against settlement. Yale Law J 93:1073–1090. Yale Law School. http://digitalcommons.law.yale.edu/fss_papers/1215/. Accessed 13 Sept 2017

Fortson R (2004) Correcting the harms of slavery: collective liability, the limited prospects of success for a class action suit for slavery reparations, and the reconceptualization of white racial identity. Berkeley J Afr-Am Law Policy 6(1):71–127

Friedlander L (1995) Costs and the public interest litigant. McGill Law J 40:55–102

Gear Rich C (2016) Reclaiming the welfare queen: feminist and critical race theory alternatives to existing anti-poverty discourse. South Calif Interdisc Law J 25:257–288

Genesis Healthcare Corp. v Symczyk (2013) 656 F. 3d 189, reversed. Legal Information Institute. https://www.law.cornell.edu/supremecourt/text/11-1059. Accessed 13 Sept 2017

Gregson v Gilbert (1783) 99 ER 629. CommonLII. http://www.commonlii.org/int/cases/EngR/1783/85.pdf. Accessed 5 Sept 2017

Grimshaw v Ford Motor Company (1981) 119 Cal.App.3d 757. Justia. http://law.justia.com/cases/california/court-of-appeal/3d/119/757.html. Accessed 13 Sept 2017

Harding RW (1964) Lord Atkin's judicial attitudes and their illustration in commercial law and contract. Mod Law Rev 27(4):434–446

Hulsebosch DJ (2006) Nothing but liberty: Somerset's Case and the British Empire. Law Hist Rev 24:647–657

Hutchinson AC (2012) Laughing at the Gods: great judges and how they made the common law. Cambridge University Press, New York

In re African-American Slave Descendants Litigation (2005) 2005 WL 1561509. Aetna. http://www.aetna.com/data/judges_order.pdf. Accessed 6 Sept 2017

In re African-American Slave Descendants Litigation (2006) 471 F.3d 754, 759–60, 762 (7th Cir. 2006). United States Courts. http://media.ca7.uscourts.gov/cgi-bin/rssExec.pl?Submit=Display&Path=Y2006/D12-13/C:05-3265:J:_:aut:T:op:N:0:S:0. Accessed 6 September 2017

In re Agent Orange Product Liability Litigation (1984a) 580 F. Supp. 690 (E.D.N.Y. 1984). Justia. http://law.justia.com/cases/federal/district-courts/FSupp/580/690/1450028/. Accessed 2 Oct 2017

In re Agent Orange Product Liability Litigation (1984b) 597 F. Supp. 740 (E.D.N.Y. 1984). Justia. http://law.justia.com/cases/federal/district-courts/FSupp/597/740/1437287/. Accessed 8 Sept 2017

Kleefeld JC (2013) The Donoghue diaries: Lord Atkin's research notes in *Donoghue v Stevenson*. Juridical Rev 3:375–450. SSRN. https://papers.ssrn.com/sol3/papers.cfm?abstract_id=2470647. Accessed 8 Sept 2017

Knight v Wedderburn (1778) [1778] Hailes 776. BAILII. http://www.bailii.org/scot/cases/ScotCS/1778/Hailes020776-0472.html. Accessed 2 Oct 2017

Krikler J (2007) The Zong and the Lord Chief Justice. Hist Workshop J 64:29–47

Lahav AD (2015) Participation and procedure. DePaul Law Rev 64:513–536

Lewis G (1999) Lord Atkin. Bloomsbury, London

Levin J (2013) The welfare queen. Slate. http://www.slate.com/articles/news_and_politics/history/2013/12/linda_taylor_welfare_queen_ronald_reagan_made_her_a_notorious_american_villain.html. Accessed 7 Sept 2017

Liversidge v Anderson (1941) [1942] AC 206. BAILII. http://www.bailii.org/uk/cases/UKHL/1941/1.pdf. Accessed 5 Sept 2017

Lobban M (2007) Slavery, insurance and the law. J Leg Hist 28:319–328

Luban D (1995) Settlements and the erosion of the public realm. Georgetown Law J 83:2619–2662

Luck G (2015) The story behind Lord Atkin of snail. Quadrant Online. https://quadrant.org.au/magazine/2015/01-02/story-behind-lord-atkin-snail-2/. Accessed 8 Sept 2017

Menkel-Meadow C (1995) Whose dispute is it anyway?: a philosophical and democratic defense of settlement (in some cases). Georgetown Law J 83:2663–2696

Morris JB (2011) Leadership on the federal bench: the craft and activism of Jack Weinstein. Oxford University Press, New York

Morris JB (2015) Jack B. Weinstein: judicial entrepreneur. Univ Miami Law Rev 69:393–428

Mullenix LS (2015) Competing values: preserving litigant autonomy in an age of collective redress. DePaul Law Rev 64:601–639

Oldham J (1988) New light on Mansfield and slavery. J Brit Stud 27(1):45–68

Oldham J (1992) The Mansfield manuscripts and the growth of English law in the eighteenth century, vol 1. University of North Carolina Press, Chapel Hill

Oldham J (2004) English common law in the age of Mansfield. University of North Carolina Press, Chapel Hill

Oldham J (2007) Insurance litigation involving the Zong and other British slave ships, 1780–1807. J Leg Hist 28(3):299–318

Paley R (2006) Imperial politics and English law: the many contexts of Somerset. Law Hist Rev 24:659–664

Parker West L (2016) Soccer moms, welfare queens, waitress moms, and super moms: Myths of motherhood in state media coverage of child care during the 'welfare reforms' of the 1990s. South Calif Interdisc Law J 25:313–346

Quéma A (2016) M. NourbeSe Philip's Zong!: metaphors, laws, and fugues of justice. J Law Soc 43(1):85–104

Rex ex rel. Lewis v Stapylton (1771) Unreported. Described in Prince Hoare ed. 1820. Memoirs of Granville Sharp. Henry Colburn and Co., London

Rupprecht A (2007a) 'A very uncommon case': representations of the Zong and the British campaign to abolish the slave trade. J Leg Hist 28:329–346

Rupprecht A (2007b) Excessive memories: slavery, insurance and resistance. Hist Workshop J 64:6–28

Schuck PH (1987) Agent orange on trial: mass toxic disasters in the courts, Enlarged edn. Belknap Press of Harvard University Press, Cambridge

Sills P (2014) Toxic war: the story of agent orange. Vanderbilt University Press, Nashville

Smith v Brown and Cooper (1701) 91 ER 566. CommonLII. http://www.commonlii.org/uk/cases/EngR/1795/3194.pdf. Accessed 2 Oct 2017
Smith v Gould (1705) 91 ER 567. CommonLII. http://www.commonlii.org/uk/cases/EngR/1795/3194.pdf. Accessed 2 Oct 2017
Somerset v Stewart (1772) 98 ER 499. CommonLII. http://www.commonlii.org/int/cases/EngR/1772/57.pdf. Accessed 5 Sept 2017
The Paisley Snail: Donoghue v Stevenson (2017) Justice Education Society of British Columbia. http://www.justiceeducation.ca/resources/paisley-snail. Accessed 8 Sept 2017
United States v Concepcion (1992) 795 F. Supp. 1262 (E.D.N.Y. 1992). Justia. http://law.justia.com/cases/federal/district-courts/FSupp/795/1262/2596395/. Accessed 5 Sept 2017
Van Cleve G (2006a) Somerset's Case and its antecedents in imperial perspective. Law Hist Rev 24:601–645
Van Cleve G (2006b) Mansfield's decision: toward human freedom. Law Hist Rev 24:665–671
Webb DA (2014) The Somerset effect: parsing Lord Mansfield's words on slavery in nineteenth century America. Law Hist Rev 32(3):455–490
Webster J (2007) The Zong in the context of the eighteenth-century slave trade. J Leg Hist 28:285–298
Weinstein JB (1995) Individual justice in mass tort litigation: the effect of class actions, consolidations, and other multi-party devices. Northwestern University Press, Evanston
Weinstein JB (2008) The role of judges in a government of, by, and for the people: Notes for the fifty-eighth Cardozo lecture. Cardozo Law Rev 30:1–244
Wiecek WM (1974) Somerset: Lord Mansfield and the legitimacy of slavery in the Anglo-American world. Univ Chicago Law Rev 42(1):86–146

Archie Zariski is Professor of Legal Studies at Athabasca University, Canada, a lawyer and an experienced mediator. He has created and taught courses in ADR, negotiation and mediation at Athabasca and at Murdoch Law School, Australia. His research includes exploring the roles of lawyers and judges in dispute resolution processes. Archie is co-editor of the book *The Multi-Tasking Judge: Judicial Dispute Resolution in Comparative Perspective* and the author of *Legal Literacy: An Introduction to Legal Studies*. He is a member of the ADR Institute of Canada, and the Resolution Institute (Australia).

Index

A
Access to justice, 2, 3, 12, 14, 15, 42, 91, 95
Active judging, 2
Advocacy organisations, 132
Agent Orange, 23, 311, 313, 319–325, 328, 329, 331
Agreement
resolving disputes by, 43, 61
Alternative Dispute Resolution
and U.S. District Court Judges, 228
restorative justice, 18, 56
Annexed-court judicial resolution, 301
Artificial Intelligence (AI), 5, 29, 87, 89, 259, 273

B
Basic Standards of the People's Republic of China on Professional Ethics of Judges, 192, 197, 205
Behavioural contract, 244
Bias rule, 26, 27
BlueWhale suicide game, 259, 260, 273
Bottom-up management, 154, 155
Branching technology, 93
Brundtland commission, 144

C
Canada judiciary, 15, 21, 30, 175, 184, 187, 189, 204–208, 210
Canadian Judicial Council (CJC), 181, 187, 188, 205
Case management, 7, 24, 45, 46, 52, 67, 73, 88, 220, 225–228
Ontario pilot project, 222, 224
Centralized vortex, 280
Change of legal culture, 280
Charter of Rights and Freedoms (Canada), 183, 207
Chief Justice Wang Shengjun, 192
Chief Justice Xiao Yang, 192
Chief Justice Zhou Qiang, 195
Child safety, 274
China judiciary, 175, 190, 191, 203–208, 210
Circle sentencing, 162
Civil litigation, 14, 26, 31, 221, 224, 236, 277, 278, 281, 296–306, 311
Civil Trials
disposition of, 218
Code of Conduct for Judges (China), 194, 199, 203, 204, 206
Code of Criminal Procedure (Cr.P.C.), 243, 245, 254
Community courts, 72, 161, 163, 232
Complex society, 23, 153
Computer code
translating law into, 101
Conciliation, 44, 53, 55, 219, 278, 282, 296, 300, 302–304
Conflict resolution, 62–67, 70, 80, 81, 163–166
Consent, 27, 64, 68, 72, 73, 75, 80, 186, 207, 208, 225, 266, 283, 303
Constitutional adjudication, 277, 278, 281, 284, 289, 293, 306
Constitutional avoidance, 293, 295
Constitutional complaints, 284, 286–289

© Springer Nature Singapore Pte Ltd. 2018
T. Sourdin and A. Zariski (eds.), *The Responsive Judge*, Ius Gentium: Comparative Perspectives on Law and Justice 67, https://doi.org/10.1007/978-981-13-1023-2

Constitutional court, 30, 242, 277–279, 281–287, 289–291, 306
Constitutional interpretation, 289, 291, 295
Constitutional review, 278, 279, 282, 288, 289, 306
Constraint of politics, 294
Control of Narcotics Substance Act (CNSA), 241
Corporate Social Responsibility (CSR), 146, 167
Court-annexed mediation
  mandatory mediation, 225, 227
  time to select mediator, 226
Courts
  and courthouse construction, 217, 218
  Ontario Court of Justice, 231–233
  Ontario Superior Court of Justice, 224
  the Aboriginal Conference Settlement Suites, 231
  Thunder Bay Consolidated Courthouse, 231
Criminal court chambers, 159
Critical Legal Studies (CLS), 105
Critiques of responsiveness, 22
Cultural genocide, 190

D
Dataism, 103, 104
Decision-making
  process design, 28, 43
  responsiveness in, 43
  strategies for, 43
Deterrence, 164, 166, 242
Dispute resolution
  communication in, 43
  compulsory, 55
  discretion in, 47
  empowering participants in, 45, 54
  encouraging agreement in, 41, 91, 92
  in tribunals, 42–44, 47, 55, 57
  mediation in, 41, 43, 44, 53, 55
  models of settlement judging in, 28
  process design, 57
  the judge's role in, 76
  timing of, 55
  weighing and balancing information in, 41, 43
Dispute settlement
  adversarial approach, 65
  collaborative approach, 69
Disruptive technology, 91
Donoghue v Stevenson, 311, 318, 319, 322–324, 328, 329
Double standard of scrutiny, 294
Drug courts, 159, 160, 219

E
Earth Charter, 143–145, 150, 163
Ethical Principles for Judges (Canada), 181, 184, 204, 205

F
First Nations (Canada), 183, 188, 189
Formalism, 18, 64, 88, 104, 105, 111, 222, 280, 286, 289, 294–296, 300, 305
Freud, 98, 105, 109, 111

H
Habeas corpus, 313, 316, 329
High Court of Australia, 29, 121, 124, 125, 129
Human capital
  strengthening, 150

I
ICC Business Charter for Sustainable Development, 146, 147
Impartiality, 2, 7, 9, 15, 16, 21, 26, 28, 30, 46–48, 57, 104, 126, 177, 180, 182, 184, 187, 188, 191, 203–205, 209, 210, 235, 236
Independence, 9, 10, 18, 30, 122, 126, 151, 157–159, 162, 164, 165, 177, 182, 185, 187, 191, 195, 196, 208–210, 220, 235, 236, 279, 280, 296, 312, 314, 326, 327
Indian higher judiciary, 259, 274
Indigenous peoples
  Gladue Courts, 229, 232
  Indigenous People's Court, 232
  over-incarceration of, 217, 218, 221, 231, 236
  Royal Commission on Aboriginal Peoples, 229
Indigenous sentencing courts, 161–163
Individual responsiveness, 4
Influence of Facebook, 134
Influence of politics, 18
Influence of Twitter, 21, 29
Internal/external perspective, 175–179, 185, 186, 208, 209
Internet service providers, 30, 259, 260, 270
ISO 26000, 143, 146–150, 168

J

Japanese Supreme Court, 281, 294, 295, 306
Jerome Frank, 3, 18, 95
Judge
    role of, 5, 6, 16, 24, 27, 61, 63, 64, 69, 74, 76, 87, 88, 90, 176, 188, 189, 207, 242, 244
Judge artificial intelligence, 5
Judge co-bot, 95, 96, 113
Judge Li Bingxiang, 197, 205
Judge quota system, 192
Judge Weinstein, 17, 23, 312, 320, 321, 323–325, 327–331
Judge's professional responsibility, 209, 299
Judge's purposive interpretation, 284
Judge's responsive activism, 283
Judges
    Chief Justice Warren Winkler, 224, 226, 228
    Regional Senior Justice, 226, 228, 233
Judging
    accountability, 15, 73, 191
    adjudicative function, 99, 113
    educative role, 97
    emotional intelligence, 239, 273
    empathy, 6, 10, 18, 20, 23, 64, 70, 71, 76, 77, 87, 164
    factors that influence, 95, 96
    impartiality, 7, 126, 180
    machine learning, 89, 100
    novelty, 100
    semantics of, 102
    societal impact, 5, 6
    unconscious biases, 95
    variance, 105, 113
Judicial academy, 241, 254, 255, 274
Judicial accountability, 73, 191
Judicial activism, 25, 267
Judicial authority, 98, 197, 208, 254, 269
Judicial chain, 150, 158, 159, 168, 169
Judicial conservatism, 306
Judicial education, 30, 241, 255, 256
Judicial empathy, 10
Judicial ethics, 25
Judicial independence, 9, 18, 30, 122, 126, 191, 195, 220, 235, 236, 327
Judicial innovation, 26, 219
Judicialization of politics, 220, 234, 236
Judicial mediation, 9, 24, 72, 149, 150, 159, 224
Judicial monitoring, 9, 156, 272, 274
Judicial passivism, 296
Judicial politics
    and Indigenous Peoples in Canada, 219, 281
    and social processes, 234
    law and development, 63, 71, 148, 193, 296
    partial connections, 235
    trial and appellate courts, 6, 25, 246, 250
Judicial pre-conscious, 109, 110
Judicial prestige, 21, 165, 203, 228
Judicial reform (China), 190, 192
Judicial responsiveness, 1, 2, 4, 28–30, 61, 63, 68, 69, 71, 74, 76, 81, 87, 88, 152, 192, 217, 220, 241, 277, 278, 306
Judicial review, 31, 54, 59, 183, 207, 208, 261, 277, 278, 281, 283, 284, 292–295, 327
Judicial speech, 196, 205, 207
Judicial training, 30
Judicial transparency, 7, 9, 21, 122
Judicial unconscious, 110
Judicial values, 164
Jurisprudential theory, 5, 6
Jurists' rent-seeking, 305
Justice, 1–3, 5, 7, 9, 11, 12, 16, 18, 19, 22, 25, 27, 29, 30, 42, 54, 59, 68, 74, 78, 87, 91, 95, 96, 98, 99, 104, 111, 112, 125–127, 137, 143, 145–152, 158, 161–168, 178, 182, 186, 187, 190, 193, 199, 201, 205, 217–219, 222, 229, 230, 232, 242, 248, 253, 267, 279, 282, 296, 305, 311–313, 315, 318, 320–322, 324–328, 330, 331
Justice Beverley McLachlin, 187–189, 209
Justice Jiang Xingchang, 197, 205
Justice objectives, 11
Justice Ted Matlow, 185–187, 203, 205
Justice Tom Berger, 183–185, 207
Juvenile, 72, 160, 242–245, 247–249, 251–253, 255
Juvenile Justice System Ordinance (JJSO), 248–256

K

Koori courts, 162

L

Legal education, 16, 79, 80, 196, 223, 280, 318, 322
Legal ego, 106, 109
Legal formalism, 104, 105, 280, 289
Legal procedure
    and Culture, 10, 277–280, 291, 295–297, 299, 300, 305
    civil justice reform, 219
    civil litigation, 14, 26, 31, 224, 236, 277, 278, 297, 298, 300, 302, 303, 306, 311

Legal procedure (*cont.*)
criminal law, 157, 158, 168, 197, 248
Fly-In Courts, 233–235
pretrial settlement, 228
Legal realism, 88
Legal Realist Movement, 222
Legal research
socio-legal research, 179
Legal super-ego, 106, 107, 109–111
Legal system responsiveness, 152
Legal training, 106, 107, 109, 204
Legitimacy, 22, 30, 64, 75, 98, 148, 175, 177–179, 185, 203, 205, 207–210, 291, 305
Litigant satisfaction, 10
Liversidge v Anderson, 327
Lord Atkin, 327, 329, 331
Lord Mansfield, 312, 315, 322, 323, 326, 329, 331

M
Ma Xiwu trial, 191, 192, 209
Mediation
role in dispute resolution, 41, 43, 44, 53, 55, 56
Mediator
choice of, 58, 137, 153, 260
Mental health courts, 160
Mixture of civil and common law system, 11

N
National Native Title Tribunal (NNTT)
case management in, 45, 46
dispute resolution in, 41–43, 47, 53, 55, 57
Natural law theory, 7, 294
Negligence, 271, 273, 316, 317, 319, 323, 325, 328
Negotiation theory, 56, 93, 297
Neighbourhood justice, 151, 161
Neighbour principle, 319, 323
Networked society, 16

O
OECD guidelines, 143, 146–149, 168
Oliver Wendell Holmes Jr, 2, 16
Online courts, 91
Online dispute resolution, 91, 92, 94
Online games, 259–262, 264, 272
Ontario Civil Justice Review, 225
Open justice, 123, 126
Organizational culture, 68
Organizational effectiveness, 148, 155, 157, 159

P
Participants
empowering, 41, 43, 45
engagement of, 42
interests of, 43, 44, 50
responsibilities of, 44, 51
Peng Yu case, 199
Phantasy, 110, 111
Politicization of judiciary, 279
Politics/Political activity, 30, 133, 134, 177, 192, 194, 205–208, 217, 218, 222, 227, 228, 234–236, 279, 280, 289, 294, 296, 302, 314, 325
Positivism, 292, 306
Pound Conference, 223
Probation, 153, 158, 162, 241, 242, 245, 249, 252–255
Probation of Offenders Ordinance (POO), 245, 248
Problem solving courts, 160, 163, 164
Procedural justice, 3, 19, 23, 42, 54, 69, 88, 163, 164, 168, 203, 330
Prosecutor, 158, 162, 194, 233, 241, 250, 283, 287, 289, 296, 305
Psychoanalytical thought, 29, 87
Public interest, 6, 25, 28, 73, 182, 259, 260, 262, 264, 267, 291, 312, 322–324
Public interest litigation, 259–262, 264, 267, 312

R
Realism, 88, 228
Recidivism, 70, 89, 151, 160, 242
Refugees, 129
Rehabilitation, 9, 30, 70, 159, 160, 162, 242, 244, 245, 248, 256
Replacement technologies, 29, 87, 90, 91
Responsive courts, 2, 22
Responsive Judges
and Extra-Disputing Judicial Activity, 220–222
in the courtroom, 219
Responsive judging
definition, 42
effectiveness of, 13
elements, 1, 13, 26, 152
Restorative justice, 18, 56, 159, 162, 164, 232, 274, 275
Restorative practices, 166
Retribution, 149, 166, 328
Role of judge, 6, 24
Rule of law, 10, 88, 97, 98, 103, 126, 147, 181, 195, 196, 203, 218, 280, 281, 289, 295, 297, 327

Rules of Civil Procedure
  Civil Rules Committee, 227
  Ontario Rule 77, 225
  Ontario Rule 78, 225

S
Separation of law and politics, 289
Settlement, 5, 6, 14, 15, 19, 23, 24, 26, 28, 29, 53, 56, 57, 61, 63, 67–69, 71–77, 79–81, 88, 100, 150, 180, 220, 221, 225, 226, 228, 230, 231, 277, 278, 296, 299, 301, 303–305, 313, 321, 323–325, 331
Settlement adjudication
  models of, 2
  narrow model, 63, 73, 74, 77, 79
  wide model, 63, 75–79
Slavery, 313–316, 323, 326, 328–330
Smart sentencing, 166
Social media, 21, 22, 29, 31, 99, 121–137, 146, 201, 210, 262, 268, 311, 312
Social responsibility, 143, 145–148, 157, 168
Social responsiveness, 4, 9, 152, 325
Social sustainability, 29, 143, 148–152, 163–167
Somerset, 311 313, 315, 316, 322–326, 328, 329, 331
Special juries, 315, 322
Substantive justice, 95, 280, 330
Supportive technology, 91
Sustainability in organisations, 147
Sustainability movement, 144, 146, 153, 157, 167, 168
Sustainable development, 29, 143–148, 150, 151, 154, 163, 167, 168
Sustainable judicial principles, 165
Sustainable justice, 29, 143, 152, 154, 163–165, 167, 169
Sustainable punishment, 166

T
Technology
  impact on judging, 89
The Limits to Growth, 143, 144, 157
Therapeutic Application of Law (TAL), 241, 244, 245, 248, 249, 252, 253, 256
Therapeutic Design of Law (TDL), 241, 244, 245, 248–253
Therapeutic judging, 69–72, 219
Therapeutic Jurisprudence (TJ), 69, 81, 241, 242, 244–247, 249, 255, 256
The Zong, 326, 329
Top-down management, 154
Toronto commercial list, 221
Traditional media, 21, 124, 126–128, 131–133
Training judges, 22
Transitional justice, 159
Tribunals
  dispute resolution in, 42, 43, 47, 57

U
United States v Concepcion, 327

W
Wu Ying case, 198, 199

X
Xu Ting case, 196, 197

Y
Yu Huan case, 201, 203

CPSIA information can be obtained
at www.ICGtesting.com
Printed in the USA
BVHW04*0216030818
523464BV00004B/9/P

9 789811 310225